B   Olsen, O
Tourgee   Carpetbagger's   5643
            crusade: the life
            of Albion Winegar
            Tourgee
                              795

SAN DIEGO PUBLIC LIBRARY

LIBRARY RULES

TIME: — Books may be kept 14 days, unless dated otherwise.

RENEWALS: — Books may be renewed once at the agency where borrowed, unless on reserve. Bring book with you.

FINES:— Five cents a day will be charged for each book kept overtime.

DAMAGES: — Injury to the book from tearing, penciling, unusual soiling or other ill-usage, will be charged to the card owner. Please report to us when a mutilated book is issued to you.

CARDS—ALWAYS BRING YOUR CARD WITH YOU.

CARPETBAGGER'S CRUSADE:

The Life of Albion Winegar Tourgée

Ignorance and neglect are the mainsprings of misrule.

Albion W. Tourgée

CARPETBAGGER'S

CRUSADE: The Life of

Albion Winegar Tourgée

by

OTTO H. OLSEN

The Johns Hopkins Press, Baltimore 1965

This book has been brought to publication
with the assistance of a grant from The Ford Foundation.

For CORINNE

This little tale is the narrative of one of Folly's failures. . . . The wise men looked on and laughed.—*A Fool's Errand*

Preface

Some years ago, the study of North Carolina Reconstruction history led me in search of the personal papers of a noted carpetbagger, Albion W. Tourgée. Although such a manuscript collection had been utilized by an earlier biographer, no trace of it was found at the site of Tourgée's home in Mayville, New York, and my next steps were directed to the local historical museum at nearby Westfield. Here I stood dejectedly one summer day in the museum office of the Chautauqua County Historical Society. A trip of several hundred miles had produced nothing more than a few insignificant display items relating to Tourgée. While I was lamenting this poor yield and probing for new leads to the missing manuscripts, a distinguished-looking elderly gentleman, Samuel F. Nixon, passed by the office and was called in as a leading authority and a probable source of additional information. Discussion of the matter soon elicited from Mr. Nixon a vague recollection that years earlier some boxes of material had been sent to the museum from Mayville, and it was agreed to set me free among the Society's unsorted accumulations. I was then conducted to a poorly lit storage room on an upper floor, where, amidst a variety of what was to me strange and ancient furniture and apparatus, wreathed in dust and cobwebs, I began rooting through an assortment of chests and boxes. After perhaps half an hour of repeatedly crushed hopes as successive boxes were emptied, I opened a cardboard carton that revealed, through dimness and dust, the exciting letters TOURGÉE. Within a few busy moments I had surrounded myself with a rich collection of manuscripts that had lain neglected, first in Mayville and then in Westfield, for many years, the one sign of recent attention being the destructive nibbling of rats. The content of the Tourgée papers confirmed my initial thrill of discovery, and I found myself determined to reconsider the life of this fascinating figure.

In the course of this reconsideration I have become deeply indebted to many people, especially to the now deceased Samuel F. Nixon for his kindness and the rare privilege he extended to me. I am sincerely grateful also to Dean H. Keller for his sympathy and assistance, to Roderick A. Nixon and the Chautauqua County Historical Society, to the Mayville Library, to Katherine Hoskins, and to Mr. and Mrs. Carl O. Jeffress and Martin F. Douglas for their gracious hospitality and for allowing me access to their family papers.

Exceptional co-operation was shown by the staffs of the Manuscript Division of the Library of Congress; the War Department, State Department, and Department of Interior search rooms in the National Archives; the manuscript and newspaper divisions of the Duke University Library; the North Carolina State Archives and State Library at Raleigh; the Greensboro Public Library; the Grosvenor Public Library in Buffalo; the Rochester University Library; and The Johns Hopkins University Library. Much of the work was completed at the University of North Carolina Library, with particular assistance from the Southern Historical Collection and the North Carolina Collection. I feel a particular debt to Sara Jackson, Caroline Wallace, Brooke Allan, James W. Patton, William S. Powell, and J. Louis Kuethe.

The friendly counsel of David Donald helped to initiate this effort, C. Vann Woodward gave encouragement and aid over many years, and the sympathetic attention of Helen and Howard Webber was invaluable. For critical commentary and assistance I also owe much to Louis R. Harlan, as well as to Ephraim Schulman, Sherman Merrill, and Alice Blakestad, and I am additionally indebted to the diligent interest of Jean Owen and the staff of The Johns Hopkins Press. The final responsibility is, of course, entirely my own.

The engraving on the title page is an emblem that was used on Tourgée's books; the engraving on page 354 originally appeared on the last page of A Fool's Errand By One of the Fools.

Table of Contents

Introduction

The great experience in the life of Albion Winegar Tourgée was his encounter with the South. This was the high point of adventure in the lives of a whole generation of northerners, but for most of them it was limited to four violent years. For Tourgée, however, the encounter was renewed, tenaciously pursued, and obstinately prolonged. The experience proved traumatic and his brooding over it later became almost obsessive. It quite filled his thoughts and emotions, furnished material for most of his novels, the subject matter for a huge quantity of journalistic writing, and the central inspiration of his personal crusades for justice and reform. Tourgée simply could not put the South out of his mind, come to grips with its distinctiveness, or accept the defeat it imposed on its conquerors. He was torn by the ambivalence of his feelings toward the South. He was repelled and attracted at the same time. He hated the South and loved it, scorned it and admired it, but he could never be indifferent to it to the end of his days. Only a year before his death a surgeon removed from his hip a piece of lead that, he wrote, "must have been wandering around in my anatomy since Perryville."

Tourgée's first encounter with the South, the military phase, came near proving fatal. He was so seriously injured in the first Battle of Bull Run that he was out of action for a year and never fully recovered. But he returned to the fight, was wounded and hospitalized again, returned again only to be captured and imprisoned for four months. Freed in an exchange of prisoners, he went back to the front a third time and sustained injuries that took him out of the war in 1864.

Cheerfully assuming that peace and victory had settled his differences with the South, Tourgée moved to Greensboro, North Carolina, with his wife and family in October, 1865, to settle down. Seeking health and economic advantage, he set up a law office and invested his money in local enterprises. The investments proved unfortunate. Tourgée had already become involved in local politics. His sympathies naturally went out to the unionists who had resisted the Confederate cause and led him to champion the white underdogs and the Negro freedmen. Shocked by the return of Confederates to seats of power and by their injustice to unionists and freedmen, Tourgée came out for Negro suffrage, took the lead in the state Union League, and quickly became known as one of the most radical and powerful members of the new Republican party of North Carolina.

Reconstruction in North Carolina contributed two of the most famous examples of the genus Carpetbagger in our history. One of them, General Milton Littlefield, pretty thoroughly deserved the odious reputation attached to the stereotype. The other, Albion Tourgée, suffered from all the odium it carried but aptly illustrates the injustice of indiscriminately applying the stereotype to all northerners who took part in the Reconstruction of the South. Fairly and dispassionately weighed, neither his public record nor his private life is found to deserve the reputation his enemies painted: "Tourgée the infamous—Tourgée the sepulchral—Tourgée the Cain-marked."

Tourgée's services to the state were extensive and sometimes heroic. He was elected a member of the Constitutional Convention of 1868 on a platform advocating civil rights, political equality, penal reform, free schools, and democratization of state and local government and successfully led the fight for their adoption. He then took a decisive hand in establishing the new democratic system of local government and framing extensive reform of the judiciary. He was one of three code commissioners who revised the law and legal procedure of the state, and he personally wrote much of the legislation passed by the Republicans. All the while he maintained a lively interest in civic affairs, especially in the founding of a Negro college.

In 1868 he was elected a judge of the state Superior Court, an office he held for six years, during which he came to be regarded as one of the best judges in the state. Even his enemies admitted that he was a most capable judge, but he was accused of showing favor to Negroes. It was a difficult and dangerous role. Many of the cases before him involved mistreatment of Negroes by the Ku Klux Klan and other white Carolinians. Completely fearless, Tourgée repeatedly denounced the Klan from the bench and handed down decisions without regard to threats he received.

The threats continued along with the insults, the ostracism, and the menacing gestures. His life was often in danger. Tourgée armed himself, defiantly named his home "Carpet-Bag Lodge," and stuck it out even after his term expired and the Republicans were overthrown. Grant appointed him pension agent at Raleigh in 1876 and he dug in for a few more years. Along with the courage, he displayed excessive pride and self-righteousness that did not help matters. By 1879 he had had enough and left the South after fourteen years of residence.

The same year appeared his sensationally successful novel, A Fool's Errand by One of the Fools, and in 1880 a sequel, Bricks Without Straw. Both novels reflect, often with literal fidelity, their author's experience in North Carolina. It was a limited experience, of course, and in many ways untypical. He pictures Reconstruction as essentially a clash between Republican equalitarianism and reform and Conservative racism and reaction. Yet for all his simplifications and stereotypes Tourgée attained a high level of detachment, understanding, and compassion. His conclusion is that the failure and tragedy of Reconstruction are largely the responsibility of the North.

One should not be misled, as some have been, by the title of A Fool's Errand. While he was disenchanted with Reconstruction policies, Tourgée never abandoned or forgot the principles and ideals of racial justice and equalitarianism for which he fought. In the eighties and nineties, when the North had turned its back on the Negro and the Civil War ideals and the struggle for civil rights was virtually friendless, he continued to fight the rising tide of racism and segregation. In the early nineties he organized, with the aid of Negro friends, a short-lived forerunner of the NAACP. And in the case of Plessy v. Ferguson, which in 1896 gave Supreme Court sanction to segregation, he wrote a brief that is reflected in both the thought and phraseology of the famous dissenting opinion of Mr. Justice Holmes.

The key to Tourgée's uniqueness as a commentator on the sectional struggle and Reconstruction is the very ambivalence of his deeper feelings about the South. Considering his personal sufferings at the hands of Southerners, his writings are remarkably free from bitterness. He had an unusual gift for maintaining a distinction between people he admired and opinions he detested. He could abhor racist doctrines and sympathize with their advocates. "One can not but admire the arrogant boldness," he writes, "with which they charged the nation which had overpowered them—even in the teeth of her legislators— with perfidy, malice, and a spirit of unworthy and contemptible revenge."

Edmund Wilson has offered an explanation for this ambivalence. "Tourgée was a special case," he writes. "He was a Northerner who resembled the Southerners: in his insolence, his independence, his readiness to accept a challenge, his recklessness and ineptitude in practical matters, his romantic and chivalrous view of the world in which he was living . . . and he evidently elicited *their* admiration or he could never have survived as so provocative an antagonist fourteen years, as he did, in their midst."

There is scarcely another northern participant in Reconstruction whose experience and whose commentary on that experience reveal so much about the character of this historic trauma. We have long needed a full-scale life of Albion Tourgée. Mr. Olsen has fulfilled this need and in doing so has shed much new light on both Tourgée and Reconstruction.

C. VANN WOODWARD

CARPETBAGGER'S CRUSADE:

The Life of Albion Winegar Tourgée

A Yankee Youth

Shortly before the Civil War, a twenty-one-year-old college student in upstate New York was bantering his pretty fiancée for her unseemly concern with the nation's slavery conflict. She displayed all the markings of "quite a rabid little petticoated Black Republican of late," the young man chided, whereas he remained devoted to the finer things and knew "absolutely nothing about Politics." He had no time for such and did not "care a copper" which side whipped which, believing it would be all the same in a hundred years one way or the other.[1]

Despite his expressed disdain for politics, young Albion Winegar Tourgée's worldly interests had often been stimulated by his Yankee ancestry and environment. Albion's father, Valentine Tourgée (pronounced Toor·zhay′), was a descendant of French Huguenots who had sought opportunity and freedom in Rhode Island late in the seventeenth century; and only a generation later, Albion's maternal ancestors of Swiss descent, the Winegars, fled the rigors of the Palatinate to settle in New York's Hudson Valley. The paths of these two families crossed a century later, after members of the Tourgée family had moved by successive steps westward to the Berkshire Mountains to become members of the laboring population of Lee, Massachusetts. Here the Winegars had already played an earlier and more prominent role. Moving from New York by way of Sharon, Connecticut, which they had helped found, the Winegars were among the earliest residents of Lee, owning land and the first grist mill in that settlement some years before the

---

[1] Albion W. Tourgée to Emma L. Kilbourne, February 4, 1860, in Albion W. Tourgée Papers, Chautauqua County Historical Museum, Westfield, New York. Unless otherwise indicated, all manuscripts cited in this chapter are from the Tourgée Papers.

American Revolution. The marriage in 1836 of Valentine Tourgée and Louise Emma Winegar, Albion's parents, was the second union between these two families.

Valentine, who later denounced "such manufacturing places as Lee where the mass become a sink of corruption and ruin," [2] was dissatisfied with his employment in the paper manufacturing industry, and the instability of that industry in the 1830's together with Jeffersonian preferences fostered his interest in homesteading farther west. At that time many New England farmers, displaced by poor conditions and a land-absorbing sheep craze and enticed by inexpensive transportation and land, were flocking to the Western Reserve of Ohio and beyond. Shortly after their marriage, Valentine and Louise Tourgée joined this movement.

A short way west of Lee, the Tourgées joined the heavy stream of migration moving north along the Hudson Valley to Albany, then west along the Genesee Road or Erie Canal as far as Buffalo, and finally down the pleasant shores of Lake Erie to the Western Reserve. Here Valentine and Louise settled in the town of Williamsfield, in the northeast corner of Ohio, and soon were worrying about their crops and their livestock and struggling against drought, frost, heavy rains, and grasshoppers. Valentine's correspondence spoke of days that were lean and hard but always filled with optimistic hopes. What appeared to distress this devout Methodist most was the neglect of religion found in the frontier area, a fault he would help the Western Reserve to overcome thoroughly. It was in the midst of these diverse problems that, on May 2, 1838, Albion Winegar Tourgée was born, a first and only child. A short time earlier the family fortune had been described as consisting of a homestead, hardships, and exactly "1 rusty cent."

The western venture proved too rigorous for Albion's mother, who had always been prone to illness, and following his birth her health steadily declined. Shortly before her son's fifth birthday she died, the loss being somewhat eased for the youngster by his having been largely under his father's care and guidance during Louise's several years of sickness. If, as Valentine asserted, Albion was soon over the impact of his mother's death, he nevertheless did not easily reconcile himself to the arrival of a stepmother less than a year later. Valentine's second wife,

2 Valentine Tourgée to ———, May 19, 1856.

Rowena Snow, was soon thoroughly estranged from her stepson. Albion's jealousy, encouraged by members of the Winegar family in Lee, Massachusetts, was a major cause of this lasting hostility, although it also has been attributed to Rowena's harsh treatment of the youth, especially as contrasted with the favoritism accorded a younger half-sister, Rosette, born in 1846. Albion's relationship with Rosette, however, was a pleasant one, although neither close nor lasting. But his hostility toward his stepmother deepened and endured, contributing to an early and conspicuous inclination to resist any unwelcome authority.

Albion's early life was not all so complex or unpleasant. In the fall of 1847, when he was nine, the family moved a few miles north, close to Lake Erie, and settled in Kingsville, so named after an itinerant whiskey salesman who had contributed four gallons of his wares for the honor. In this promising location, "without a doubt a better agricultural district than any other in the county," Valentine, who had been rather successful since his son's birth, invested fifteen hundred dollars in the house and farm that remained his home until death. It was a comfortable home, indeed. The two-story dwelling included seven rooms, a cellar, and a porch and was plastered upstairs and down and painted outside and in. The farm boasted fifty acres of improved land, ten acres of forest, and plenty of good water as well as a barn, stable, and shed and an orchard with peaches, pears, cherries, butternuts, walnuts, and a variety of decorative trees. The front yard was filled with colorful locust trees, lilacs, roses, cinnamon, sweet briar, almond trees, snowberries, and flowers "too numerous to mention." Years later in the plantation South, Albion would fondly recall small-scale independent farming as he knew it in Ohio.

Valentine was proud of his son, "fat as butter," "healthy and robust," ever willing to do his chores, and always anxious to read. Boastfully noting that if Albion could "get a book or newspaper he [was] satisfied hot or cold," Valentine prophesied to relatives in Lee that perhaps "we shall come out some distinguished Literati as we are near a flourishing academy," [3] a prediction partially expressing earlier aspirations of his own. He had written verse in his youth and retained a respect for literature which he succeeded in conveying to his son. Albion benefited from a small but respectable family library of classics, and his writings

[3] Valentine Tourgée to Sophronia Winegar, September 19, 1847.

would often resemble the flowing and flowery letters of his father. Valentine also stimulated an interest in affairs and in the art of controversy with serious and sometimes heated discussions over the family dining table, and, esteeming his own reputation for enthusiastic independence, he especially cultivated self-reliance and assertiveness in his son. This was an emphasis later sometimes rued as the high-spirited Albion left his chores without warning to hie off to the woods with his rifle or rod, returning when he pleased.

A healthy and active youth, Albion was a "great help" on the farm but fond of sport and play and prone to a good share of mishaps. At the age of six, he was temporarily blinded by a fall from a ladder, and five years later he was the victim of a literally harrowing experience. While Albion was driving his father's harrow, part of the rig became unhooked, and he dismounted to make the required repairs. As he bent before the team of horses they suddenly started forward, throwing him over the whippletree and beneath the onrushing sharp teeth. Before Valentine could reach his shouting son, Albion had been dragged about fifty yards, and when he "came out at the back end of the harrow, he was completely harrowed from one end to the other, some 15 teeth at least passing over his head; he was completely bruised and some cut up about his head, breast, and legs." [4] A few years later the fourteen-year-old Albion was the victim of a less dramatic but more serious mishap when a playmate exploded a percussion cap, a piece of which tore Albion's right eye and left it permanently blind.[5] These exploits secured Albion a certain distinction among his friends, as is the way among youth, and he responded to his blindness with an aggressiveness intended to rebuff any suspicion of weakness.

Young Tourgée was also moulded in part by the New England environment into which he was invited by relatives who resented the "parental tyranny" their nephew endured in Ohio. He spent several years in the early 1850's in Lee, Massachusetts, but to Valentine's delight, the Winegars found Albion more than they cared to handle, and in 1856 they gladly sent him back. During his stay, he had benefited

[4] Valentine Tourgée to Sophronia Winegar, June 4, 1848.
[5] Albion W. Tourgée to his father, May 9, 1852. (In the possession of Dean Keller of Kent, Ohio. I am indebted to Mr. Keller for several items relating to Tourgée's early life.) See also obituary clipping, Boston *Transcript*, May 23, 1905, Tourgée Papers.

from the public high school and library and, contrary to his father's fear that Albion might be debased by his urban associates, had probably absorbed a good amount of the democratic spirit and religious morality that characterized the Berkshires. On his return home the eighteen-year-old Albion was beset by similar currents in the Western Reserve.

The Western Reserve of the 1850's had been settled "almost wholly by persons of New England stock," whose peculiar heritage was strengthened as well as altered by the impact of the frontier. The area was populated predominantly by small independent farmers; extremes of poverty or wealth were rare; and economic, social, and political democracy was the fashion. Habits of religious toleration and a devotion to public education also characterized the Reserve, while one of the strongest traditions inherited from the East was that of local self-government. Albion had seen his father in stentorian voice direct the communal construction of the Kingsville village square, and he had also been touched by the excitement accompanying the opening of canal and railroad connections and the various industrial developments of the 1850's. The value of these and other events was doubly impressed on the youth by the reformism and intellectual ferment then besetting the nation and the Western Reserve. Women's rights, political and educational reform, prison and legal reform, and temperance were among the lofty, sometimes foolish, goals, and although such contemptible doctrines as Know-Nothingism and white supremacy were also apparent, the general spirit in northeastern Ohio was uniquely positive and idealistic. One of the strongest forces in the area was that of anti-slavery, and the Tourgées' home town was a station on the Underground Railroad.

Nevertheless, although young Albion's ancestry did encourage a noticeable interest in the struggles for freedom of the Huguenots and Swiss, he remained aloof from much of the contemporary ferment, most noticeably from the slavery dispute, an agitation frowned upon by the family Methodist church. As Valentine had predicted, it was the formal intellectual and literary ferment—the lyceums, the literary societies, the popularity of poetry and prose—that had the most noticeable impact on his son, even encouraging a certain aversion for the worldly concerns of the reformers. On the other hand, although Albion was not captivated by the more popular political interests of the Reserve, their lasting impact would be sharply revealed as his own interests changed in the future.

Following his return from Massachusetts, Albion began working his way through Kingsville Academy, alternately attending the Academy and teaching school. The town's flourishing coeducational academy in various ways reflected the spirit of the age of reform. Board, room, and education were provided for approximately 150 students from throughout and beyond the state for as little as one dollar per week, and the intellectual activity of the faculty and students stimulated the town's life. Here, from 1856 to 1858, the "hustling, witty, one-eyed stripling" Tourgée was a popular and respected student. Considered a promising scholar by his teachers, he was one of the most active members of the Didaskalion Society, an association that presented weekly educational entertainment. Aided by a spirited boldness and piercing stare, which his blindness enhanced, he also won renown as an orator and was elected to the presidency of the debating society. In the midst of one debate, the audacious Albion walked across the room, took up and glanced over his opponent's notes, and replaced them with a contemptuous snort that left his more proper opponent quite paralyzed in the midst of speech. Another tale of academy days reveals that Tourgée's unpredictable initiative was sometimes accompanied by an energetic knack for failure. Anxious to secure the passage of a certain resolution at a society meeting, Albion ascertained that the members were equally divided in sentiment. Securing a deferment of the vote, he then slipped out of the meeting and hurriedly ran two miles to return with an absent member, who promptly voted against Tourgée's measure.[6]

As a student, young Tourgée was clearly in a central and commanding position, although in some ways his own interests were uncommon. While political and practical interests dominated academy activity (typical student orations dealt with "The Moral Responsibility of Political Action," "Political and Social Revolution," and the "Utility of Botany"), Albion stood among an artistically inclined minority. Four public addresses that he delivered as a student, two of them addresses for graduation ceremonies, indicated his preferences: "The Literary

[6] W. J. Gibson to Orlando Luce, December 27, 1899 (copy in the possession of Dean Keller).

Influence of Lord Byron," "Gentleman's Part of LeBouquet," "Mental Culture Favors Poetry," and "A Love for the Beautiful, Its Cultivation and Effect." Albion also composed a number of poems, several of which were published in the local press or read at public meetings. His poetry was artificial, immature, and heavily sentimental, but occasionally original, as in his depiction of the trials of a stormy boat trip on Lake Erie: "While every sea-sick sinner poured / Immense libations overboard."

A tall and slender youth with dark hair, bright blue eyes, and gentle features, the dashing Albion attracted a good share of admiration from the young ladies of Kingsville, and following several minor flirtations he became enamored of a comely student, Emma Lodoilska Kilbourne, the daughter of a Conneaut farmer. Although Emma and Albion wrote and rhymed to one another for a year prior to their engagement in 1858, their relationship was supposedly a case of love at first sight. For the following five years Albion and Emma saw little of one another, but aided by an avid correspondence, in which every particle of space was usually filled with crisscrossed script, a strong and intimate bond grew between them.[7] The two were wonderfully matched. Emma, though inquisitive and talented, was of stable and practical bent and served as somewhat of a check and support for the wildly energetic, imaginative, and emotional Albion. Proud of his superior talent and aspiration, she retained an intelligent independence, which was quick to reject his haughty advice or counter criticism with her own humorous jibes. During a long and devoted marriage, she would offer invaluable encouragement and aid to a husband whose life was marked by strenuous successes and depressing failures.

After exhausting the offerings of the Academy, Albion wished to attend college, but his father, now somewhat skeptical of his son's impractical artistic bent, refused to "squander" his own meager fortune on Albion's further schooling. But the death of a relative left an inheritance of four hundred dollars, and with this, his head, and his hands, decided Albion, he would secure the desired education. After toying with thoughts of Harvard, he chose instead to attend the more convenient university at Rochester, where the cost would be about

[7] The remainder of this chapter is based largely upon correspondence between Emma and Albion.

half that of Harvard and where he obtained admittance as a Sophomore, thus saving an important year. So, in the fall of 1859, this Ohio farm boy arrived in Rochester with a trunk and carpetbag for his first encounter with a city, one he found dusty and noisy and filled with uncouth figures, hideous sounds, and "outrageous stenches." The accommodations that he and a fellow student secured were more pleasant—a freshly papered and pleasant room, linen, board, and unlimited gas illumination, all for $2.25 apiece per week.

At this small and still new university Albion encountered the same dedicated spirit that had prevailed at the Academy, and it was this that dominated his life. Commercial and industrial activity, the famed work of Frederick Douglass, and other local urban forces had a minimal impact, for although the University's system of discipline was rather lax for that day, time was scarce for the diligent student. Classes were held from nine until noon, and afternoons and evenings were usually spent in study. Except for an evening lecture and a fraternity meeting each week (the latter usually concerned with serious literary discussion) Albion's main extracurricular activity was reading, an imposed routine which was sometimes hard on his one good eye.

But there was play, too, especially holiday carousals and student pranks, in which Albion frequently played a leading role. He delighted in the school's competitive camaraderie, which was marked by intense rivalries and clashes of sharpness and wit. Repartee was highly valued, while the quiet, timid, or dull were mocked and relegated to disgrace. At times the students were hard on professors:

> We have Chemistry under Dr. Dewey. It is glorious sport. He is an old man—76 years old but we do have much fun in his room. He has a funny sort of habit of asking a question and answering it himself. Thus he will say, "*Oxygen* united with another substance forms—what? Oxides—are they not? Eh. *Yes*." He does this so much that we have become accustomed to roar out—*Yes*—just as soon as he says "Eh?" Sometimes when his back is turned from us in performing an experiment we all leave the room.[8]

---

[8] Tourgée to Millie Kilbourne, September 26, 1860.

Albion's college curriculum included literature, logic, and rhetoric (three subjects which he enjoyed and excelled in) as well as language, mathematics, and science. Although he greatly admired his professor in Greek, Asahel C. Kendrick, and later formed a close friendship with the University's president, Martin B. Anderson, Albion was often at odds with his college superiors. Able, original, and devilish enough to form many independent opinions, he was too proud and impetuous to curtail them, and resultant clashes with the faculty or administration were somewhat of a problem. Albion complained of being treated unfairly at times because of this, and on occasion he assumed a self-imposed silence to secure fair treatment. Wherever the fault lay, he did suffer for his unruliness.

Albion's attitude toward grades fluctuated. At one moment fired by fraternity rivalry to seek high grades, at another he cared "but precious little about those marks anyhow." The still unresolved problem of the real meaning of grades contributed to this ambivalence, but so, too, did self-doubt, and it was a sensitivity about failure that did much to make Tourgée a popular and successful student. His marks, except in mathematics (which he detested), were very high, and he acquired a reputation for wit and hearty laughter as well as for the familiar ability in debate. During his first year at Rochester he read his poetry at commencement, became a member of the Psi Upsilon fraternity, and led the Sophomores in their rivalry with the Junior class. The following year he was elected class poet, composed verse for the University Glee Club, and furnished both songs and speeches for the campus Republicans. Adhering to its motto "from the heart," Albion's literary fraternity no doubt added a bit more to his inclination toward independence. Though not always the best scholars, thought he, the Psi U's were staunch and well-read fellows, "strong rugged men who dare oppose the views even of the Omniscient Faculty itself, and set aside all authority but right & reason." [9]

Encouraged by teachers and continued local recognition, Albion's literary aspirations grew stronger during the years at Rochester. William H. Prescott's account of Spanish conquest inspired an interest in sixteenth-century expansionism as an exciting field for fictional romance, and Albion actually began a novel based upon De Soto's exploits. His

[9] Tourgée to Emma L. Kilbourne, November 26, 1859.

concepts of the task (one of "mighty effort," "refined taste," and "thorough scholarship") were ambitious but artificial, and most of his formal writing was typically collegiate, with pretense far exceeding sincerity or depth, and there was a marked lack of learning. Albion's letters, however, most of which were written to Emma, were exceptional. Overcoming touches of affectation and conceit, they were readable and honest and revealed a rare gift for narration in their delightful and picturesque depictions of such incidents as giving a speech, guiding an expedition through the dangers of an icy gorge, or perpetrating some college prank.

An attachment to literature also helped form Albion's general pattern of values, as did familiar world and national currents of revolution and reform. His admiration for Milton, Burns, and Byron both reflected and amplified an idealistic concern for humanity, and from the novels of Scott he absorbed an early appreciation of the shaping power of environment. A related but somewhat different impact provided by the literature of the Romantics was reflected in young Tourgée's addiction to lauding the fine, the beautiful, and the wise, or to idolizing the noble man. Ambition along with collegiate rivalry contributed to this reverence for "manly" character and behavior, but the reverence was none the less sincere and strong. Albion prayed that he might "be ever honorable, trustful, pure" and vowed that he would come to the wedding couch as pure as his wife ("I am almost an anomaly in this respect and am truly glad to be so"). Quite characteristic was the tone of his refusal to cultivate the good graces of his fiancée's parents: "I would not sail under false colors, or win love by false pretenses. My motto is not, as you know, seem, but *be*. . . . That they may know what I am, I must *appear* to *them* as I *am*." [10]

Albion Tourgée also persevered in a strong, basic Christianity, although he was not much concerned with theology, failed to join a particular church, and considered the theology students at college "radical young fanatics." As an ardent defender of free speech, he also insisted upon the right of Freemasons and Unitarians to be heard, and he found the teachings of the latter group rather to his liking. Both Albion and Emma observed the Sabbath irregularly, attended a variety of churches, and were impressed by practical sermons rather than denominational dif-

[10] Tourgée to Emma L. Kilbourne, March 8, 1859.

ferences. The core of Albion's own Christianity was simply the conviction that God saw to the ultimate triumph of His justice on earth, a belief instilled especially by his father and by the poetry and prose of that puritanical New Englander, Josiah G. Holland. In later years, this elementary faith would furnish hope and inspiration in the face of much injustice and despair.

On occasion Albion's attention reluctantly veered in a more mundane direction, especially toward considering the more certain rewards of a legal career. His real interests, however, remained elsewhere, and he perceived, but never conquered, his aversion to practical business affairs, a weakness that would limit his economic success and eventually carry him into several financial disasters.

By the eve of the Civil War, Albion W. Tourgée had clearly revealed a number of personal strengths and weaknesses. Troubled somewhat by insecurity and self-doubt, he was unduly sensitive and proud, but he was able and ambitious enough to make a mark on his world. That mark was, and would continue to be, greatly influenced by a humanitarian idealism and a rebellious independence. Although burdened by quixotic conceit and exaggeration, Albion would retain the lofty goals and much of the charm of Cervantes' worthy knight.

II

Liberty, Union, and War

A lbion's absorption in literature and college long isolated him from that political turbulence preceding secession, and prior to the autumn of 1860 his only suggested interest in sectional issues appeared in the lines of a poem he had written on his twenty-first birthday:

> How sweet and glorious 'tis to be—
> A man and *white*—(by courtesy)
> In this great nation of the free.[1]

The sociable Emma reflected the political leanings of the Reserve more readily, and by early 1860 her antislavery enthusiasm was earning Albion's good-natured ridicule. What, asked he, will you do "in view of the immense responsibilities which are resting on the women of America in the 19th century as regards the crying sin of Negro slavery"? Will you discard crinolines, shorten your skirts, put on cowhide, and "endeavor to kick your northern brethren into compliance with your peculiar tenets and beliefs, as some of your amiable sisters have done?" He suggested marriage and many offspring as an effective and pleasant manner of propagating good Republicanism, but his own cares were not of society. He longed for a house in the mountains or by the sea with an abundance of "fruit, flowers, books & music," where he could "live & love and write & study without ever thinking of what the world called Society." [2] One notes in these and other comments an emphasis upon

[1] Tourgée to Emma L. Kilbourne, May 31, 1859, Tourgée Papers. Unless otherwise indicated, all manuscripts cited in this chapter are from the Tourgée Papers.
[2] Tourgée to Emma L. Kilbourne, February 4, 19, 1860.

personal freedom which, reflecting his own rebelliousness and allegiance to the Romantics, became increasingly important in Albion's thought. Although he was concerned with civil liberties,[3] his extolment of freedom had not yet become tied to national political issues, and as late as September, 1860, Albion advised his roommate, a Douglas Democrat, against wasting valuable time on politics. But within a month Albion was himself caught in the whirl.

The administration of Rochester University successfully discouraged organized student Republicanism until the fall of 1860, when a popular Republican organization, the Wide Awakes, offered free caps, capes, and lanterns to students who would contest this state of affairs. Meanwhile Emma had been saturating her beau with Republicanism, sectional antagonisms had become sharper, and the Republican party had become more palatable to the previously Whiggish Albion. Probably more decisive, however, in inducing Albion and some of his companions to launch a Rochester University Wide Awake Club was the offer of free materials, the opportunity for leadership, and the challenge of administrative opposition. An enthusiastic response of some seventy members quickly prompted an order from the University's president to disband, to which the students responded with a threat to resign from school en masse, thus forcing a compromise whereby the organization continued without using the University's name. For the remainder of the fall, Albion Tourgée, Captain of the Wide Awakes, wrote, sang, cheered, and spoke for Republicanism, and with Emma and her seminary companions rejoiced at the news of Lincoln's victory.

In the midst of these new political commitments, Albion had to abandon college. Efforts as a book and picture salesman the previous summer had not earned enough to finance another year at the University, and in December he accepted a position as assistant principal and teacher at Wilson Collegiate Institute in northern New York. Here the disheartened Albion taught a variety of subjects, excelling in, of all things, "that detestable science" mathematics and deriving some satisfaction from encouraging what "little flame of zeal" he found among his students. His political interests meanwhile did not flag, and

[3] Written manuscript, n.d., by Tourgée on the persecution in North Carolina of recipients of Hinton Rowan Helper's *The Impending Crisis of the South: How to Meet It* (New York, 1857).

foreseeing disunion, war, and revolution, Albion planned to share in the turmoil, "for one will then either make or lose much in a very short time." [4] Obviously excited, he complained of restlessness and a longing to write so that the world might hear him.

In March the school term at Wilson ended and Albion re-entered the University. The following month Fort Sumter fell and the martial fever rose. Troops drilled on the city streets, ministers preached war on the Sabbath, and the recently pacific president of the University delivered a patriotic exhortation from the Baptist pulpit. Albion, of course, exulted in the excitement, and as Emma feared, the temptations of duty, patriotism, adventure, and glory proved irresistible. Soon Albion and a classmate enlisted together in a regiment of dragoons led by their mathematics professor, Colonel Isaac F. Quimby. They were two of four students from their entire class sufficiently aroused to volunteer for the cause. "Go and Heaven bless my soldier love, and keep him safe from harm and danger," wrote the distressed Emma, and at her insistence Albion agreed to their immediate marriage. But the regiment was off to the front before they could be wed.

There were no provisions for dragoons in the rapidly growing Federal army, and to Albion's chagrin, his regiment was converted into the Twenty-Seventh New York Volunteer Infantry. Trim in an army crew cut and proud of his election as a sergeant, this new infantryman was also worrying about the possibility of being discharged because of his blind eye and busily penning patriotic verse:

> Let Union be your battle cry
> For Union suffer, toil or die.[5]

Union volunteers were apparently as prone to complain as soldiers anywhere, and Sergeant Tourgée soon displayed his ability to disrupt affairs when, catering to the soldier's major grievance, he conducted a company funeral over some old and wormy beef. With all the honors of war, a large piece of beef was encased in a wooden box and interred to the tune of "The Rogues' March." Tourgée preached the funeral sermon and was soon severely reprimanded, but this and subsequent

4 Tourgée to Emma L. Kilbourne, March 3, 1861.
5 Tourgée to Emma L. Kilbourne, May 19, 1861.

demonstrations against the food (the most dramatic of which was the prearranged kicking over of the eating tables, sending cutlery, cups, plates, and food flying) finally secured the helpful intervention of the regimental colonel.[6] Thereafter the regiment enjoyed excellent fare, and Tourgée would remember that radical action could win positive results.

Less than two months after being sworn in, Albion wrote Emma from the vicinity of Fairfax Court House, Virginia, where the Twenty-Seventh New York Volunteers, with very little training, were in one of three divisions moving forward under General Irvin McDowell to launch the disastrous battle of Bull Run. The movement into the Confederacy, protested Albion, was accompanied by plundering "carried on to a most shameful extent . . . pigs, poultry, knives, forks, spoons, wine, sugar, tobacco, &c." His objections marked the beginning of a growing compassion for the sufferings of the South and a lasting contempt for Union plundering. He admitted, however, to having himself succumbed to a daring theft of honey from a beehive, only to be relieved of the hard-won prize by army pickets.

At 2 A.M. on July 21, 1861, after exactly two months of service and two days of dysentery, Albion moved into battle with his regiment, a part of the main attack force of the Union Army at Bull Run. Following a long, slow march of eight hours, without rest, water, or food, the exhausted regiment was quickstepped an additional mile directly into the heart of battle. "In the face of a scorching fire," the Twenty-Seventh Infantry successfully charged the center of the enemy line to rout a rebel force, and during most of the day's long fight, though suffering heavy losses, "the men of the regiment behaved coolly and gallantly, promptly obeying every order, and . . . never once retreated or gave way before the enemy without a positive command." [7] After the Union retreat began, Albion's regiment was the first to rally, but after three unsuccessful attempts to re-form the Union line, it joined the pathetic rout.

[6] Charles Bryant Fairchild, *History of the 27th Regiment N.Y.* (Binghamton, N.Y., 1888), 3–4.

[7] U.S., War Department, *The War of the Rebellion: A Compilation of the Official Records of the Union and Confederate Armies* (Washington, D.C., 1880–1901), Series I, II, 389; hereafter cited as *Official Records*. See also Fairchild, *History of the 27th Regiment N.Y.*, 11–15, and Charles Elihu Slocum, *The Life and Services of Major General Henry Warner Slocum* (Toledo, O., 1913), 12–16.

Six hours of bloody fighting amidst dust and heat, wrote Albion, were followed by an order to retreat "and save ourselves if we could for Gen. Johnson had come up with a reinforcement of 40,000 new troops for the rebels." Men in our fatigued condition could not retreat, he continued, and "we only ran and back went through all those long weary miles with the expectation that our enemy would be upon us every moment." "Oh! you cannot imagine the horrors of that day and night," he lamented, "that was a terrible day, a horrible battle, a more terrible retreat and a far more horrible night. I am preserved, God only knows how but I do know that it can only be by his power and mercy." [8]

During the battle the captain and first lieutenant of Tourgée's company disappeared, and it was rumored that they were on an errand after a bottle of brandy, an incident contributing to Albion's belief that "the men won the day; the officers lost it." [9] The second lieutenant had taken command and with Tourgée's energetic assistance kept the men together during the retreat. As the company approached Washington, it entered a narrow forest road, where "a retreating Battery passed through the ranks at full speed, and before Sergt. Tourgée could get out of the way, one of the wheels of a gun carriage struck him a severe blow in the back, from the effects of which his spine was injured. . . ." [10] Like the more gloriously wounded hero of his future novel *Figs and Thistles*, the injured Tourgée managed somehow to reach Washington, where he collapsed. The exertions of the retreat had compounded the effects of his back injury. Paralyzed from the waist down and "*wholly unfit for military duty*," he was discharged from the army.

Lightly dismissing predictions that he might never again walk, the paralyzed and frightened, but still spirited, youth returned to Kingsville and the tender ministrations of his devoted Emma. A frustrating year of alternating recovery and relapse followed. Less than a month after returning home, he was elated over the unexpected extent of his recovery. Somehow aided by a jolt received in a mild horse-and-buggy accident, he was already able to hobble about on crutches. His high hopes were then shattered by renewed paralysis and predictions of a

[8] Tourgée to Emma L. Kilbourne, July 23, 1861. The rumored 40,000 was greater than the entire army in the field on either side.

[9] *Ibid.*; Tourgée notebook.

[10] Affidavit of Edward P. Gould, February 11, 1862, Federal Pension Records, National Archives, Washington, D.C.

long convalescence. A slow but steady recovery was followed by another relapse in the early spring and orders to refrain from all mental and physical activity.

Albion's attitude and action fluctuated along with his physical condition. With each recovery he burst into a hopeful but dangerous rush of activity—speaking and reading patriotic poetry from a wheel chair at military rallies, attempting to become an army recruiting officer, studying law, and considering marriage on a teacher's salary of $350 a year. But each relapse brought despairing fears of a long or permanent paralysis and the rejection of any thought of burdening Emma with a helpless husband. Sometimes hopelessly distressed by her hero's changing moods, Emma did her best to help him.

The warmth of spring and the ministrations of a back specialist in Cleveland, who treated Albion with doses of strychnine, happily brought him more permanent relief. "I think you may *dismiss all your fears*," Albion joyfully wrote Emma in June. "I cannot come down there now, but I can *walk*." Accompanying these happy tidings was the unwelcome news that Albion was a lieutenant in the Union Army busily recruiting a company of infantry volunteers. In a few days Albion was again off to war. Emma wept openly as he left.

At twenty-four years of age, awarded an A.B. degree from Rochester University on the strength of his military service, Tourgée was appointed a lieutenant in the 105th Ohio Volunteer Infantry on July 11, 1862. He was active during the next few weeks recruiting men from the Western Reserve to serve in the regiment for less pay than farm laborers were then receiving. Many of those who did volunteer, so Albion believed, did so because of their devotion to "Liberty and Union," especially the former. By August the regiment was bedded on hemlock boards in spartan barracks near Cleveland, and on the twenty-first of that month the men were sworn in. On that same day urgent orders were received to move to the front in response to a threatened Confederate penetration as far north as Louisville, Kentucky, or even Cincinnati, Ohio.

With only three or four hours' drill and forty-six experienced soldiers in its ranks and without any equipment, the 105th Infantry was sped by train to Covington, Kentucky. Here three days were spent securing arms and equipment, whereupon the regiment continued by train through parched bluegrass country to Lexington. On August 30, these green troops pushed forward to engage the enemy, only to meet defeated Federal forces in full retreat.

The indignant Albion once again found himself in the midst of an ignominious Union retreat. The 105th, with nine days of official service, formed the rear guard for the famous "Hell March," which took them back through Lexington and ninety-five additional miles through hot sun and limestone dust to Louisville. Although the contributions of wayside Negroes afforded some relief, food and water were scarce and the rear guard found little succor remaining. In one of the hardest marches in the history of the war, the 105th marched 140 miles in six days with approximately twenty-seven hours' sleep, and Lieutenant Tourgée, who was troubled by his back, fell out as one of five hundred stragglers among the eight thousand making the march. Most of the stragglers, including Tourgée, arrived a day late at Louisville, and those from the 105th were deprived of six months' pay by order of their colonel, an inconsiderate punishment that was later revoked by the governor of the state.

Tourgée's exhausted regiment spent the following month in much-needed training. Digging, drilling, erecting fortifications, standing guard, and engaging in maneuvers, they toughened up and learned the duties and tricks of army living, which included conquering portions of "the ubiquitous and indestructible 'hard tack,' " part of a lot reportedly left over from the war of 1812. Then in October the regiment joined General Buell's pursuit of the Confederate Army toward Perryville, a march that provided a pleasing contrast to the recent retreat. Albion wrote of delightful weather and firm roads and vividly described trees aflame with autumn and herds of cattle, stalks of corn, and stacks of hay and oats which dotted the landscape. "Never fear for me," he admonished Emma on October 7, for "I am tough, hearty and strong and just as happy as a clam at high water *seems* to be." The following day he participated in the bloody battle of Perryville.

At Perryville, the 105th Ohio Volunteers were part of the brigade that bore the brunt of the main Confederate attack. After repulsing an initial Confederate movement, the regiment found itself in an exposed position, which, in addition to the poor placement of the brigade's artillery, forced it to fall back under a hot fire, suffering

many casualties but in turn taking a heavy toll among the enemy.
With approximately 500 men in the field, the 105th suffered 203
casualties. In Tourgée's company of less than 100, 9 were killed
and 25 wounded. During the regiment's ordeal "not an officer and but
few of the enlisted men flinched from the hail of death or left their
positions until ordered. . . . Citizen soldiers with not twenty days
drill, they . . . exhibited the coolness and efficiency of veterans." [11]

Tourgée was slightly wounded and retained a piece of shell from
Perryville in his hip for many years. Hospitalized at Danville, he complained of poor treatment and a diet of corn bread, chitterlings, and
pork, and unsuccessfully sought leave to recuperate at home. The
refusal, he quipped, probably reflected the army's need to keep patients
on hand to ensure employment of its undertakers, but two months
after the battle, Albion returned to his regiment plump and healthy
and manfully sporting a mustache and whiskers.

The 105th spent the succeeding months maneuvering in Kentucky
and Tennessee, sometimes in pursuit of the annoying and elusive
Confederate cavalry of General John H. Morgan. In January, 1863,
the regiment camped at Murfreesboro, where Lieutenant Tourgée fell
victim to Morgan's horse soldiers.[12]

Albion was assigned second-in-command over 128 soldiers sent out
with a wagon train to secure corn and fodder. Claiming to know a
particularly choice spot, the wagon master urged haste lest others reach
it first, and standing army orders were therefore violated, over Lieutenant
Tourgée's objections, by having the entire detail ride inside the wagons.
The wagon train proceeded out beyond the pickets and into a densely
wooded hillside, where, with the entire guard still inside the wagons,
it was ambushed by about 160 of Morgan's cavalry. Hearing shots
forward, Tourgée, who was in command of the rear wagons, quickly
ordered the men out, but before they could act the Confederates were

[11] *Official Records*, Series I, XVI, Part I, 1064–65. See also Tourgée, *The Story
of a Thousand: Being a History of the Service of the 105th Ohio Volunteer Infantry,
in the War for the Union from August 21, 1862 to June 6, 1865* (Buffalo, N.Y.,
1896), 108–36. The history of the 105th can be easily followed in Tourgée's history,
which has proven accurate whenever checked against standard military histories and
official records.
[12] The following is based upon a manuscript account by Tourgée, May 30, 1863;
Tourgée, *Story of a Thousand*, 175–86; *Official Records*, Series I, XXIII, Part I, 15–
16; *ibid.*, Part II, 21–22.

upon them. Almost the entire detail was shamefully captured with hardly a shot fired. Only 20 men and the wagon master escaped, the latter under suspicious circumstances.

Little is known of the four months that Albion spent in Confederate prisons, except that he was at Atlanta, Salisbury, and Libby. In a subsequent account of his Ohio regiment he ignored prison experiences as of "little interest and no value" today, but elsewhere he mentioned crowded conditions, a lack of shelter, foulness, and neglect,[13] and in an unfinished fictional manuscript he portrayed a sadistic guard but tolerable though uncomfortable conditions at Atlanta. In some respects, prison proved beneficial to Albion, giving his back a needed rest and enabling him to read Carlyle's account of the French Revolution and Cervantes' Don Quixote. When he was finally exchanged, he returned damning the Confederacy and full of fight. For four months he had claimed "but two enjoyments—cursing the Confederacy and smoking," and he emerged with torn and dilapidated clothing, one shoe, one jackknife, "one bone toothpick, and 540,000 lice." [14]

Before returning to war, Albion traveled to Columbus, Ohio, where he and Emma were finally wed on May 14, 1863. Two weeks later he was back with the regiment at Murfreesboro.

The following month the 105th moved against the enemy to discourage Confederate assistance from being sent to either General Lee, who was then invading Maryland, or to Vicksburg, which was besieged by Grant. Though traveling through rain and mud, Albion reported himself to Emma as in the best of condition, and after outstanding service in the Battle of Hoover's Gap and the days of skirmishing which followed, his regiment joined in pursuit of the Confederates toward Chattanooga. Once again Albion enjoyed a delightful march "through the most romantic country and the richest scenery that our American Switzerland can furnish." He also found time for a fascinating canoe trip through Nickajack Cave and endorsed the prevalent view that "Old Rosey" and "Pap Thomas" would soon lead them to a victory.

As the Confederates abandoned Chattanooga in September, the

---

[13] Tourgée, Story of a Thousand, Preface; Roy F. Dibble, Albion W. Tourgée (New York, 1921), 26–27.

[14] Tourgée to Emma L. Kilbourne from aboard the flag of truce ship "State of Maine," May 6, 1863.

eager Federals pursued them into the confusing and bloody Battle of Chickamauga. The battle was fought mainly amidst dense woods and foliage, where central control was minimized and the burden of action rested heavily upon independently acting units. Albion found himself "wild with excitement" and caring "no more for bullets or steel than for a shower of feathers," [15] and he participated in the 105th's gallant bayonet charge against the flank of Longstreet's army, which, by delaying the turning of the Union wing, saved many Federal troops.

After the battle the Union Army returned to Chattanooga, where the sound of ax, spade, hammer, and saw, punctured by occasional musketry, marked the digging in of the Federal forces. The greatest hardship of the moment was a drastic but temporary shortage of rations. Amidst this quiet, Albion's army career was pushed to a close.

During his second enlistment, Albion had retained his qualities of leadership and in many ways had been "well known and recognized as a brave and efficient officer." [16] But soon after the battle of Perryville, he noticed that men were being promoted over him. Although he attempted in vain to be "too dignified to fret," he was increasingly annoyed at his failure to secure a captaincy. This failure was attributable to a variety of causes. Tourgée's obstinate independence aroused hostility, and he also held controversial ideas on discipline. Idealistic and conscious of his previous service as an enlisted man, Albion did not approve of slavish discipline but believed that obedience should and could be based upon confidence and understanding. Although claiming disciplinary success with his own men, he discovered that his views conflicted with standard belief and aroused resentment among his superiors. Of greatest significance in hindering advancement, however, was Tourgée's injured back. He never complained, said a close comrade-in-arms, but he walked with difficulty and always sat down the moment march was halted, and when free he frequently rested lying down.[17] Although Albion fought against admitting any incapacity, even to himself, his weak back undoubtedly contributed to his collapse on the Hell March and to his extended hospitalization following the wound received at Perryville. But until years later he fought against any such admission,

---

[15] Tourgée to his wife, September 29, 1863.
[16] Affidavit of Charles G. Edwards, April 24, 1906, Federal Pension Records.
[17] Affidavit of Joseph R. Warner, March 11, 1890, Federal Pension Records.

instead attributing his difficulties in the army to various clashes with his superiors.

That there were such clashes was beyond dispute. For instance, he engaged in a protracted controversy with his regimental colonel over the captured wagon train. Accepting the escaped wagon master's account of the incident, the colonel blamed the disaster on the captured captain, Byron W. Canfield, and had him summarily dismissed from the army. Tourgée, upon his return from prison, defended the captain, attributed the capture to an order from the colonel, and implied that the wagon master was in league with the enemy. Soon a letter praising the cashiered captain was being signed by the officers of the regiment. Personally affronted and with his authority endangered, the colonel threatened dishonorable discharge for the officers involved and arrested two officers and had their quarters searched to secure the controversial letter. Tourgée and ten other officers thereupon threatened to resign, and as others prepared to join them, the colonel backed down. We have "conquered our tyrant" proclaimed the vexatious Lieutenant Tourgée, and wherever the fault for the captured troops lay, the arbitrarily convicted Captain Canfield was subsequently cleared.[18] Albion had again shown his propensity to disrupt, but there was point and purpose to his protest.

The jubilation aroused by this victory was short-lived. A few days later Albion threatened to resign because of his discontent with the "infernal regiment," and three days later he was arrested for his behavior while serving as lieutenant of the guard. With drawn sword, the doughty Albion blocked a formation of soldiers that a major attempted to march through the area of gun stacks that Albion was guarding. One of the soldiers, out of similar bravado, marched into Albion's sword and was slightly pricked, and at his court-martial, Albion was also accused of calling the major "a damn fool." [19] Tourgée's appropriate defense, that he was defending a "sacred trust," won a verdict of not guilty on all counts, but he was reprimanded for having thrust too readily with his sword.

[18] See Tourgée's manuscript account, May 30, 1863; Tourgée to his wife, May 30 and June 3, 1863; Tourgée to his father, June 4, 1863; Tourgée's War Diary, June 3, 1863, and resignation dated June 2, 1863; and Tourgée, *Story of a Thousand,* 175–86.

[19] Tourgée to his wife, June 8, 11, 1863. See also Court Martial NN 78, Judge Advocate General's Records, National Archives; Tourgée to his father, July 16, 1863; Tourgée notebook, 1863.

Albion was also annoyed by certain difficulties with the captain of his company, and the sum of all his discontent provoked an application for transfer to a Negro regiment. But as the troops moved out of Murfreesboro, Albion's difficulties dissolved amidst the pleasant marches and exciting battles which followed. In July, 1863, he felt honored by his appointment as a judge advocate, and difficulties with his captain subsided when Albion was given command of a separate company. Although he had not received the usual promotion to captain with this command, Albion was delighted with his men and his new authority and reported to Emma that he was in the best of health and spirits.

Again Albion's contentment was brief. Shortly after the army moved into Chattanooga, he lost his footing while leaping over a deep excavation and fell backward into it, seriously re-injuring his back. Lame and chagrined, doomed to the most unglamorous of war injuries, the gallant young lieutenant was confined to camp as the Federals moved out for their dramatic successes at Lookout Mountain and Missionary Ridge. As Albion watched the exciting mountain battles from the plains below, his army career approached its end.

Perhaps fittingly, Albion's final dispute with the army concerned his resignation. The army suggested that the lieutenant resign because of his injured back, but unwilling to admit the significance of this disability, Albion refused. Instead he submitted an indignant resignation based upon his failure to secure a promotion. This was rejected with orders to report for possible transfer to the Invalid Corps, an insult that prompted Albion's proposal to resign "for the good of the service," [20] on the grounds that the continued promotion of junior officers over him would ultimately undermine his authority. This was reluctantly accepted, and on December 6, 1863, his army career came to an end.

There is no doubt that Albion's injured back was a source of continued difficulty in the army and the major reason for the termination of his service, and, despite his reluctance to accept the seriousness of his handicap, this disability troubled him for the remainder of his life. The once athletic Albion remained unable to walk long distances, to lift weight, or engage in manual labor. He could not remain standing for long periods and when sitting had to shift position frequently and lean against his desk for comfort. On occasion a misstep or a fall would

[20] United States Army Muster Roll Records, National Archives.

leave him temporarily prostrate, paralyzed, and depressed. The impact of this injury became especially acute in the later years of his life.

A tragic physical disability was not Albion's only heritage from the war. His wartime letters reveal, for example, an intensified religious faith, which appeared to provide inner security against the dangers of war and an increased confidence in the triumph of a righteous cause. The cause itself had a momentous impact also. Upon first enlisting in 1861 Tourgée's only apparent concern had been national reunion, but he proved ready prey for the glorious slogan of Freedom as well. While Tourgée was recovering from the injuries received at Bull Run, anti-slavery sentiments pervaded his poetry and oratory, and several incidents during his second term of service further awakened an interest in the Negro and the South.

Negroes endeared themselves to the soldiers of the 105th by supplying water to the parched troops along the route of the Hell March, and many escaped slaves joined this journey to Louisville. As the army entered that city, civilian deputies were waiting to seize runaway Negroes, but Albion's regiment, with the encouragement of its aboli-tionist colonel, protected the slaves within its ranks with lowered bayonets. Holding firm against a brief flurry of violence, the regiment won from an unsympathetic Union general the title "abolition nigger-stealers." [21] Albion supported such regimental activities, although he did object to the colonel's forceful encouragement of abolitionist sentiment within the ranks.

Tourgée's employment of a runaway slave as a servant (the model for the hero of *Bricks Without Straw*, one of Tourgée's famous Reconstruc-tion novels) additionally stimulated his interest in the Negro, and after attending a meeting of escaped slaves in the spring of 1863, he professed an unexpectedly favorable impression of their abilities. It was at this time that he requested a transfer to a Negro regiment, and he discussed slavery and emancipation in several poems written during the war.

The war also developed Albion's political thinking, as revealed in his letter to a fraternity brother early in 1863: "I think the oft repeated maxim of the Administration—'We are fighting but for the Union as it was'—A most sublime hoax. For one, I don't care a rag for 'the Union as it was.' I want & fight for *the Union better* than 'it was.'

[21] Tourgée, *Story of a Thousand*, 91.

Before this is accomplished we must have a fundamental thorough and complete revolution & renovation. This I expect & hope." [22] The significance of this statement should not be exaggerated. It is perhaps the only political expression in Albion's entire war correspondence and occurred at a time when he was striving for maturity. But, conforming to Albion's turbulent idealism, the comment revealed an attitude which would easily incline him toward radical Republicanism, if and when he became involved in politics.

[22] Tourgée to a fraternity brother, January 19, 1863.

III

South to Emancipation

After resigning from the army, Albion returned to Ohio and experimented indecisively with a variety of occupations. Securing admittance to the Ohio bar in the spring of 1864, he entered a Painesville law office and sought legal work in several surrounding towns, but limited returns soon prompted his acceptance of a journalistic position with the Erie, Pennsylvania, *Dispatch*. Little is known of Albion's duties for the *Dispatch*, other than that he traveled constantly by railroad, while Emma tended farm in Conneaut and kept him involved by mail in farming affairs. Following several months of this, the travel-weary Albion welcomed an appointment to the *Dispatch* office in Erie, and the young Tourgées established their residence in that city in the fall of 1864. This position also lacked lasting appeal, and in March, 1865, Albion became a teacher and principal at Erie Academy, but remained dissatisfied. During this time he also secured an M.A. degree from Rochester University, and he may have obtained an appointment as an officer in a Negro army regiment in the spring of 1865, although the conclusion of the war ended any such possible resumption of a military career.

Of greater consequence during these months than fluctuating employment was Albion's growing interest in the South. Although his army experiences and a concern with the outcome of the Civil War contributed to this interest, other decisive stimulants included Albion's unsettled condition, medical advice that the cold aggravated his troubled back, and speculative business discussions with some close friends. Inspired by some combination of these factors, early in 1865 Albion directed a fateful letter to the governor of North Carolina inquiring as to the opportunities available to a group of prospective Yankee immigrants. An encouraging reply from Provisional Governor William W. Holden revealed that the futile efforts of the Confederacy had reaped their usual bitter harvest in his state but noted that fertile land was available at low prices, that many investment opportunities existed, and that there was a demand for skilled labor. North Carolina needed capital and men, Holden urged, and promised the prospective carpetbaggers that "every favor [would] be shown to them by our people and our laws." [1]

Holden's letter enticed Tourgée into a tour of inspection in the summer of 1865, and he left Erie somewhat fearful lest he "find some insuperable obstacle in the way" of his "southern scheme." But shaking off the pessimistic counsel received from "some heavy capitalists" in New York City, he invested twenty-five dollars in a boat passage to North Carolina. On July 22, 1865, this sanguine and noble Union veteran of twenty-eight boarded the southbound steamer "El Cid," a name far more prophetic than his own thoughts. "I believe my aim is as good as a poor man's may be," he wrote Emma shortly before embarking, "and I have faith that God will open a way for its accomplishment or if not that some other as good or better." [2]

The sea voyage south was stormy (a fitting omen), but the undisturbed Albion disembarked at New Berne and eagerly proceeded overland to Raleigh, the state capital, which was bustling with activity and filled with southern unionists flocking after privileged places and with recent Confederates seeking to restore lost fortunes or secure needed pardons. Two days in the capital provided Albion with a hopeful impression and with more information than he had expected to obtain in a month. He was greatly encouraged by two "satisfactory interviews" with Governor Holden and by such an abundance of prospective legal clients that his stay was extended by his first court case in the state, the defense of a Union soldier accused of stealing Federal cotton.

Albion returned north in August with intentions of settling in North Carolina, and that fall he and Emma returned to the state with several thousand dollars in saved and borrowed capital. They were soon joined by Emma's family, which had helped finance the venture, and by

[1] William W. Holden to Tourgée, June 16, 1865, Tourgée Papers.
[2] Tourgée to his wife, July 20, 22, 1865, Tourgée Papers.

Albion's two young business associates, Seneca Kuhn and R. T. Pettingill. The group settled on the outskirts of Greensboro, one of the state's leading towns and the county seat of the prosperous and pleasant piedmont county of Guilford. A moderate climate and a sturdy and unusually literate yeomanry contributed to the county's attractiveness, and certain national and liberal traditions of the region boded well for Tourgée. Support for the colonial Regulator rebellion and for the American Revolution had been strong in the area, and before and during the Civil War, Guilford and her neighboring counties had abounded in unionist and antislavery sentiment.

In 1865 the idealistic traditions of Guilford were, however, of less moment to Tourgée than the problem of securing a livelihood. Four miles west of Greensboro, he and his associates leased the West Green Nursery and seven hundred and fifty acres of plantation land, for a yearly rental of $1,000, from Cyrus P. Mendenhall, a prominent Greensboro unionist, who had recently invested $17,000 in the nursery without much success. Nevertheless these Yankee partners were encouraged by recollections of Rochester's famed and prosperous nurseries. A subsequent contract between Tourgée, Kuhn, and Pettingill established the firm of "A. W. Tourgée & Co.," which was to operate the nursery and plantation, practice law, and engage in any other venture agreed upon. Each partner contributed equal shares to a joint capital of $4,500 and shared equally in the profits. Negro freedmen were soon employed upon the plantation, large advertisements of the nursery's products appeared in the local press, and Emma's father was engaged as salesman for the firm. As legal clients were secured, Albion became involved in suits by southern unionists against the United States for damages inflicted by Sherman's army, but such claims were to be unexpectedly frustrated by the indecisive, even unsympathetic, attitude of the Federal government. "A. W. Tourgée & Co." also became involved in a small railroad speculation, from which the hopefully anticipated "snug little fortune" would never appear.

Ultimately, the most significant aspect of Tourgée's business activity was the contact it provided with southern unionists and Negroes who later became his political allies, although this was not apparent in 1865. As Tourgée later stated, he ventured south unaware of the approaching political turmoil or the complexities of emancipation, naïvely anticipating the benefits of an "incursion of Northern life, thought, capital, industry, [and] enterprise." He expected an economic boom whereby that great Yankee cure-all, the "plaster of profit," would heal the sores left by slavery and war, and he trusted that his own education and belief would contribute to the wealth of the nation, the South, and last and by no means least, himself. Tourgée did envisage some difficulty in effecting the transition from slavery to freedom and had speculated on the status of the freed slave, but he assumed that this would be essentially a mechanical task—"Yesterday the Southern planter had owned his labor; tomorrow he would pay him wages: that was all." [3] Quite ironically, the same oversimplification by the white South aroused Tourgée's anger and helped impel him into Reconstruction politics.

The fate of the emancipated southern Negro was one of three prominent issues provoking Tourgée's entrance into politics (the other two concerned the questions of national loyalty and popular government). Although there is a paucity of source material dealing with his initial response to race relations in the South, Tourgée's subsequent writings, especially his two autobiographical novels, A Fool's Errand and Bricks Without Straw, provide a strong clue to his reaction. What evidence does exist confirms the autobiographical accuracy of his fictional accounts.

Northern free-labor concepts almost always inspired some conflict with southern ways, but Tourgée's position became particularly provocative because of his acceptance of the Negro as an equal. Certain fragments of poetry written during the war revealed this inclination and displayed a combination of penetrating realism and romanticized fancy which would continue to characterize his writings. Several of these poems dwelt upon the clash between the state of slavery and the dignity, emotions, and desires of the individual slave, and one poem completed in 1862, "The Answer," suggested the wisdom of helping lift the Negro out of his heritage of oppression and ignorance. Clearly attempting to counter the reluctance of even northern whites to recognize Negro capabilities, Tourgée depicted a glorified group of slaves who welcome the invading (not yet liberating) Union Army with remarkable displays of piety and industriousness and aspirations for freedom and knowledge:

[3] Tourgée, An Appeal to Caesar (New York, 1884), 56–59.

And the rough blaspheming soldiers
Stood rebuked before the slave,
As they listened to their worship
And the deepest reverence gave,
And they felt how great the shame is
That these men of Christian mind,
Others, for unholy profit,
In vile servitude should bind.
Then there came the kindly feeling
Swelling every patriot-breast,
That to lift these trodden children
From the dust, was God's behest.

Such idyllic visions help explain Tourgée's subsequent behavior, but they were of little aid in solving the problems presented by emancipation. Tourgée soon learned that habitual southern behavior and belief were not abolished simply by proclamation or constitutional amendment and that the task of readjustment was particularly difficult because "the boundary-line of servitude [had] marked also the distinction of race. Only the white man had the right to freedom in the South." [4] Of course racism did exist without slavery, as witness the North, and perhaps the most important distinction of the South was merely the size of the Negro population. More racial contact could mean more racial conflict, which, in turn, could intensify prejudice. Also, racist beliefs had been strengthened and spread in the South by the ante-bellum defense of slavery, and Tourgée was justly appalled at the extent to which pseudoscience, theology, and rationalization had inculcated convictions of Negro inferiority and of the necessity for white leadership and control. The condition of freed Negroes, whose morality and education had been perverted by slavery, contributed to the continuance of white supremacy, but Negro shortcomings were never quite the same rigid barrier as what one North Carolinian referred to as the "social prejudice of centuries." [5]

The national government became deeply involved in this problem,

[4] Tourgée, An Appeal to Caesar, 31.
[5] Robert P. Dick to T. D. Cox, July 7, 1867, James A. Padgett (ed.), "Reconstruction Letters from North Carolina," North Carolina Historical Review (hereafter cited as NCHR), XVIII (1941), 374.

primarily through the army and the Freedmen's Bureau, as it attempted
to ensure the establishment of a free-labor economy. Federal authorities
were devoted to free enterprise and were not overly inclined to interfere
with the economic prerogatives of landowners or to be overly sentimental
toward a landless, laboring class; nonetheless, the policies of these
authorities were favorable to the Negro simply because they were directed toward removing vestiges of slavery. Although there were
innumerable clashes between northern and southern views concerning
the requirements of freedom, much encouraging progress was made.
Federal policies, high prices, the Negro's need of a livelihood, and the
planter's desire for profit all contributed to economic recovery, and
within a year of the conclusion of the war, the Freedmen's Bureau was
convinced that free Negro labor was a proven success and that over
three-fourths of the planters were disposed to treat the Negroes fairly.
The Bureau, in turn, was complimented by employers for its contributions to this transition. Furthermore, in North Carolina during this
period, race relations were often friendly, the legislature passed "Black
Codes" which were comparatively moderate, and the higher courts dealt
justly with Negroes. But, paradoxically, racism remained a glaring problem, and the precise status of the Negro remained a subject of heated
dispute. The very Bureau agents who admitted impressive progress remained dissatisfied and frightened. They agreed with Tourgée that
Negro interests were inadequately represented, that the moderate white
majority was not disposed to curtail the racial extremists, and that a
partial return to slavery threatened.[6]

Many facets of this problem vexed Tourgée during his first years in
North Carolina, and the representatives of white supremacy quickly
drifted into his category of major foes. Anti-Negro behavior was
particularly noticeable among the ante-bellum slaveowning gentry, a
group accustomed to almost unlimited power over Negro labor and
thoroughly imbued with proslavery theories of Negro inferiority. In their

[6] Conclusions respecting the Negro's status are based especially upon the local
records of the North Carolina Freedmen's Bureau (in the National Archives), the
vicious attitude of much of the state press, and the views expressed in the private
papers of state leaders. Hundreds of reports from throughout the state testify to the
conscientious application and observation of most Bureau agents, and their activities
are accurately summarized in such North Carolina reports as those found in U.S.,
Congress, Senate, *Senate Executive Document 27*, 39th Cong., 1st Sess., and *Senate
Executive Document 6*, 39th Cong., 2d Sess.

attempt to restore the productivity of the often annoying free Negroes, these recent slave masters found the methods and prejudices of slavery useful and appealing. Although seldom so impoverished as Negroes or poorer whites, landowners had suffered great losses and humiliating defeat, and they were in no mood to tolerate further challenges to their authority or their profit from a people they considered inferior. Honest differences and mutual abuses easily provoked thousands of conflicts between these planters and Negro laborers. Negroes were guilty of instability, insolence, and theft, and their masters of coercion, dishonesty, and fraud. In such disputes, however, economic, political, and intellectual forces overwhelmingly favored the planter, and Tourgée correctly complained that vestiges of slavery were being preserved (a fact of which some planters boasted [7]) and that the Negro was being reduced to a helpless, semifree, inexpensive laboring class. This echoed a common complaint of Freedmen's Bureau agents. Not only did some whites restrict the significance of emancipation to the mere payment of wages, but "an almost universal determination [was] expressed to make [the Negroes] politically and socially an inferior and degraded caste." [8]

Violence frequently accompanied and dramatized the dispute over the status of freed slaves. Negroes complained that sometimes they were treated more cruelly than when they had been slaves, that they were whipped, cheated, driven from the land or their livelihood, shot at, and killed. Soon after the close of the war, a meeting of North Carolina Negroes requested protection against "our former rebel masters, who have taken the oath, but are filled with malice, and swear vengeance against us as soon as the military are withdrawn"; [9] and later in the year a state Negro convention sought proper wages and protection against the landowners of the state. The moderate head of the Freedmen's Bureau in North Carolina affirmed such complaints: "Some refuse to employ negroes except at very low wages. Others claim the right to whip

[7] Testimony of William K. Lane, Court Martial OO 1705, Judge Advocate General's Records, 91–103, 112. See also Greensboro *Patriot*, September 9, 1865, and Central District Report, October 10, 1865, North Carolina Freedmen's Bureau Records, Box 423, hereafter cited as NCFBR.

[8] Eliphalet Whittlesey to Oliver O. Howard, August 21, 1865, NCFBR, VII.

[9] *National Anti-Slavery Standard*, May 27, 1865; see also *ibid.*, July 29, October 14, 21, 1865.

and 'buck' them at will, as in former times. And a few openly declare that they will either have them slaves again, or exterminate the whole race." [10]

To Tourgée such occurrences were unacceptably reminiscent of slavery, and both his and Emma's inclinations were well revealed by their activities with the West Green Nursery and Plantation. Albion's two Yankee business partners, on the other hand, proved to be profit-minded and anxious to exploit Negro labor, and they strongly objected to the generosity and kindness of the Tourgée family. When Emma and Albion endangered business profits by actively representing the freedmen, tempers flared and the business partnership drifted toward dissolution.

Postwar economic rivalry was central to racial conflict, but the streams of prejudice ran much wider and deeper, with the state and local leadership of North Carolina displaying an intense prejudice against the supposedly inferior Negroes. Emancipation was viewed with great skepticism, and any violation of the traditional submissive status of the Negro was sharply resented. In essence, Tourgée's many fictional illustrations of the various phases of this phenomenon can be easily documented by manuscript sources. For example, certain accounts in A Fool's Errand remind one of the question of a planter who asked whether there "was ever such a crime committed against humanity as by their liberation?" [11] Or consider a gentlewoman's description of the "general feeling of indignation" directed against a native white woman who taught Negroes. "The school in Greensboro has ruined the poor creatures," she wrote; "it puts notions of equality into their heads that wholly unfit them for any kind of servitude." [12] It is true that the more benevolent North Carolinians endorsed a degree of legal protection and rights for Negroes (Jonathan Worth even accepted qualified Negro suffrage at one moment), but there was a dread of substantial equality between the races, and thoughts of intermarriage were the climax of such fears. In 1865 Governor Jonathan Worth, soon a bitter foe of

[10] Whittlesey to Howard, August 21, 1865, NCFBR, VII.

[11] A Fool's Errand (New York, 1879), 73; Weldon N. Edwards to Thomas Ruffin, October 11, 1866, J. G. de Roulhac Hamilton (ed.), The Papers of Thomas Ruffin (4 vols.; Raleigh, 1918–1920), IV, 132–34.

[12] M. C. Avery to a friend, February 21, 1866, Patterson Papers, Southern Historical Collection, University of North Carolina.

Albion Tourgée, summed up the issue quite clearly: "We who were born here will never get along with the free negroes, especially while the fools and demagogues of the North insist they must be our equals. This will not be tolerated." [13]

Similar feelings were evident on many levels. Efforts at Negro improvement were scoffed at and opposed, the Black Codes retained inequities based upon race, police authorities ignored violence directed against Negroes and participated in outrages upon them, and the lower courts dealt out even less than the law to the degraded race. Tourgée's subsequent writings would reveal his sensitive reaction to this state of affairs. Particularly galling was the only newspaper in his home town, the Greensboro *Patriot*, which constantly maligned the Negro during 1865 and 1866. Negroes were ridiculed and slandered in viciously stereotyped articles and poems; the affectionate "Cuffee, Sambo, Gumbo or Squashie" was depicted as akin to a pet parrot or monkey; the right of whites to aversions of "taste or smell" was defended; imprisonment was suggested and violence against insolent Negroes approved of; and Yankees were denounced for encouraging Negro impudence.[14] Even paternalism could be annoying, as when objections were raised against any ill-treatment of the "lazy, heedless, thriftless" race. "If they cannot (as they never can)," wrote a late slaveowner, "occupy the places of legislators, judges, teachers, &c., yet they may be useful as tillers of the soil, as handicraftsmen, as servants in various situations, and be happy in their domestic and family relations. I repeat, it is our Christian duty to encourage them to these ends. . . ." [15]

With the potential colored voter numbering about one-third of the state's total, the question of Negro political participation was one of particular sensitivity and importance. Multiple factors, including emissaries from the North and theories of democracy, inspired the Negroes to organize, seek reform, and agitate for voting privileges during 1865; and before the end of the year the question of Negro suffrage was being openly discussed in the state, perhaps because the climate for it was so unfavorable. The Raleigh *Progress* [16] insisted, with mistaken but

[13] Worth to B. G. Worth, September 11, 1865, J. G. de Roulhac Hamilton (ed.), *The Correspondence of Jonathan Worth* (2 vols.; Raleigh, 1909), I, 417–18.
[14] Greensboro *Patriot*, June 3, July 22, August 26, December 23, 1865; March 9, April 13, 20, May 4, 1866.
[15] Greensboro *Patriot*, September 9, 1865.
[16] Quoted in *National Anti-Slavery Standard*, June 17, 1865.

indicative confidence, that not one white person in North Carolina favored Negro suffrage, and both political parties in the state advised the Negroes to improve themselves but not to trifle with politics. Only a small minority accepted the thought of eventual full citizenship, with some of the most astute comments on the subject being made by William P. Bynum, State Solicitor and later a Republican and judicial colleague of Tourgée. Because this nation was committed to the philosophy of political equality, declared Bynum, emancipation would not be the end of Negro advancement, for the principles of popular sovereignty supported the claims of the black as well as the white: "A wise statesmanship would seem to require of us, to anticipate danger by providing against it, to allay discontent before it swells into convulsion, by providing a gradually ascending scale of political right, which will disarm clamor, encourage the black race, and also strengthen the state." [17]

But no such steps were taken. Black and white advocates of Negro political equality were left to await the drastic Federal steps in this direction taken by the Reconstruction Acts of 1867. Prior to this, Tourgée had become sufficiently aroused by racism and other issues within the state to advocate the wisdom of full Negro suffrage. Unfortunately, such a radical challenge to southern whites would inspire bitter resistance and ignite a flame that destroyed much of the kindness that had accompanied white supremacy in the past.

The status of the Negro was certainly a central problem in the postwar South, although prevailing attitudes in that region were not as unique as many imagined. The North, which could manipulate with relative ease because of its small Negro population and the absence of slavery, would take significant steps toward equality with obvious reluctance, and, far from united, it would drag its feet on the matter for generations. Furthermore, it was a northern Democratic party's cry of white supremacy, during and after the war, which southern leaders rushed to endorse. At that time, the humiliated and impoverished South was not

[17] Raleigh *Tri-Weekly Standard*, July 14, 1866. In January, 1868, the *Tri-Weekly Standard* became the Raleigh *Daily North Carolina Standard*; each will hereafter be cited as Raleigh *Standard*. Eventual Negro citizenship was also endorsed by Alfred M. Waddell, a Conservative, and Victor C. Barringer, a member of the Union and Republican parties. See Raleigh *Daily Sentinel*, August 9, 1865, cited hereafter as Raleigh *Sentinel*, and J. G. de Roulhac Hamilton, *Reconstruction in North Carolina* (New York, 1914), 151.

in a favorable condition or mood to handle the problem of a large and backward population of emancipated Negroes. Custom, belief, and self-interest all encouraged rigidity. The honest critics of the South, on the other hand, lacked imagination and tact, and many of their supporters would prove to lack sincerity or determination. Postwar challenges from within and without inspired southern resentment and resistance rather than reform. The Negro was relegated with marked determination to a status of inferiority, and injustice and violence were freely utilized to keep him there. Intensifying the plight of the Negro was his own condition. "A race despised, degraded, penniless, ignorant, houseless, homeless, fatherless, childless, nameless," wrote Tourgée, which "had neither property, knowledge, right or power." [18] Tourgée's perception included compassion as well as criticism:

> He [the southern white] simply regards the Negro as an inferior, with an inherited belief which amounts almost to an instinct, even if it be not actually instinctive. He wishes only good to that inferior; has no desire to do him harm, to lessen his comfort or prevent his success, within what he deems the proper sphere of his existence. He is a Christian man, and he desires to see the colored man improve in morals, industry, and the virtues of a Christian life. All these things he may most earnestly and sincerely desire for the colored man, whom he calls, with effusive and perhaps delusive warmth, "our brother in black." It is only when the necessity arises for considering this race as the equal of the white race in power, in freedom, and in opportunity, that we discover that beneath this sentiment of kindness lies the indefinable feeling that the colored man may not, must not, shall not, stand upon the same level of right and power as the white.[19]

Tourgée's conception of race relations in the South was accurate, if intolerant, and initially it was not as sophisticated as it later became. His contempt for racist doctrines always exceeded by far any compassion he held for the advocates of such beliefs. He attacked this evil with the

[18] Tourgée, *Bricks Without Straw* (New York, 1880), 34.
[19] Tourgée, *An Appeal to Caesar*, 96. Because Tourgée fought long and hard for the capitalization of the word Negro, it has been thought fit to do so wherever he is quoted in this book.

same crusading ardor that had characterized his participation in the Civil War, and to an exaggerated extent he identified this new enemy, racism, with slavery. The question of the Negro's position in society became of ever-fascinating concern to Tourgée and would largely motivate his involvement in Reconstruction politics, dominate his future writings, and remain the frustrating central focus of his life's work until his very death.

IV

White Man's Politics

R ace relationship was not the only southern problem affecting the newly arrived immigrant Albion W. Tourgée. He was also greatly influenced by several portentous political controversies among the whites, one of which involved southern hostility toward secession and the Confederacy. Despite the initial martial enthusiasm of 1861, it had not been long before unionism in North Carolina, reinforced by the strains of war and by older class and sectional antagonisms, had sparked noticeable opposition to the Confederate cause. Discontent expressed itself by desertion, guerilla activity, secret unionist organization, resistance to conscription, aid to escaped Union soldiers, and enlistment in the northern army. An openly functioning peace movement in North Carolina helped promote such disaffection and attracted the support of consistent antisecessionists as well as of those southerners who began to despair of the Confederate cause. By 1864 the peace movement was powerful in many areas, and although its candidate lost the gubernatorial race of that year, it may have had the support of a majority of the home population. Several Confederate leaders in the state bemoaned their lack of popular support, and the energetic war governor Zebulon B. Vance concluded "that the great *popular heart* is not now & never has been in this war. It was a revolution of the *politicians* not the *people.*" [1]

It would be almost two years after the collapse of this Confederacy before the well-known congressional plan of Radical Reconstruction was launched, but in the interim political rivalry and civil government were

[1] Vance to David L. Swain, September 22, 1864, quoted in Richard Bardolph, "Inconstant Rebels: Desertion of North Carolina Troops in the Civil War," *NCHR*, XLI (April, 1964), 167.

essentially restored in North Carolina under the milder auspices of President Andrew Johnson. Elevated to the presidency by Lincoln's assassination, Johnson was not a wholly appropriate replacement for the martyred Republican. A life-long Democrat from Tennessee, the new President was a man whom belief and political calculation would gradually impel toward an unconcealed sympathy for the defeated white South and its racial traditions. In response, Republican leaders increasingly viewed the postwar policies of this southern Democrat with distrust and dismay. They were more inclined to feel compassion for the black and the unionist South, and they resented the President's pretensions and feared a Confederate-Democratic resurgence. An intense and lasting wrangle as to the proper means of reconstructing the nation was soon under way and this conflict centered in a clash between the Chief Executive and the Republican Congress. Southern events would both reflect and affect this tale.

The initial step of Johnsonian Reconstruction in North Carolina was the appointment of the recently defeated gubernatorial peace candidate, William W. Holden, as provisional governor of the state. Although an early secessionist and reluctant signer of the ordinance of secession, the prominent Holden had become a Douglas Democrat who fought secession until the firing at Fort Sumter; during the war he became a peace advocate and ardent critic of the Confederacy and the leader of the peace movement. As postwar provisional governor, Holden ambitiously began building a new Union party, largely an offshoot of his peace movement and ante-bellum Democratic following. Unfortunately, however, most of the powerful economic and political leaders of the state had remained staunch Confederates and bitter opponents of Holden during the war, and they continued to consider him a betrayer of their own sectional beliefs and interests. Immediately following defeat, these ex-Confederates were fearful and quiet, but they were soon encouraged to reassert themselves by such factors as Federal leniency and indecision, divisions between the President and Congress, and overtures from the northern Democratic party. A rivalry between anti-Confederates and unionists on the one side and consistent Confederates or "latter day war men" on the other soon became a central focus of North Carolina politics, and this rivalry retained much of the emotionalism and rancor that had existed during the war.

This division was not absolute and was sometimes obscured, especially by the history of a wartime conservatism that opposed and overpowered more centralist and fire-eating tendencies. The Conservatives represented traditional leaders of the state who had labored for both slavery and union, but who finally felt driven by events to endorse secession and cast their lot with the Confederacy. They retained control of the state and became determined supporters of the Confederate cause, but they regretted the entire state of affairs and attributed it to the radicalism of original secessionists and abolitionists. This attitude alienated many early secessionists (some of whom later supported Holden) and, together with the popularity of antiwar sentiment, helps explain why both postwar parties disclaimed responsibility for secession. It was ironic that those who dominated the state before, during, and soon after the war never desired or considered themselves responsible for the position of North Carolina. They attributed all evils to radicalism. Opposed to any postwar innovation, whether by state or nation, they fittingly retained the title of Conservatives.[2]

The Union party repentantly accepted defeat and Federal omnipotence after the war and advocated compliance with whatever terms the victors prescribed. It correctly cautioned that failure to cooperate might incite more radical demands and that North Carolina could not freely handle its internal affairs or influence Federal policy until it secured readmission to the Union.[3] But Holden's plea for "silence and hope" had little appeal to the proud and rather aristocratic Conservatives, who were accustomed to rule and feared suggested changes. They accepted emancipation, union, and, after some resistance, the repudiation

[2] Jonathan Worth, soon elected governor, was a natural leader for this group. A consistent unionist until 1861, Worth preferred secession to abolition. Additionally influenced by ties of property, family, and sentiment, he finally acquiesced in secession and, although flirting with the peace movement, remained a consistent Confederate. Worth blamed radicals in both sections for secession and continued the fight against radicalism in the postwar period, preferring as much of the status quo ante bellum as possible. Although his allies were the core of Confederate strength during the war, his postwar appeal was heightened by his initial resistance to secession, his continued unionism (in 1864 he actually hoped that reunion might yet save slavery), and his minimal war role. See Hamilton (ed.), Jonathan Worth, I, 131, 135–37, 148–52, 245, 282, 285, 298, 351, 438–39, 510, 536, 557, 576–77, 639; II, 749–52.

[3] Raleigh Standard, March 24, April 28, August 14, 1866. This account of postwar political rivalry is based largely upon the positions revealed by two Raleigh newspapers, the Union party and later Republican Standard and the Conservative Sentinel.

of the Confederate state debt, but nothing more. In response to Holden's plea for "unconditional re-Union," Conservatives demanded "the old Union" and the old Constitution without "any punishment, which fanaticism or political hatred or revenge may inflict upon them." [4]

The Union party achieved electoral victories immediately after the war, but when the powerful Confederate-Conservative coalition re-entered the political arena, power began to shift into their hands with the election of Jonathan Worth to the governorship late in 1865. The Union veteran Albion Tourgée was much perturbed by the apparent ascent of prominent Confederates, whom he considered traitors, and he would later complain that opposition to the Federal government became as "bitter and hostile as when it [the South] was united under the banner of rebellion." [5] Furthermore, as ex-Confederates regained confidence and control, southern unionists, whom Tourgée considered patriotic heroes, became a maligned and mistreated group. The press, private correspondence, army and Freedmen's Bureau reports, and North Carolina leaders and legislators testified to such persecution, and the strongly unionist western portion of the state was even pro-voked into seeking separate statehood. Undoubtedly Confederate sympathizers were also persecuted in unionist areas, but the picture was usually the reverse.

The piedmont area, where Tourgée had settled, was deeply immersed in these disputes. Some of the greatest strength and most talented leaders of the peace movement came from this area, including Thomas Settle of Wentworth and Robert P. Dick of Greensboro. After the war Settle and Dick became Union party leaders; and local figures such as the Reverend George W. Welker, a pastor of the German Reformed church since 1841, and Dr. W. P. Pugh, a member of the gentry, were active in local unionist meetings during 1865.[6] All these gentlemen later became close friends and political allies of Tourgée. During the war the sentiments of such men had inspired intense and sometimes violent opposition, and the continuing antipathy toward unionists, which so infuriated Tourgée, was evident in the laments of David F. Caldwell of

[4] Raleigh *Sentinel*, August 1, 1866. The cry for "the old Union" was, of course, the slogan of northern Democrats during and after the war.

[5] *An Appeal to Caesar*, 63. For example see Raleigh *Standard*, May 15, August 16, 1866.

[6] Greensboro *Patriot*, June 24, July 8, August 26, 1865.

Greensboro. A wealthy planter, lawyer, financier, and railroad promoter, Caldwell had remained a union man but was too conservative to endorse the Union party. Honest and consistent union men, Caldwell reported to his good friend Governor Worth, "have been singled out and are today hated and denounced in the most bitter and malignant manner. And the decree has gone forth from the lips of your great leaders, that all who thought and acted with you, as union men during the war shall be branded as *Cain and sink*, to rise no more as *politicians*. They are all traitors, Tories, Redstrings, so called Union men, or poor white trash." [7]

Already annoyed by the Negro issue, Tourgée was enticed into this political dispute by the spring of 1866. Recently meek and submissive ex-rebels were becoming defiant and oppressive, he protested, and he described the three predominant political elements in the South as consisting of: original secessionists, passive accepters of the Confederacy, and consistent unionists. While most of the second group became disillusioned by the war and viewed it as a "rich man's war and a poor man's fight," thought Tourgée, they still blindly followed "certain men who had led them by the nose from infancy to manhood, and these men are the leaders of the late rebellion." [8] Tourgée trusted only wartime unionists and Yankee immigrants. He refused to endorse Holden's Union party because Holden and other leaders of that party had acquiesced to Confederate authority, and he doubted their general sincerity. Tourgée's position paralleled an important rift within the state, since outright wartime unionists, known as "unionists of the straitest sect," looked upon Holden and his followers as Confederates and resented their own minimal postwar power. Holden's organization sought to smooth over this difference with only limited success, for it was unwilling to accept such extreme "straitest sect" measures as harsh proscription (this would bar many Union party men from political leadership) or complete repudiation of the state debt. Although the straitest sect remained a vocal minority, the more moderate Union party was of much greater significance in the state.

Tourgée affiliated himself with the minority of staunch unionists, which included men who resisted Confederate authority, fled conscription, deserted the Confederate Army, joined secret unionist organizations

[7] Caldwell to Worth, July 31, 1866. Hamilton (ed.), *Jonathan Worth*, II, 711–15.
[8] Notebook, April, 1866, Tourgée Papers.

or guerrilla units, or fought with the Union Army. Such men were comrades in arms and the only reliable population in the South, and in Tourgée's novels their heroic exploits suggest his admiration. Although his fictional unionists included upper-class gentlemen like Colonel Nathan Rhenn of *A Fool's Errand* (modeled after Colonel James Wren, a Guilford union man), they were usually southern yeomen who combined their opposition to the Confederacy with a class antagonism toward the slaveowning gentry.

Unionist feats such as draft-dodging, which Tourgée found ingenious or heroic, inspired lasting contempt from Confederates, and after the war hatred was kept alive by contemptuous descriptions of "unqualified Union men" as traitors or "weak and ignorant" men "too cowardly and base to fight." [9] "We could not persecute such a people," asserted the Raleigh *Sentinel*, "much less be afraid of them, but we simply despise their cowardice and infidelity to their own people." [10] It is not difficult to imagine such men discriminating against the straitest sect, and by 1866 this group found itself, like the Negro, subject to official and personal abuse, including violence, throughout the state. With irritating hypocrisy, state amnesty acts protecting Confederate veterans actually left civilian unionists criminally liable for pro-Union activities, until Federal authorities intervened in their behalf.[11]

To Tourgée the treatment of southern unionists was not only dastardly but downright treasonous, and he became involved in a unique case of persecution, illustrating the triangular conflict between straitest sect, Conservative, and Union parties. One of those involved in this case was Thomas Settle, formerly a supporter of the peace movement as well as a Confederate Army officer and solicitor, who during the war prosecuted the consistent unionist Rev. George W. Welker for delivering a Union speech. After the war Settle joined the Union party, but as state solicitor he now became involved in prosecuting a Union Army veteran.[12]

This case concerned William M. Johnson, a laborer from Rockingham

[9] Salisbury *Banner*, quoted in Raleigh *Standard*, April 7, 1866.

[10] Raleigh *Sentinel*, September 7, 1866.

[11] Edwin R. S. Canby to Ulysses S. Grant, November 14, 1867, Letters Sent, Second Military District, and General Order, November 15, 1867, Second Military District, War Department Records, National Archives.

[12] For the following account see Canby to Grant, November 14, 1867, and J. W. Clous to Tourgée, April 17, 1867, Letters Sent, Second Military District, War Department Records; Letters Received, Second Military District, War Department

County, who had deserted the Confederate Army in 1863, and while in flight to the Union lines had, with two accomplices, broken into and burglarized a house. Johnson subsequently reached the Federals and served honorably in the Union Army, especially as a scout during raids into his native state. Meanwhile he and his accomplices had been indicted for breaking and entering a dwelling and stealing five dollars' worth of bacon and two dollars' worth of other items. Johnson's two accomplices were soon apprehended, tried, and convicted of larceny, but were released upon their enlistment in the Confederate Army. However, when Johnson returned to the state after the war, he was arrested under the old indictment, tried, found guilty, and sentenced to be hanged.

Infuriated by this absurdity, Tourgée sought Federal military intervention, which was refused on the ground that civil justice had been restored in North Carolina and Johnson was not officially connected with the Union Army at the time of the crime. This was an outrageous abandonment of a civilian unionist to recent rebels. Not only had Johnson's military service not aided him, in ironic contrast to the fate of his accomplices, but according to Tourgée, the prosecutor had kept "it prominently before the court and jury, that Johnson had been a deserter and traitor to the Confederate cause." [13] Not only did Tourgée continue to implore further investigation by the military, but he offered four thousand dollars' security for the indigent Johnson's release. The military finally did respond, and after confirming Tourgée's account, exerted pressure upon Governor Worth. Meanwhile, certain residents of Rockingham County presented a petition for pardon, the tenor of which was that despite an impulsiveness and lack of morality that had led Johnson to oppose the Confederacy he should be released.[14] In April, 1867, after a year in prison, Johnson was unconditionally pardoned.

No doubt this was an extreme case, but it reflected an all too prevalent atmosphere that Tourgée equated with a betrayal of Union victory. Such incidents also hindered cooperation between the straitest sect and the Union party, although, as time passed, other issues began to loom

---

Records, Box H. 138; Court Martial OO 2610, Judge Advocate General's Records; NCFBR, XCVII, 26, 48; and various letters, April, 1867–January 1868, Governor Worth Papers, State Archives, Raleigh.

[13] Tourgée to Daniel E. Sickles, April 11, 1867, Letters Received, Second Military District, War Department Records, Box 138.

[14] Pardon petition, Governor's Letter Book, LIII, Governor Worth Papers.

larger than the criterion of wartime behavior and encouraged the merging of these two groups. The most important of these newer issues was, perhaps, the question of state political reform.

The spread of democracy and reform, which had been so apparent in Tourgée's childhood environment, had lagged in North Carolina. Two upper classes, a gentry and a more numerous middle class, had dominated the state politically since its beginning, and their supremacy was emphasized by obvious caste concepts. Tourgée concluded that the state was politically and economically backward. Former slaveholding aristocrats, who were still relatively rich landowners, dominated the state and oppressed the majority of whites and blacks, complained Tourgée; he also detected an annoying political intolerance reminiscent of the ante-bellum era.[15] As a student in 1860, Tourgée had been shocked by the arrest of recipients of Hinton R. Helper's *Impending Crisis* and a mob burning of 150 copies of this book in the very county where Tourgée was living five years later. Although etched too sharply, Tourgée's complaints of a caste-ridden and backward South were for the most part accurate (for a judicial post, Governor Worth preferred "the merest tyro in the law to one not to the manor born"),[16] but, as with race prejudice, Tourgée exaggerated the responsibility of slavery.

Tourgée also minimized previous political progress within the South. In North Carolina "throughout the ante-bellum period there was a constant effort on the part of the yeomanry to take from the upper classes the control of public offices," and many reforms had been accomplished.[17] A demand for change was becoming critical on the eve of secession, only to be checked as the defense of slavery and the needs of war secured precedence, but the peace and union movements inclined to represent the older reformism. Both unionism and peace sentiment were strong among the same group, the yeomanry, and in the same areas (especially the west) as the earlier reform movement, and such leaders as Holden and Settle were identifiable with both forces. By the conclusion of the Civil War a link was forged between the unionist and democratic movements, and Tourgée had a strong affinity for each. Although Tourgée never adequately appreciated the older origins of this struggle

[15] Notebook, April, 1866, and Tourgée and Kuhn Daybook, n.d., Tourgée Papers.
[16] Worth to Thomas S. Ashe, August 7, 1867, Hamilton (ed.), *Jonathan Worth,* II, 1018.
[17] Guion G. Johnson, *Ante-Bellum North Carolina: A Social History* (Chapel Hill, 1937), 76. See also *ibid.,* 33–36, 73–79.

for democratic reform which he now joined, he did succeed in becoming one of the first writers to appreciate the stature of the non-slaveowning southerner and to debunk the stereotype of the poor white.

Tourgée's piedmont straitest sect strongly represented reformism, since it was composed largely of poorer whites who were neglected by, or who resented, the existing caste and political structure. In Tourgée's novels they would be "of that class who are neither rich nor poor, who were land-owners but not slave-owners" and "'misters,' not 'colonels' or 'squires.'" [18] Such men might be less likely than substantial or slaveowning unionists, like Jonathan Worth, to finally endorse the Confederacy. Recollecting their consequent wartime sufferings, they would often favor proscriptive measures against ex-rebels. They were also favorably inclined toward legislation for the masses at the expense of the classes, although Tourgée complained that they were unaccustomed to participating in politics. While Tourgée and the piedmont straitest sect remained reluctant to endorse Holden's Union party, their position was soon identified with the more markedly unionist and reformist western division of that party.

The Confederate-Conservative coalition represented the traditional opposition. "The people who felt most bitterly at the close of the war," said one of them, Cornelia Phillips Spencer, "were not the majority *in numbers* at the South, but they were the majority so to speak in social rank and influence, refinement, intelligence, and wealth." [19] The preservation of the privileges of these people understandably rivaled considerations of secession and war in postwar politics, especially after the Union party declared its opposition to certain dominant families and interests and called for a government controlled by "the honest hard-working people of the state." [20] One scholar has concluded that in Holden's party the Conservatives "were afraid of a government conducted in the interests of the masses," [21] and they were also resisting challenges from a variety of growing urban and business interests.

[18] Tourgée, A Fool's Errand, 41, 126.
[19] A Sketch of the University of North Carolina, Cornelia Phillips Spencer Papers, III, 69, Southern Historical Collection.
[20] Raleigh Standard, May 15, 1865.
[21] Horace W. Raper, "William Woods Holden: A Political Biography" (unpublished Ph.D. dissertation, University of North Carolina, 1951), 173. See also Robert D. W. Connor, North Carolina: Rebuilding An Ancient Commonwealth, 1584–1925 (4 vols.; Chicago, 1929), II, 82, 155–56, 205–7, 225–29.

Little wonder, then, that some conservative unionists began to consider the challenges of radicalism of greater consequence than the issue of union, which was already essentially settled. David F. Caldwell, for example, ultimately overcame his grievances against "secessionists and ultra old line War Whigs" and joined with them. Some unionists were also alienated from the Republican national government because of the lack of consideration they received for their loyalty during the war: Tourgée noted a deep resentment on the part of union men who were just as arbitrarily deprived of their slaves without compensation as was the "open and avowed rebel." The resultant loss to the future Republican party of the state, which would suffer from a shortage of able leadership, may have been of decisive importance.

Others, however, remained to support the Union party, and the inclinations of that party were well revealed in the constitutional convention of 1866. Union party delegates to that convention denounced property representation and property qualifications for office, demanded more popularly elected officials, sought debtor relief, and debated questions of loyalty to the Federal government and the repudiation of the Confederate debt. "A spirit of radicalism is at work," objected one Conservative, "which will not cease until the Judges are made elective for short terms, and until all property qualification for office is destroyed." [22] Nevertheless, the convention's accomplishments were mild, a proposed white basis of representation for the state legislature becoming the major issue of debate. Union party leaders might accept Negro representation when Negroes voted, but until then they were anxious to weaken the eastern gentry's control of the state. Their opponents defended virtual representation and the need to protect property against "the demoralizing radicalism of the day." A final convention compromise granted the reformers their demand in the lower house but retained taxation as the basis of apportionment for the Senate. Even this proposal, together with several lesser democratic and anti-Confederate measures, encountered determined Conservative opposition in the popular election of August, 1866, and all were defeated. The west had overwhelmingly voted for the changes and the east overwhelmingly against them. Conservatives had ignored the perceptive warnings of

[22] Edward Conigland to Thomas Ruffin, June 26, 1866, Hamilton (ed.), *Thomas Ruffin*, IV, 61–62.

Samuel F. Phillips that if these proposals were not accepted, more radical ones were in store: "the white basis in both Houses, or a negro-suffrage in both, the abolishment of all property qualifications for office, the election of Judges for a term of years by the people and many other inventions of that American democracy which is surging and hissing at white heat, throughout this continent." [23]

Sentiments of union and reform were native to North Carolina, as they were to all of the United States, and the carpetbagger Tourgée stepped south into a political struggle already under way. In 1866 Tourgée opposed Holden and his party as neither unionist nor sufficiently democratic, but there was an affinity between Tourgée and the Union party men, and they were destined to be more firmly united. When, following the Reconstruction Acts of 1867, a new Republican party entered the North Carolina political conflict, Tourgée, along with at least thirty-four of the delegates to the constitutional convention of 1866, would be numbered among its leaders.

[23] Quoted in *ibid.*, 107.

V

Entering the Vortex

Tourgée entered Reconstruction politics with an ample share of self-righteousness. Just as strongly as ex-Confederates believed in the justice of the Lost Cause, the honorableness of their course, and their continued right to self-rule, so did Tourgée believe in the necessity to fulfill the Union's cause. To him this meant more than forgiveness and reunion: it meant the eradication of the caste, class, and racial heritage of the South and the establishment of the democracy and freedom of the North. Bolstering Tourgée's zeal was the conviction that his ways were the ways of God and must, therefore, triumph, and helping to guide him were not only his own experiences in North Carolina but the writings of radical northern Republicans and the crusading spirit of the Methodist Episcopal church.

While unionists and reformers were experiencing political defeat within North Carolina during 1866, their opponents were achieving new national strength by combining with the supporters of President Andrew Johnson, who was sharply at odds with the Republican Congress over the question of Reconstruction. Meanwhile, the Union party drifted toward an endorsement of the Fourteenth Amendment, which had become the heart of Republican Reconstruction by the autumn of 1866. Other unionists, dejected by Conservative victories, were becoming more radical, and that fall Tourgée joined a number of citizens in meetings to protest existing conditions and to encourage stronger Federal measures. The first such Guilford meeting requested Federal "protection of the Union men of the South until order shall be fully restored" and was believed to have elected Tourgée to attend a proposed national gathering of southern unionists.[1] A few days later, Tourgée attended a similar meeting presided over by Colonel Abram Clapp and W. M. Mebane and addressed by Colonel James Wren, a respected member of the gentry. After Wren thankfully welcomed this open meeting of unionists and denounced Governor Worth as "the great leader of the Secession or Rebel party," the meeting proceeded to adopt resolutions criticizing President Johnson; complaining of persecution, oppressive taxation, and poor economic conditions; and calling for democratic political reform in North Carolina. Before these resolutions were adopted, the recent immigrant Albion Tourgée spoke in their behalf. But Tourgée proceeded beyond the sentiments of the meeting to introduce the question of Negro suffrage. He was "opposed to universal and in favor of impartial suffrage" and "willing any man should vote who knew the worth of a ballot and was loyal." [2] Such suffrage without distinctions of race, which might include other qualifications, was advocated by certain northern Republican circles at that time, and Tourgée's speech corresponds to an incident related in A *Fool's Errand*: if the South would "give the elective franchise to every colored man who owns a hundred dollars' worth of real estate, and every one who can read and write," the nation would be satisfied, the Fool advised his neighbors. "Wait, hesitate, refuse, and all will be enfranchised at the same time by the General Government." [3]

Tourgée's first political address displayed a characteristic frankness, which he discovered was not often tolerated, especially when race was involved, in the sensitive South. When the Greensboro *Patriot* disparagingly reported this unionist meeting,[4] it singled out Tourgée for attack as an unknown speaker who had recently arrived from Pennsylvania. Tourgée's call for a new loyal newspaper in Greensboro, which, with typical immodesty, he offered to edit, increased the *Patriot*'s ire. Southerners deprecated the presence of strangers whose only aim was to excite dissension and discord, the weekly warned, adding that the South

[1] Raleigh *Standard*, September 1, 1866; J. Worth to Nereus Mendenhall, September 10, October 2, 1866, Hamilton (ed.), *Jonathan Worth*, II, 772–74, 808–9. Prominent men in attendance included Nereus Mendenhall, Dr. W. P. Pugh, R. F. Trogden, and A. H. Holton.
[2] Raleigh *Standard*, September 4, 1866.
[3] A *Fool's Errand*, 56. See also N.Y. *Weekly Tribune*, May 30, 1866.
[4] August 24, 1866.

already dealt honorably with Negroes whereas the speaker cheated his own Negro tenants.

Such attacks would goad rather than silence Tourgée. When the leading Conservative daily in the state, the Raleigh *Sentinel*, haughtily dismissed these gatherings of "obscure individuals" from Guilford, one "Obscure Individual" angrily responded in a style suggestive of Tourgée. They were citizens too, it was noted, and a number of prominent men, including former state legislators, had participated in the meetings. The writer also endorsed the equal right of Negroes to testify in court (a standing subject of controversy) and added sarcastically that such a privilege would probably reduce the frequent miscegenation of the past, which the *Sentinel* appeared so worried about in the present. The "Obscure Individual" concluded by mocking the *Sentinel*'s threats— there might be *"assassins* abroad, but open warfare most of you have had enough of." [5]

Southern unionists, like their opponents, also sought national unity, and in the summer of 1866, twenty-eight union men from the southern and border states summoned an anti-Johnson convention in behalf of their "loyal" followers. Two North Carolinians participated in the call —Byron Laflin, who entered the state with the Union Army and was originally from Massachusetts, and Daniel R. Goodloe, a North Carolina abolitionist who had lived in Washington, D.C., since the 1840's, where he edited the antislavery *National Era*. Holden's Union party cautiously ignored this convention call, but unionist meetings in several counties approved the proposed convention and elected delegates. Tourgée and eight others attended from North Carolina. Four of these were carpetbaggers, at least three of whom were Union Army veterans, including the Reverend G. O. Glavis, previously an army chaplain, a representative of a northern benevolent association, and a Freedmen's Bureau agent.[6] The five prewar residents of the state were the Reverend Hope Bain; Alexander H. Jones, a radical westerner; the Reverend James Sinclair, who left a Confederate lieutenant colonelcy to become a

---

[5] Raleigh *Standard*, September 6, 1866.

[6] Glavis' career was spotted by his military conviction for theft and dishonorable discharge, but a reading of the record reveals that he was not guilty of anything other than indiscretion in advising a subordinate. In 1893 he was cleared and honorably mustered out of the army (General Court Martial OO 1705, Judge Advocate General's Records).

Union chaplain and later a Freedmen's Bureau agent; Daniel R. Goodloe; and J. W. Wynne.

A Quaker unionist from Greensboro, Jonathan Harris, was scheduled to accompany Tourgée to the Philadelphia meeting, but whether from sickness or, as Tourgée suspected, disinclination, the moderate Harris did not attend. Tourgée was the first delegate to arrive from his state and was delighted with what he found. Accommodated at the Union League headquarters and dutifully impressed by his elegant lodgings and free franking privileges, he was pleased above all at meeting several old army comrades and being "among loyal warm-hearted Union men again." Tell our "loyal friends" they "need have no fear," he informed Emma with assurance. Everything was "right," and he had not dreamed "that such enthusiasm could grow up over anything less holy than religion itself." [7]

The idealism that Tourgée encountered in Philadelphia helped to crystallize his own radicalism, but his optimism respecting the convention was excessive. It was true that Frederick Douglass and Theodore Tilton marched arm in arm in symbolic answer to the procession of northern and southern whites a few days earlier at the pro-Johnson National Union convention, and idealistic phrases were abundant, but equalitarianism proved weak. Only one southern Negro was present, and, to Tourgée's disgust, even proposals for qualified Negro suffrage were discouraged by prominent northern Republicans and suppressed by the border state delegates, who controlled the convention.[8] These unionists were already powerful in their states, and like Holden's party in North Carolina, they feared that any endorsement of Negro suffrage would alienate many of their white followers. The convention majority did condemn the southern aristocracy and the persecution of Negroes and unionists in the South, but the only remedy it would endorse was the pending Fourteenth Amendment. This was considered inadequate by delegates from those states not yet restored to the Union, who had been promised an opportunity to air their views—a pledge that was rudely

[7] Tourgée to his wife, August 31, 1866, Tourgée Papers.
[8] Tourgée to his wife, September 5, 1866, Tourgée Papers. The account of the convention is taken from *The Southern Loyalist Convention: Call for a Convention of Southern Unionists* ("Tribune Tracts," No. 2, Philadelphia, 1866); "Proceedings of the Southern Loyalist Convention" (*The Reporter*, Nos. 33–34, Washington, D.C., 1866); Philadelphia *North American and United States Gazette*; Philadelphia *Daily News*; and Philadelphia *Inquirer*.

violated by an attempt to adjourn the convention. When this was blocked, almost all of the border state delegates simply departed. The radicals from the unreconstructed South remained, and, urged on by a distinguished group of northern abolitionists, they presented a program of their own.

Tourgée was the chairman of the North Carolina delegation and a member of the convention committee that then presented the radicals' program. According to their report, a rebel aristocracy wielded absolute power in the South, aided by the policies of President Johnson and by its control of that section's fiscal, agricultural, and railroad wealth. Neither Union nor freedom would be secure in the South, the report concluded, until the cornerstone upon which this aristocratic edifice rested was removed. That cornerstone was "Negro serfdom." To secure such removal, the Federal government was urged to confer upon all citizens their "American birth right of impartial suffrage and equality before the law." Included with this demand was a naïve hope that the "final realization of the promises of the Declaration of Independence" would soon mollify any "unchristian" opposition to Negro suffrage.[9]

Several southern unionists spoke in opposition to impartial suffrage, and an "eloquent address" in its support was delivered by Tourgée, who dramatically portrayed the plight of Negroes and unionists in North Carolina. Tourgée declared that after rejecting the feasibility of disfranchising rebels his constituency of two thousand Union men endorsed the enfranchisement of all loyal citizens, including Negroes. The issue was "not justice merely for the black man, but justice, liberty, protection and salvation for the white." "No other plan will ever give the Union men of the South a majority there"; it was "a matter of success or complete extermination."[10] Principles and expediency had nicely merged.

This handful of southern unionists approved impartial suffrage by a vote of sixty-eight to eleven, but their action was of minor significance, since they did not, except in Louisiana, represent tangible political power. Their laments may have helped to impel the nation toward Negro suffrage, but as one North Carolinian warned Governor Worth, the intransigent attitude of powerful Conservatives was aiding radi-

[9] *North American and United States Gazette,* September 8, 1866.
[10] Philadelphia *Herald,* n.d., clipping, and speech manuscript, Tourgée Papers.

calism much more than the activities of this handful of southern unionists.[11]

It is impossible to determine how representative Tourgée's views were. He was the only North Carolinian at Philadelphia to vote for impartial suffrage, whereas at least four opposed it, and not one unionist meeting in the state ever openly endorsed the principle. Nevertheless, Tourgée's views were not unknown when he was delegated, he claimed that his constituents supported him, and there were no subsequent denials of this claim by his constituents. Caution on this touchy topic was common during the period, and Tourgée believed that most whites who did favor Negro suffrage feared to say so openly. Consistent Union men, he later complained, "could look at danger and death very calmly, but they could not stand forth openly and face the glare of social proscription." They, in turn, could not understand a boldness in Tourgée which invited "proscription, broils, mobs, and innumerable risks which might be avoided by a prudent silence." [12]

Tourgée's prominence at Philadelphia secured him an appointment to a speaking tour for the fall elections in the North, and he spent the following weeks traveling and stump-speaking along the back roads of Pennsylvania. In Pittsburgh he attended the anti-Johnson Soldiers and Sailors Convention and then prepared for a tour into New York following the early Pennsylvania elections. A northern Republican victory in 1866 was essential to the success of radicals like Tourgée, who sought a stronger program from Congress, but Tourgée joined those few Republicans who openly championed Negro suffrage. He would later criticize his party for not having squarely fought for this issue in 1866, but at that time he was only optimistic. "I have to speak almost every day," he reported to Emma, "and would not stop if I could. I know I am doing good for the great cause. . . . Tell Lark [a Negro friend] that he will have a chance to vote and all other rights in less than two years." [13]

Meanwhile new tempests raged back home in North Carolina because of Tourgée's activities. The Philadelphia unionist meeting had been

<hr>

[11] Benjamin S. Hedrick to Worth, September 16, 1866, Hamilton (ed.), *Jonathan Worth*, II, 781–85.

[12] *A Fool's Errand*, 130–31.

[13] Tourgée to his wife, September 16, 1866, Tourgée Papers.

denounced by Conservatives, even before it convened, as part of a despotic effort "to reduce the white people of the nation to the level of the black race in all civil and political rights; which must end in the social degradation of the white race and consequent miscegenation." After it did convene, it was described as "made up of Southern white trash, without character or means and representing only Negroes, and of Northern fanatics and agitators." [14] Conservatives were prepared for provocation, and Tourgée's speech did not disappoint them. He was quickly marked and maligned as the North Carolina spokesman of a dastardly crew.

While he was still electioneering in Pennsylvania, Albion learned from Emma and others of a weekly "hurricane of indignation and falsehood" directed against him in the press and in addition, that his Yankee partners had dropped his name from the firm and were annoying Emma with their hostile behavior. The *Patriot* described him as a mean, dastardly, contemptible liar with a "forked, slimy, vicious tongue"; [15] several threatening letters were received; and there was one friendly note pleading with Emma to keep her husband away until matters quieted down. The writer, seemingly a cultured lady, claimed that certain leading citizens were arousing the poorer white rowdies and were perhaps designing to do away with Tourgée. Even ladies, she noted, are saying he should be tarred and feathered, and we "who have always lived in the South know what such hints mean." Another letter condemned Tourgée as a liar who "knew that Southern Loyalists and Negroes *are* safe here provided they behave themselves," but since Tourgée had misbehaved he would "not be suffered to come back and insult us. Your stay in North Carolina had better be short if you expect to breathe the vital air." [16] This all added spice to Tourgée's campaign speeches in the North, and as he dauntlessly prepared to return to Greensboro, both Emma and admirers in the North provided him with pistols to insure his safety.

Tourgée's Philadelphia speech was marred by a repetition of second-hand information and an adolescent exaggeration of just complaints,

[14] Raleigh *Sentinel*, August 31, September 6, 1866.

[15] Mrs. Tourgée to Tourgée, October 7, 1866, Tourgée Papers; quoted in Raleigh *Sentinel*, September 29, 1866.

[16] Unsigned to Mrs. Tourgée, October 16, 1866, and unsigned to Tourgée, September, 1866, Tourgée Papers.

but it hardly warranted the clamor it aroused. Intense political differences lay behind the reprobation directed against this carpetbagger, and the condemnation of Tourgée was accompanied by distorted depictions of his speech. Perhaps his most interesting provocation was the assertion that a petition for relief by seven or eight hundred unionists had been treacherously returned by President Johnson to the Conservative governor of North Carolina. Governor Worth publicly and privately repudiated "this vile wretch Tourgée" as a liar, asserting that only two petitions of protest had been sent to him "by the Prest.," and that the greatest number of signatures involved was forty-six.[17] This alone vindicated Tourgée's central point, but in addition, while Worth's statement was literally correct, it concealed some essential facts. The petition Tourgée referred to did exist, although signed by close to four hundred unionists, but a copy of it had been sent to Worth by a close friend of the President rather than by the President himself.[18] Southern gentlemen were apparently as capable of questionable behavior as were their radical opponents, and several months later Worth would actually manufacture false facts to further discredit Tourgée.[19]

Thus, as a representative of ostracized elements and unpopular doctrines, Tourgée was roundly denounced as he entered southern politics. The threats he represented were additionally annoying because they came from a conquering but youthful outsider, and sincere resentment soon merged with political calculation to cultivate the carpetbagger stereotype. This enraged Tourgée, who grew to cherish North Carolina and who always considered himself a citizen of the entire nation, North as well as South, with the "right to live where he chose." He also resented such intolerance because it interfered with the democratic political process, and he responded with the same proud assertiveness that characterized his opponents. As a matter of national and personal honor, he remained open and direct, often aggressive and self-righteous, in his speech and behavior. Defiantly he named his home in Greensboro "Carpet-Bag Lodge," and his Negro friends were not strangers there. Tourgée's lack of tact, patience, and self-restraint contributed unneces-

17 Worth to Greensboro *Patriot*, September 10, 1866, and Worth to N. Mendenhall, September 10, 1866, Hamilton (ed.), *Jonathan Worth*, II, 772–76.
18 Hedrick to Worth, July 23, 1866, Worth to Hedrick, August 6, 1866, and Worth to Mendenhall, August 30, 1866, *ibid.*, II, 690, 731–32, 756–57.
19 See below, p. 116.

sarily to his difficulties, but it was not easy in that era to draw the line between propriety, recklessness, and surrender. In later and mellower years, he would describe well his difficulty in choosing between needed courage and useless provocation in the postwar South,[20] and it was a welcome irony that his gallantry sometimes aroused a lasting admiration among his romantic-minded foes.

Tourgée would remain a determined partisan during the Reconstruction period and forever retain a belief in the value of such partisanship. "All the great reforms of the age," he observed in 1897, "have been accomplished through the efforts of men who were partisans. Passiveness never accomplished anything. A strong man will be a partisan." [21] Yet he also possessed an unusual ability to appreciate his opponents' point of view, and Tourgée's fiction combines an intense partisanship with both an understanding of his southern foes and an admiration for their fine qualities and lamentable success. Once the Tourgées became involved in politics, however, they received little such acceptance or graceful appreciation. Ostracism and insult pervaded their private as well as public life, and when the sensitive and amiable Emma walked in Greensboro, southern women took pains to avoid her, some even drawing back their skirts to prevent them from touching her own. While Emma was neither so strongly inspired as her husband nor so often isolated by study and work, she remained faithful to Albion's beliefs and supplied needed consolation and support during these increasingly troubled years.

In Reconstruction politics, Tourgée would continue to be a combatant and propagandist rather than a politician or statesman. Devoted to ideals and candid in expressing them, he perhaps lacked the constraint and calculation suitable to political machinery, but he was energetic and able as a thinker and debater and exerted a strong influence on some of the most momentous questions of Reconstruction in North Carolina. When the "higher" principles were at stake, as in the campaigns of 1867 and 1874 and the conventions which followed, Tourgée would have decisive influence.

Tourgée's greatest weakness during his early southern years was a personally and politically motivated exaggeration. In its most innocent

form this was merely poetic license, which reflected his bent for literature
and his dramatic imagination. To a greater extent it reflected Tourgée's
aggressive readiness to cast careless words into heated dispute, and this,
in turn, reflected his devotion to the cause, a self-righteousness that was
too determined to carry its point. Finally, desiring to be really good,
successful, noble, and brave, Tourgée made a common youthful error in
trying too hard to prove that he was. Thus, his army lieutenancy had
never seemed quite adequate, so he encouraged or allowed the rank
of captain, to which he had only a quasi-brevet title. Moreover, in
two instances, he appears to have been guilty of simple deceit. The less
serious instance occurred in response to the epithet "Cain-marked,"
when he implied that his sight had been taken by a Confederate shell;
the other was prompted late in 1867, when William W. Holden recommended him to the military authorities for appointment to a judicial
post. Although, in a letter to Holden, the then impoverished carpetbagger pointed to his youth and lack of "practical training" and advised
that "if possible men better acquainted with the practice of the state
should hold these places," he also falsely boasted of having obtained a
legal training at Cambridge. This was not only despicable but hazardous,
for a dispute soon flared over the proposed appointment, and Holden's
Raleigh *Standard* openly proclaimed that Tourgée had been educated
at Harvard. Certainly Tourgée must have fretted lest his claim be tested,
and, unknown to him, his Conservative foes were checking the college
roster. Luckily for Tourgée, the entire matter was then dropped when
the military bowed before Governor Worth's initial objections.[22] The
fright may have been a boon, for although far from free of subsequent
error, never again could Tourgée rightfully be accused of any such
blatant falsehood. The tale of his eye did persist, however, primarily
because its immediate popularity allowed no convenient escape.

[22] Raleigh *Standard*, April 10, 1868; Tourgée to Holden, December 20, 1867,
enclosed in letter of N. A. Miles to E. R. S. Canby, December 26, 1867, Letters
Received, Second Military District, War Department Records; Richard L. Zuber,
"Jonathan Worth—A Biography of a Southern Unionist" (unpublished Ph.D. dissertation, Duke University, 1961), 522.

VI

For the Straitest Sect

Tourgée's political activities remained outside the main stream of North Carolina politics for many months after his trip North. The "loyal" convention he attended in Philadelphia had received no support from the Union party (it was even denounced by some segments of that party), and the controversial report from the unreconstructed South, which Tourgée had helped prepare, was mentioned in Holden's *Standard* with the sole comment that it was binding on no one. One significant endorsement of the radical position did occur, however. A Negro education convention held in Raleigh proceeded to reject advice from both Conservative and Union party leaders by voicing eloquent pleas for Negro suffrage.

Meanwhile, the ratification of the proposed Fourteenth Amendment became a major issue. Conservatives opposed the terms of this amendment, which was somewhat proscriptive of Confederates and denied congressional representation for unenfranchised Negroes; and they viewed the entire endeavor as a form of continued "illegal" intervention in state affairs. They also injected the Negro issue into state politics by inaccurately denouncing the amendment as establishing Negro suffrage, equality, and domination, and they concluded that therefore the Union party, which endorsed the amendment, was *ipso facto* in favor of Negro equality.[1] The Union party, it is true, had been more tolerant of Negro ambition than had the Conservatives, and some Union party men supported the Fourteenth Amendment as a means of making "haste slowly"

[1] Raleigh *Sentinel*, September 4, 1866; J. Worth to C. C. Clark, October 1, 1866, Hamilton (ed.), *Jonathan Worth*, II, 806–7.

toward political equality.[2] But officially that party was "for the white basis and for white voters," a stand reminiscent of the state constitutional controversy a few months earlier. Nor did the Union party shy from racist arguments in its own behalf, arguing that Conservative opposition to the proposed Federal amendment was inviting more severe Federal measures and helping "unintentionally—to force negro suffrage on our people." "May a kind Providence avert these evils from our unhappy country! But if they should come, remember that our skirts are clear. We have done our duty. We have done it in the face of opposition and excitement. *When negro suffrage comes, as it will, if these warnings are not regarded,* let no man say that we are to blame for it." [3]

The logic of the Union party position could not conquer its weaknesses. Little aid came from the North, conservative unionists continued flocking to the opposition, and many radicals, including Tourgée, were anxious for Conservatives to provoke harsher Federal measures and feared the moderating effect of any Union party success. There was little to fear. The Conservatives easily swept the October, 1866, elections, and in succeeding weeks their objections to the Fourteenth Amendment became, if anything, stronger. In December the amendment was overwhelmingly rejected by the state legislature.

These had been fateful months for North Carolina and the South. Proud and determined Confederate-Conservatives had continued to dominate the state, but in their own way they had become as extreme as the radicalism they opposed. Indignant and overconfident, they maintained convictions hostile to the democratic process and hardly conducive to the art of pragmatic politics, and they helped impede any realistic compromise with the Federal government. The failure to at-

[2] Raleigh *Standard*, September 27, November 6, 1866. Of those now favorably disposed toward Negro rights, Victor C. Barringer, William P. Bynum, Samuel F. Phillips (who all later became Republicans), R. S. Donnell, and W. S. Mason were close to the Union party. B. F. Moore appeared neutral, and A. M. Waddell, Conservative. In contrast to the *Standard*, the Conservative newspapers were very racist in tone, and the Union party had a legislative record friendlier toward the Negro. See *Senate Journal* (1866), 164, 179, 240. Also Holden's appointees to prepare the state's Black Code were moderate men, and as early as 1865 a northern journalist believed Holden was disposed to treat the Negroes fairly but feared that the ex-Confederates were anxious to ride into power with the cry, "Down with the Nigger party!" (see *National Anti-Slavery Standard*, July 1, 1865, quoting the N.Y. *Tribune*; cf. Raleigh *Standard*, March 20, 1866).

[3] Raleigh *Standard*, September 29, 1866.

tempt the moderate program represented by the Fourteenth Amendment, which was the path the nation finally followed, fundamentally rests with the Conservatives. They share with the North much of the responsibility for the failures of that era.

During this time Tourgée remained opposed to both state parties and to the moderation represented by the Fourteenth Amendment. Realistically assessing Conservative thought and power, he anticipated that they would refuse to vote political damnation upon themselves and that more radical measures would be required. The proposed constitutional amendment was but "a makeshift, inspired by fright at what had been done, and a desire to avoid what must be done." [4] He had planned his own continued political activities during his visit North, and the prominence that Tourgée gained from that trip, his ability and initiative, and the shortage of capable men among the straitest sect helped propel him into a new position of leadership in North Carolina.

Tourgée's initial project was establishing and editing a radical unionist newspaper in Greensboro. With his literary ability and newspaper experience, he was a logical man for such a venture, and a newspaper to represent the active unionists in that area had been sought since 1865. Tourgée and the native unionist David Hodgin eagerly promoted the proposed newspaper but secured little financial assistance. Union party men were reluctant to aid a paper sponsored by the straitest sect, and Federal officeholders declined to assist because the paper intended to oppose the President and they feared the official ax. At Philadelphia Tourgée circulated a fund-raising appeal, which the Union League had gratuitously printed, without apparent success, while Hodgin repeatedly complained from Greensboro of continued poverty. But somehow, in November, a new Greensboro weekly, the *Union Register*, was launched, "devoted to the consistent and manly vindication of true Union principles 'with malice toward none and with charity for all.'" Subscriptions were $3 per year or $2 for six months, *"payable invariably in advance,"* [5] and the editors were A. W. Tourgée and A. B. Chapin. The latter was a native of Michigan and a recent Union Army surgeon, who represented an independent faction of conservative unionists.

Although Tourgée has also been credited with organizing the first

[4] *A Fool's Errand*, 115.
[5] Raleigh *Standard*, November 13, 1866.

Union League of the state about this time, his actual connection with this well-known organization was unclear in 1866. He was the leading spirit in the establishment of an independent and radical Loyal Reconstruction League, which held its early meetings in an ex-Confederate workshop that had been converted into a school for freed slaves. The sentiments of the LRL were illustrated by its oath admitting "pioneers":

> I will ever, as now uphold the hands of loyal brothers, maintain and defend the union of states, its constitution and Laws, free speech, a free press, elective judges, equal justice to all men and an *everlasting* reconstruction.
>
> I will not favor or conceal fraud, treason or corruption toward the government of the United States. I will not countenance any social or political aristocracy, but will do all in my power to aid in elevating and educating the people, to wrest power from the rich as such, to crush out nepotism and fraud, to prevent the leaders of rebellion from holding offices of trust and emolument, to the end that treason may be rooted out, and our country may be saved.[6]

While the *Union Register* was primarily devoted to promoting similar doctrines, it also sought to become a first-class literary and business journal, and in his encouragement of immigration and economic development, with particular emphasis upon the great potential of Greensboro, Tourgée was an early, enthusiastic advocate of a New South. Politically, the *Register* acknowledged that its "advocacy of Union principles; or if you prefer the word, radical principles" was not very popular in the South and rather arrogantly added its intention of releasing that section from its "slough of ignorance and prejudice." The weekly pledged to struggle for a government which would "fulfill and demonstrate the declaration of the fathers that 'all men are created equal,' and exemplify in its laws the spirit and teaching of that Divine

---

[6] Proceedings for the "Institution of a Pioneer" into the Loyal Reconstruction League, Tourgée Papers. Officers were: Rev. G. W. Welker, President; R. F. Trogden, Vice-President; Hiram Worth, Treasurer; David Hodgin, Secretary; Tourgée, Corresponding Secretary; C. C. Causey, Marshal. Tourgée's War Diary lists also W. C. Hill and W. P. Pugh as officers.

Master, who 'is no respecter of persons,' but sendeth His Holy Spirit alike unto rich and poor, black and white." [7]

Following North Carolina's rejection of the Fourteenth Amendment, Holden's party swung toward the acceptance of qualified Negro suffrage, pointing out that President Johnson had once endorsed impartial suffrage and that free Negroes had voted in North Carolina prior to 1835. Arrangements were also being made with northern radical Republicans for a special reconstruction plan for North Carolina on such a basis. By this time, Tourgée and the *Union Register* had moved further on. Audaciously modifying Lincoln's immortal words, the *Register* stood "fairly and squarely upon the doctrine of 'a government of the people, by the people and for the people' who are (and have been) sincerely and faithfully devoted to the Union, the Constitution and laws." It bluntly rejected the Union party, including most of the future Republican leadership of the state, by maintaining that *the act of rebellion disfranchised all who participated in it voluntarily.*" [8] Tourgée also refused to ally the Loyal Reconstruction League with the Union Leagues in the state when Holden was appointed state head of the latter organizations.

Although Tourgée's position was alienating northern Republicans who looked to Holden for support, he remained on friendly terms with the northern radical George W. Julian. Tourgée had apparently met Julian during his trip north, and Julian, who was the son of a North Carolina Quaker, was privately receiving Tourgée's support for a stronger Federal role in the South and the impeachment of President Johnson. An indication of the spread of such views came in February, 1867, when a meeting of unionists from Guilford and Randolph counties denied the possibility of organizing a loyal government in the South under existing conditions. This meeting recommended "the establishment of a territorial government in said district," together with the disfranchisement of "all who originated or voluntarily aided and assisted the late rebellion." [9] These policies were extreme but not illogical. Understandably doubting the possibility of overcoming Conservative opposition, southern radicals believed that only Federal tutelage would guarantee the estab-

[7] Clipping, *Union Register*, n.d., Tourgée Papers; Dibble, *Tourgée*, 37.
[8] Manuscript salutation of the *Union Register*, Tourgée Papers; *Register*, quoted in the Raleigh *Sentinel*, February 12, April 29, 1867.
[9] Greensboro *Patriot*, February 22, 1867.

lishment of urgently needed democratic reforms, and they accepted the recent rebellion as a logical justification for extensive and lasting Federal intervention.

In seeking these radical ends as editor of the *Union Register*, Tourgée produced his first substantial literary creation and first fictional depiction of the Reconstruction South, the "Lagby Papers." These were a series of humorous dialect poems, modeled after James R. Lowell's "Bigelow Papers," which presented the rationale of the straitest sect and were printed in the *Union Register*.[10] "Jehu Lagby Unioner" was an old, illiterate southern yeoman, of the type Tourgée frequently encountered, whose views were transcribed by his more moderate and less illiterate friend, a justice of the peace, David Wiggleworth. The Justice believed in being "modderit, always, modderit gentlemen, modderit," but was often inclined to believe that Jehu was right after all. Although greatly encumbered by dialect, the poems presented a thoughtful and incisive, if intensely partisan, picture of early Reconstruction.

In the first Lagby Paper, Jehu welcomed the *Union Register* as a needed "squar an' strait" Union paper, and after sorrowful complaints over the sufferings and losses of the war, he denounced the past and present policies of Confederate leaders:

> We've bin a follerin on, jest sorter willy nilly,
> A set uv men about haf-rascal, an' haf silly,
> Who've allers bin a blatin about "Suthun Rite,"
> An' yellin' "Nigger," "Abolishinist," an' "Fight!"
> Proclaimin thet the pore men orter go an' bar
> The burdin an' the danger uv the rich man's war,
> Fight fer "Stait Rights" an' "Cotton," "Slavery" an' sich,
> Becos thay kep' the pore man down, an raised the rich;
> Thet "Yankee mud-sills" hadent neethur pluck ner wurth,
> And that the Staits wuz God's viceregents upon earth.
> But now we kno right well, sence all's ben dun and sed,
> Thet evry polytishin'd dun more gud, ef 'stead
> Uv putting "Cotton" in the ears uv all the South,
> He'd jest a staid at hoam, an' put it in his mouth.

---

[10] Proof copies of three poems, January 1 and 10, 1867, and n.d., Tourgée Papers.

Jehu objected to the continued power and dominance of southern aristocrats. Annoyed by their overbearing behavior toward unionists and reformers, he appealed to these two groups to fight for their rights but feared that the only cure for the South's ills was a good dose of "Territorial Bitters." Although old Jehu had no special magnanimity toward rebels ("Ev thay don't get a roastin' 'twould be just as well, / In my opinion, if we didn't have no hell"), his motive, he asserted, was not malice or any desire to "punish *them*," but only to "save *ourselves*" and secure full and permanent freedom. The following selection from the Lagby Paper of January 10, 1867, is representative of the series and of Tourgée's analysis of the postwar South.

> Now thar's my nighest nabor, Godsaninted Phue,
> Who thinks the world was made for his espeshil crew,
> An' that a thousan' pawpers died that he might live,
> An' rule an' guidance to his needy fellers give.
> He's one uv them ar lucky ones thats born tu rule
> Jes, as it seems I wuz, to be their thing an' tool;
> Thet thinks pore men an' niggers haint no vested rite,
> In ennything, unless it be tu help them fite.

> . . . .

> [He sez] I want up t' the mark in eighteen sixty-one,
> An' thet in sixty-four I tried tu hide my son;
> Thet I wuz jes' a shirkin, triflin, "Red String" then,
> An never will be much uv ennything agen;
> Thet every wun shud jest speak out an' show,
> The cussed Yankees, thet the South haint got so low,
> As jes' tu take whatever terms they chuse to give,
> Providin' they'll be kind enuff to let us live;
> He fit fur "Suth'arn Rights" an' hates a sneakin coward,
> He wuz'ent ever whipped, but jes' was overpowered;
> Thet when they all surrendered, mung' em *him* an' Lee
> They didn't yield "State Rights" nor "Soverinty."
> They jes' give up ther arms, and held tu all the rest,
> Tu say an' du with, 'zactly ez they thot it best.
> That Cungress haint no right tu offer enny terms,

But jest must take em back with open arms;
An' ought to be content tu du it jest, tu git
A few brave "gemmen" wunst more inter it.

. . . .

Admit thet ther aint menny, yit they'r jest the men,
That's always led the peeple rong and mean t' du't agen.
They haint got no more care, for common weal an' good,
Than vulturs hev, for beasts, thet dyin, giv 'em food.
They merely want to live an' hold the ole time rule,
An' hev the laborin man ther crittur and ther tool.
It makes no diff'rence whether hirelin or slave,
The same his hopeless life, the same his nameless grave.
Ther aint no freedum known, whar sich men hold the power,
We lerned that when confed'racy, was at its noon-tide hour.
An' now I don't believe, thet human right demands
The puttin' uv ourselves agin inter thay're hands.
Now that's my notion Squire, it aint no use tu prate,
Of usin' such ere timbur, in building' up a stait.

While expressing such harsh beliefs, it was characteristic of Tourgée
that he simultaneously lauded the valor and sacrifice of Confederate
soldiers. One of the first issues of the *Register* called attention to the
neglected Confederate graves in the Greensboro cemetery and initiated
a fund to care for them.

Straitest sect Carolinians welcomed the *Union Register*. One reader
from Alamance County was gratified to read "a Union paper once more
in my native state" and was determined to remain a Union man "in
defiance of all the Rebs out of Hades." [11] Others told of their sufferings
during the war. There were also complaints of continued persecution
and of the lack of money among Union men for subscriptions. Because
of this poverty, Tourgée also published an inexpensive weekly "for circulation among the poorer whites and blacks," the *Red String*, which
was the official publication of the Heroes of America, or Red Strings, a
secret unionist organization established during the war.[12]

[11] W. A. Patterson to editor of the *Union Register*, February 6, 1867, Tourgée
Papers. See also other similar letters, Tourgée Papers.
[12] Raleigh *Standard*, March 26, 1867; Benjamin F. Wade to Union Executive
Committee, April 1, 1867, Tourgée Papers.

Conservatives and Holdenites each greeted the appearance of the *Union Register* kindly. Holden's party, which continuously endeavored to heal the breach between itself and the straitest sect, wooed Tourgée as a patriot whose paper was "very popular with the Unionists and will wield a strong influence in the western portion of this state." At the same time, Conservatives appreciated the *Register's* denunciations of the Union party, politely attributing the skillful editorship of the new weekly to northerners "with very radical opinions" and happily reprinting Tourgée's warnings against placing any trust in "those who were the first to back out of the rebellion, though they may have been the first to embrace it and the most influential in inducing others to go with them." [13] There may even have been a serious hope on the part of the Conservatives of winning over Tourgée. Staunch unionists and Republicans such as Daniel R. Goodloe and Benjamin S. Hedrick were conservatively inclined, A. B. Chapin of the *Register* represented a similar tendency, and Tourgée had openly stated a preference for conservative unionists over Holden's followers. The Conservative press even lauded the *Register* for "indications of ability, sincerity and honesty, and a temper and decency far superior to any paper in the State advocating Radical principles." [14]

Nevertheless, Tourgée's antipathy toward Confederates, his encouragement of stronger Federal policies, his advocacy of Negro equality, and his promotion of democratic reform conspired against any accommodation with the Conservatives. More indicative of his future relationships with that political faction were instances of hostility. Early in 1867 he complained that "the principal citizens of Greensboro" condoned and encouraged the malicious destruction of posted advertisements for the *Register*,[15] and one irate opponent called Tourgée a "damn scoundrel" and a "liar" and blamed Tourgée and Holden for the evil condition the state was in: "All such men ought to be hung or shot whenever they have the impudence to open their mouths. Your sheet is generally used for Bung paper at this office and nothing else. . . . Go back home you dam Yankee & stay there." [16]

[13] Greensboro *Patriot*, January 11, 1867.
[14] Raleigh *Sentinel*, January 5, 23, 1867.
[15] *Union Register*, quoted in Raleigh *Standard*, March 23, 1867.
[16] Unsigned to editor of the *Union Register*, n.d., Tourgée Papers.

VII

A Maverick Republican

For two years following the conclusion of the Civil War the terms of reunion remained undecided. During these years the bold restoration to power of recent Confederate leaders and the persecution of Negroes and unionists in the South caused increasing concern in the North. Many northerners apparently feared that a coalition between northern and southern Democrats might capture control of the Federal government and negate the moral, economic, and political results of the war. To prevent this, several groups—including Republican officeholders, economic interests fearful of the agrarian West and South, sympathetic allies of southern Negroes and unionists, and intense anti-Confederates —were prepared to unite in support of stronger Federal policies. The South's rejection of the Fourteenth Amendment strengthened this tendency and helped promote the Reconstruction Acts of 1867, which temporarily restored Federal military supremacy in the South and summoned conventions to revise the constitutions of the southern states. Those Confederates proscribed by the terms of the rejected Fourteenth Amendment were barred from participating in this procedure, delegates were to be elected by all males over twenty-one without distinction of race, and the states were instructed to enfranchise the same electorate in their new constitutions. Negro suffrage had arrived and could obviously control the balance of power in North Carolina.

Many Conservatives reluctantly accepted these acts as law, but Tourgée discovered that to others "the humiliation that came through the enfranchisement of the Negro was a new aggression, an inconceivable insult and degradation." [1] The lawyer and planter David

[1] Tourgée, An Appeal to Caesar, 46.

Schenck, who would publicly debate against Tourgée during the year, confided prophetic words to his journal. This great evil of Negro suffrage will not be tolerated, wrote Schenck, "for the white race will not suffer this outrage without bloody resentment and if it cannot be done by force it will be done by assasinations [*sic*] and secret means of revenge." Why, Schenck wondered, was he thus debased beneath his former slaves, when he had always discharged his duty to society and family and had "eaten no man's bread, or taken ought unjustly from anyone." [2]

The reaction to Negro suffrage was actually less rigid than the words of Tourgée and Schenck suggested. Some Conservatives had earlier endorsed qualified Negro suffrage, and for several months the Conservative party seriously wooed the Negro vote. Negro leaders were lauded, Negro meetings were described as "quiet, orderly and attentive" with a "uniform appearance of order and decorum," the sentiments of these meetings were approved, and even Negro laborers were accorded new respect.[3] According to a northern reporter, an optimistic hallucination prevailed among the landowners of the state regarding their ability to win Negro votes.[4] Their illusions were soon to disappear.

The Union party had endorsed qualified Negro suffrage before the Reconstruction Acts were passed, and, consistent with its policy of "unconditional submission," it readily accepted the new Reconstruction program. Although Conservatives had hopefully predicted that many men would desert Holden over the issue of Negro suffrage, most of his followers accepted the new radical measure as the necessary result of Conservative recalcitrance or continued to endorse submission as the wisest policy. Others were more jubilant, welcoming the Reconstruction Acts "with feelings of Joy" and seeing in the Negro voter a possible means of political victory,[5] and for a number of reasons, Holden's following would seek Negro support with greater success than the Con-

---

[2] Journal of David Schenck, V, 84–85, David Schenck Papers, Southern Historical Collection.

[3] Greensboro *Patriot*, March 29, April 26, May 11, 31, 1867; Raleigh *Sentinel*, March 1, July 15, 1867; Wilmington *Daily Journal*, May 23, 1867; Plymouth Report, September 16, 1867, NCFBR, Box 423.

[4] Washington *Chronicle*, quoted in *National Anti-Slavery Standard*, April 20, 1867.

[5] William F. Henderson and others to Thaddeus Stevens, March 4, 1867, Padgett (ed.), "Reconstruction Letters," *NCHR*, XXI (1944), 242–44. But for the increasing importance of caste and racist beliefs in alienating other unionists, see especially the Benjamin S. Hedrick Papers, Duke University Library.

servatives. Union party leaders accepted the Negro with greater grace and unanimity, their past record was better, they were in closer harmony with northern Republicans, and, as reformers, they could promise the Negro more. Above all, perhaps, was their participation in a new party, the North Carolina Republican party, whose name alone had almost irresistible allure.

Tourgée was perplexed by these developments. He was reluctant to ally himself with the Holdenites, and he was not enthusiastic about the Reconstruction program. Believing that Congress had finally endorsed the correct principles, but fondly harkening back to the territorial plan, he doubted the possibility of success. Despite his skepticism, there was little choice for Tourgée. The Holdenites now endorsed all his principles, and a new and powerful union was being forged between Negroes, unionists, reformers, and Union party men. He could join and help direct this coalition, or remain in a political wilderness. There was a fighting chance of victory, and since Tourgée's major objection to the Reconstruction program was that it might fail, he could hardly let it go by default. Reluctantly accepting his new allies, Tourgée entered the fray with vigor.

Of course old hostilities between the straitest sect and the Holdenites lingered, and Conservatives continued to recall the previous Confederate and anti-Negro activities of Holden, Settle, and other Union party men.[6] Conservative reminiscences contained more half- than whole truths, but Tourgée and others were anxious to take the bait. Having pioneered in the demand for a radical reconstruction, they were suspicious and resentful of the leading role seized by Holden's political machine. But northern Republicans now viewed Holden as an ally and Tourgée as a disruptor, and a national Union League leader, James M. Edmunds, tactfully criticized Tourgée. Holden was greatly needed, advised Edmunds, as they were all in a common struggle and "the general good of the cause" demanded a "united front." [7] Apologizing for its past discord, Tourgée's *Union Register* bowed in the desired direction: "Now is the time for Union among Unionists. A strong, hearty pull and a pull all together is what is needed now. Let the L.R.L., the U.L.A. and what-

[6] Rufus Y. McAden to Tourgée, [early 1867], Tourgée Papers.
[7] Edmunds to Tourgée, March 3, 1867, Tourgée Papers.

soever else there may be, 'red strings' or 'hemp strings,' whose animating principle is loyalty to the Union, muster in force." [8]

A month later Holden appointed Tourgée a deputy member of the Grand Council of the Union League, but embers still smoldered.

Meanwhile the state Republican party was in the process of formation. Immediately after the passage of the first Reconstruction Act, various Union party legislators summoned a convention to meet on March 27, 1867, to discuss the implementation of Reconstruction. One hundred white delegates representative of various factions were designated by name (they included Tourgée and his coeditor, A. B. Chapin), and Negro leaders were contacted to secure Negro representation. The interracial gathering that assembled on that date, under the slogan "Union, Liberty, Equality," made a conspicuous display of the new equality between Negro and white, and against the tactical protests of some moderates, the convention proclaimed the creation of the North Carolina Republican party.[9]

The prominence of the Holdenites in this convention rekindled old suspicions. A. B. Chapin attended and complained that debate was suppressed. Tourgée was unable to attend, as he was then in Washington, D.C., seeking financial assistance for his tottering newspapers. However, a letter from him was read before the convention, which apologized for his absence and stated certain reasons why he did not approve "of the assembling of this Convention or transaction of business by it as constituted." This marked a resurgence of animosities that again filled the columns of the *Register*. While approving the sentiments of the March 27 meeting, Tourgée denied the right of a minority of an "illegal" legislature to appoint the delegates to such a convention arbitrarily, considering it a far cry from democracy for a small group of politicians to arrange, control, and manipulate a purportedly representative political organization. According to Tourgée, the Reconstruction Acts had released a flood of opinion favoring "absolute political and civil equality," and ante-bellum rulers were cleverly acquiescing in this sentiment in an endeavor to maintain the strength of "aristocracy and caste." The Holdenites were merely more subtle and less reactionary than the Conservatives, and pointing to their past behavior, Tourgée

[8] Quoted in Raleigh *Standard*, March 12, 1867.
[9] *Ibid.*, March 16, 28, 1867. The latter contains the convention proceedings.

cautioned the Negroes to "shrink from their caress." These criticisms were further stimulated by the fact that Holden's *Standard* had a Federal printing contract that Tourgée desired for the *Register*.[10] Conservatives again enjoyed the wrangling among their rivals, and complimenting the *Register's* "bona-fide" union men for their "honest straightforward course," expressed a desire "to cooperate with them as far as possible in the work of Reconstruction." [11]

While some Republicans endorsed Tourgée's course, others were again distressed. W. Dunn, Jr., of Kinston, wrote two persuasive letters complimenting the *Union Register* on its ability and principles but objecting to its bickering and discord. The Republicans were weak, warned Dunn, and if they were split they would be overridden. Conservatives viewed Holden as the tower of Republican strength, so why should he be attacked if he was now on the right side and against the aristocracy? Men such as Holden, Settle, Dick, John Pool, said Dunn, "and others in this state have stood up & stood out against them [the aristocrats] in this state in the face of heavy odds. It was *worth something* to stand against that party in this state during the war. It was different at the North. It was easy—*easier than any other* to be a Union man there. Opposing & endeavoring to thwart the secessionists here was about all we *could* do." [12]

The convincing protests of Dunn were ineffective, and Tourgée remained more devoted to his own principles than to pragmatic politics. But by June the *Register* collapsed and moved to Raleigh, where under the control of Daniel R. Goodloe, A. B. Chapin, and H. H. Helper (brother of the famous author of *The Impending Crisis*), it represented conservative rather than radical opposition to Holden. The impact of Tourgée's attack was thus sharply curtailed, but the issues he raised continued to disrupt the Republicans.

There was some justification for Tourgée's criticism, and as a result of his attacks upon the March convention the formal organization of the Republican party was credited to a more representative meeting

[10] Manuscript editorial, Tourgée Papers; *Union Register*, quoted in Raleigh *Sentinel*, April 12, 1867; Raleigh *Sentinel*, April 27, 1867.
[11] *Ibid.*, May 8, 1867.
[12] W. Dunn, Jr., to A. B. Chapin, April 20, 25, 1867, Tourgée Papers.

held in September. But in certain respects Tourgée's course appears unwise. With little recognition of the difficulties involved, he relied excessively upon allegiance to the Confederacy as a postwar criterion, and he failed to appreciate the wisdom and effectiveness of subtle opposition to the Confederacy. In any event, secession and war were dead issues in 1867, and it is surprising that Tourgée, who appreciated Republican weaknesses, did not readily welcome able allies. Because of his distrust of the Holdenites, he seriously misjudged their sincerity. Thomas Settle, Robert P. Dick, William P. Bynum, Ralph P. Buxton, Edwin G. Reade, and other native Republicans were able, educated, and unusually enlightened men who displayed an effective and persistent attachment to democracy and reform. Without such leaders the Republicans would have been in worse straits than they were, and Tourgée eventually did develop an admiration for his once mistrusted allies. Although such intelligent native Republicans were a constant refutation to the scalawag myth, they had little success in modifying the Reconstruction stereotype. The comments of the Greensboro *Patriot* about Robert P. Dick were indicative: "Personally we did have, and still have a high regard for him; in the social and private relations of life he is unexceptionable, but as a politician he is as deep in the dregs and as low in the mire as any of them." [13]

Carpetbaggers, too, were considered as "low in the mire" as any, and by 1867 Tourgée was experiencing many adverse effects of his political prominence. Exasperated over the results of Tourgée's activities, his business associates terminated the partnership and sold out to him. Tourgée then attempted to continue the nursery with a new partner, George L. Anthony, but harassed by political enmity, poor general conditions, and a legacy of trouble left by his previous partners, the business did poorly. One partner, R. T. Pettingill, had secretly given his uncle a mortgage on the nursery as security for a private loan, and in the name of the partnership, Pettingill had also collected, but never paid, a claim for a Union veteran. This veteran attempted, without success, to collect the claim from Tourgée in 1867, and the matter was used politically to discredit Tourgée during that year. In the spring Pettingill's uncle foreclosed the mortgage, and whether for that or other

[13] Greensboro *Patriot*, July 6, 1872. See also *ibid.*, August 31, 1871, May 30, 1872.

reasons, Tourgée was forced to surrender the business, losing his investment and remaining several thousand dollars in debt.[14]

From Ohio, Emma's sister offered the distressed Tourgée family consolation—they all knew Albion had tried to do right by everyone, but
with his business, his newspapers, and his politics, perhaps he had "too
many irons in the fire." [15] This was true, and business was the iron
Albion tended least. Further intensifying his plight was a sense of
honor; in imitation of his literary idol, Sir Walter Scott, Albion refused
bankruptcy and vowed to pay off all his debts. Fortunately, the rewards
of Republican success would enable him to do so in the near future.

Tourgée's newspapers had also experienced persistent economic difficulties. "Opposed in sentiment by nearly all the public business men,"
both Conservative and Holdenite, Tourgée found it "impossible to get
advertising patronage," and early in 1867 he desperately sought congressional aid.[16] Although the *Register* received a favorable recommendation from the Federal district judge, George W. Brooks, two
Union party papers, Holden's *Standard* and the Hendersonville *Pioneer*,
were preferred over the radical Greensboro weekly for the two available
Federal printing contracts. "God only knows what will become of
everything," the distressed Albion complained to Emma in March as
he left for the national capital to seek aid. There he conferred with
George W. Julian and with the Congressional Executive Committee,
and in April he was enthusiastically endorsed as a "thoroughly Radical
and Union" editor by the prominent Republican Benjamin F. Wade.
Despite the influential Wade's solicitations, there is no evidence that
assistance was secured for either the *Register* or the *Red String*, probably
because the political situation in North Carolina had by now all but
eliminated Tourgée's previous importance to northern Republicans. The
last number of the *Register* appeared on June 14, its demise coinciding
with the collapse of Tourgée's nursery. Sadly, Tourgée bade goodbye
to his readers—"the forlorn hope of true Republicanism in the state." [17]

[14] Tourgée to U.S. Treasury Department, January, no day, and July 9, 1867, and
biographical manuscript, Tourgée Papers; sketch of Tourgée, no author, no date,
Greensboro Public Library; B. S. Hedrick to E. R. S. Canby, January 10, 1868,
Letters Received, Second Military District, War Department Records.

[15] Angie Kilbourne to Mrs. Tourgée, June 21, 1867, Tourgée Papers.

[16] Benjamin F. Wade to Union Executive Committee, April 1, 1867, Tourgée
Papers. The succeeding quotation is also from this letter.

[17] Quoted in Dibble, *Tourgée*, 37.

Hitherto, Reconstruction had brought the carpetbagger Tourgée little benefit. Radicalism had contributed to economic failure and debt, editing had provided little, if any, remuneration, and politics had secured neither important office nor leadership. The Tourgées would recall 1867 as a year of poverty, cold, and hunger amidst the spartan surroundings of an old log cabin, and other North Carolinians would recall a shabbily dressed Yankee who rode about to political meetings on an old and skinny white nag, blind in one eye like its master. There was some income from real estate and law, but the principled Tourgée could practice only in Federal cases because he refused to apply for a state law license to a provisional government whose authority he did not recognize. He also held an insignificant post as a Federal deputy collector, apparently a political gratuity from some local officeholder.[18]

Tourgée's poverty failed to cool his ardor, and during these troubled months, he added to his understanding of the problems of Reconstruction. Through his political and legal activities, he remained ever aware of the race problem, and in one revealing case, he fought the continuing effects of the burdensome apprenticeship laws that had been pressed upon ante-bellum free Negroes. For some reason, a free Negro, Washington Watkins, had been obliged to keep his son in apprenticeship before the war, but in return for a loan, one Jason Thompson, a white man, secretly agreed to execute an indenture over the boy but to leave him in Watkins' care. There were witnesses to this illegal agreement. In 1867, because of some dispute between the parties, Thompson sought to force Watkins' son to work for him under the indenture, while Tourgée fought to abrogate the contract of indenture by securing recognition of an agreement that had been illegal under ante-bellum law. Another irritating expression of race prejudice was the ostracism of northern white women who taught in Negro schools, a form of hostility which came from as high as the governor of the state.[19] The discomfort suffered by the Tourgées did not stem only from their close association with such teachers, but from the entire family's direct involvement in Negro

[18] *Ibid.*, 36; Mrs. Tourgée to Tourgée, December 18, 1875, Tourgée Papers; Tourgée to Nathan H. Hill, June 7, 1867, Nathan H. Hill Papers, Duke University Library; interview with Katherine Hoskins, local historian, Summerfield, N.C.

[19] Watkins case, NCFBR, CVIII, 11–13; J. Worth to Lydia Maxwell, November 15, 1867, Hamilton (ed.), *Jonathan Worth*, II, 872–76. Cf. Tourgée, *A Fool's Errand*, 44.

affairs. Emma's parents, whose presence sometimes compounded the personal problems of Reconstruction for Tourgée, were "socially, mentally and religiously" educating the recent slaves, and in Pennsylvania Emma's sister was collecting relief money for their benefit. Tourgée encouraged greater Negro participation and leadership in the Republican party, and the *Register* paid unusual attention to happenings in Warnersville, the Negro suburb of Greensboro. One of the builders of Warnersville, Harmon Unthank, a well-respected ex-slave and local Republican leader, became a friend of the family and was the model for Tourgée's fictional character Unthank in the novel *Hot Plowshares*. Tourgée also reputedly taught in the Warnersville school, wrote parts of his first novels in one of the schoolrooms of what later became Bennett College for Women, and assisted Negroes in the purchasing of land.

Negro ownership of land was a subject in which Tourgée displayed a unique interest in 1867. Although rejecting the confiscation advocated by many Negroes and radical Republicans, he was convinced of the advantages of Negro ownership and suggested a vast Federal program aiding Negroes to purchase land.[20] Tourgée pointed out that most freed slaves were anxious to purchase land, and that over two hundred had done so in Greensboro and had proven to be reliable purchasers. He feared, however, that Negroes were so frequently handicapped by ignorance, prejudice, and distrust that they might be kept "hirelings" forever. Landowners had "little if any confidence in the Negro as a buyer and almost universally refuse to sell to him on time or at a reasonable price," Tourgée reported, while Negroes displayed a reciprocal distrust and disliked the prevalent custom of having to pay money down while receiving in return only "a bond for a deed on payment of the remainder," which threw "all the risk upon the purchaser." Furthermore, Tourgée believed that if Negroes were "left to buy subject to the caprice or knavery of the landowners," they would "be subject to the greatest imaginable fraud." Federal intervention might solve the problem, and, pointing to the success of the Freedmen's Bureau in providing mutually acceptable laboring contracts, Tourgée suggested a

[20] Tourgée to Nathan H. Hill, July 17, 1867, Hill Papers. The following plan is in Tourgée to Mr. Armstrong, Bureau agent, n.d., Tourgée Papers, which includes the observation: "It is useless to think of locating the freedmen in communities by themselves. They prefer to live as now, interspersed with the whites, the business interests of the people demand it and there is no doubt it will be continued."

similar Federal role designed to give confidence to the landowner in selling and the freedman in buying. He proposed that Federal land agencies negotiate contracts and execute titles and that a nine-year installment plan be provided to enable the freed slaves to purchase land. Federal endorsement of the contracts would offer needed security to both whites and Negroes. As a final inducement, Tourgée pointed out that such a plan would "bring clearly to the attention of Northern capitalists the astonishing opportunities which now exist for the profitable investment of capital in land at the South." Thousands of acres could be purchased, at "from $1.50 to $5.00 per acre cash" and resold at "from $6 to $10 upon the terms before given." It all seemed so clear —the indebted landowners needed money, the Negroes needed and wanted land, and the capitalists desired profits; but the Federal government failed to respond, and the vision came to naught.

Tourgée was also interested at this time in the development of water power, but the most curious enterprise that his economic enthusiasm led him into was of a public nature—the National Anti-Monopoly Cheap-Freight Railway League. Tourgée was a member of the national council of this League, whose president, the Texas Republican Judge Lorenzo Sherwood, he had met at the Philadelphia convention; and the League's vice-presidents included such notables as William G. Brownlow, Henry Carey, James Speed, Daniel E. Sickles, and William W. Holden.

Largely motivated by hostility toward the exploitive practices of private railroads, the Railway League advocated a publicly owned system of double-track railroads modeled somewhat after the earlier state canal systems. Cars on each track would proceed in one direction at a uniform speed, with shippers placing any desired number of cars upon the tracks and being charged according to tons per mile shipped. The League especially proposed to build up the railroads of the South with the aid of Federal subsidies accompanied by local or state investment, ownership, and control. It was urged that Federal aid for such a purpose would serve to regain the loyalty of the once rebellious section, and it was promised that such a system would avoid collisions, cut costs, increase carrying capacity, destroy monopolies, and provide "a thousand other good things." This scheme, too, drifted into oblivion, and two years later the Conservative press would comment that perhaps this was all "a good idea, but we have looked in vain for government aid to any state enterprise." [21]

Tourgée's enthusiasm for economic projects was characteristic of Reconstruction Republicanism. Humanitarianism has rationalized more than it has characterized free enterprise, but the post-Civil War period in the South witnessed an unusual combination of faith in political democracy, free labor, and free enterprise. The Republican party issued ardent calls during 1867 for the development of the mines, mills, industries, railroads, schools, and even churches of the South, which helps to explain its popularity in urban centers.[22] Conservatives, who still dominated the private wealth and enterprise of the section, also encouraged progress, but they had less interest in the general welfare, feared higher taxes from increased public expenditures, and viewed with misgiving the faith that some southerners, including members of the Railway League, had in state and Federal government. Perhaps unduly influenced by their appreciation of postwar Federal intervention, southern Republicans had great expectations for democratic government, and in North Carolina they would soon undertake railroad and other projects that were accompanied by extensive state investment and control. The patronage that this provided to an indigent Republican party was also an important aid to power, whereas the taxation, interference, and political threat this represented to Conservatives became another basis for their hatred of Reconstruction.

[21] Greensboro *Patriot*, December 23, 1869. A pamphlet and circulars of the Railway League may be found in the Tourgée Papers.
[22] Raleigh *Standard*, July 9, August 8, 13, 17, September 7, October 19, 1867.

VIII

Campaigning for Reconstruction—1867

Politics increasingly occupied Tourgée in 1867, and his political organizing, editing, and speaking were far more significant than his bickering with the Holdenites. But here, too, there was disagreement with a Holden following that preferred to do little more that year than to endorse the Reconstruction Acts and Negro suffrage. To Tourgée, these questions had already been settled by the Federal government, and he was among a number of North Carolina Republicans eager to commit the party to further specific reforms.

Tourgée complained proudly to Emma of being busy day and night during the year with a continuous round of writing, traveling, and speaking; with characteristic boastfulness he claimed to have attended, at his own expense, more Republican meetings than any other man in the state, with the possible exception of the prominent Negro James H. Harris. Simultaneously he continued to flaunt his radicalism by successfully promoting local Negro representation and equality and by vigorously attacking the existing state administration of Jonathan Worth. Oppressive taxation, the harassment of debtors, the legalization of Confederate crimes, and the persecution of unionists were included among his many complaints against the state government, but he especially bemoaned leaving the implementation of the Reconstruction Acts in the hands of such hostile authorities. The recognition, even temporarily, of such a government, pleaded Tourgée, would make the national government "a *particeps criminus* in a most damning tyranny." "We can endure a good deal," he concluded tactlessly, "but the idea that Uncle Sam is to stand god-father to these secession bastards is too much for our equanimity." [1] His equalitarianism and clamor soon alienated a number of potential Guilford Republicans.

Less pompous was Tourgée's activity among the three different mass Republican organizations—the Union League, the Loyal Reconstruction League, and the Heroes of America—whose very existence also suggested continued division. Despite such division, the response to Republican recruitment among the lower-class blacks and whites was most enthusiastic, with the various leagues playing a leading role in instructing the Negroes in their new political rights and shaping them into an effective political force. "As yet unused to political assemblages, but with an indistinct impression that their rights and interests were involved," Tourgée would recall, the Negroes welcomed the leagues as a source of security and strength and participated eagerly in politics.[2] Their sympathies were soon apparent, one Republican reporting happily that while the recent slaves politely listened to them, it was "impossible to lead them to vote for their former Masters." [3]

Also impressive to the equalitarian-minded Tourgée was the blossoming of political leadership from the lower classes and the cooperation between the blacks and whites that accompanied the spread of the leagues in the state. Many of the lower-class whites who assumed Republican leadership in 1867 had been (very appropriately in Tourgée's opinion) unionists or active in the Freedmen's Bureau, and local Negro leaders had often sought education, advancement, and justice for their people. One commendable heritage of slavery that Tourgée overlooked was the number of competent Negroes available for leadership. Represented among sixty politically active and respected Negroes in six counties surrounding Greensboro were such skilled occupations as minister, baker, mechanic, mason, blacksmith, coach-maker, shoemaker, carpenter, tinsmith, tanner, cabinetmaker, harness-maker, barber, merchant, painter, cooper, miller, butcher, waggoner, jeweler, millwright, farmer, and grocer.[4] While the prejudices of many whites were being hardened by the burgeoning activity of these Negroes, other southern

[1] *Union Register*, quoted in Greensboro *Patriot*, May 18, 1867.
[2] *A Fool's Errand*, 135–36.
[3] Thomas Conway to Salmon P. Chase, April 23, 1867, Padgett (ed.), "Reconstruction Letters," *NCHR*, XXI (1944), 233–35.
[4] List of registrars, NCFBR, Box 423.

whites were repudiating their "past prejudices." Joel Ashworth, a League organizer in Tourgée's neighborhood, confessed that since mingling with the Negroes, "my opinion is that there is but little if any difference in the talents of the two races and I am willing to give them all an even start in the race." [5] Tourgée's appreciation of the growth, effort, and accomplishment of the many untutored whites and Negroes would ultimately inspire such fictional heroes as Uncle Jerry of *A Fool's Errand* (who was modeled in part after Wyatt Outlaw, a Negro mechanic from Alamance) and John Walters in the same novel (who was based upon the notorious Caswell scalawag John Walter Stephens). But Tourgée also suggested the limited abilities of these political novices in the character of Jordan Jackson in *Bricks Without Straw*, an uneducated and disillusioned Confederate veteran who turned to Republicanism and became a member of the state legislature, "where he did many foolish, some bad, and a few wise things in the way of legislation. He knew what he wanted—it was light, liberty, education and a 'fair hack' for all men. How to get it he did not know." [6] In defiance of their own degree of responsibility for the plight of these uneducated Negroes and whites, Conservatives would mock and shun their limited learning, experience, and ability. The conceited refusal of the state's traditional leadership to cooperate with her "lesser" sons would contribute decisively to the tragic blunderings of Reconstruction.

By the summer of 1867 it was obvious that the Republicans were winning the Negro vote. Conservatives had largely undermined themselves. Tourgée's assertion that former slave masters often viewed Negro equality with "distrust and aversion if not with positive hatred" was accurate, and Conservatives confessed publicly to "the shudder of disgust which thrills through a Southern gentleman's frame when he contemplates the contingencies of sitting in convention, and arguing and debating with those whom his education, his associations and the promptings of his nature have always taught him were his inferiors by the infallible decree of Almighty God." [7] Many similar assertions, con-

---

[5] Ashworth to Nathan H. Hill, April 15, 1867, Hill Papers. Governor Holden's Papers, State Archives, Raleigh, also provide excellent illustrations of the impressive efforts of unlettered whites and Negroes, e.g., Rev. S. Lewis to Holden, January 4, 1869.

[6] *Bricks Without Straw*, 344.

[7] Weldon *State*, quoted in Raleigh *Standard*, April 20, 1867.

stant browbeating, Negro caricatures, and tales of Negro atrocities in the Conservative press nullified Conservative appeals. Only if Negroes were submissive were they considered fit to vote. The race was first paternalistically advised what it must do, then warned, and finally threatened.[8] But, commented Tourgée, these whites soon rediscovered a "contrariness and contradictoriness of character" that had been rather prevalent among the Negroes since secession.[9]

It was not only racism, as Tourgée was inclined to assume, that led Conservatives to take their final stand on the platform of white supremacy. The ultimate provocation was the consolidation of the Negro vote in support of a party led largely by the already hated Holdenites at the very moment when the radical impetus of Reconstruction had sharpened the class character of North Carolina politics. Sharing Tourgée's conclusion that "there were ignorance and poverty and a hated race upon one side and upon the other, intelligence, wealth and pride," the Conservatives viewed the Republicans as a dangerous alliance of inferior Africans, incompetent whites, and traitorous unionists. What Tourgée welcomed as the elevation of the people, his opponents dreaded as the rising of "the mongrel scum" or "the dregs and filthy scum of society,"[10] and this presumptive threat to property and social stability left the Conservatives largely unable or unwilling to accept the modern political process. In Republicanism they recognized a threat to their power and their purse, and rather desperately they denounced as a fallacy the idea that the voice of the people was "the unrestrained absolute sovereign . . . to which all must bow." Also rejected was "that infidel and unfounded assumption in the Declaration of Independence, that 'all men are created free and equal,' "[11] and the governor of the state firmly clarified his belief that "civilization consists in the possession and protection of property." "I abhor the Democratic tendency of our government. I use the word in its proper—not its party sense. The tendency is to ignore virtue and property and intelligence—and to put

[8] Raleigh *Sentinel*, March 1, July 1, 1867; Greensboro *Patriot*, March 29, May 3, 1867; *North Carolina Progress*, quoted in *National Anti-Slavery Standard*, October 26, 1867.

[9] *A Fool's Errand*, 295.

[10] Henderson *Index* and Lincoln *Courier*, quoted in Raleigh *Standard*, September 19, 1867.

[11] Raleigh *Sentinel*, July 18, 1867.

the powers of government into the hands of mere *numbers.* . . . The majority in all times and in all countries are improvident and without property. Agrarianism and anarchy must be the result of this ultra democracy." [12]

In their panic, Conservatives had exaggerated the threat, just as had their Yankee counterparts in earlier generations. Moderates actually controlled the North Carolina Republican party, which, like its northern parent, was as sympathetic to property interests as to democracy and was not inclined to welcome confiscation, repudiation, or other extreme doctrines, or even heavier property taxation. Republicans expressed sympathy "as much [but no more] with the humblest as with the highest." For nine months preceding the November election of 1867, the *Standard* carried accounts daily of local Republican meetings, almost every one of which expressed moderate sentiments and rejected economic ultraism. Suggested political reforms simply sought more democracy, the one common proposal of local Republican meetings being the establishment of a public school system. Even the state's most prominent Negro leader was considered too cautious by an interested northern observer,[13] and the much-maligned leagues appear to have been mild. Despite the desires of watchful Conservatives, not one instance of criminal activity by the leagues was ever established in North Carolina, and the few charges that were made were almost entirely "founded on hearsay evidence spread by political opponents or through the reporting of a bitterly partisan press." [14] The leagues may actually have had a widespread moderating influence. They sought to dispel a heritage of illegality and anarchism among the Negroes and unite them into a legitimate political force, and in so doing they cultivated a respect for principles of both property and politics and helped dispel ignorance, radicalism, and criminality among the league membership. It was

[12] Worth to William Clark, February 16, 1868, and Worth to A. M. Tomlinson & Sons, April 11, 1868, Hamilton (ed.), *Jonathan Worth*, II, 1154–56, 1185.

[13] Conway to Chase, April 23, 1867, Padgett (ed.), "Reconstruction Letters." *NCHR*, XXI (1944), 233–35. The preceding quotation appears in Raleigh *Standard*, May 14, 1867.

[14] Austin Marcus Drumm, "The Union League in the Carolinas" (unpublished Ph.D. dissertation, University of North Carolina, 1955), 59. None of the cases in North Carolina had substantial evidence. The League's major violation of its principles was political coercion, which was opposed by leaders and insignificant in its political effects (*ibid.*, 48, 62, 92–117).

probably their legitimate effectiveness, rather than any evil or failure, that inspired Conservative resentment, and other accusations against the leagues were the weapons rather than the causes of political warfare.

Tourgée was certainly one of the most radical Republicans in the state and was constantly attending meetings identified with the lower classes and the leagues, but while undoubtedly offensive in manner, neither Tourgée nor these meetings endorsed substantial extremism.[15] For example, Tourgée addressed a meeting in May in which all three mass organizations participated—the Union League, the Loyal Reconstruction League, and the Red Strings—which merely endorsed the Republican party and the elevation of the Negro. Another meeting addressed by Tourgée resolved that all men were free and equal, advocated free public schools to prepare the masses for industry, and commended the Negroes for their educational efforts. On the Fourth of July, Tourgée was the main speaker at a mass meeting at Lincolnton, reportedly attended by about 1,500 Negroes, but only about 70 whites, since the "respectable" whites kept away. Although Tourgée was denounced by the Conservative press for sowing the seeds of strife at this meeting, the only specific criticism of the young carpetbagger was that he was turning the Negroes against "their *only true friends*," their former owners. For many this was more than enough.

As the Negro vote swung Republican and racial and class fears fused, both resentment and political expediency encouraged Conservatives to endorse white supremacy. Conservatives who had once supported qualified Negro suffrage or had opposed the idea of a white man's party eventually joined the rush, and during the latter half of 1867 the most specific criticism of the Republicans was that they fostered Negro equality and domination. Whatever its merit, this criticism did contain some substance. But as earlier respectable descriptions of Negroes in politics disappeared and efforts to arouse emotional hostility against the race became legion, both the Republican position and the danger of Negro control were grossly exaggerated. By October the *North Carolina Progress* defined the trend when it called for a "white

[15] Raleigh *Standard*, May 21, 23, 1867; clipping, Lincoln *Courier*, July 5, 1867, in Journal of David Schenck, V, 102, Schenck Papers.

man's party" and advised that *"these black Radical upstarts and popin-jays be discharged by wholesale from plantations, workshops, house-holds and counting rooms*, and the test of prowess now begin." [16]

What merit there was in opposing either votes for the ignorant or Republicanism was soon submerged by the race issue. This issue conveniently mitigated responsibility for decades of slavery and oligarchy by attributing the results to racial characteristics and provided an excellent basis for weakening the Republicans. By preserving unqualified suffrage for the whites, Conservatives minimized their challenge to the nation's democratic philosophy while still catering to the interests and beliefs of the gentry. Ignorance remained fit to vote, if it voted Conservative and was white, and many whites thereafter voted for racial prejudice and little or nothing else.

Republicans recognized and dreaded the racist tactics of their opponents and were perplexed by a desire to cater to both prejudice and equality. While Republicans remained firm in support of Negro political and civil equality, they were too wary or too biased to go further; they rejected assertions of social equality as a humbug, declaring that social relationships were outside the realm of politics or law. Negroes would not "trench on the social rights or status of the white race," promised the Republican party's *Standard*,[17] and this newspaper also condemned interracial marriages, insisting that political equality would actually reduce the extensive amalgamation that had been encouraged by slavery. With some reluctance, Tourgée took a similar position, while Conservatives deliberately ignored the express limitations of the Republicans.

Tourgée's effective Republicanism during this tense campaigning brought him increasing odium. While some Conservatives were still utilizing his articles in the *Register* to promote factionalism, it was Tourgée himself who became the special object of attack in the Greensboro region. By June the once respectable *Register* had become a "sickly sheet" and Tourgée the "editor of a dirty newspaper printed in this town." Unjustly abused and accused of various political shenanigans, Tourgée became sufficiently disturbed by community hostility to apply

---

[16] Quoted in *National Anti-Slavery Standard*, October 12, 1867.
[17] June 27, 1867. See also issues of March 16, September 7, 1867.

to the Federal authorities for permission to carry a pistol.[18] It was his new local success that inspired this state of affairs. Led by Tourgée, Reverend Welker, and David Hodgin, and supported by the lower-class Negroes and whites, the Loyal Reconstruction League was capturing control of the Republican party in Guilford, a development that alienated a number of moderate Republicans and unionists. The rank and file and most of the leadership of these piedmont radicals were still prewar residents of the state, both Negro and white. In fact, Tourgée appears to have been the only prominent carpetbagger identified with this group in Guilford County. Of course ambitious immigrants were generally welcome in all wings of a Republican party that lacked capable leadership, and although only a handful in numbers, carpetbaggers were to be of great importance in that party, some effectively promoting reform and others selfishly contributing to eventual Republican ruin.

In September, 1867, the Guilford Loyal Reconstruction League nominated Tourgée and Welker as candidates for election to the approaching constitutional convention, and in the following month they were both endorsed by the influential Negro community of Warnersville. Precisely what occurred at these meetings is unknown, since the local press, which was Conservative, had by then given up any pretense of rational political reporting and merely ridiculed radical meetings as being composed of all races, names, and shades. Meanwhile, a rival meeting of moderate unionists nominated Jonathan Harris and Nereus Mendenhall as convention delegates, both antislavery Quakers and unionists who had been co-operating with Tourgée since 1866. Also under way at this time was a statewide revolt of moderate Republicans, led by Daniel R. Goodloe and the Raleigh *Union Register* (Tourgée's former paper). This revolt was aided by an erroneous insistence that the confiscation of rebel land had been endorsed by the Republican state convention of September, and several prominent Republicans, including Thomas Settle and Robert P. Dick, were reportedly leaving the Guilford party. Holden's *Standard*, obviously perplexed, failed to carry an account of affairs in that county during the fall of 1867, and it was over a month before Tourgée and Welker were recognized as

[18] Greensboro *Patriot*, June 7, 14, 21, 1867; Tourgée to Major Worth, May 24, 1867, Tourgée Papers.

official candidates by their state party. Once this recognition took place, Guilford Conservatives threw their support behind the moderate candidates Nereus Mendenhall and Jonathan Harris.[19]

Tourgée was undisturbed. Writing under a pseudonym for the northern *National Anti-Slavery Standard,* he welcomed the sharpening party division and even applauded Republican defeats in the North because they had helped drive weak-kneed North Carolina Republicans out of the party. The real issues had been concealed, he complained, with only a few bold Conservatives openly opposing the Reconstruction convention and only a few Republicans, including himself, urging a straightforward fight for major reforms. Weak Republicans and frightened Conservatives had been standing together on a noncommittal state platform until the current of progress had grown so strong that the respectable fled from the ranks. Praise their flight, Tourgée advised, for real Republicans could now stand on their own feet and establish a government of, by, and for the people. The party had rested content with the opportunity to build a new state and had ignored the problem of *how* to build it for too long, "never once thinking that the great struggle between aristocracy and democracy, between freedom and slavery, is but half won; that emancipation is not complete until the 'master' is abolished as well as the slave." There were specific questions that Republicans must answer:

> Will they give to the landless voters the right to sit upon a jury with the owner of a hundred barren acres? Will they allow the landless voter to be a candidate for office? or will they require two hundred acres of red clay to give a man sufficient dignity and intellect to represent a county in the Assembly? Will they shape the fundamental law of the State to favor the hundred thousand voters who do not own land enough to bury them in, or the fifteen hundred inhabitants who own more than *two-*

[19] Raleigh *Standard,* November 5, 28, 1867; Greensboro *Patriot,* November 8, 1867. The Republicans *had* threatened that further resistance to Federal desires might bring confiscation, and they *had* refused a prior repudiation of such possible congressional action, just as they refused to interfere with Congress in their own behalf (*Standard,* January 3, March 21, 22, September 7, 10, 12, October 3, 8, 1867).

thirds of the lands of the State? Will they seek to put a tax of one-and-a-half dollars upon the polls of her poor men, or *one-half* cent per acre upon the lands of her rich ones? [20]

Tourgée feared that the desired answers to these questions meant opposition from landlords and capitalists and eventual failure. The removal of property representation, the shifting of the burden of taxation from the poll tax to land, and such costly innovations as free public schools were recognized as endeavors in which the laboring poor would "act as the political opponent of the very men whose patronage is necessary to secure to-morrow's bread." The results could be disastrous.

> Hunger is more potent than patriotism. . . . No law, no constitution, no matter how cunningly framed, can shield the poor men of the South from the domination of that very aristocracy from which rebellion sprung, when once States are established here. Anarchy or oligarchy are the inevitable results of reconstruction. Serfdom or bloodshed must necessarily follow. The 'Plan of Congress,' so called, if adopted, would deliver the free men of the South, bound hand and foot, to their old-time, natural enemies.[21]

Again he urged in vain the old territorial plan, and he detected as a great threat that decline in idealism and emphasis upon expediency which had increasingly characterized the northern Republican party since the war.

But Tourgée would still attempt the fight, and while lamenting the lack of more effective national assistance, he did his best to mobilize his allies in the South. "Laborers of Guilford," he asked with typical flourish, "are you not as capable of self government as those men who with the motto rule or ruin, did both rule and ruin all this glorious Southern land? The aristocracy of slavery is dead. Shall we now build up an aristocracy of land? Shall we have a government of a few, by a

---

[20] *National Anti-Slavery Standard*, October 19, 1867. Also see issues of November 9, December 14, 1867, and January 4, 1868, letters signed either Wenckar or Winegar.
[21] *Ibid.*, October 19, 1867.

few and for a few?" [22] To prevent any such development, the convention candidate Tourgée pledged to support ten specific constitutional reforms:

1. Equal civil and political rights to all citizens.
2. No property qualifications for jurymen.
3. Every voter eligible for every office.
4. Popular election of all state legislative, executive, and judicial officials.
5. A humane criminal code without whips or stocks.
6. Free public schools from the primary to the university level.
7. Uniform ad valorem taxation upon property.
8. A poll tax not to exceed three days' work or the equivalent.
9. Prohibition of the assumption of any county, city or other political debt "contracted in aid of rebellion, directly or indirectly. . . ."
10. Extension of full citizenship to the present excluded classes as soon as Congress removes their disabilities.

In reality, Tourgée was even more strongly opposed to the existing poll tax than his program suggested. He would later boast of having flatly opposed the poll tax during the campaign and he certainly did fight against any poll tax at all in the constitutional convention of 1868. Significantly, however, he also supposed himself to have been "the only public man in the State who had openly advocated (perhaps the only one who sincerely believed in) the abolition of the poll tax." [23] Newly freed slaves, whose income was at a bare subsistence level, resented the taxation that accompanied freedom, especially when political leaders pointed out that the tax on the labor of the poor man was proportionately much higher than the tax levied on property. The total poll tax in some counties was as high as a month's wages, and Tourgée estimated that the property tax was somewhere between one-third and one-tenth of one per cent, whereas the average poll tax was between four and five per cent of a year's wages. Adding to the antagonism aroused by this issue was the fact that landlords were responsible for and collected their tenants' poll taxes. Indignant over this power of the landlords and the general inequity of the tax, Tourgée also composed an

[22] Tourgée's election circular, October 21, 1867, Tourgée Papers.
[23] Raleigh *Standard*, July 23, 1870.

anti-poll tax song, which he claimed was sung "with much gusto" by the politically active freedmen.[24]

Once again Tourgée's position is worthy of special note because he was one of the more radical Republicans and would be perhaps the strongest leader of the radical wing in the approaching constitutional convention. Relying heavily upon class appeals, he had sought more democracy, increased social services, and a shifting of the tax burden onto the shoulders of the wealthy. Such measures were undoubted challenges to the power, pocketbooks, and beliefs of Conservatives, but they did not begin to approach the danger or crime that Conservatives claimed. Probably Tourgée's one still controvertible suggestion was that of the popular election of judges, while restraint was apparent in his rejection of progressive taxation and acceptance of a limited poll tax. Furthermore, all of Tourgée's proposals repeated suggestions made by North Carolinians in the constitutional convention of 1866.

Antagonisms remained sharp enough, however, to reduce rational political argument to a minimum in the Greensboro press. Under a new owner, the unionist-Conservative David F. Caldwell, the *Patriot* thoroughly exploited the Negro supremacy theme, maligning and ridiculing the darker race, emphasizing the racial division between the parties, and printing the influential white supremacy address of the Conservative titan William A. Graham. On the other hand, the forces of liberalism were, and would remain, unusually strong in the county, and the *Patriot* sought to cultivate the moderates by endorsing eventual Negro suffrage; this concession was qualified by the demand that Negroes "establish a character for sobriety, honesty, industry, truthfulness, patience and charity" before seeking the rights of white men.[25] Little was said about Tourgée's specific constitutional proposals. Instead, Conservatives inveighed in general against confiscation, repudiation, and taxation, although the one great future Republican extravagance, aid to railroads, was not even thought of. Defeat "A. W. Tourgée & Co." with his party of "*agrarian radical* confiscators," implored the *Patriot*, as it accused Tourgée and his allies of poisoning the minds of the lower-class Negroes and whites and warned that never in history had the poor

[24] *National Anti-Slavery Standard,* November 9, 1867.
[25] Greensboro *Patriot,* November 8, 1867. See *ibid.,* August 30, September 13, 20, November 22, 1867, for more vicious racism.

bettered their condition by combining "to make war upon capital or capitalists." [26]

Despite the unity between Conservatives and moderates and their control of the local press, the radicals carried the Guilford election. Tourgée had squeaked through to victory by only 43 votes (the estimated 100 voters disfranchised by Congress could have changed the result), but the strength of liberalism could be seen in the fact that 1,766 votes were cast in favor of holding a convention and only 638 votes against. This was a tacit acceptance of the Reconstruction Acts.[27] In the state as a whole there was an impressive display of biracial unity as twenty to thirty thousand whites joined about twice that many Negroes to give the Republicans 107 of the 120 convention seats.

Defeat did not cow the Conservatives. In Guilford County, where the Negro vote had been decisive, they angrily denounced the Negroes for arraying "themselves against the whites" and expressed a wish that the race would leave the state. The editor of the state's leading Conservative daily, the *Sentinel*, and the governor of the state now took the recalcitrant stand that the Negro should "have no part in the civil government." Racist propoganda increased, and white tenants were punished for putting themselves "down with the niggers." [28] Soon resentment and determined opposition to the Republican victory engendered an irrational denunciation of the approaching convention even before its sentiments were known and an irreconcilable opposition to the new constitution even before it was prepared.

Republicans, in contrast, were jubilant, and especially pleased at how well the white unionist counties in the west had resisted the demagogic cry of "negro supremacy." Tourgée was not only pleased but somewhat more confident. Threats notwithstanding, the election had gone peacefully, he noted, and although the odds were still adverse, the extent of the victory was most encouraging. The Negroes had proven unwilling to believe that those who opposed emancipation, denounced the Freed-

[26] *Ibid.*, November 1, 22, 1867.

[27] *Ibid.*, November 29, 1867. Welker, 1,347; Tourgée, 1,231; Menhenhall, 1,188; and Harris, 1,044.

[28] Greensboro *Patriot*, November 29, 1867; W. E. Pell to W. A. Graham, November 25, 1867, William A. Graham Papers, Southern Historical Collection; Worth to Clark, February 16, 1868, and Worth to W. A. Graham, February 27, 1868, Hamilton (ed.), *Jonathan Worth*, II, 1154–56, 1165–67; Complaint, December 2, 1867, NCFBR, Box 447.

men's Bureau, and resented equality were their best friends. In addition, a gratifying number of whites were apparently convinced that the men who had led the state to destruction were not those best qualified to rebuild it. Yet Tourgée fretted still. There remained powerful opponents to be feared, whose only "hope of success lies in arousing the cowardly fear of the masses, and appealing to their basest passions and most unmanly prejudices. They are daily growing more despicable." [29]

[29] *National Anti-Slavery Standard*, December 14, 1867.

IX

The Reconstruction
Convention of 1868

The constitutional convention which met in Raleigh on January 14, 1868, was, as one Republican delegate bragged, truly an innovation, "both in its purpose and in the kind of men composing it." The old political leaders of the state and the Confederacy were conspicuously absent, and one prominent North Carolina visitor found only Negro men and women in the gallery, and in the hall itself, he commented, "every here & there is dotted a woolly headed Negro—& oftener than is proper the voice of the African is heard—where none but the anglo saxon voices have been heard before— Such is *Progress*." [1] Of the 120 delegates, all but 13 were Republicans. Surely the convention would be an indication of the results of Negro suffrage, of the attitudes and abilities of black and white Republicans, and of the validity of Conservative fears.

Seventy-four of the Republicans were prewar white North Carolinians. Many former leaders in Holden's Union party were prominent among them, while others, such as George W. Welker and John Quincy Adams Bryan, had been consistent unionists or even Union veterans. The sentiments and votes of these native whites controlled the convention, and they chaired eight of the original thirteen committees drafting constitutional articles. Tourgée, the youngest man present (he was only twenty-nine), was one of eighteen recent immigrants or carpetbaggers, a group that included at least eight Union veterans and a number of able and influential men—two generals, a major, two previous members

[1] Joseph R. French, quoted in Raleigh *Standard*, January 28, 1868; Rufus L. Patterson to his wife, February 21, 1868, Patterson Papers.

of northern state legislatures (including an editor), two Federal officials, and a minister active in educational work among the freedmen.
Because of their experience, ability, and ambition and their familiarity
with a type of political structure that Republicans often desired to
emulate, these white carpetbaggers played a much more prominent role
than their number suggests. The fifteen Negro delegates present included
both the previously slave and free, with only one known to have been
born in the North, and a high proportion of them were active and able
men who played prominent roles in the convention. The two perhaps
most active Conservatives, Plato Durham and John W. Graham, were
recent Confederate officers, and the latter was the son of William A.
Graham, ex-governor and chief architect of the white supremacy
program.

From the first, Tourgée was prominent in the convention. On the
second day he was elected assistant secretary pro tem and eagerly ex-
pedited the launching of the convention's work. He was appointed a
member of the initial committee of sixteen to report on the best way
to frame a constitution for the state, he was chairman of the committee
that wrote the constitutional article on local government, and he was
a most influential member of the committee framing the judiciary
article. Tourgée also served on the committees on printing, recommend-
ing citizens to Congress for relief from political disability, preventing
the intimidation of voters, and preparing an address to the people on
the new constitution. In the major debates and issues of the convention,
Tourgée was always to be heard, and he often suggested various
simplifications or modifications (some quite momentous) of constitutional articles. He complained to Emma of quarreling and windy
speeches, and he tried to speed up the convention's accomplishments
and to encourage efficiency by proposing (unsuccessfully) that full pay
be provided for only thirty days and only half pay thereafter (the convention sat for fifty-five days). After numerous failures, he finally did
secure both day and night sessions. But Tourgée also favored legislative
action by the convention, which occupied additional time, and he
remained prone to wrangle with both friend and foe.[2]

---

[2] The official proceedings are in the *Journal of the Constitutional Convention of
the State of North Carolina at its Session 1868* (Raleigh, 1868), hereafter cited as
Journal. Debates can best be followed in the Republican *Standard* and the Con-

Tourgée clashed with the Republicans, for example, by championing the right of Conservatives to be heard. Whether from principle, or to expose demagoguery, or to promote a suitable compromise, he opposed the practice of calling the previous question to shut off Conservative debate. In one instance this led him into such a heated altercation with the convention president that Tourgée was arrested. Such boldness captured admiration, however, and following an almost unanimous convention demand for his release, the bellicose carpetbagger returned to his seat amidst great applause. A somewhat different willingness to compromise was illustrated during the debate over the proposed constitutional phrase, "all men are created equal," when Tourgée yielded to Conservative objections by suggesting the less controversial phrasing that all men were "created free and equal in rights." But the Republican majority considered this quibbling, and Jefferson's famous words were retained. Conservatives, for different reasons, had rejected Tourgée's version as well, and the illustrative comment of their leading newspaper, that he who sought to prove "that God teaches the equality of rights of the several varieties of the human species, goes on a fool's errand," may have furnished Tourgée the title for his most famous novel.[3]

As this incident indicates, party conflicts during the convention remained centered on issues of race and class. "The property and earnings of the industrious would not be safe under universal suffrage," complained the Conservatives, as they sought property representation, property qualifications for office, and other curbs on democracy.[4] Their constant objections to "dangerous innovation" finally prompted from Tourgée the sarcastic suggestion that the delegates adopt the oldest constitution they could find and declare it inviolable and unamendable forever. Conservatives especially dramatized the race issue. Their press ridiculed the "Gorilla Convention," "Black Republican Convention," "Nigger Convention," and "Bones and Banjo Convention," and the policy-making *Sentinel* asserted that, although Conservatives were in a

---

servative *Sentinel*; the latter was, however, too often concerned with discrediting, rather than presenting, the proceedings. See also Hamilton, *Reconstruction*, and the more sympathetic Jack B. Scroggs, "Carpetbagger Influence in the Political Reconstruction of the South Atlantic States, 1865–1876" (unpublished Ph.D. dissertation, University of North Carolina, 1951), 121–87.

[3] Raleigh *Sentinel*, February 15, 1868.

[4] *Journal*, 49, 159, 183–84, 195–96; Raleigh *Standard*, February 1, 14, 1868.

hopeless minority, by correct tactics they could emphasize Republican hostility to *"the rule of the white race in North Carolina."* [5] This became the predominant role of their convention delegates.

Plato Durham, subsequently a Ku Klux Klan chieftain, introduced the first racist note into the convention with an appeal for white supremacy and the preservation of racial distinctions. He also bewailed the presence of Negroes in seats once occupied by eminent whites, while J. R. Ellis delivered what Tourgée considered a lengthy, unscientific speech "on the anatomical and physiological differences between white and black races. A grand copperhead effort." [6] Thereafter, Conservatives demanded constitutional provisions for a segregated militia, where "no white man shall ever be required to obey a negro officer"; segregated schools; a ban on intermarriage; and a ban against Negro guardianship of any white ward. Native white Republicans and their allies responded by overwhelmingly rejecting every proposal for racial provision in the new constitution. When Conservatives sought to bar persons of African descent from any executive office, Tourgée countered that it was un-charitable for ex-slaveowners to seek to exclude the blood that they had mixed. He also suggested a challenging substitute for the Conservative proposal for segregated schools: "That separate and distinct schools may be provided for any class of citizens in the State: *Provided,* That in all cases where distinct schools shall be established, there shall be as ample, sufficient and complete facilities afforded for the one class as for the other, and entirely adequate for all, and in all districts where schools are divided, the apportionment to each shall be equal." [7] This, said Tourgée, would allow prejudice to be catered to, but it would have to be paid for. But Conservatives wanted each race to support its own schools and refused to endorse the principle of separate but equal facilities. Tourgée was satisfied that their motives had been exposed.

Conservatives were logical about Negroes only in their arguments that recently emancipated slaves were unfit to exercise the franchise. Of course here they encountered firm Republican resistance, as Negro and white, native and immigrant, joined in an able defense of universal male suffrage. Pointedly denying that Negroes were more inclined to

5 Raleigh *Sentinel*, January 15, 20, 1868; Hamilton, *Reconstruction,* 256–57.
6 Tourgée to his wife, February 19, 1868, Tourgée Papers.
7 *Journal,* 342–43.

follow demagogues than whites had been in 1861, Republicans dismissed talk of social equality and amalgamation as nonsense. "Man is man is the keynote of our civilization," argued Tourgée, and insisting that the poor needed power against privilege and wealth and that there could be "no color before the law," he predicted a world-wide acceptance of political equality as the crowning glory of the century.[8] Actually, as Tourgée noted, Congress had alredy determined who should vote, but the convention's adoption of universal suffrage reflected an enthusiastic endorsement of popular sovereignty and equality.

Nevertheless, there were limits to this resistance against Conservative demands for constitutional guarantees that "the Negro was the social, moral and intellectual inferior of the white man." Few Republicans attacked segregation and the efforts of one Negro delegate to forbid it in all public conveyances and public places received practically no support. In response to race-baiting, the Republicans even passed a resolution, introduced by a Negro, which stated "that intermarriage and illegal intercourse between the races should be discountenanced, and the interests and happiness of the two races would be best promoted by the establishment of separate schools." [9] While Republicans thus shied from attacking segregation (and there were Negroes who anticipated its benefits), they also stoutly refused to place any racial provisions in the constitution, believing that such provisions had no place in the supreme law and would imply and encourage an inferior status for the Negro.

Conservatives were energetic and annoying critics, but the actual creation of a new state constitution was carried out almost solely by the Republicans, with Tourgée contributing to a number of important constitutional reforms, including the institution of a new form of local government. Prior to 1868, local self-rule in North Carolina had been sharply limited by the legislative appointment of the powerful county magistrates, and demands for more locally elected officials had existed since the ante-bellum era and had been strong in the convention of 1866. Tourgée considered local democracy the political key to northern progress, and as later stated, he felt its absence in the South "had

---

[8] Speech manuscript, Tourgée Papers.
[9] *Journal*, 473, 483–88. For an extreme instance of defensive Republican racism, see Raleigh *Standard*, August 29, 1868.

suppressed free thought and free speech, had degraded labor, encouraged ignorance, and established aristocracy." [10] Quite fittingly, he chaired the committee which prepared a new system modeled after the "township and county commissioner plan" of Pennsylvania. In an attempt to provide more local independence and a greater separation of powers, the committee took county political control from the magistrates and placed it in the hands of five locally elected county commissioners. The counties were divided into townships which elected a clerk and two magistrates, who had judicial and various local administrative duties. Tourgée also secured an amendment placing school control in the hands of an elected school committee in each township. Although a northern model had been followed in this plan, the demand was indigenous to the state. The Pennsylvania system itself had earlier been approved by the prominent Conservative David F. Caldwell,[11] and twelve of the thirteen members of Tourgée's committee, including one of two Conservatives, approved this plan when it was submitted. Tourgée and seven other members of the committee also submitted an additional section providing that no county, city, town, or other political corporation should pay any debt "contracted directly or indirectly in aid or support of the rebellion." This proposal was one of Tourgée's campaign pledges and had earlier been rejected by the convention, but he now succeeded in having it endorsed as part of the constitutional article on local government. Three Republicans joined nine Conservatives in a final unsuccessful effort to revert to the previous system, and with all the Conservatives and one Republican opposed, the new system was adopted.[12] Subsequently this reform became quite popular, especially in the western portion of the state.

Tourgée was of even more decisive influence in the preparation of a new judicial system for a state that was still using the two separate legal procedures of equity and common law. During the nineteenth century a reform movement in the United States and Europe was steadily under-

[10] See *Bricks Without Straw*, 460–64, 506–13.

[11] Caldwell to Worth, November 2, 1866, Hamilton (ed.), *Jonathan Worth*, II, 829–31.

[12] For the preceding account, see *Journal*, 44, 204, 314–20, 352–53; Raleigh Standard, February 15, 1868; Charles Christopher Crittenden and Dan Lacy, *The Historical Records of North Carolina*, Vol. I: *The County Records* (Raleigh, 1939), 21.

mining this dual system and substituting a single, simplified, written code of procedure. These reformers also sought, with less success, to minimize technical procedural requirements in pleading cases. This legal movement had additional appeal to such equalitarians as Tourgée because it supposed itself to be establishing a more democratic code of law, a law of simple and direct justice, written in plain language, and intelligible to those who were governed by it. Ohio had followed New York as one of the first states to adopt the reform, and Tourgée, trained in both these states, was well acquainted with, and enthusiastically in favor of, the newer code system. He was also in communication with David Dudley Field, the most influential promoter of code reform in the United States.

Early in the convention session, Tourgée had printed and distributed his own state judicial plan, which was "based upon the hypothesis that the distinction between actions at law and suits in equity should be abolished—a distinction accidental in its origins, cumbrous and artificial in its nature, tedious and expensive in practice and not infrequently mischievous and unjust in its results." [13] Also included in Tourgée's proposal was another major innovation, the popular election of Superior and Supreme Court judges. All these suggestions were strongly opposed by the native Republican delegate William B. Rodman, an able lawyer and the chairman of the judiciary committee, but Tourgée, who was a member of this committee, provoked such division and furor among its members that they finally went before the entire convention to request a settlement of certain "fundamental points respecting the proper organization of the Judiciary Department."

The matter of judicial elections became the first topic for open debate, and Tourgée delivered the major speech in its favor. He maintained that if the people were competent to elect the makers of the law they were competent to elect its interpreters, and that the mass of voters were less liable to corruption than legislatures, parties, or other smaller groups. Rodman urged adherence to the method followed by the national constitution, and almost every prominent delegate who spoke, native or carpetbagger, opposed Tourgée and accused him of a lack of proper reverence for tradition. Tourgée's experiences in academy

[13] "A Plan for the Organization of the Judiciary Department, Proposed by A. W. Tourgée, of Guilford, as a Section of the Constitution," Tourgée Papers.

and collegiate debate now served him well. Sharply countering criticism and capturing the democratic predilections of the convention, he secured approval of the electoral principle. He had succeeded in bypassing the majority of the judiciary committee, which had preferred some form of appointed judiciary but had been divided within itself. The great majority of the carpetbaggers and a majority of the Negroes had also preferred appointed judges, while the most equalitarian pressure had come from native whites. This entire reform had some native roots dating back to at least 1800. In 1850 the Democratic party had advocated a popularly elected judiciary and Whigs had been willing to endorse it, and in 1866 it had been urged by the prominent Robert P. Dick.[14]

The following day Tourgée was again the main champion of legal change when the proposed single system of procedure was discussed, and he was apparently supported in debate only by his codelegate from Guilford, Reverend Welker. Rodman and others resisted the change as destructive and accused Tourgée of a mania to import northern ideas. But again he captured the convention, as the change was approved by a vote of 50 to 38. A majority of carpetbaggers, Negroes, and members of the judiciary committee had finally supported the change, but nevertheless the momentous and beneficial abolition of North Carolina's system of dual procedures had been carried through almost solely by the young carpetbagger, Tourgée. "A stranger boy," lamented the Conservative delegate John W. Graham, had succeeded in overturning a time-honored and revered legal system, and he had done this despite the opposition of the authoritative legal opinion in the convention. This change was to be the one major innovation in the new Reconstruction constitution not specifically based upon native sentiment, and is illustrative of both Tourgée's influence and the reluctance of Republicans to import alien ideas.

There were other debates over the details of the final judiciary article, which, in addition to the changes already discussed, required proceedings to be in writing, abolished feigned issues, increased the number of judges, abolished the old county courts and transferred most of their functions to the Superior Court, gave the Superior Court clerk probate functions, and provided for a code commission of three to prepare the

[14] Connor, *North Carolina*, II, 68; Johnson, *Ante-Bellum North Carolina*, 627–43; Raleigh *Weekly Standard*, June 13, 1866.

new code of procedure and "a Code of the laws of North Carolina." Also, the courts, which had previously been "creatures of the Legislature," were given a needed independence. Conservatives particularly opposed the abolition of the old county courts and the expense of increasing the number of higher judges, but Tourgée, now supported by Rodman, convincingly argued that the new system would pay for itself by eliminating complexity, delay, and cost. Negroes especially welcomed the curtailment of the old county courts, said one of their delegates, A. H. Galloway, because the untrained magistrates had so frequently been unjust.

"If there had been nothing else objectionable in the new Constitution, its provisions as to the Judiciary would have made me view it with horror," exclaimed Jonathan Worth while he was still governor of the state, and yet, despite many such complaints, these were logical reforms and frequently represented ante-bellum demands. Prominent attorneys had long sought general reform, greater judicial independence, curtailment of the county courts, simpler methods of pleading, written records, and more judges. Although the new judicial article was almost identical to Tourgée's original plan (seven of the thirty-five sections in the article were almost verbatim copies and thirteen others repeated the essence of sections of his plan), he himself considered the judicial reforms, except for the new codified procedure, strictly *sui generis*. Only two delegates born outside of North Carolina, he stated, dared advocate any interference with the county courts. The pressure against these courts was overwhelming, and "that pressure came almost entirely from the native North Carolinians." [15]

Tourgée also contributed to two other reforms with ante-bellum roots by assisting the chairman of the Committee on Punishments, Penal Institutions, and Public Charities, his codelegate Reverend Welker. These two Guilford Republicans helped establish increased state responsibility for the needy and an amelioration of criminal punishment. Republicans seriously split over the latter, Tourgée insisting that the law should seek to reform as well as to punish, while his opponents spoke of the need to strike terror into the hearts of criminals. Particularly

[15] Manuscript on *McAdoo v. Benbow*, 63 N.C. 112 (1869), Tourgée Papers. For the preceding quotation, see Worth to B. S. Hedrick, May 11, 1868, Hamilton (ed.), *Jonathan Worth*, II, 1200–1.

resisted was a suggested limitation of the death penalty to "wilful murder," with many Republicans joining Conservatives in a desire to retain the supreme penalty for burglary, arson, and rape as well, although, as Welker pointed out, white men were seldom executed for those crimes. A final compromise did provide punishment by death for all these crimes, but only "if the General Assembly shall so enact." Tourgée had secured this qualification in hopes of convincing the Assembly not to do so, and after the convention adjourned he promoted a series of petitions to the General Assembly advising that the supreme penalty be limited to willful murder. Tourgée preferred, but considered unobtainable, the complete abolition of the death penalty, and he hoped that a petition campaign, together with the favorable attitude of half the state judges, the code commissioners, and certain leading Republicans, would bring this much success. "Such another opportunity to humanize our laws may not present itself in half a century," he advised his cohorts, and thereafter they did see the confinement of executions to murder and rape.[16]

Another past practice of the state undone by the carpetbagger Tourgée was that of the levying of costs in criminal proceedings against innocent defendants. This custom was not only unjust to the poorer whites and Negroes, but in the bitter era of Reconstruction it invited persecution. After initial failure, Tourgée obtained a constitutional provision that defendants in criminal cases would not be compelled "to pay costs or jail fees or necessary witness fees of the defense, unless found guilty." [17]

It is obvious that Tourgée was giving full and effective play to his idealism in the constitutional convention, yet in other instances his activities were coldly practical, and even devious. Unlike many of his allies, he remained acutely aware of the strength of the opposition and was prepared to go to great lengths to prevent Republican failure. Fearful of any taint being attached to the convention, he even attacked Republicans, and his complaint that some delegates, including the convention's president, appeared to be disqualified by the Reconstruction Acts prompted an investigation to determine whether or not the

[16] Tourgée to Mendenhall, April 28, 1868, and Tourgée to William J. Allinson, May 2, 1868, Tourgée Papers.
[17] *Journal*, 43, 47, 50, 214; Raleigh *Standard*, January 22, 1868.

president's signature might possibly invalidate the convention's actions. While thus insisting that everything about the convention must be just, legal, and manly to prevent its being discredited, Tourgée's own activities were at times rather unmanly. He had been disturbed to learn that a Conservative minority in Alabama had apparently defeated a new Republican constitution simply by not voting, since the Reconstruction Acts provided that a majority of those registered must vote. When news reached him that Congress was preparing to amend the Reconstruction Acts so as to validate the Alabama results, Tourgée advised Senator Benjamin F. Wade as to how the Republicans might have their cake and eat it too: "Might it not be well to defer action upon that until after the election in other states? If this is done the inaction policy will be adopted everywhere, otherwise they will do their best to vote down the constitution and may succeed in some." [18] Tourgée's justification for such chicanery was that intimidation by the Conservatives was already preventing a fair expression of the popular will in the South. Here was undoubtedly a man whose tactics Conservatives might closely watch.

Sanguine of Republican success in the initial elections, Tourgée also sought to establish the Reconstruction regime more firmly by extending the term of office of various officials. Therefore, while his democratic-minded allies urged shorter terms for judges, Tourgée joined with Conservatives, who desired to check the popular will, in demanding lengthy terms. It was by Tourgée's motion that the term of Superior Court judges was extended from six to eight years, and he was also responsible for some ambiguous terminology in the judiciary article that added two additional years to the term of the first group of judges elected. Tourgée was also involved in the inclusion of a similar clause in the article on the legislature, the literal meaning of which was that the first legislature elected, which was to be a Republican one, was to sit for four years rather than the normal two. When this was first grasped by Conservatives, more than a year later, a great furor arose, and Tourgée stood alone in supporting the meaning of the clause, claiming that such had been its intended meaning and that it had been offered by certain colleagues as a substitute for a more explicit deferment that he had prepared. Tourgée's convention colleagues denied this account; either

[18] Tourgée to Wade, February 13, 1868, Padgett (ed.), "Reconstruction Letters," *NCHR*, XXI (1944), 247.

Tourgée was desperately striving to check the resurgence of the Conservatives in 1869 or there had been a misunderstanding in the convention. Wherever the truth lay, Tourgée displayed suspicious delight in 1869 over the wool having been held so long over Conservative eyes.[19]

Tourgée also differed with many Republicans over questions of political rights, and convention disagreement over requirements for voting and holding office were expressed in four separate committee reports. The majority report essentially granted universal male suffrage but required of officeholders a belief in God and a mild oath to uphold the state and national constitutions. A report by two Conservatives opposed Negro suffrage, while a carpetbagger desired to bar from office Confederates who had previously sworn to uphold the national Constitution. A harsher report by two native whites (one from the mountains and one from the coast) proposed to deny state suffrage and office to those so denied nationally by the Fourteenth Amendment, to those who would not "accept the political and civil equality of all men," to those who interfered with anyone's right to vote, and to those who had committed crimes during the war against a citizen or soldier of the United States. Tourgée was partial toward this severe attitude, although he also desired the removal of all religious qualifications and the retention of full rights for consistent unionists who were hostile to the Reconstruction program. He was not as tolerant of the heretics of the Confederacy. To his admission that no man should be "deprived of any of the rights or privileges enjoyed by his fellow men," Tourgée added, "except as may be necessary to secure the rights of others." He would include in this exception ex-Confederates who continued to oppose civil, political, moral, and educational rights for the Negroes, as he considered them obstinate aristocrats who had recently shown the entire nation how far they were prepared to go. Tourgée warned the delegates that God never converted an adult generation and urged them not to open the way for the destruction of the "poor man's party." [20] Mockingly, but correctly, the *Sentinel* stated that he wanted rights only for those who were sincerely repentant and "willing to give to a poor, humble and downtrodden race, recently emerged from bondage, the

[19] Tourgée to W. H. S. Sweet, December 22, 1869; V. C. Barringer to Tourgée, December 20, 1869; Sweet to Tourgée, December 17, 22; and D. Heaton to Sweet, December 27, 1869; all in Tourgée Papers.

[20] Speech manuscript, Tourgée Papers; Raleigh *Standard*, February 25, 1868.

same rights and privileges which they asked for themselves." [21] But the prevalent idealism and desire to appease the opposition were against Tourgée, and the convention defeated all proscriptive requirements as well as every attempt to establish an oath upholding civil and political equality. The convention, however, would not go out of its way to petition Congress for the benefit of Conservatives. Throughout, Negroes and carpetbaggers had divided their votes, while the strongest support for proscription had come from the piedmont and western white delegates.

In addition to framing a new political system for the state, the convention of 1868 dealt with various economic problems, and in contrast to their stubborn disruption of the political activities of the convention, Conservatives participated intelligently in these economic proceedings. The most pressing problem was the need for relief from the continuing impact of the tragic years since 1861 and from the crop failure of 1867, and the first significant proposal made in the convention was one for relief from the existing burden of debt. A pattern had already been established by a variety of civil and military stay laws in the state during the past seven years, and the convention quickly adopted a temporary stay on debts contracted before 1865. Tourgée had somewhat different desires. Since the courthouses of the state were plastered with notices of the sale of land for debts, he wondered why a man should be beggared for new debts any more than for old ones, especially when many new debts were renewals of the earlier ones or had been contracted in expectation of the payments of old debts that were now stayed. Tourgée unsuccessfully fought for a temporary stay on all debts, whether contracted before or after 1865, and appeared primarily interested in relief for the needy rather than in the technicalities of credit.[22] When carpetbaggers David Heaton and Joseph C. Abbott objected that his suggestions would be ruinous to commerce, Tourgée abused Abbott for opposing debtor relief while industriously promoting financial aid for a railroad that was over its head in debts contracted since 1865, and asked why a railroad should be offered a type of relief that was denied the people. The convention did approve a request that the military

[21] Raleigh *Sentinel*, February 22, 1868.
[22] *Journal*, 57, 139–42; Raleigh *Standard*, February 3–6, 1868. See also Kenneth Edson St. Clair, "Debtor Relief in North Carolina during Reconstruction," *NCHR*, XVIII (1941), 215–35.

authorities halt ruinous executions on debts contracted since the war, but the military refused to intervene in such civil affairs, and Tourgée was left to write a stinging protest (signed by six other delegates and himself) against the convention's stay on war debts alone.

Meanwhile certain sentiments promoted by the Conservative John W. Graham were gaining favor. Although Graham described stay laws as unconstitutional, he advocated a form of stay laws allowing the gradual payment of debts over a period of years. Obviously somewhat equitable, this plan was particularly appealing to large landowners who were heavily in debt, and the essence of Graham's idea was contained in a law presented by William B. Rodman, frequently a spokesman for conservative and propertied Republicans. A lengthy and stormy struggle ensued when Tourgée mustered support against Rodman's proposal as one that primarily protected the "upper-crust," the fifteen hundred citizens who owned two-thirds of the land and were in debt. This act would prevent their land from coming on the market and thus hinder the poor in obtaining land, Tourgée argued, which was not needed relief, but a method of allowing the land to be retained by the wealthy. He preferred to guarantee only a frugal living for a man, enough to maintain his family. After this was secured, the rest should go to pay his debts. Tourgée also expressed sympathy with the middle classes who had placed their few dollars in trust with the wealthy landowners and were now threatened by the proposed stay. Rodman, with perhaps more accuracy than Tourgée, retorted that land was moving into the hands of absentee landlords rather than into the hands of the poor. It was small wonder that some delegates could not decide just whom these stay laws were meant to help.[23] Tourgée did not succeed in blocking the measure, and with the acceptance of Graham's idea, the Conservatives achieved their most substantial contribution to the results of the convention. This suggests that one of the least differences between the two parties was in matters economic.

Tourgée also supported a minor relief measure prohibiting the distillation of grain because of the crop shortage of 1867, and at the urging from Greensboro of Robert P. Dick, he secured an ordinance relieving sheriffs of financial liability for having upheld a stay law later judged

[23] Raleigh *Standard*, January 22, March 5, 1868; Raleigh *Sentinel*, January 30, March 6, 1868.

unconstitutional. A much more significant accomplishment, as well as a compensation for his defeat on the matter of stay laws, was Tourgée's sponsorship of a retroactive homestead law. He wanted a law preserving to every family a small amount of landed or personal property against all debts, whether old or new, and he had fought for his proposed stay law primarily for the purpose of delaying all foreclosures until he could secure homestead protection for all North Carolinians. A homestead law was one thing, but its retroactive application was something else, and when Tourgée introduced his suggestion, it was at once condemned by leaders of both parties as an illegal lure, an unconstitutional ex post facto law, and an unconstitutional violation of the obligation of contract. Tourgée himself was accused of communist tendencies. There was no support for retroactivity from any member of the homestead committee, and Negroes, few of whom had old homesteads to protect, showed little interest in the measure. Some strong support was voiced by westerners, and, desirous of the broad relief promised by such a measure and unwilling to see the small landowner suffer because of the less liberal laws of the past, Tourgée marshalled arguments in support of his proposal. The gist of his clever legal case was that private contracts remained subject to the supreme law of the state and that there were conditions of public requirement superior to private contracts. One of these conditions was the right of the state to combat poverty:

> To secure these ends the right of eminent domain may be used in giving a homestead, retrospective and unassailable, for the property thus protected is left in the hands of the debtor, simply as a trustee for the state, the income derived therefrom being supposed to go entirely to the support of the otherwise impoverished family of the debtor. In exercising the right in this manner the state only renews the tenure which had been for a time alienated for the purpose of devoting the profits of the exempted property to its own use, viz. the support of its needy citizens—instead of taxing the property of the state—including the creditors to accomplish that end.[24]

[24] Speech manuscript, Tourgée Papers. See also Raleigh *Standard*, March 2, 1868.

But it was sympathy for the poor rather than legal logic that was Tourgée's inspiration and strength. Stay laws would not stand, but he insisted that here was a real measure of relief that would also preserve the small farmer and hinder the further concentration of land owner-ship. If there was a legal doubt, the people should at least be given the benefit of the doubt and the matter left for the courts to decide. His diligent efforts finally swayed Rodman and others hitherto opposed, and the measure was approved, Tourgée having meanwhile secured additional guarantees for a landowner's wife.

The final fate of both the stay law and the retroactive homestead was decided by the higher courts. In 1869 the state Supreme Court nullified stays but upheld the retroactive homestead on the precise grounds argued by Tourgée. Eight years later, however, the United States Supreme Court declared the retroactive provision unconstitutional. Nevertheless, Tour-gée could still claim victory, since retroactivity had been honored for nine years and had afforded most of the desired relief, and the home-stead law remained otherwise intact.

As promised in his campaign circular, Tourgée also fought the tradi-tional head or poll tax. The justice of the complaints against this arbitrarily determined and frequently high tax secured them abundant convention support. The delegates approved the proposal that a limited tax be established "equal on each head to the tax on property valued at three hundred dollars . . . but the State and county capitation tax combined shall never exceed two dollars on the head." When the dis-satisfied Tourgée attempted to push the convention further, his sug-gestion that the capitation tax be abolished was denounced by one Republican as the first gun of "agrarianism" because it would destroy the principle of a fixed proportion between the tax on property and on per-sons. Without a fixed balance between the two, some Republicans feared the war between numbers and property that Conservatives had long predicted. Tourgée's motion that the poll tax maximum be reduced to one dollar was then soundly defeated, as only four carpetbaggers and no Negroes joined its supporters, who were mainly western delegates. An effort to set the maximum at a dollar and a half fared the same. Tourgée next attempted to have the entire poll tax allocated to the public schools and succeeded in having a minimum of seventy-five per cent of the tax so utilized, the remainder to be used for poor relief.

Somewhat more difficult to interpret than Tourgée's democratic orientation on economic policy was his vacillating role on the question of fiscal aid to railroads. The ante-bellum government of North Carolina had been active in promoting railroad development, and as railroad companies began to fail after the war, sympathy for further state aid increased. The incoming Republicans were engulfed by this demand and by a feverish and optimistic postwar desire to build the economy of the South rapidly. Only a few days after the convention of 1868 opened, its members were approached by the Conservative president of the Wilmington, Charlotte, and Rutherford Railroad, who reported that his road lacked money and that if it were not assisted New York bond-holders would foreclose.[25] Largely at his inducement, Republicans presented their first ordinance on behalf of a railroad, emphasizing the need to protect a second mortgage of two million dollars that the state already held on this road. This act reduced the road's capitalization and provided state endorsement of one million dollars in the bonds of this reduced stock. Thus did Republicans begin a policy that became a major basis for subsequent denunciations of the entire Reconstruction epoch.

Tourgée at this time desired to have the entire state debt repudiated, which would eliminate the need to protect any state investment in the railroad, and he vigorously opposed the measure. Upon seeing that the ordinance would pass, he secured an amendment providing that half a million dollars of the road's bonds would be deposited as security with the state. With this added protection the ordinance passed by a close vote, with eleven Conservatives, ten carpetbaggers, and nine Negroes voting for it, while three Conservatives, four carpetbaggers, and three Negroes opposed. The Conservative *Sentinel* endorsed the measure. Tourgée remained convinced that it was a dangerous bill, even with his amendment, and concluded that his effort to stop it "was killed by cowardly weak-kneed-ism alone. If men had not been afraid of the sound of their own voices its fate would have been different," he complained to Emma, and it was apparently his encounter with railroad pressure that led him to add that he would do "nothing more to secure a nomination for anything whatever." [26]

[25] Letter of Joseph C. Abbott, Raleigh *Standard*, April 6, 1868. Abbott's assertions were never contradicted.
[26] Tourgée to his wife, February 8, 1868, Tourgée Papers.

The prosperity of North Carolina railroads was also closely connected with the state's debt, since the railroads held many old state
bonds. Conservative political and business leaders had feared repudiation since the collapse of the Confederacy, and these fears had increased
with Republican success. As the convention of 1868 approached, Samuel
McDowell Tate, a Conservative and a railroad president, the Conservative political leader Augustus S. Merrimon, the banker and businessman George W. Swepson, and other Conservatives arranged to secure
a definite acknowledgement of the state debt and to obtain aid to certain
railroads. They had less to fear than they imagined. Free enterprise-
minded Republicans were morally opposed to repudiation, except of the
Confederate debt, and one influential convention delegate, the carpetbagger General Joseph C. Abbott, had formed a ring with six other
men "to purchase a large amount of these bonds and sell them on the
rise." [27]

But the sentiments that Conservatives feared also existed, and they
were centered in the carpetbagger from Guilford County, Albion W.
Tourgée, who, with little hope of success, began a spirited fight against
acknowledging the state's old debt. Tourgée was in good part motivated
by four desires: to punish secession, to weaken the gentry, who held
much of the debt, to lighten taxes, and to contribute to the stability
of the new democratic government by casting off a burden. Why
assume this debt? Tourgée asked. The credit of the new state would
depend upon its constitution and laws, upon the future and not the
past, and he would be happy "to give to bondholders all she [the state]
had in railroads and swamplands, and the people would be glad to be
rid of them." The state was already impoverished, and he saw no
reason why ex-slaves should be taxed to save the honor of the slave
state, or the people further beggared to fatten bondholders. If the state
assumed this debt for what Tourgée described as the "whistle of honor,"
he predicted a debt of over twenty-eight million dollars in ten years.
Let repudiation indicate the price of treason, he concluded. Recognizing

---

[27] Tate to Swepson, December 5, 17, 1867, George W. Swepson Papers, State
Archives, Raleigh; Merrimon to Tate, January 24, March 11, 1868, and Swepson to
Tate, February 23, March 1, 1868, Samuel M. Tate Papers, Southern Historical
Collection; *Report of the Commission to Investigate Charges of Fraud and Corrup-
tion. . . . 1871–72* (Raleigh, 1872), 399, 523–34. Bribery gained the vote of the
carpetbagger Byron Laflin (*ibid.*, 527).

where many of the state bonds were held, he maligned northern and foreign bondholders for having aided the rebellion. Wall Street could have stopped the war in twenty minutes, "but no—they saw a chance to buy bonds of this section of the country far below their par value," and now they want the "principal and accrued interest." [28] Once again Tourgée provoked a burst of indignation, as Negroes, carpetbaggers, and native Republicans joined with Conservatives to rebuke him for "forever tearing down everything, and building up nothing." The bond-holding Abbott understandably considered his proposals "infamous." Seeing the convention obviously and overwhelmingly against him, Tourgée sought to have the question submitted to a popular vote; but a popular decision on such a matter was understandably feared and was crushed by a vote of 56 to 15. Instead, the old state debt was declared inviolable, in no less a place than the constitution's bill of rights.

After repudiation failed, Tourgée's position, logically enough, changed. He became anxious to protect the state's railroad investments and displayed all the characteristics of a sound money man. To enhance the market value of state bonds, he urged that the legislature be ordered to provide at once for taxes to pay the interest on the state's debt and to begin paying off the principal after 1880 by means of "a specific tax upon the real and personal property of the State." Accusing some delegates of trying to sneak out the back door to repudiation, Tourgée insisted that if the debt were assumed it should be paid, and he did not think it was too much to begin doing so in twelve years.

Meanwhile, more state aid to railroads was being promoted. Both parties entertained visions of building up the state, the west was especially desirous of long-denied railroad connections, many citizens anticipated rapid progress as a consequence of emancipation, and railroad presidents and directors were desperately requesting assistance. Consequently, several moderate loans, supported, and often initiated, by Conservatives, were made to various railroads, all accompanied by attempted safeguards for the state. Tourgée now displayed some sympathy toward state aid wherever state investments were endangered, but on all these measures except one he voted only once, and then only to call for a reconsideration. He also helped to establish a con-

[28] Raleigh *Sentinel*, February 15, 17, 1868; Raleigh *Standard*, February 15, 17, 1868.

stitutional article curtailing the power of the legislature to contract new debts or to extend any further aid except to unfinished roads in which the state already had an interest. Pressure from home, however, did force him further in support of one appropriation.

Both parties in the Greensboro area lobbied for convention aid to a completely new road running westward from Greensboro to Salem, and that section of the state was on fire with the idea. Tourgée was at this time seeking a Republican congressional nomination, and he could hardly hope to obtain it if he opposed a railroad destined to run through the heart of his congressional district. Besides, this particular measure was unusually sound, and the temptation was enhanced when a Salem Republican assured Tourgée that his major rival for the nomination, I. G. Lash, would withdraw if Tourgée supported the railroad. Not only did Tourgée desire the nomination, but he considered Lash a Copperhead who should be out of the race.[29] When an ordinance incorporating this road came before the convention, Tourgée spoke enthusiastically in its behalf, stressing the economic benefits it would bring the state and the political support it would bring the Republican party. The measure was passed by an almost unanimous vote, which included the bulk of the Conservative delegation. This was the only state railroad project that Tourgée supported.[30] It had unusually strong protective guarantees (all profits going toward paying off the debt before any dividends were paid), and it never cost the state a penny.

Thus far there had been no sign of party division over the convention's fiscal policies, but the final action of the convention in respect to the state debt did produce a decided party split. This arose over a proposal, originating with Joseph C. Abbott, to begin paying the interest in cash on certain bonds falling due in 1869. Abbott later testified that he had been advised in favor of this policy by Conservative railroad leaders, but he himself was also speculating in state bonds. Although the measure was similar to what Conservatives had suggested earlier in the convention (they proposed beginning such payments two years later), they now denounced Abbott's proposal, which passed, as an attempt to enrich northern bondholders. They objected especially to

[29] Tourgée to his wife, February 19, 1868, and Tourgée to D. H. Starbuck, March 21, 1868, Tourgée Papers.
[30] But he may have called for a reconsideration. See *Journal*, 371.

the immediate rise in taxes that would be required, and in view of the prevalent poverty there was some justification for their position, although they also appeared anxious to make political capital out of higher taxes and Yankee bondholders.[31]

Those aspects of the convention that have been discussed were typical of the whole, and the new constitution clearly continued the political trend of the century. Universal manhood suffrage, no property representation, judicial and penal reform, a mechanic's and laborer's lien, a limited poll tax, local ad valorem taxation, increased women's rights, more local self-rule, and the basis of a state-supported system of public schools were among the admirable additions to the state's constitution. Most of these changes had previously been sought in the state and soon gained a popularity that was sufficiently embarrassing to Conservatives to force them to acquiesce. The one momentous exception was Negro civil and political equality. Questionable interests and methods had also been at work in the convention, especially on matters of fiscal and railroad policy; but here the convention's action had also reflected a faith in political and economic progress, and no extravagant steps had been taken. But too many Republicans were less concerned than Tourgée with the dangers of further legislative aid to railroads.

In their fifty-five days of power, Republicans had certainly not justified the vituperation hurled against them during the preceding year. While they had encouraged democracy and liberalism, they had displayed caution and catered to Conservative desires, and they had not lived up to the dreadful expectations of their opponents. Republican delegates had proven rational and able in debate and action. Native and immigrant Republicans had displayed ability and independence, and the much-maligned Negro had shown unexpected ability and moderation. Conservative fears had been realized only in the extension of democracy and social welfare and the affirmation of civil and political equality for the Negro. The actions of the convention, elected under Negro suffrage, proved that such suffrage might not be as disastrous as Conservatives claimed.[32]

[31] Raleigh *Sentinel*, March 14, 16, 1868.

[32] Charges of fraud and extravagance in Hamilton, *Reconstruction* (258–62) do not stand up well. The convention's length was hardly excessive in view of the extent of revision, the criticized per diem salary was supported by Conservatives, and the doubling of the per diem rate and mileage allowance since 1865 indicates no

The carpetbagger Tourgée had been an outspoken, independent, and influential delegate, and perhaps no one exerted more individual influence in open debate than he. He had displayed a devotion to democratic, political, and economic reforms and a strong sympathy for the lower classes; anxious to guarantee the permanence of the changes being made, he had championed the economic heresy of repudiation and had favored proscriptive actions. Here he differed from the majority of his allies, who, through a combination of political idealism and fear and an identity of economic beliefs with Conservatives, sought to conciliate or even appease the opposition. Although Tourgée had sometimes supported Conservatives in their rights, he was clearly a leader of the most radical Republican wing and became a special object of ridicule and attack. He was falsely accused of a criminal past and maligned, and one newspaper referred to the convention of "Baboons, Monkeys, Mules, Tourgée and other Jackasses." "Who is the blackest man?" queried another, and answered "Tourgée," while also referring to "The Tourgée (Nondescript animal, something between an ass and a lion judging from his voice)."

On March 17, the last day of the convention, Republicans celebrated their accomplishments and sought to mend their fences with speeches, songs, and general celebration. The Republican press reported that General Milton S. Littlefield (a notorious carpetbagger and lobbyist as well as an accomplished gentleman) sang "The Star Spangled Banner," while the opposition, reflecting its differing orientation, credited him with such songs as "John Brown," "Hang Jeff. Davis," and a variety of "Negro melodies." Tourgée, a gadfly and frequent antagonist of the convention president, was appropriately honored with the convention chair, from which he apologized for remarks uttered in the heat of debate and appealed to Conservatives to meet the Republicans halfway for the good of the state. The Conservative delegate Plato Durham

---

more than its doubling between the conventions of 1861 and 1865. Accusations of excessive mileage charges are not proven, and some are false. Thus, Carey did charge for 150 miles each way, but this appears to have been the railroad distance and was also charged by the Conservative delegate from Carey's county. It is not true that Eppes and Hayes charged 223 miles each way, but another delegate, O. S. Hayes of Robeson, did charge this amount, which was about right, since he probably had to travel by way of Wilmington. See *Executive and Legislative Documents* (1868–69), No. 18, 62–63, hereafter cited as *Public Documents*.

reciprocated, to strong applause, but outside the hall such niceties were being negated by the insulting manner in which the Conservatives greeted adjournment and launched their bitter campaign against the constitution's ratification.

Tourgée returned to Guilford pleased with the convention's work. All but one of his ten campaign pledges had been secured. In a public letter supporting the new constitution, he stressed its grant of *"equal and ample facilities for all,"* the aspect Conservatives most opposed. "Its main fault in my estimation," he wrote privately, "is, too great liberality—a fault decidedly inclined to virtue's side." [33]

[33] Tourgée to A. G. Wilcox, April 2, 1868, Tourgée Papers; Raleigh *Standard*, March 19, 1868.

X

Continued Triumph

Shortly before the constitutional convention of 1868 convened, William W. Holden recommended Tourgée to the Federal military authorities for a vacant state Superior Court judgeship. It was Tourgée's response in this instance that contained both the modest disclaimers and the spurious educational claims discussed earlier.[1] Meanwhile Holden's recommendation again aroused Governor Worth, whose wrath led him to compound the dishonesty already contributed by the ambition of Tourgée. Worth's denunciations of "this vile wretch Tourgée," "the meanest Yankee who has ever settled among us," became the focus of a dispute that Worth expected might well culminate in the removal of either himself or the military commander, General Canby. To substantiate his charges against Tourgée, the Governor presented the General with a long list of men who would supposedly endorse his views, the last named being, Worth noted elsewhere, a freedman, "as much as to say, if these names will not satisfy you, Genl., I close with one you can't fail to respect." Worth's entire list was a suspicious one. It was prepared without, and never received, substantial verification, it contained the names of several of Tourgée's friends, and one of the individuals included, William L. Scott, flatly denied ever having given Worth cause for such an estimate of Tourgée.[2] Canby, however, bowed before Worth's objections.

Tourgée acquired a lasting distaste for Governor Worth through this

[1] See above, p. 58.
[2] Hamilton (ed.), *Jonathan Worth*, II, 774–76, 1069–72, 1085–86, 1113–27, 1141–43; Tourgée to Scott, January 6, 1869, and Scott to Tourgée, January 11, 1869, William L. Scott Papers, Duke University Library; Richard L. Zuber, "Jonathan Worth—A Biography of a Southern Unionist," 521.

incident, but he was far too immersed in constitutional reform to give the matter much thought. Besides, his dreams for the future envisioned a much more active political role than that promised by a judgeship, and during the convention he began promoting his candidacy for the national House of Representatives. Convinced that the new constitution would be ratified, Tourgée believed a Republican nomination would be "nearly equivalent to an election," and he and Emma organized Guilford meetings in his behalf, while friends also worked for him in other counties. In March, Albion reported to Emma that the entire matter was still "pretty much of a lottery," but he imagined he had as good a chance as anyone and advised Emma to save every penny she could for his possible campaign. Tourgée's hopes were greatly boosted when the influential Thomas Settle, soon a Republican nominee for the state Supreme Court, promised to work for him; and Tourgée further enhanced his chances by his convention speech supporting the proposed district railroad. But other Republicans were working against him, including two moderate Greensboro carpetbaggers, Thomas B. Keogh and one of Greensboro's early industrial promoters, a Mr. Lawson.

At the district congressional convention a three-way race developed between Tourgée, I. G. Lash (who had not dropped out as promised), and the uneducated Red String leader William F. Henderson. The nomination finally went to Lash, with Tourgée angrily attributing his defeat to "an infamous breach of faith" and the careless confidence of his supporters. The influential Settle had unfortunately been absent due to illness, and the Greensboro stalwart Robert P. Dick had not been "worth a wet dishcloth." [3] Lash's nomination was clearly a concession to that extensive moderation which Tourgée feared. Conservatives expressed surprise that the respected Lash would even accept a Republican nomination, and during the campaign Tourgée felt impelled to urge Lash to dispel confusion among the Republican voters by openly declaring his Republicanism.

Meanwhile other honors helped relieve Tourgée's chagrin over his collapsed congressional aspirations, honors attributable to his effective role in the convention and, perhaps, to the desire of moderates to push him out of politics. First he unexpectedly found himself appointed one

[3] Tourgée to D. H. Starbuck, March 21, 1868, and Tourgée to G. W. Welker, March 23, 1868, Tourgée Papers.

of the three commissioners to prepare the new law codes for the state, and the extent of the convention's faith in him was revealed by its rejection of efforts to replace him with Samuel F. Phillips, a man respected by both parties and probably the best legal mind in the state. The commissioner's monthly salary of two hundred dollars was warmly welcomed by Tourgée's long-impoverished family. At last they were "tolerably well provided for," he joyfully wrote to Emma. "Bon Dieu is good to us sometimes my darling. Let us thank him for his mercies."

A more momentous honor followed when one of the original Republican judicial nominees declined to run on the Republican ticket and Tourgée was selected as his replacement—Republican candidate for Superior Court judge of the Seventh Judicial District. The position denied him by Governor Worth, and for which he had doubted his own qualifications, might be at hand, a possibility that evoked from the *Sentinel* the nasty response that "a more loathsome, scurvy, low-down Yankee cannot be found in the State." [4]

Some citizens began to wonder whether Tourgée had been pushed out of politics or politics pushed into the courts, especially when he accepted the judicial nomination with declarations of his continued political commitment to Republicanism. A judge must be nonpartisan only so far as his judicial duties were concerned, he asserted, and under the existing critical conditions he could not forget a citizenship which was "higher in dignity and importance than any official place, its duties more important, its functions more sacred." While he revealed sufficient propriety to declare that he would not canvass for election as a judge, he also announced that the new constitution was of such importance that he would actively campaign for its adoption.[5] For several weeks he toured the state with other Republicans, glorifying the result of the recent convention and rebuking the Conservative opposition, and he remained harsher than most in denouncing ex-Confederates.

Conservatives were adamantly opposed to the new constitution, a position they had officially taken even before the instrument had been

[4] Raleigh *Sentinel*, March 27, 1868.
[5] Tourgée to the Republican State Central Committee, March 21, 1868, Tourgée Papers. Cf. Raleigh *Standard*, March 26, 1868, and for Tourgée's speeches see *ibid.*, March 19, 20, 21, 24, April 9, 1868.

produced. "Chaos is preferable" to it, concluded Governor Worth. The greater democracy, the expenses of increased state offices and services, and the beginning of interest payments on the state debt, all were resented, and Conservatives still feared "gradual but rapid confiscation of all the property of the State, by onerous and oppressively heavy taxation." [6] Unfortunately for the Republicans, they were assuming power in years of economic distress, some of which they were unjustly blamed for, but Conservative complaints in the spring of 1868 were essentially unjustified. The number of state officials had not been increased to the extent Conservatives implied, the increases that were made were justifiable, some of the new expenses of the state had merely been shifted from local shoulders, and it is difficult to conclude that a system of public schools was not worth the cost. Finally, Conservative wrath over interest payments on the state debt appears hypocritical when one recalls that two years earlier these same Conservatives had sought to assume the entire Confederate debt, an act that would have doubled the burden faced in 1868.

But these matters were all secondary, and the main Conservative theme in the spring election of 1868 was officially enunciated as follows: "The great and all absorbing issue, now soon to be presented to the people of the State, is negro suffrage and negro equality, if not supremacy, and whether hereafter in North Carolina and the South, the white man is to be placed politically, and as a consequence, socially, upon a footing of equality with the negro." The leading Conservative newspaper agreed: "THE GREAT and paramount issue is: SHALL NEGROES or WHITE MEN RULE NORTH CAROLINA? All other issues are secondary and subordinate and should be kept so." [7] Reflecting this advice, every imaginable accusation, prejudice, and rumor was utilized to inspire support for white supremacy. Segregation was a daily theme, dismissal from employment for political activities continued, and a Greensboro paper advised that lists be made of every white man "ashamed of his color and in favor of negro supremacy." [8]

[6] Worth to A. S. Kemp, March 26, 1868, Hamilton (ed.), *Jonathan Worth*, II, 1175–77; Greensboro *Patriot*, March 27, 1868.

[7] Raleigh *Sentinel*, February 7, March 10, 1868.

[8] Greensboro *Times*, March 5, 1868. For evidence of increased economic intimidation, see also Freedmen's Bureau reports, NCFBR, XCVIII, CVIII, and Boxes 441, 445.

Also, Ku Klux Klan notices first appeared, those in Greensboro written in elegant style and threatening blood, vengeance, and death. The force of such pressure is clearly illuminated in the experiences of David Schenck, a stump opponent of Tourgée's during the preceding year. Schenck initially decided that the new constitution was quite admirable, and although he continued to "loathe the Negro," he decided to support it. As a result he found himself ostracized, forced to part with friends, obliged to keep aloof from political discussions, and frightened by the Klan. Schenck thereupon decided that the issue was one of whites against Negroes and scalawags and prudently reversed his stand.[9] Republicans bowed to the pressure in a different manner. The unusually able Negro James H. Harris surrendered his unanimous congressional nomination to an unsavory carpetbagger, much to the state's loss, and elsewhere the removal of a Negro candidate was decreed because he had married a white woman.

The bitterness of the campaign, together with the assassination of a Georgia Republican, contributed to Tourgée's continued desire for strong Federal measures. Still he enjoyed the excitement and gloried in "talking down a cocky reb" or "giving as good or as bad" as he received, and he boasted of having broken a platter over the head of an opponent who had called him a rascal at a public dinner, fearing that, had he not so reacted, "the crowd would have set me down as a coward." Less beneficial to the cause was Tourgée's note to Holden complaining that the Guilford ticket was weak in forensic ability. Holden foolishly allowed this note to fall into the hands of the opposition, which made the most of Tourgée's complaint that *our ticket here is a VERY WEAK ONE.*" Conservative denunciations of Tourgée also reached a new high during the campaign. The Greensboro *Times* asked its readers how they would "like to be arraigned before such a shallow-brained, revengeful yankee judge?" and according to the Wilmington press,

This Tourgée is the meanest looking man it has ever been our misfortune to meet. The pirate; the cutthroat; the despicable, mean, cowardly, crawling, sneaking villain have been portrayed by nature, with a master hand, in every lineament of his countenance. The mark of infamy is stamped indelibly on his brow

[9] Journal of David Schenck, V, 195, and VI, 1–4, Schenck Papers.

in the shape of a large protuberance that strikes the beholder
with ineffable disgust. In a deep, sepulchral voice he proceeded
to deliver himself of a most infamous, violent and incendiary
harangue. It was an appeal to all the baser passions of his more
ignorant hearers, but was so intensely virulent that it utterly
failed to produce any permanent influence on the misguided
people whom he hoped to work up to a pitch of frenzy against
the Southern whites.[10]

But all was not odium and error for the Republicans. Not only were
they strong, but many moderates, including the Quakers, were pleased
with the new constitution and with the Republican candidates. The
distinguished Edward Cantwell, a previous secessionist and Democrat,
publicly declared that the constitution embraced "all the cardinal principles" of democracy and progress, that Negro equality was a false cry,
and that the real enemy was aristocracy.[11] Once again the Republicans
swept the state, securing ratification of the constitution and firm control
of all branches of the state government, and Holden was now Republican governor of the state. The victory was not as overwhelming as that
of 1867, however, and Republicanism was weakening in the west, where
twelve of the counties that had supported the proposed reforms of 1866
voted against the constitution of 1868. In Guilford the Republicans
exceeded Tourgée's expectations, and although he ran 100 votes behind
the county ticket, he secured a majority in Guilford and in the seven-
county judicial district, and became a Superior Court judge. One
ominous sign was that the Republican Negro candidate for county
commissioner in Guilford ran over 300 votes behind the ticket, almost
enough to defeat him.

Tourgée, who had turned thirty just after the election, was now a
judge and code commissioner, and his time was to be increasingly
occupied at these tasks. But the continued instability of the Republican
reforms also kept him involved in politics. Conservatives would not
gracefully accept the popular election results; Governor Worth surrendered the governorship only under "military duress" and continued
to lament that the "red Republicans" were "undermining civilization."

[10] Wilmington *Morning Star*, March 25, 1868.
[11] Raleigh *Standard*, April 7, 1868.

Ironically, if portentously, this Conservative gentleman concluded that "if there be any rational hope of future good government here it must be looked for in Revolution." [12] Conservatives had high hopes, however, of overthrowing the entire Reconstruction program through the election of a Democratic President and Congress in 1868, and this desire was in good part endorsed by the national Democratic party in the campaign of that year. Not only did this possibility disturb Tourgée, but he had taken a trip north that spring, at the request of Governor Holden, to seek relief funds for the state, and had been struck by the growing northern disinterest in southern poverty and politics. He was also worried by the failure to impeach Johnson, and from a carpetbagger friend in Tennessee he received alarming reports about the activities of a Ku Klux Klan. All these considerations contributed to Tourgée's intensive political efforts during the summer of 1868. He served on the state executive committee of the party and was chairman of the congressional district executive committee, and he was eagerly sought and active as a campaign speaker. He was on the committee of arrangements and grand marshal of the state party convention held in September, and he retained contact with the still active leagues.

The presidential campaign in North Carolina was as slanderous, abusive, and irresponsible as the one that just preceded it. Conservative newspapers again urged their adherents to impress upon the Negro that "he is quarreling with his meat and bread," and economic reprisals were carried out and publicly defended. Of course, observed Thomas Settle, landowners would not carry this so far as to seriously interfere with profits, but they might intimidate enough voters to turn the scales, and then "the very devil would be to pay—it would be good-bye, home, government, country, & all." [13] Denunciations of the Reconstruction Acts by the Democratic vice-presidential candidate contributed to the emotionalism, and the slogan of the Conservative Greensboro press was alarming: "THE PATRIOT AND TIMES advocates the election of SEYMOUR AND BLAIR as the only hope of averting ANOTHER WAR." Some Republicans helped provoke such determination. Particularly harmful were some idiotic editorials in the *Standard*, which, not content with alienating Negroes by accusing the Conservatives of

[12] Hamilton (ed.), *Jonathan Worth*, II, 1201, 1218, 1222.
[13] Settle to Tourgée, August 8, 1868, Tourgée Papers.

practicing social equality, proceeded to arouse general wrath by in-
decently advising Republican campaigners how to "go after" Conservative women: "And don't hesitate to throw your arms around their
necks now and then, when their husbands are not around, and give
them a good ———. They all like it, and the Yankeer you are the
better it takes." [14] It is doubtful that any other item had as great an
anti-Republican impact as did this editorial. Although it was exploited
for years, this atrocious article was a rarity in Republican campaigning,
which, compared to that of the opposition, was a model of reason-
ableness.

Fearful of Conservative threats but confident of popular support,
most Republicans strove to restore a rational tone to political rivalry
in the state, the most noticeable effort being that of Governor Holden
in his eloquent inaugural address. This tactic scored impressive successes
during the summer, and among those sufficiently repelled by Conservative extremism to support the new state constitution and Ulysses
S. Grant for President were Richmond M. Pearson, just elected Chief
Supreme Court Justice on both party tickets; Nathaniel P. Boyden,
the only Conservative congressman elected in the April contest; and
the Confederate war hero General Rufus Barringer. While these
moderates were hostile to Conservative tactics, they were not opposed
to Conservative principles, but the majority of their natural associates
lacked sufficient appreciation of the democratic political process to
heed advice from Justice Pearson that might have lessened many subsequent unpleasantries. "When the storm is over," predicted Pearson,
"the Conservative party, representing as it does, the property and
intelligence of the State, will take the guidance of affairs, and all will
be well." [15] This would be the final result, but not by the peaceful
means Pearson envisaged. Nor has all been well since.

As these developments were taking place, Tourgée became involved
in an embarrassing Republican imbroglio over the new congressional
nomination in his district. Upon Tourgée's order as chairman of the
district executive committee, a Republican nominating convention,
apparently composed entirely of native North Carolinians, met to

[14] Raleigh *Standard*, September 19, 1868. The tone of the address of the general
assembly was not incendiary, as charged by Hamilton (*Reconstruction*, 364–70).
[15] Pearson letter, Raleigh *Standard*, August 11, 1868.

nominate a candidate for Congress. Tourgée, who displayed no sign of renewed interest in the seat, was again being supported, although, according to Reverend Welker, the Negroes were unwilling to have Tourgée take the post. They consider you their judge, reported Welker, "and on the Bench they are determined to keep you." Tourgée and Lash again drew votes, but on the second ballot the Red String leader, William F. Henderson, was nominated by a majority of one, a nomination that immediately disrupted the party. The uneducated Henderson was distasteful to the "substantial Republicans," he had incurred Tourgée's distrust through some obvious deception in recent correspondence, and, reflective of the tactics of that era, Henderson carried the liability of having been recently (but falsely) indicted for stealing a mule. Upon Henderson's nomination the chairman of the convention, the secretary, the entire delegation of three counties, and other delegates withdrew and formed a rump convention which condemned the nominee as a man of unfavorable character and of "an incapacity and ignorance which would bring disgrace upon any party whose candidate he might be." Tourgée joined in opposing the controversial candidate, pointing out that the Conservative, David F. Caldwell, was "as nearly unexceptionable as any man of that party can be to Republicans. An honorable man, a scholar and a gentleman, an undoubted union man and an 'iron-clad.' " [16] The rump convention then selected Tourgée as a nominal candidate and approached Henderson with the suggestion that both he and Tourgée withdraw in favor of some mutually acceptable nominee.

Conservatives gleefully made a great to-do over the Republican crisis, ridiculing both factions and printing large cartoons of the carpetbagger and scalawag rivals, whose behavior contributed excellent opportunities for ridicule. At one meeting Tourgée's attempted speech was drowned out by shouting and band music, and Henderson popularized, perhaps originated, the thereafter prevalent accusation that Tourgée was an escaped Ohio convict. It was reported that the two even came to

[16] Convention manuscript, Tourgée Papers. For the preceding see also Welker to Tourgée, August 28, 1868, D. H. Starbuck to Tourgée, August 25, and Settle to Tourgée, August 29, 1868, Tourgée Papers. For accounts of the entire affair, see Greensboro *Patriot*, September 24 through October 22, 1868; Raleigh *Standard*, October 7, 9, 13, 20, 23, 1868; D. H. Starbuck to Tourgée, September 29, 1868, Tourgée Papers.

blows, and the entire affair aroused the wrath of the Republican state leadership. In a nasty editorial, the *Standard* depicted the affair as a selfish personal quarrel between the two men, and the Republican state executive board arbitrarily appointed I. G. Lash as the regular party candidate for the district. These denunciations, partially encouraged by Tourgée's past record of disruption, were unfair. It had been Tourgée who originated the movement to secure a third candidate upon whom the party could unite, and it was understood from the first that his name was being used only for that purpose. After protesting the dictatorial and irregular nomination of Lash, Tourgée withdrew his own candidacy in support of Lash. The latter was then nominated in a new district convention, which also gave "a vote of thanks" to Tourgée for his role in the affair. Henderson subsequently withdrew. Although he had perhaps less ability and training than was desirable, Henderson had been unfairly treated, and when he later did secure a congressional nomination, the Republicans had great difficulty in swallowing the assertions made in 1868.

Republicans overcame their difficulties in the fall of 1868 and carried the state and the nation. The implementation of Reconstruction appeared somewhat better assured, although North Carolina Republican strength had declined from a majority of over nineteen thousand to one of about thirteen thousand, largely because Conservatives gained those voters previously banned by the Reconstruction Acts. Strong white support for Republicanism was still apparent in some western counties, and Guilford Republicans had actually increased their vote and their majority. It was in this piedmont area that Republicans appeared to be achieving their greatest success. Since April the Republicans had lost thirteen counties scattered throughout the state, while the only two counties they gained were both in Tourgée's judicial district, Alamance and Caswell, the former containing a large white majority and the latter a slight Negro majority.

While Republicans too optimistically hoped that Grant's victory would ensure continued success, their opponents were undecided. A new indecision on the questions of Reconstruction and Negro suffrage was noticed among Conservatives throughout the South, with many inclining toward moderation, and within North Carolina a conflict raged between moderate and radical wings until the 1870's. Greensboro

Conservatives inclined toward moderation, and, apologizing for the bitter campaigns of 1868, the Greensboro *Patriot* advised that "the political past be forgotten and never again called up." But a hollow sound was provided by an article approving of Ku Klux justice that appeared in an adjoining column. A Negro who had eloped with a white woman was hung by the neck, drenched with turpentine, and ignited. When the flames severed the rope and the burning Negro fled, he was shot to death.[17] The future would apparently be much like the past.

[17] January 28, 1869.

XI

A Code Commissioner

Tourgée's career in the South had thus far been entwined with many central threads of state and national history, but after 1868 his activities were of a more confined nature. Before dealing with these activities, however, it would be well to look at the subsequent history of Republicanism in North Carolina. Very much as Tourgée had feared, the national government refrained from decisive interference in the South, and the success or failure of southern Republicans was left primarily dependent upon their own ability, strength, and conduct. They were ill-prepared for the task, and following a steady decline in status and power, they lost legislative control of North Carolina in the election of 1870. Although a Republican governor and judiciary remained, Republican rule was, in effect, at an end in the state.

Historical interpretations of this phenomenon have usually attributed it primarily to Republican evil and extravagance between 1868 and 1870. Undoubtedly there were evil and selfish Republicans, but they may have been the exception rather than the rule, and the traditional picture of a corrupt, immoral, oppressive, and greedy coalition of Negroes, scalawags, and carpetbaggers is an unconvincing one. Although Republicans did introduce new and costly state services, this was a modern trend that has continued to the present. The one really momentous and controversial Republican expenditure consisted of continued state loans to railroads, a policy intended to benefit the state, but which was accompanied by a deleterious enthusiasm that desired "the end without caring for the means" [1] and was tainted by fraud,

[1] Henry E. Colton to G. W. Swepson, November 16, 1868, Swepson Papers. See especially Charles Lewis Price, "Railroads and Reconstruction in North Carolina" (unpublished Ph.D. dissertation, University of North Carolina, 1959).

bribery and greed. But Conservatives were very prominent in promoting and profiting from these grants, and when Conservative party opposition did solidify, it was based in good part upon political opportunism and the selfish interest of private stockholders.[2] Republicans cannot, of course, escape responsibility for measures that they passed (partly to secure patronage for a poor party), but the reasons for the failure of their attempt to build the railroads and increase the prosperity of the state remain unclear. Although Conservatives denounced the resultant debt as impossible to maintain, they themselves had been willing to assume a war debt just as large, incurred for a somewhat less positive cause. The various reasons for the collapse of the Reconstruction railroad program included careless expenditure, fiscal mistakes, sectional poverty, Conservative repudiation propaganda,[3] and a national depression; and although loud cries against excessive taxation accompanied the entire venture, the state's main burden was the old debt and certain grants in its behalf that were honored by both parties. Republicans finally agreed with Conservatives that the debt was a burden the state was unwilling, if not unable, to pay immediately, and after 1869 there was little difference in the fiscal policy of the two parties. Meanwhile, the disputed new debt's interest continued to accumulate and was periodically quoted to discredit the Republicans, but this debt, ironically, was no problem at all because it was never paid.

There are other puzzling aspects of the purported impact of Republican misbehavior. Why should a degree of misrule or corruption which was actually quite slight in comparison with similar activities throughout the nation during that era have so lastingly eliminated the Republican party from effective political participation in the southern political process? Or how can the final collapse of Republican power in the state be attributed to the policies followed between 1868 and 1870, when this

[2] Perhaps the most bitter critic of Republicanism was Josiah Turner, Jr., irascible editor of the Raleigh *Sentinel*, who would later assert that the "state was not robbed by negroes and carpet-baggers but by Democrats who filled high stations" (Turner to editor of Raleigh *News and Observer*, n.d., Holden Papers, Duke University Library).

[3] There was much Conservative dissension over this, e.g., Greensboro *Patriot*, October 21, 1869, quoting Wilmington *Journal*. In 1881 the state's governor would assert that the state tax could be tripled without unduly burdening the state (H. T. Lefler and R. A. Newsome, *North Carolina: The History of a Southern State* [Chapel Hill, 1954], 504).

final collapse did not occur until 1876? One should note in this connection that the Republicans, though never recapturing control of the state, carried a majority of the state's voters in the constitutional dispute of 1871, the gubernatorial and presidential elections of 1872, and the convention elections of 1875. These majorities necessarily included a sizable minority of whites. Republican strength had been continually undermined during these same years, but this had been accomplished largely by intimidation, by the race issue, by the Negro-carpetbagger-scalawag stereotype, and by distorted recollections of the period of Republican power. It was Conservative power and propaganda rather than righteousness that played the central role in completing "redemption."

After the convention of 1868, Tourgée was not connected with any further promotion of state aid to railroads. He continued to fear that such financial burdens might undermine the entire Republican experiment, and when the danger of excessive debt became apparent, Tourgée advised Governor Holden to withhold bonds already granted by the legislature. This, he said, "is the only course which can save the Republican party and the State from defeat, ruin and disgrace. There must be some end to the road on which we have entered." [4] Whether due to Tourgée's advice or not, Holden did cease issuing bonds, but matters had already proceeded too far to save the party, and the issue intensified an enervating split between eastern and western Republicans. Tourgée was also probably connected with the code commission's preparation of an act to restrict further bond issues and to recall all unsold bonds. Thereafter, in typical free-enterprise fashion, Tourgée distrusted any tie between political and economic activities. He favored the sale, at prices set by the legislature, of all the state's interest in public works, a step that he believed would increase efficiency, eliminate political jobbery, and furnish proceeds with which to reduce the state's debt and restore her credit. [5]

The controversial railroad matter was only a small item in Tourgée's life, however, and his activities as a code commissioner more adequately

---

[4] Tourgée to Holden, May 11, 1869, Tourgée Papers.
[5] Tourgée to C. L. Harris and others, n.d., Tourgée Papers. Here he agreed with many Conservatives, but the subsequent end of state interference was accompanied by gross favoritism to business at the expense of the public.

reveal the relationships between this carpetbagger and the rise and fall of Republican Reconstruction. Two very competent North Carolinians, William B. Rodman and Victor C. Barringer, were on the code commission with Tourgée. Neither Rodman, a Democrat, nor Barringer, a Whig, had been very prominent in politics before the war, although (as an indication of the surprising backgrounds of some Republicans) each had endorsed secession and served as a Confederate Army officer, and Barringer had been elected a state senator in 1860. Rodman was rather prominent after the war; he was elected a member of the convention of 1868 and a state Supreme Court justice on the Republican ticket of that year. Despite the prominence of his colleagues, Tourgée was the best known and perhaps most influential member of the code commission. He had launched the code movement and was well acquainted with it, he was secretary of the commission, his persuasions attracted Rodman and many other lawyers and judges to codification, and one opponent even advised the proud carpetbagger that "it is admitted by all, that the Constitution and Code—are yours." [6] But Tourgée was only one of three capable men, and the emphasis upon the contributions of the carpetbagger often reflected an effort to discredit the commission's work altogether.

The most urgent task of the commission was the preparation of a code of civil procedure, the state meanwhile lacking a civil court system, but the constitution also specified that the commissioners were to prepare "as soon as practicable, a Code of the laws of North Carolina." That this meant more than a mere revised code of legislative law, such as had been prepared previously in the state, was indicated by a convention ordinance that had been copied from David Dudley Field's plan for complete codification of both substantive and procedural law. The commissioners had been presented the task and opportunity of creating the complete body of law for the state, and this effort was to be implemented not only by their code work but also by their preparation of a vast number of particular acts for the Republican legislature. Complicating the immense task of thus "collecting and arranging the jurisprudence of a people" was the need to define the results of the social upheaval that had disturbed the state since 1861.

[6] George V. Strong, quoted in Tourgée to his wife, January 12, 1873, Tourgée Papers.

It was another touch of Reconstruction irony that while Tourgée and others sought to carry out these legal reforms in the South, the father of code reform, David Dudley Field, was promoting Federal court decisions that were helping undermine the entire Reconstruction program.

By mid-July, about a month after beginning their work, the commissioners presented their first report, along with some legislation and portions of the civil code. The following month, after "constant and assiduous labor" (in the words of a subsequent Conservative legislative committee),[7] the commission presented its completed code of civil procedure. Admitting their haste, the commissioners urged "a generous criticism" of their work, but reflecting an incisive appreciation of the new system and of the need to adapt it to local conditions, they had prepared an admirable code. They had also been concerned with "opening the forum, the bar and the bench, to the honorable competition of the colored man," and with tactless ardor they later defended their much-criticized utilization of the state code of New York as a model by expressing doubt that "a system suited to the highest civilization would be unsuitable to ourselves." [8] Tourgée valued the new system as conducive to simplicity, efficiency, and dispatch, and devoid of the rigid and artificial formalism of the past. The code spirit, he asserted, "seeks to discard form in favor of substance." During August the new code of civil procedure was enacted by the legislature.

Great hostility greeted this work of Tourgée and his fellow commissioners. As had happened in New York, older lawyers resented a simplification that vitiated a mass of knowledge that they had spent their lives in learning, and in the Reconstruction South opposition to Republican reforms was a matter of course. The commissioners and their code were insulted and ridiculed. Almost the entire legal profession opposed the new code, and the *Sentinel* professed to know not one citizen who approved it. It was condemned as alien, costly, and un-

[7] North Carolina, House of Representatives, *House Bill, No. 307, Session 1871–1872* (n.p., n.d.).

[8] Barringer, Rodman, and Tourgée, *The Code of Civil Procedure of North Carolina to Special Proceedings* (Raleigh, 1868), iii–xvii. For the commissioners' work, see also *Documents of Code Commission 1868–1871*, bound volume, University of North Carolina Library, and *Public Documents*, No. 28 (1869–70) and No. 5 (1870–71). For Tourgée's views, see also his *The Code of Civil Procedure of North Carolina with Notes and Decisions* (Raleigh, 1878), v, 21, 43, 75, 77.

necessary, and with obvious reference to Tourgée, one newspaper objected that the new simplicity was designed "to do away with the necessity of legal learning, so that negroes and carpetbaggers might be qualified to come to the bar, or sit upon the bench." Conversely, another paper complained of a complexity that was intended to force the people to "go to lawyers for information." The influence of Tourgée, "who is powerful for evil," was particularly deplored, and the Greensboro press hopefully saw signs that "even Radicals are disgusted with the N.Y. 'Code of Civil Procedure' so recently palmed off upon this state by the Code Commissioners—Judge Tourgée & Co." It was asserted that "no man of sense" could expect such a ridiculous system to be borne by the people, who preferred "the speedy restoration of our former *cheaper* and *safer* system." [9] Although the commissioners did not hesitate to admit errors and weaknesses in their work, their efforts to make reasonable revisions were often frustrated by such emotional and irrational opposition.

The reception of the code was not always so hostile. The Salisbury bar received it favorably and was inclined to give it a fair trial, and after practicing under it, many former opponents, especially the younger lawyers, began to appreciate its merits. The astute Conservative lawyer Samuel F. Phillips (who became a Republican in 1870) provided an interesting commentary:

> I have been reading my primer in the new law. Barring the circumstances which surround its *imposition* upon us I am disposed in its favor. All the lawyers in *old* N.C. would never have framed as good a code—in a century. *Old* lawyers (like myself for instance) are too fond of the conundrums, Chinese puzzles & quibbles & "quillets" (see grave-digger in Shakespeare's Reports) which they pick up in 20 or 30 years' conversancy with the Common law, to be pleased with, or even to acquiesce in any system however simple or scientific, that rifles *their* treasures. Nine tenths of the objections to the Code will have this extent. Meanwhile without committing myself to its details—this much is to be said in its favor—that it is a modern scientific system for

[9] Wilmington *Daily Journal*, July 29, August 13, 1868; Raleigh *Sentinel*, August 8, 13, December 9, 18, 1868; Greensboro *Patriot*, December 24, 1868.

administering justice—a system produced with great labor and the result of consideration given to the subject by very learned gentlemen who were trammelled by the past no further than it had reason with it, & who have been very liberally aided by the "censures" of lawyers, English, Continental & American, in framing it. I think this is a great deal to be said *for* it. Nor are the gibes of a gibing profession, nor the invectives of a profession exercised in invective—much to be weighted *au contraire*.[10]

It was in response to the commissioners' own request for criticism that a meeting of the bench and bar was held in the state capital a few months after the adoption of the Code, a meeting greeted by the *Sentinel* with the comment that objections to the code "were endless and serious." Such was not quite the case, though, since the real objection was not to the commission's work but to the change to a code system itself, and this was a constitutional matter beyond immediate remedy. The dilemma was revealed when a committee of lawyers, including many vociferous opponents of the code, studied the commissioners' work for weeks but could recommend little more than that as few changes be made from the past as possible. At a second meeting, Tourgée presented "an able and forcible defense of the code," while the state's chief justice, Richmond M. Pearson, attempting to smooth over existing antagonisms, suggested some minor modifications and "complimented the commissioners on the very excellent work performed by them in the short time they had to do it in." According to the sympathetic *Standard*, "The conclusion generally arrived at seemed to be that the new Code, though defective in some of its parts, was not liable to any criticism upon its intrinsic merits." [11] The commission then set about correcting the "several deficiencies and imperfections" that had been pointed out.

During these two meetings of the state bar, one serious and lasting dispute did arise. It involved the interpretation of the constitutional clause that "the Superior Courts shall be at all times open for the transaction of business within their jurisdiction, except the trial of issues of fact requiring a jury." Because each Superior Court judge presided over

---

[10] Phillips to D. L. Swain, August 20, 1868, Spencer Papers.
[11] Raleigh *Standard*, January 8, 1869; Raleigh *Sentinel*, December 19, 1868.

a number of individual courts, the code commission desired to implement this phrase by allowing the clerk of each court to handle, throughout the year, almost all matters preceding the actual trial of facts before a jury. This would obviously speed up procedure and relieve the great amount of litigation crowding the dockets. But many, if not most, members of the legal profession objected to the courts' handling matters at all times, or to the clerks' handling some of them at all. Reasons for these objections included a mere sense of inconvenience, scepticism about the capabilities of the clerks, and, most important of all, a desire to delay litigation.

Significant post-bellum economic considerations were involved in this dispute. The commissioners believed that promptness and punctuality were imperative for justice, but they also associated this necessity with the maintenance of credit, the sanctity of contract, and the encouragement of investment. In effect, the position of the commissioners would facilitate the operation of the free-enterprise process. "Legal development," they asserted, "must keep step with commercial and industrial development," [12] and this clear expression of a capitalist orientation did little to allay certain fears of an agricultural society. Assuming that private contracts would make needed adjustments, there may be nothing intrinsically harmful to an agricultural population in speedy procedures, but such adjustments are not always easily made, and, in addition, southern farmers and planters were still heavily in debt and desired to stay the hands of northern and southern creditors. Thus there was reason for the complaint of one Carolinian that the new code system was "too short and rapid for an impoverished agricultural people." [13] Tourgée appeared eager to promote the economic survival of the fit, and although he tempered this belief with respect to the poor, he revealed less compassion for the substantial farmer or planter. His lack of sympathy for "the potentates of the South" with their "ill gotten gains" was increased by the fraudulent protection of property that he frequently encountered on the bench. Since the war, Judge Tourgée complained, "the nonpayment of debt has become an epidemic and our Legislature has a perfect *scabies* of *nil debit*." But such sentiments on the part of the commissioners should not be exaggerated. Tourgée and his colleagues primarily sought modernization and efficiency in the law rather than advantage to any

[12] Commissioners' Report of March 20, 1869, Raleigh *Standard*, March 25, 1869.
[13] *Ibid.*, January 25, 1869.

one group. There were interesting qualifications in their position, and the code itself allowed old cases to proceed under the older slow procedure. Barringer considered Tourgée's judicial decision implementing this provision of the code "a better stay law" than any other, and Tourgée was actually credited by Conservatives with the comparatively better economic conditions in his judicial district.[14] Also, Justice Rodman, who championed speedy procedure under the code, wrote a vigorous dissent to the Supreme Court's rejection of the stay law passed by the convention of 1868.

Nevertheless, Tourgée remained adamant in opposition to "any 'Stay-law,' 'Suspension Law,' 'Jurisdiction Law,' or any other legislative humbug." Admitting that immediate final settlements would be hard on some citizens, he still believed it best "for the people." But pressure for delay was growing in both political parties. When early in 1869 the courts nullified the stay law, Reverend Welker, now a state senator, informed Tourgée of confusion and consternation in the capital and appealed for suggestions as to how to avoid the threatened foreclosures. But Tourgée would accept nothing beyond the implementation of the constitution's homestead measure, which he considered fully adequate to protect the really needy· debtor, and to ensure the success of the homestead, he engaged in his only known lobbying activity among Republican legislators. He wrote numerous letters to leaders in the general assembly urging the quick passage of a simple clarifying bill submitted by the code commission, and he angrily denounced efforts to complicate the measure, as by registration requirements: "We might as well have no homestead as have one fettered, cut up and cramped by such absurd conditions. It is all that stands or can stand between thousands of our people and untold misery. Let its provisions be plain, simple and effective, as I know those of my bill to be." [15] To Tourgée's dismay, the bill that passed was a compromise. He had desired a simple exemption from sale, and many years later the courts did interpret the constitution's homestead as he had suggested.[16]

The homestead law offered little to the wealthier debtors. While it was

[14] Tourgée to Judge J. S. Henry, March 13, 1869, and Barringer to Tourgée, March 26, 1869, Tourgée Papers; Tourgée to Martin B. Anderson, February 13, 1873, Anderson Papers, University of Rochester; Raleigh *Standard*, March 17, 1869.
[15] Tourgée to G. W. Welker, February 26, 1869, Tourgée Papers.
[16] William B. Aycock, "Homestead Exemption in North Carolina," *North Carolina Law Review*, XXIX (1950–1951), 145.

admitted that over seventy-five per cent of the debtors in the state were fully protected, many citizens failed to see any equity in thus allowing the poor to escape their debts completely, while not allowing even a delay for the wealthy. The power and influence of this prosperous debtor group was felt in both parties and did secure new legislation, but most such laws "to postpone for the relief of the debtor" were quickly overruled in the courts.

Although further efforts to legislate stays were considered hopeless because of the attitude of the courts, one decisive law remained, which was connected with the disputed questions of keeping the Superior Courts open at all times and increasing the functions of the court clerk. This law foiled the desires of the code commission by suspending certain portions of their code. Summonses were to be returnable and defendants were to appear only when a judge was holding court; thus the courts were in effect closed eleven months of the year to such proceedings, affording an easy lengthy delay. When these provisions came before Judge Tourgée's court in March, 1869, he promptly ruled them in violation of the disputed constitutional provision. His decision was immediately taken before the state Supreme Court and reversed, Chief Justice Pearson adding to the technical justifications for his decision certain smug references to northern importations that could not work in North Carolina.[17]

The Supreme Court's decision was a questionable one, and Associate Justice Rodman, also a code commissioner, strongly dissented, claiming that the law violated both "the letter and the spirit of the Constitution." Rodman was well qualified to judge thereof because the disputed constitutional section had been inserted not from New York, but at his own insistence, in order to relieve the overcrowded dockets of the court. Tourgée also criticized the higher court for declaring, in effect, that *"the plain unmistakable words of a constitutional provision . . . must be modified in their application by a subsequent act of the legislature."* [18] The Supreme Court's most convincing technical argument was that the legislature could define the jurisdiction of the court clerk, and Tourgée reluctantly conceded this point in hopes of allowing at least min-

17 *McAdoo v. Benbow*, 63 N.C. 461.
18 Manuscript on the McAdoo decision, and Tourgée to E. G. Reade, November 6, 1869, Tourgée Papers.

isterial activities by the clerk the year round. In the present case, he argued, jurisdiction of the clerk was not involved, as he had merely to deposit the returns in the court files. Pessimistically, the commissioners continued this struggle for several years, and an attempted compromise, originally prepared by Tourgée, was rejected by the Conservative legislatures of 1870–1871 and 1871–1872, although in the latter instance it was strongly recommended by the House judiciary committee. Not until thirty-five years later were the provisions sought by the commission restored.

During these disputes, the commission also continued with such other work as the drafting of at least forty-six specific bills for the state legislature, including acts on state and local government, liens, fence laws, the homestead, the University, and the state Bureau of Statistics and Immigration. Tourgée had prepared one item that involved him personally, a convincing defense of a proposed increase in judicial salaries, which was defeated by the demand for economy. The commissioners estimated that their acts displaced three-quarters of the previous legislation of the state, and they had enhanced their influence by securing the privilege of addressing the House of Representatives directly. Conservatives objected that the commission was originating practically "*all* the important legislation," although eventually they applauded the intelligent influence in such matters "of the one or two sensible lawyers [excluding the carpetbagger, of course] on the Code Commission." [19]

The final fate of the commission's work was determined by the decline of Republican strength during 1869 and 1870. Consistently under Conservative attack, frightened by Ku Klux Klan atrocities, and disturbed by railroad failures and exposures of fraud, Republican policies became weak and dilatory during these two years. Idealistic Republicans neglected party success to root out taint from their ranks, while others appeared immobilized by fear or inability, and the Republican legislature was often guided by its Democratic minority. Reflecting this state of affairs, a financial investigation was launched that extended to the code commission because of complaints that it was a waste and that Tourgée and Rodman were receiving pay as both commissioners and judges. The latter, while true, was traditional procedure. The three com-

[19] Raleigh *Sentinel*, August 8, November 6, 1868.

missioners ably defended themselves in a reply that was never seriously challenged and reported that at that moment, late in 1869, they had almost completed a penal code and code of criminal procedure.[20] The success of the commission, however, was approaching an end. Its further legislative activities were effectively opposed, and attempts were made to abolish it—the *Sentinel* actually insisted that the commission had been abolished, but that the bill *"got lost by the indiscretion of somebody!"* [21] That somebody, by implication, was Tourgée. Politically motivated denunciations of the commission as part of that "corruption and stealing foistered upon us by Radical carpetbaggers and scallawags" were soon frequent and were closely connected with Conservative desires to alter the constitution of 1868. Bowing before these desires, the frightened Republican legislature obsequiously appointed a committee dominated by Conservatives to study the need for constitutional revision, and this committee singled out the new judicial system as the most objectionable feature of the constitution. Should North Carolina follow the ancient and honored past, asked their quite unintelligent report, or should it "be led by the nose by one or two freshly imported innovators far more remarkable for *pertinancy* and *self-assertion* than for *sound sense* or *legal learning?*" [22] A return to the old law and to "the time-honored distinction between law and equity" thereupon foolishly became the main plank in a Conservative movement for constitutional reform that was defeated by popular vote in 1871.

Despite these attacks, the commissioners happily recognized that their new code of civil procedure had already become a success within the legal profession, that even its "greatest enemies" would now "admit that it has some merits over the former system," and that only occasional opposition to this code continued within the bar. The commissioners' further work, however, came to naught. Early in 1870 they completed their code of criminal procedure and penal code, and they were prepared to submit to the next legislature a general law for corporation charters

[20] Commissioners to Senate, January 25, 1870, *Documents of Code Commission.* Law codifiers before and after Reconstruction received compensation while holding other official positions, e.g., the Chief Supreme Court Justice in 1821, the reporter of the Supreme Court in 1837, and a state senator and the head of the law department of the state university in 1883. Tourgée and Rodman might be criticized, however, in that they were each receiving two separate salaries.

[21] Raleigh *Sentinel,* July 30, September 29, 1870.

[22] North Carolina, *Public Documents,* No. 34 (1869–70).

(eliminating the time-consuming legislative charters), a law defining women's property rights, a compilation of the internal improvement laws of the state, and "a codification of the whole *statute* [emphasis added] law of the State, arranged in a convenient form for reference, and making a single volume about the size of the Revised Code." "When this shall be done our labors will have finished," they declared, apparently having dropped the idea of complete codification.[23] But the timid Republican legislature postponed consideration of the completed criminal codes, and hostile Conservatives captured legislative control in the election of 1870.

Barringer resigned from the commission in the summer of 1870, and an effort was made to restore its prestige by securing Chief Justice Pearson as his replacement. Pearson, however, further undermined the commission by declining with the assertion that Rodman and Tourgée desired to reduce the entire common law to a written code, which he considered an "impossibility." In view of the commission's latest published report, this statement was inaccurate, a fact that Rodman took pains to point out. Tourgée initially had sought complete codification; however, he was not only willing to surrender this goal but offered to resign and did resign in the hope that Pearson would join the commission and help salvage its work. Pearson did not do so, but a moderate, William H. Bailey, joined Rodman to prepare the commission's final report of November, 1870. This report sought only the adoption of a mildly revised code of civil procedure, one that Tourgée had prepared earlier and that included an attempted compromise on keeping the superior courts open throughout the year. Although Tourgée's absence was apparent in the report's unusually apologetic tone, its humility was ineffective. The legislature ignored the commission's work, curtailed its printing privileges, and treated it as abolished. Following one more unsuccessful attempt by Rodman and several leading Conservative attorneys to secure acceptance of the revised code, the code commission itself was abolished by constitutional amendment in 1873.

In the face of many difficulties, Tourgée and his fellow commissioners had labored diligently and had decisively influenced legal development within North Carolina. Their code of civil procedure was a lasting and

23 *Ibid.*, No. 28.

momentous contribution to the state, while their many legislative contributions have never received a scholarly evaluation. The commissioners' own view of their work (including the rejected criminal codes) was most complimentary:

> These acts, with many others such as those concerning the settlement of the estates of deceased persons, guardian and ward, landlord and tenant, fences, draining low land, etc., prescribing just rules and convenient modes of procedure in all these important subjects, form a body of law, the enactment of which will, for at least a century to come, mark an era in our history. We may be permitted to believe that this body of law, by the certainty and economy it has introduced into the administration of justice, has saved, and will save, millions of dollars which otherwise would have been spent in unnecessary legislation.[24]

With the possible exception of the disputed railroad grants, Republican legislation in general, whether initiated by the code commission or not, had not displayed the destructive characteristics that Conservatives had predicted. For example, concessions to the state's landowners were apparent in the attempted stay laws, the act suspending portions of the code of civil procedure, the lien law, and the landlord and tenant act. Once again the more equalitarian-minded Tourgée had displayed greater concern for the lower classes than the majority of Republican legislators, and his effort to abolish the customary local practice of forcing people to work upon the roads was rejected by the Republican legislators. Instead, in what appears to have been a violation of the constitution's ceiling upon the head tax, the Republican regime continued to allow as much as thirty days' labor per year in some counties.[25] Nevertheless, it can be maintained that Republicans were somewhat more solicitous of the interests of the poorer whites and Negroes than were the Conservatives, who would subsequently pass an even harsher law on road work, rewrite the lien law and the landlord and tenant acts to be more firmly in favor of both landlords and merchants, pass elec-

---

[24] *Ibid.*
[25] Greensboro *Patriot*, September 2, 1869; North Carolina, *Public Laws* (1869–70), 66.

toral laws disadvantageous to the poor, and encourage the degradation and exploitation of the Negro.[26] Such laws, including one that arbitrarily made it a misdemeanor to sell cotton between sunrise and sunset, were later critically exposed by Tourgée in his novels.

While most of the code work prepared by the commissioners was shamefully wasted, the Republicans had succeeded in establishing in North Carolina a codified civil procedure, "the most sweeping legislative contribution in the nineteenth century to the law of private relations." [27] The significance of this contribution was suggested three decades after Reconstruction by a North Carolina Supreme Court justice, who stated that since 1868 "the time formerly wasted by the Profession and by law students on technical and ingenious works on pleadings . . . has been economized for a study of useful principles of the law, save by those curious to delve in the most useless waste and ashes of the past." [28] In addition, the absence of legislative tinkering with the code (as urged by the initial commission) and the influence of an eventually friendly Supreme Court left the North Carolina civil code unusually unencumbered and gave that state one of the most flexible and informal legal procedures in the Union.

Some mild objections to the new legal system did continue, the most significant, perhaps, pointing to a decline in legal accuracy and care. While this defect existed, it appears to have been the result of a misunderstanding and was certainly contrary to Tourgée's desires. The code's emphasis upon fact rather than procedure was utilized by the state Supreme Court to excuse carelessness and error, and in one of the first of his decisions appealed to the higher court, Judge Tourgée's emphatic objection to thus extending flexibility of form to the point of condoning actual error was overruled. Other objections to the code were of a minor nature, and the state increasingly turned toward paths that the code commission had urged. While several substantive codes prepared by the initial commission were all rejected, the state soon prepared new versions of each. Similarly, the wisdom of speedier procedure con-

---

[26] North Carolina, *Public Laws* (1870–71), 74; *ibid.* (1872–73), 133; *ibid.* (1873–74), 62; *ibid.* (1874–75), 20, 209; Raleigh *Standard,* February 4, March 28, 1870.

[27] James Willard Hurst, *The Growth of American Law: The Law Makers* (Boston, 1950), 71.

[28] Walter Clark, *The Code of Civil Procedure of North Carolina with Notes and Decisions to July 1900* (Goldsboro, N.C., 1900), v–vi.

tinued to gain support, and in the twentieth century the disputed provisions of the code of 1868 were, in effect, restored. Even Tourgée's desire for complete codification of substantive law won increased and significant support.

The history of legal reform in North Carolina during Reconstruction is suggestive, and the frequent asininity of the attacks upon this Republican endeavor suggests that some good was being accomplished despite, rather than because of, the opponents of Reconstruction.

XII

A Carpetbagger Judge
and the Ku Klux Klan

As code commissioner and judge, with a combined salary of five thousand dollars per year, the carpetbagger Tourgée attained a measure of both prestige and wealth. In the suburbs of Greensboro, adjacent to that city's Negro community, he and Emma purchased a lovely but modest house, to which the familiar enthusiasm of the Tourgée family quickly extended. Soon remodeled, abundantly flowered, and boasting one of the city's first stone sidewalks, the Tourgée residence was considered one of the prettiest in Greensboro, and the Judge was almost as proud of his home as of his politics and was so attached to the several huge oaks which shaded the house that he diverted his fence unsymmetrically to avoid interfering with their growth. A less pleasant feature of the Tourgées' new home was that it had been purchased with thirty-five hundred dollars borrowed from two men, Milton S. Littlefield (a Republican carpetbagger) and George W. Swepson (a Conservative native North Carolinian), who shortly garnered notoriety as Reconstruction railroad promoters. Although it appears that the Judge borrowed this money honestly at a standard interest rate, he unwittingly compromised himself by dealing with such a source, and the loan later became a particular source of embarrassment because it was never paid back. According to Tourgée, this default was due to his complete financial collapse in the depression of 1873.[1]

---

[1] There is no specific indication of fraud in this transaction, and as Tourgée pointed out, the existence of this loan was public knowledge from the very first and no attempt was ever made to prosecute. It is clear from Tourgée's correspondence

Judge Tourgée began riding his court circuit of eight piedmont counties in the fall of 1868. A great lover of horses, he frequently traveled in his own buggy. The old one-eyed nag of 1867 had been replaced by a team of fine thoroughbreds, and the Judge's horses were apparently as spirited as those fondly described in his fiction, since they twice broke loose in downtown Greensboro and created considerable havoc. The Judge's powerful horses and his love for a fast ride, combined with the bumpy rural roads of his circuit, meant frequent emergency buggy repairs, and Tourgée soon learned to make "all but the wheels" from roadside hickory and complained of having had practice enough to master that art as well. While thus attending to the courts, the code, his horses, and his buggy, Tourgée also kept an eye on the family's agricultural activities in Greensboro.

Tourgée's first court was held in Guilford County on September 6, and the decidedly Conservative legal profession awaited the unknown carpetbagger with mingled hostility and concern. They were greeted by perceptive and conciliatory words. Admitting his youth, inexperience, and unpopularity, Tourgée promised to spare no effort to be friendly and fair, and he requested generous assistance from the wisdom of the bar to assure full justice. Displaying a discernment that later became the basis for his literary success, Judge Tourgée also spoke realistically of the problems of Reconstruction. He decried an obvious laxness in public order and morality and attributed it to the impoverishment brought by war, the many years of military supremacy, and the sudden emancipation of Negroes "unaccustomed to self-direction and self-control." That these freed people, who as slaves had condoned theft from the white, "should be improvident, thriftless, and in many instances should resort to theft"

---

with his wife and with Swepson that at least two thousand dollars of the amount was a bona fide loan to be used to purchase a house and secured by four notes, and Tourgée had borrowed and repaid a small sum to Swepson earlier. The precise character of the additional fifteen hundred dollars, which was secured from Littlefield, is unclear, although two years later Swepson recalled the entire amount as a loan arranged by Littlefield (see Tourgée to Swepson, September 17, 20, 27, 1868, April 7, May 30, 1869, and four notes dated May 22, 1869, Swepson Papers; Tourgée to his wife, May 10, 1869, and Swepson to Tourgée, November 20, 1871, Tourgée Papers). The loan was contracted too late to involve the convention, and there is no trace of Tourgée's influence being employed in behalf of Littlefield or Swepson, but rather the reverse (see also Tourgée letter, New York *Sun*, December 9, 1880, and the attack by William L. Royall, *A Reply to "A Fool's Errand By One of the Fools"* [New York, 1881], 87–95).

Tourgée's boyhood home, situated on a sixty-acre farm about two and one-half miles from the center of Kingsville, Ohio. The wing at the left is a later addition. Courtesy of Dean Keller, Kent, Ohio.

Lieutenant Albion W. Tourgée, 105th Ohio Volunteer Infantry, 1862–63. Tintypes in the Tourgée Papers, Westfield, New York.

Civil War Dress Uniform   "On the March"

Emma and Albion Tourgée
at about the time of
their marriage.
Tourgée Papers,
Westfield, New York.

was not surprising, the Judge declared, adding, nevertheless, that this "evil must be checked at once." "The very prevalence of this crime is an aggravation of every offense and must awaken your special vigilance," he continued, but neither enthusiasm nor racial and political prejudice should be allowed to taint the law.[2] While clearly those of a Republican, Tourgée's words revealed an appropriate humility, a desire to conciliate his political opponents, and a determination to stamp out postwar crime. With significant cooperation, the obvious desire of Tourgée and other Republicans for harmony and stability might well have been attained. Instead, vocal segments of the opposition resisted the establishment of normal political or social relationships and launched a bitter campaign to malign everything Republican.

The denunciation of the Republican judiciary began before its courts were even held. "In the main," the Raleigh *Sentinel* asserted, our judges "are a disgrace to the bench, a mockery of dignity and decency, a laughing stock for the legal profession and a curse and blight to the people . . . they have no legal learning, or any other sort of learning, and what is worse, they have no *capacity* to learn." [3] Disrespect for Tourgée was encouraged by implying that he was an escaped convict and by depicting his efforts to provide heat in the local jails as an encouragement to crime, and, in a distorted presentation of his initial court addresses, Tourgée was abused for criticizing slavery and believing that Negroes should steal from their late masters. Even more horrendous was his attribution of crime to the war, an intended "slur upon the Confederate soldiery" by a veteran from the army corps "of one of the most noted pillagers that ever robbed a henroost or made war upon the smokehouses and pantries of defenseless women." [4] When these falsehoods prompted public apologies from several Conservative attorneys, the press ignored the apologies. This attack corresponded to what became the standard method of creating the popular image of Republican debasement and villainy in North Carolina—irresponsible slanders were freely made and circulated by the Conservative press (there were few Republican newspapers), but when they were exposed as erroneous, little or no effort was made to correct them publicly. As Judge Tourgée made

[2] Manuscript, first court address, Tourgée Papers.
[3] Raleigh *Sentinel*, September 26, 1868.
[4] Greensboro *Patriot*, September 10, 1868.

his first circuit tour, he was a frequent victim of this procedure, though among innumerable instances of petty ridicule and calumny the only significant criticism of the Judge involved his several late arrivals at court. This particular criticism was stingingly echoed in a court decision by Chief Justice Pearson, and Tourgée took special pains to avoid any further opportunity for the rebuke. There were other complaints of substance, but not necessarily of justice, such as those against Tourgée's efforts to obtain Negro jurors or against his involvement in the disputed congressional race in the fall of 1868, the latter criticism convincing the Judge that his involvement in that affair was a major tactical error. The nastiest Conservative comment occurred when a young Negro girl was adopted into the Tourgée home: "This is generous in the Judge—very generous! Is Tourgée a married man?" [5]

The stigmatizing of Judge Tourgée did not, however, prevent his capturing further respect and friendship, a development that annoyed some Conservatives as much as it pleased the Judge. In several letters to Emma, he happily described his court conquests, and at the conclusion of his first circuit, he publicly offered "hearty thanks . . . to the bar of the Seventh Judicial District (*with one exception*) for the uniform kindness and courteous deference with which they have aided me in the performance of new and onerous duties, the manly forbearance which they have exercised toward unavoidable defects, and the cheerful grace with which they have yielded in cases of difference." [6] The one exception was Josiah Turner, Jr., irascible editor of the *Sentinel* and the source of many attacks upon the Judge. On occasion even the Conservative press paid tribute; the *Patriot* once concluded that Tourgée's judicial conduct was "fair, full and unbiased by party prejudice" and that he was "about as good a judge as we have under the new constitution." [7] Angry denunciations, however, were more prevalent and influential than occasional praise, and they were also instrumental in arousing some citizens to the point of violence.

Following the formation and rapid success of the North Carolina Republican party, members of that party became increasingly concerned

[5] Raleigh *Sentinel*, April 20, 1869.

[6] Raleigh *Standard*, December 29, 1868.

[7] Greensboro *Patriot*, July 8, 1869. See also *ibid.*, October 14, 1869; Tourgée to his wife, May 16, 1869, and James McCleery to Tourgée, May 24, 1869, Tourgée Papers.

with a variety of coercive threats and acts, particularly those of the Ku Klux Klan. Threatening Klan notices had appeared during the elections of 1868, and Klan terrorism erupted before the end of the year. Eastern North Carolina was the scene of the first assassinations committed by the Klan, but it was the piedmont counties of Judge Tourgée's judicial district that soon became the center of Klan violence in the state. Early in 1869 it was reliably reported from Rockingham County that the "state of affairs . . . was simply intolerable," and, properly indignant, Tourgée urged immediate action and secured a special session of court to deal with the difficulties in that county. Although he found Republicans there "the worst frightened men you ever saw," Tourgée successfully prompted indictments against about twenty supposed Klansmen and entertained some hopes of stamping out their organization *at once, here and now.*" At the succeeding trial, the perplexing skill of the Klan was revealed when all the defendants "proved a *perfect alibi* without a particle of trouble," and the jury, the angered Judge reported, "very properly rendered a verdict of 'Not Guilty.' " [8] The terror continued.

By the summer of 1869, disguised bands had perpetrated a series of beatings, cuttings, shootings, and other outrages, usually against Negroes, and an undeniable "reign of terror" continued in Tourgée's judicial district, until at least fifteen murders and hundreds of lesser atrocities had been committed by the Ku Klux Klan. Republican leaders went armed in fear of their lives, barricaded and fortified their homes, and slept uneasily behind locked doors, while the unarmed Negroes often slept in the woods or fields for protection. The law appeared impotent. Effective disguises and the Klan's clever system of arranging raids by distant dens hindered the identification of suspects, and when such identification was made, Klansmen furnished sworn alibis for their comrades and intimidated or killed hostile witnesses. Police officials belonged to the Klan, its members sat on juries to obstruct indictment or conviction, and mysteriously altered words nullified indictments. "All the law that could be, would be worth nothing, that is the civil law," concluded one Negro magistrate in disgust, while a number of state judges, including Tourgée,

---

[8] Tourgée to T. Settle, June 24, 1869, Tourgée Papers; Tourgée to W. W. Holden July 3, 1869, Governor Holden Papers. The following account is based upon O. H. Olsen, "The Ku Klux Klan: A Study in Reconstruction Politics and Propaganda," *NCHR*, XXXIX (July, 1962), 340–62. Permission has been graciously granted to reprint much of that article, and a repetition of the documentation has been avoided.

despaired of enforcing the law against the Klan. Warning of potential civil war in his judicial district, Tourgée desperately urged Governor Holden to take more decisive action and recommended several competent detectives as perhaps the most effective response.

Contributing to this state of affairs was a Conservative press campaign encouraging and excusing vigilante justice. Hatred of Republicanism had been whipped into a frenzy, and of central significance was a purported Negro crime wave that Republicans would not or could not control. There is "no reasonable safety for life or property" and "crimes of the most bloody and terrible character are perpetrated, and the perpetrators of these crimes go unwhipt of justice," Conservatives charged. Who was responsible for this crime? The Union Leagues were blamed directly for four-fifths of it and indirectly for it all, and compounding the evil was the prejudice of "League Judges" who dealt lightly with "League rogues." "Who could be surprised that this has given rise to, if it has not created, that other terrible organization, the Ku Klux? The wonder is, that there are not more Ku Klux." It was concluded that "very often in the present condition of southern society . . . nothing but lynch law will do." Whipping was encouraged as "the one great incentive" to Negro morality, brutal lynchings were calmly described, and surprise was expressed that summary vengeance was not dealt out more often to lustful Negroes. While so indignantly concerned with a supposed Negro crime wave, most Conservatives were gladdened or unperturbed by the obvious atrocities of the Klan. The very existence of the Klan was long denied or treated as a grand joke, and when its atrocities became of such notoriety as to demand deprecation, the victim was depicted in a manner that condoned the crime.

Conditions in Tourgée's district suggest that this Conservative portrayal, despite its persisting effect, originated almost entirely in the minds of political propagandists. Consider, for example, the asserted relationship between crime and the Ku Klux Klan. Due to poverty, want, turmoil, and war, criminal activity did increase in the South during and after the Civil War, and undoubtedly the prevalence of crime, along with demagogic exaggerations of Negro crime, did contribute to Conservative desperation. But this increased crime had existed from the middle of the war up to the time when the Republicans assumed control of the state, and it would continue long after Republican Reconstruction collapsed. There is no evidence that crime (other than that of the

Klan itself) increased or that chaotic lawlessness existed in the areas of Klan rampage during the Republican regime. Investigation of many sources has failed to reveal any telling sign of unusual Reconstruction crime, and North Carolina Conservative newspapers, which were adept at securing information and anxious to display outrages by Negro men against white women, did not reveal any crimes that were not adequately handled through the courts. Charges of rampant thievery were suspiciously general rather than specific, and the few specific accusations usually proved to be false. Then too, there was seldom any connection between a Klan outrage and criminal activity by the victim. There appears to have been but one major crime known to have motivated a Klan atrocity, an instance wherein three Negroes were hanged for barnburning, although evidence suggests that at least two of them were innocent.[9] Sufficient outcry was made over this case to suggest that if there had been other similar cases they would have been prominently displayed in the Conservative press.

It is also pertinent that not even occasional instances of criminal activity by the Republican leagues were ever established in North Carolina. The only two known specific accusations were based solely upon the accounts of a bitterly partisan press, and neither occurred in an area of subsequent Klan concentration. Even some Conservatives believed that the leagues were engaged only in legitimate political activity, and paradoxically, the leagues were teaching respect for legality at the very moment when the law was failing to protect league members against the outrages of the Ku Klux Klan. In Tourgée's entire judicial district, the only known organized Negro criminal activity for political purposes occurred in retaliation against the Klan and two years after its initial appearance. These Negroes were quickly arrested, tried, and convicted before Judge Tourgée, who sentenced them to unusually harsh prison terms.[10]

Further suspicion of Conservative assertions is aroused when it is noted that in the three counties of greatest Klan activity (Caswell, Orange, and Alamance), political and legal control was mostly in Conservative hands. The Caswell County commissioners, sheriff, deputies,

---

[9] *Trial of William W. Holden, Governor of North Carolina* (3 vols.; Raleigh, 1871), II, 1793–1805, cited hereafter as *Holden Trial*; Greensboro *Patriot*, August 12, November 4, 1869.

[10] U.S., Congress, Senate, *Senate Report No. 1*, 42d Cong., 1st Sess., Part 2, 39–48, cited hereafter as *Senate Klan Report*.

and other local officials were Conservatives. The county commissioners, court clerk, sheriff, and deputies of Orange County were Conservatives; and in Alamance many of the county officials, including the sheriff, were Conservatives. The Alamance sheriff and his deputies were actually members of the Klan. In none of these counties was there any unusual obstacle to the arrest, indictment, and prosecution of criminals, unless they were Klansmen.

One remaining Conservative justification for vigilante justice in Tourgée's judicial district was the accusation that Judge Tourgée did not adequately enforce the law. A state senator asserted that Tourgée was indirectly, at least, assailable "as the cause and origin of all the [Ku Klux] trouble in the county of Orange." [11] While cultivated hatred of the carpetbagger judge undoubtedly did assist in inspiring the Klan, the validity of the pertinent accusations against him is something else again.

Following many petty slanders, the first specific criticism of Tourgée's judicial behavior appears to have been an editorial in the *Sentinel* entitled "Judge Tourgée's Revenge." Written by Josiah Turner, Jr., this editorial accused the Judge of a partisan and revengeful decision in a legal case wherein Turner was the defeated attorney. Two respected Conservative lawyers promptly and emphatically repudiated this charge and described Tourgée's decision as the only equitable one possible, but in conformity with brutal partisanship their statement did not appear in the Conservative press.[12] Shortly thereafter, the *Sentinel* chose to condemn Tourgée for undue leniency when he twice set aside the conviction of a Negro for larceny. Klansmen in Orange County would subsequently refer to this case as the major reason for their existence, although in actuality the Orange County Klan had made its appearance before the first trial of this Negro and had committed most of its atrocities, including three murders, before his second trial. It was again racial prejudice that was being exploited. Judge Tourgée was guilty only of having agreed with the defense attorney, who was a Conservative, that no "white man would have been convicted upon the evidence in the case." [13] The state Supreme Court ultimately would endorse the technical grounds upon which Tourgée acted, and meanwhile he was typically

[11] Raleigh *Standard*, February 1, 1870.
[12] Raleigh *Sentinel*, May 4, 1869; Raleigh *Standard*, May 11, 1869.
[13] Henry K. Nash to Tourgée, January 25, 1870, Tourgée Papers.

defiant in his own defense, publicly pledging never to do "evil in the seat of justice from a cowardly fear of the slanderer," but to do his honest duty "whether the same please friend or foe, or accords with the administration of 'wild justice' in the County of Orange and elsewhere or not." [14]

Also unsubstantial was the Greensboro *Patriot*'s only explicit charge of Tourgée's incapacity in a criminal case: "A *white* boy is sentenced to the penitentiary for ten years for defending himself against a man; a colored *boy*, for wantonly killing another, is neither fined nor imprisoned." This declaration was prompted by a political dispute, and Tourgée pointed out that the "*white* boy" of sixteen had been so clearly guilty of murder that the defense requested and received permission to plead guilty to manslaughter. The "colored *boy*" of nine was tried for murder, but no evidence was presented, and the jury, "*more than two-thirds* of which were conservatives, rendered a verdict of 'Not Guilty.' " The *Patriot* neither retracted nor repeated the tale.[15]

Judge Tourgée was also denounced for collaborating with the Republican governor to pardon hundreds of dangerous criminals, although the only specific instance encountered involved a pardon recommended by two noted Conservatives, one of whom later became governor of the state. If this accusation were true, one would expect a significant number of pardons in Tourgée's district. Instead, in North Carolina's twelve judicial districts only 5 of the 127 pardons and commutations granted by Governor Holden before 1870 were from Tourgée's circuit, and during 1870 there was only one pardon and one commutation. All apparently had good reasons for being pardoned, with the possible exception of a Conservative whose pardon Tourgée had opposed. Not one of all these pardons suggested any need for Klan revenge, nor was there ever any connection established between a Klan raid and a pardon. In the two counties of greatest Klan activity prior to 1870 there had been no pardons in one and all those in the other had been urged by Conservatives.

It was distorted trivia and fabrication upon which the indignant condemnation of Republicanism and justification of the Klan was

[14] Tourgée letter, Raleigh *Standard*, February 1, 1870.
[15] Greensboro *Patriot*, September 2, 1869; Tourgée to Greensboro *Register*, September 6, 1869, and Superior Court Record Book, Tourgée Papers.

primarily based. When prejudice was affecting justice, it was usually that familiar prejudice against the Negro, and the general cultural climate lends support to Tourgée's complaint that when Negroes were on trial "the most trivial offenses secured conviction upon the most doubtful evidence," whereas whites were easily acquitted of proven outrages against Negroes. "There is no crime can be committed by a *white* conservative," the Judge angrily complained to his wife: "Yesterday three men were tried for cutting a colored man in pieces almost—stabbing and beating and maltreating in every possible manner—but it was all of no avail—'Not guilty' was the verdict." [16] Sometimes conditions were more satisfactory, as when members of both parties cooperated to find a Negro defendant innocent in a celebrated case of arson that had driven a white planter to suicide. No outcry was made over this verdict, perhaps because public feelings were sufficiently assuaged by the three retaliatory murders already committed by the Klan.

Several of Judge Tourgée's court cases suggest that although Republican officials were plagued by difficulties they were not remiss in their responsibilities. In a murder case tried amidst great clamor and tension, one of three Negro defendants appeared innocent, and the Judge privately advised the defense to request removal of the case to another county. Fearing an immediate lynching, the worried defense counsel rejected this advice (he would later remind Tourgée that had he not done so "the Fool's Errand might have ended right there"),[17] and the trial proceeded more successfully than Tourgée had anticipated. A racially mixed jury was accepted and found two of the Negroes guilty and the third innocent. The convicted men were sentenced to death and executed shortly thereafter. A Negro woman had also been convicted and sentenced to death by Tourgée during this court session. Obviously criminals were being punished in Republican courts, but even this was used to political advantage: Tourgée was reported to have "sentenced two colored members of the League . . . to be hung." [18]

Despite his idealistic attachment to the Negro, Tourgée was not inclined to be overly merciful toward Negro criminals. In his enthusiasm

[16] Tourgée to his wife, June 9, 1869, Tourgée Papers.
[17] Ike R. Strayhorn to Tourgée, June 22, 1887, Tourgée Papers.
[18] Wilmington *Daily Journal*, February 9, 1870.

to stamp out crime among the freed slaves, he was inclined toward sternness, and he proved anxious to inflict harsh punishment upon Negroes as a deterrent to any Klan-like criminal activity. But when he sentenced three Negroes to six years at hard labor for whipping another Negro while in disguise, Conservatives concluded not that Republicans were impartially administering justice but that "Judge Tourgée [had] ascertained . . . that all the murders, whippings, and barn-burnings had been done by Loyal Leaguers under the garb of Ku Klux!" [19] Tourgée also sentenced five Negroes to as much as twenty years' imprisonment for an arson committed in retaliation against the Klan, and in a milder case he sentenced two Negroes to five years in prison merely for going masked and disguised. While Republicans were securing these convictions, they were unable to prosecute successfully a single Klansman.

It appears, then, that neither excessive crime nor the collapse of legal authority can be held responsible for inspiring the Klan, and certain impressive Conservative testimony also suggests as much. Klan terror was incited, however, by the belief that such conditions did exist, as well as by the prevalent emotional denunciations of Republicanism. The most pertinent contribution of the Republicans to this situation was probably the inspiration that they furnished for such verbal attacks. Judge Tourgée's challenges to racial prejudice, his involvement in various political disputes, and his persistently outspoken and aggressive behavior, for example, often did invite criticism. In the fall of 1869, he aroused anger in a disputed county election case when he declared certain elections void and upheld the continuance in office of a number of Republican magistrates. Paradoxically, the nullification of these elections had been initiated by a defeated Conservative candidate. Adding to the exasperation aroused by this case were several other matters, including Tourgée's legal criticisms of the county road tax, his threats of possible private retaliation against Klansmen, and his suspected connection with the Republican press and with the military preparations of Greensboro Negroes against the Klan. Slanderous characterization of Tourgée, "the self-constituted Tycoon of the 7th judicial district," again

[19] Greensboro *Patriot*, August 1, 1870. For Tourgée's severity, see Greensboro *Patriot*, March 17, June 23, 1870, September 14, 1871; *Senate Klan Report*, Part 2, 39–48. Tourgée later sought a pardon for those Negroes guilty only of going disguised and was censured for his severity by Governor Tod R. Caldwell.

appeared: "A partisan judge upon the bench—administering laws made by partisans for partisan party purposes. Laws which can be construed to mean just what the exigencies of the judge's party demand." [20] Charges of rampant crime and judicial leniency followed, and the local press announced a deliberate campaign to publicize "all the diabolical outrages being committed all over the South by Negroes." Denunciation ceased only when conciliatory Republican officials ignored Tourgée's decision and appointed Conservatives to certain disputed posts. The Judge's legal opinion, however, was never discredited, and his objectivity had been indicated in two earlier cases in which he had ruled against the Republican state administration in behalf of Conservative county officials.[21] It was several months after this incident that Tourgée became the center of the state-wide imbroglio over the question of whether the Republican legislature was to sit for two years or four, and he simultaneously aroused local hostility by correctly refusing to grant an injunction against the building of a Republican-sponsored bridge across the Dan River.

In sum, there was certainly little substance to the many criticisms of Judge Tourgée, and there was apparent validity to his belief that Reconstruction was characterized by "a general plan of slander, vituperation and personal assault upon every representative of the government, which is entirely unparalleled in the history of political damnation." He himself became one of the most hated Republicans in the state, especially in areas where he had little opportunity to counteract frequently irresponsible propaganda with personal contact—as, for example, in the Tarboro press, which declared: "We believe him to be venal and vicious as a man; undignified, partial, and unlearned as a judge; who would, without hesitancy, prostitute the powers of his official station to the purposes of party or of personal revenue. A mere adventurer. . . ." [22]

From equalitarianism to railroad scandal, Republicans in North Carolina had inspired angry opposition, and the pugnacious tendencies of Tourgée did little to calm the storm. But neither Tourgée's behavior nor Republicanism in the piedmont warranted the extent or nature of the criticisms made nor such a vicious response as that of the Ku Klux

[20] Greensboro *Patriot*, September 2, 1869.
[21] Raleigh *Sentinel*, April 5, 1869.
[22] Clipping, Tarboro *North Carolinian*, February 1, 1870, Tourgée Papers.

Klan. Behind the breakdown of law and order was not evil so much as obstinate opposition to Republican reform, and while the persistent poisoning of the public mind against Republicanism may not have been, as Tourgée believed, deliberately intended to promote violence, there is no doubt that it contributed to that end.

XIII

The Klan and
Republican Collapse

Judge Tourgée's explanation of the Ku Klux Klan differed greatly from that offered by Conservatives. Some combination of pride, prejudice, and chagrin, he suggested, inflamed by convictions of injustice and oppression, had led to Klan violence, and this did appear to be the case. Many of the leaders of the Conservative party in North Carolina were still smarting from military defeat and Federal intervention and were still horrified by Reconstruction equalitarianism and reform. They had soon experienced enough "of this thing called SUFFRAGE. Whereby the people as a mass (who are always silly things when taken collectively) vote like idiots for the very worst men over the very best." Some even professed to prefer a monarchy under Robert E. Lee.[1] Incited by emotional propaganda and as determined as they were convinced, many Conservatives were prepared to accept almost any means, including violence, for overthrowing Republican rule.

The Klan is very easily connected with what Tourgée called this "great and holy aim." The Klan oath was racially and politically oriented, and while many Klansmen did believe that their atrocities were necessary to stop Negro crime or impudence, their more perceptive cohorts spoke of the necessity "to keep down the style of the niggers and to increase the Conservative party." One of its leaders in western North Carolina noted that the Klan was formed not to achieve "a white man's government only, but—mark the phrase—an *intelligent* white

[1] Milton *Chronicle* and Wilmington *Star*, quoted in Raleigh *Standard*, April 27, May 3, 1869; Hillsborough *Recorder*, April 28, 1869.

man's government." [2] Hearsay evidence from a Klansman that a majority of the Democratic legislature elected in 1870 were Klansmen was, perhaps, an exaggeration, but this did approximate the situation in Judge Tourgée's circuit, where a veritable galaxy of Conservative luminaries, ranging from state legislators to local policemen, belonged to the Klan. It is also indicative that, when they so desired, Conservatives of "responsible position" quickly and easily secured the dissolution of the Klan. But the rarity of such efforts,[3] the role of prominent Conservatives in Klan organization and terror, the characteristics of Klan literature, and the precision of troops of Klansmen mounted on valuable horses all confirm Tourgée's opinion that the Klan "originated with the best classes of the South, was managed and controlled by them, and was at all times under their direction. It was their creature and their agent to work out their purposes and ends."

Conservatives also justified the Klan to the extent of supporting it, and they exploited its existence. Until the leagues were dissolved, said many citizens of Chapel Hill, they would not "condemn good citizens and true men, who, in self-defense, resort to other means because they fail to obtain from the law that protection and security which they have a right to demand." This public resolution appeared immediately after one murder and preceded four additional murders by the Klan in that county. What was demanded was the end of Republican rule. "Negro savages and white ignoramusses wearing the ermine of office" must abdicate willingly, the Conservative press threatened, or they would be removed forcibly by the Klan.

The Klan's choice of victims also suggests its purposes and motives. Instances where the Klan punished actual crime were rare, although accusations to the contrary were frequent and historians have repeated

[2] *Third Annual Message, W. W. Holden, Governor of North Carolina* (Raleigh, 1870), Appendix, 257, hereafter cited as *Holden Message*; Hamilton (ed.), *The Papers of Randolph Abbott Shotwell* (3 vols.; Raleigh, 1929–39), II, 376. For the following account, see O. H. Olsen, "The Ku Klux Klan," *NCHR*, XXXIX (July, 1962), 340–62.

[3] Thomas Ruffin did advise his son against the Klan (see Hamilton [ed.], *Ruffin Papers*, IV, 225–27). Tourgée credited John Birney Gretter of Greensboro with being the only Klansman he knew of who voluntarily repudiated and denounced its atrocities without fear or favor. Gretter, model for the rollicking John Burleson of *A Fool's Errand*, later became a Republican (Tourgée to R. M. Douglas, July 29, 1880, Douglas Papers [in the possession of the Douglas family, Greensboro, N.C.]).

several very doubtful illustrations that this was the case.[4] Conservatives, by the way, had an excellent opportunity, during an impeachment trial of Governor Holden, to determine whether or not crime inspired the Klan, but they made no attempt to do so. Klan atrocities motivated by other considerations, however, have been abundantly established. Negro departures from segregated or submissive behavior—ambition, independence, impudence, eating with whites, and the possession of firearms—frequently provoked assaults, and whites were beaten for challenging racial mores or for assisting Negroes to better their position. Tourgée perceived the anomaly that a Klan supposedly directed against evil persisted in attacking the most ambitious, able, and independent members of the darker race; "uppity" Negro victims of the Klan in his circuit included three schoolteachers, three shoemakers, two blacksmiths, a mechanic, and a miller. Political activity was also an invitation to attack, and league leaders, as well as Republican magistrates, postmasters, and lesser officials, were common victims. One white man was assertedly whipped merely for not voting in his effort to keep clear of the bitter political struggle. Almost all of these atrocities were committed against individuals of only local prominence, thus attracting a minimum of attention outside the immediate area. Plots against more prominent Republicans often failed or were blocked by cautious leaders, and reputed attempts on Tourgée's life included an attempt to hang him in downtown Greensboro, to waylay him as he rode his circuit alone in his buggy, and to create a court row during which he was to be shot.[5]

The unusual intensity of Klan activity in Judge Tourgée's judicial district was also suggestive. The North Carolina Klan appears to have originated in the only safely Conservative county in the district (Orange County, the home of a chief architect of the white supremacy program, William A. Graham) and then radiated outward, first into counties

[4] Hamilton (*Reconstruction*, 467–69) concludes that Caswell Holt was whipped for "exposing his person" before a white girl, but the record suggests that Holt's opposition to the Klan and his strength of character were the sources of resentment (see Raleigh *Standard*, February 27, April 7, 1869; *Holden Trial*, II, 1311–28, 2002; *Senate Klan Report*, 341–46). Hamilton's view is also contradicted by the only direct testimony, that of a Conservative, in another case (see Hamilton, *Reconstruction*, 468–69; *Holden Trial*, II, 1785–87).

[5] See especially Tourgée to his wife, March 20, 1872, and the confessions of William T. Troy and Willis C. Truit, Tourgée Papers.

with a sizable Negro minority. The counties of heaviest Negro population or greatest Republican strength remained free of Klan violence the longest. Meanwhile, in two counties in this piedmont area, Alamance and Caswell, an able and moderate Negro-white Republican leadership, which Tourgée had helped to establish, was making an unusual contribution to Republican success. Between the spring and fall elections of 1868, it was these two counties that the Republican party gained, while losing thirteen counties elsewhere in the state. As the elections of 1870 approached, it was precisely in these two counties that Klan terrorism reached its greatest extreme.

Official Republican response to the Klan, which ranged from pleas for law and order to ineffective police action, accomplished little. More telling and dramatic was the action of a Negro woman who successfully defended her home against the night raiders by cleaving the head of a Klansman with an ax. Although Judge Tourgée considered clever police action the best way of dealing with the Klan, he also warned juries that if the law were not effectively enforced, victims of the Klan would be justified in providing for their own protection. Various private defensive preparations were made, and following extreme violence in the fall of 1869, including five murders in Orange County, one Republican advised in exasperation that "assassination must be met by lynching and midnight murder by midnight execution." [6] It must have been about this time that Tourgée himself seriously considered forming a band of armed men to track down Klan raiders and fell them upon their thresholds. Such counterthreats did reduce terrorism, especially in areas of heavy Negro population. But in Judge Tourgée's circuit, wherever order was successfully restored, counterthreats had been combined with Conservative efforts to disband the Klan, and the relative effect of each action is impossible to determine.

The idea of forceful action of any kind generally made little headway among the divided and drifting Republicans. Their legal efforts remained ineffective, and they continued to rely heavily upon general pleas for law and order and for Conservative assistance. Years later Tourgée concluded that more effective private retaliation would have developed but for the great restraint applied by Republican leaders, but during the crisis, he, too, had feared to encourage a test of force. "It will be

[6] Greensboro *Union Register*, October 20, 1869.

hard for you to conceive how such things can be," the Judge wrote a friend in 1870, but our entire party is composed of poor whites and Negroes, "without arms and without the habits of self assertion so natural to Yankees—& in a thousand forms too intricate to detail here we are bound down and shackled in our action and can do but little for ourselves against this Klan of secret-murderers." [7] Tourgée was thus induced to turn away from his earlier forceful attitude and adopt moderate tactics, and Republicans soon hopefully reported that his court addresses were "yielding nothing of principle, but by their advisory and conciliatory tone, working wonders in his judicial district." [8] It was in conjunction with such a policy that the Judge severely punished instances of private Negro retaliation against the Klan. This approach did have some success, not only in discouraging the Klan but in dividing the Conservative party, a moderate faction of which both repudiated the Klan and denounced the Raleigh *Sentinel's* "little, proscriptive, vindictive, spiteful clique." [9] Partially to avoid spreading this schism, the Conservatives, despite approaching elections, avoided holding a state convention in 1870. Meanwhile, neither force, moderation, nor law succeeded in fully stopping the nefarious operations of the Klan.

Anticipating an eventual test of force, Governor Holden sought a more efficient militia law and appealed quietly for assistance from the Federal government. The latter effort was fruitless, but the Republican state legislature did reluctantly pass the desired militia measure, which, like all anti-Klan legislation, was bitterly opposed by Conservatives and was passed under circumstances that aroused antagonism against Judge Tourgée. Although the Judge preferred efficient detective measures to armed force and was confident that he "could easily arrange to detect and capture a crowd *en masque* in a month," his description of the state of affairs in the Seventh Judicial District had been used to justify the disputed militia law. Conservatives responded indignantly that law and order prevailed everywhere and accused Tourgée of "barefaced and unmitigated falsehoods"; the local Greensboro press actually insisted that "this Ku Klux cry is all a humbug!" Two days later, however, the

[7] Tourgée to R. M. Tuttle, May 26, 1870, Tourgée Papers.
[8] Raleigh *Standard*, October 9, 1869.
[9] Charlotte *Democrat*, quoted in Raleigh *Standard*, February 3, 1870. See also Greensboro *Patriot*, March 3, 1870; Salisbury *Old North State*, March 11, 1870.

Klan cruelly verified Tourgée's account. About midnight of February 26, 1870, a large body of robed horsemen bodily took over the county seat of Alamance County and hanged the leading Negro Republican in that county, Wyatt Outlaw, from the branch of a huge oak tree, whose branch pointed in silent mockery toward Judge Tourgée's courthouse less than a hundred feet away.

This murder was soon covered with a veil of obscurity and distortion. A lurid tale was told of Outlaw having exchanged wives with another Negro, whom the Klan reputedly had been pursuing, and the deed was attributed to Republicans, on the grounds that Outlaw had stolen money from the Union League. Except for such misleading speculation, the event was thereafter largely ignored, and three weeks later the entire matter was denounced in a distant area of the state as a fabrication. The most lasting explanation of this atrocity was either that Outlaw's character was bad or that he had previously exchanged gunfire with the Klan, although, in truth, the latter was not believed in Alamance, even by Klansmen, and the character and reputation of this Negro were exceptionally good. Wyatt Outlaw's real sins were his ability and leadership. He had been publicly active in behalf of his people as early as 1866, the following year he participated in the formation of the state Republican party, and in 1868, in close cooperation with a pre-Civil War Whig, merchant, and slaveholder, William R. Albright, he was instrumental in swinging Alamance County to the Republican party. Outlaw had also served as town commissioner, and no criticisms of his capabilities in that position have been revealed. As president of the local Union League, he had promoted the establishment of a school and church for the Negro population. Ironically, he also was described as "the most active man in opposition" to proposals for violent retaliation against the Klan, although he may have been active in seeking legal redress against that organization.

Outlaw's murder was soon compounded by the killing of another Negro who was alleged to have uncovered evidence concerning the atrocity. Governor Holden then reacted by declaring Alamance in a state of insurrection, but no forceful steps accompanied this declaration. Instead, Republicans continued to plead for Conservative cooperation and even offered to disband the Union Leagues. A favorable Conservative response did secure an end to Klan activity in two of Judge

Tourgée's counties, but elsewhere Klan raids continued, and Tourgée's "questionable character . . . and his more questionable conduct" were often blamed for the disorder.[10] One group of moderate Conservatives suggested that Tourgée's resignation, together with the appointment of a Conservative judge in his place, would facilitate the restoration of order. Although the Republicans would not endorse such an abject surrender, Tourgée's various Republican party titles were suddenly removed. The worried Judge by now had fortified his home against attack, and he rode to court heavily armed and via circuitous buggy routes. Meanwhile, despite desperate negotiations by the Governor, violence was increasing in Caswell, a county with a slight Negro majority. Two efficient politicians, Wilson Carey, a Negro, and John W. Stephens, a native white artisan, had recently captured that county for the Republican party.

Often depicted as one of the most unsavory of Reconstruction scalawags, John W. "Chicken" Stephens has remained one of the most controversial figures of that tragic era. Born in Guilford County in 1834, of poor but respected parents, Stephens became an excellent harness-maker and engaged in the tobacco trade before secession. His war record is unclear, but he supposedly dodged conscription—according to his friends, because of hostility to the Confederacy, and according to his enemies, because of cowardice—and out of some wartime dispute, which was anything but a case of theft and may have involved the question of his loyalty to the Confederacy, arose the subsequent malignment of "Chicken" Stephens as a chicken thief. After the war, Stephens displayed a particular hostility toward the ex-slaveholding gentry, whom he blamed for the war and for many of the ills of the poorer population, and he became involved in Freedmen's Bureau work and was soon in the Republican ranks. During this postwar period he was successful in politics, business, and law, and his success at passing the bar examination before Tourgée provoked several denunciations of the Judge. Stephens was also a minor official in the Methodist church until he was expelled because of his politics, and his two brothers, Confederate veterans who achieved local prominence, recalled him as a good and honest man. On one matter many a friend and foe agreed, that Stephens was a man of unusual courage and ability, reputedly "a

[10] Wilmington *Daily Journal*, March 17, 23, 1870.

stalwart in every sense [who] could not be overcome physically, mentally or legally, by any one of his jealous political enemies." [11]

Stephens' political policies were effective but not reckless. In 1868 he helped quell threatened violence between the races and pledged his life for the good behavior of the Negroes. Under his leadership (and he was often advised by Judge Tourgée), Caswell Republicans followed a policy of moderation, promoting cooperation with, and the support of, some Conservative candidates. There was little talk of rampant crime or injustice in Caswell before 1870, and there was certainly no Republican barrier to the execution of the law, since the county commissioners, the sheriff and his deputies, and other local officials were Conservatives. On the other hand, the Republicans held a voting majority as well as various local and state offices, and Stephens himself was one of the county's two state senators. As the election of 1870 approached, Klan violence erupted in Caswell.

Following many atrocities there, some cases of arson occurred, for which Stephens was considered in some way responsible, very likely because of his pledge of good Negro behavior. There were other considerations more definitely endangering Stephens. He was the party stalwart, he was very close to the Negro population, he had incurred Conservative displeasure as a Freedmen's Bureau agent and as a magistrate handling controversies between Negro laborers and the tobacco planters of the county, and he had been active in ferreting out information against the Klan. Early in 1870 Stephens received warnings of plots against his life, but he would not back down. The "poor, ignorant, colored Republican voters in that county had stood by him and elected him, at the risk of persecution and starvation," Tourgée reported him as saying, and "he had no idea of abandoning them to the Ku Klux." Instead, he armed himself with three pistols and fortified his home against attack, and Judge Tourgée joined a band who at one time lay in ambush for an expected Klan raid that never occurred. In February, 1870, Stephens insured his life to provide for his wife and two children, and in April Tourgée helped him to prepare his last will and testament.

Meanwhile, proceeding with his political work, Stephens approached the respected and seemingly moderate ex-sheriff Frank Wiley and

[11] W. L. Brinkley to Katherine Hoskins, May 30, 1946 (in the possession of Miss Hoskins, Summerfield, N.C.).

urged him to run for sheriff with Republican support. Wiley, secretly a member of the Klan, asked time for consideration and prepared to use these negotiations to entice Stephens to his death. On May 21, 1870, a Conservative party convention was held in the Caswell County courthouse, and as Stephens sat busily taking notes on the proceedings, Wiley approached and suggested that they step out to discuss the proposed candidacy for sheriff. The unsuspecting Stephens was led into a downstairs room, where he was surprised, overpowered, and disarmed by a group of waiting assassins. He was then strangled and stabbed to death and his body thrown upon a woodpile. Locking the door behind them, the assassins departed.[12]

Some of the leading citizens of the county had participated in this cowardly killing. Wiley, the ex-sheriff, "a large and successful farmer, a gentleman of the very highest moral character, a peaceable and law abiding citizen . . ." had betrayed Stephens to his death. One of the most prominent landowners in the county had engineered the plot and helped carry it through. Another planter, who was the son of the chairman of the board of county commissioners, a state university graduate, and one of the most cultured men in the community, had played a prominent part. So also had a Conservative candidate for office, a respected coach-maker and merchant, an ex-Confederate captain, and a gentleman bearing the name of a prominent family of planters. Four, perhaps five, of the men participating in the murder were Conservative political leaders, and the two men most prominent in the assassination had helped write the party's county platform, which, of all things, denounced secret organization and illegality and urged the maintenance of law and order. The final irony was that one, if not two, of the assassins appeared on the Republicans' compromise ticket of 1870.[13] Wiley would have been the third.

After the deed, Conservatives, in their usual fashion, denounced

[12] Confession of John G. Lea, State Archives, Raleigh. Released posthumously in 1935, a copy is available in Greensboro *Daily News*, October 2, 1935. Tourgée's narration of the murder in *A Fool's Errand* was based upon the sworn testimony of a Negro servant who overheard an account by Frank Wiley (statement of Patsie Barton, December 12, 1872, Tourgée Papers).

[13] Raleigh *Sentinel*, June 8, 1870; Greensboro *Patriot*, July 21, August 4, 1870; Hillsborough *Recorder*, June 1, 1870; Caswell County Republican ticket of 1870, Scott Papers. Patsie Barton's statement included Thomas Johnson, who may have been T. D. Johnson.

murder but tried to deny, palliate, or distort the crime. Stephens' murder "is fully justified by every conservative . . . in Greensboro," complained the exasperated Tourgée. " 'Oh!' they say, 'he was a man of bad character'—and that seems to cover more sins of others than charity was ever reputed to do." While Conservatives could adduce many reasons why Stephens deserved death, they were certain that "the good and honest conservative citizens of our state" could not be connected with the crime. When circumstantial evidence did link three of the assassins to the murder, the *Sentinel* was indignant: "We say positively, after having known Messrs. Wiley, Mitchell, and Roan for years, that they are as innocent of the charge of murdering Stephens as their children three years old. . . . It is high time that such men . . . who are above reproach among respectable men, should be free from the censures of those whose judgements are biased by political prejudice. . . ." [14] To remove every trace of guilt from themselves, Conservatives found numerous reasons for attributing the deed to Republicans. The assassins readily lied under oath, not only to save themselves but to cast suspicion upon Negro Republicans, and others lied to substantiate these false accounts.

The murder of Stephens inspired a drastic response. Risking expected adverse political repercussions, the aroused Republicans resorted to military force. State troops moved into Alamance and Caswell and arrested suspected Klansmen, while Conservatives responded with wrathful objections to militarism. Many were the tales of outrage, atrocity, and indignity committed during this notorious "Kirk-Holden War." There was, indeed, misbehavior, but not one drop of blood was shed, and the military movement as a whole was quite moderate. The most substantial outrage was the temporary denial of the writ of habeas corpus to some imprisoned Klansmen; however, the individual who suffered most was not a Klansman but a Republican imprisoned by his own party for 94 days because he was accused by Klansmen of suspending men by the neck in an effort to extort confessions.

Tourgée feared that the entire military program was making more fanfare than progress, and he opposed Governor Holden's suspension of the writ of habeus corpus. Such suspension was in conflict with both Republican promises and the state constitution and inspired widespread

[14] Raleigh *Sentinel*, October 21, 1870.

public disapproval on the eve of the election. More momentous than Tourgée's opinion, however, was that of the Federal judiciary, which, with doubtful legal propriety, undermined Governor Holden by granting writs to the imprisoned Klansmen. President Grant then advised Holden to bow before the Federal courts, and the Republican program collapsed. Paradoxically, this Federal judicial intervention, so beneficial to, and lauded by, Conservatives, was based upon the Fourteenth Amendment.

Republicans lost more than a legal dispute. In the midst of the furor the Conservatives carried the election of 1870 and achieved firm control of the state legislature. The defeat Tourgée had long expected seemed at hand, and the Judge despondently censured the Federal government for having placed southern Republicans in a hopeless position and then having abandoned them to the Ku Klux Klan. There would be "anything but good news from this state for some time to come," he gloomily predicted. Democracy and public education would probably fall: "If it were not for a most abiding sense of the Mercy and goodness of an Over-ruling and sleepless providence, I should almost despair."

Judge Tourgée thought that the Ku Klux Klan was largely responsible for this result, but the actual contributions of that organization to Republican collapse are rather uncertain. The Klan was known to have been active in ten of the fifteen counties that swung to the Conservatives in 1870; and in the Judge's circuit the only two counties that went Republican were those where troops were present. These troops allowed, if they did not guarantee, a peaceful and fair election. It was also suggestive of the power of intimidation that the Conservative victory was due less to an increase in their vote than to a decrease in the Republican vote. Nevertheless, the most significant contribution of the Klan may have been an indirect one—the indignant public response to the militia movement. The Klan did illustrate how far the opponents of Reconstruction would and could go, but its decisiveness is questionable. Political power was already swinging toward the Conservatives, and by 1870 there was nothing to threaten the source of their power. The Klan was not so much a necessity as an illustration of the inability of certain elements to accommodate themselves either to Negro equality or to the democratic political process. They would soon learn to accept the latter, and when, in 1875, the final defeat of

Republicanism occurred, it was dependent upon political rather than terroristic procedures.

There was some sunshine for Republicans among these dark clouds of 1870. Tourgée credited the militia movement with having averted a reign of bloodshed on election day; and the Klan had almost disappeared, which was attributable to the military movement, to growing national interest, and to the fact that Conservatives had achieved much of their desired political control. It also appeared that Republicans might profit from information secured by the militia movement, and various confessions, which Conservatives denounced as "too monstrous to believe," had already frightened a good number of young men into flight. Tourgée thought this might all "be good editorial thunder and bring moral conviction to impartial minds," but he was soured by a failure to secure substantial evidence. "The thing has been bungled, just as Holden has bungled everything he has touched since his election," concluded the Judge, but a few weeks later he was entertaining optimistic hopes that revelations being secured in a Supreme Court hearing might "bring the Ku Klux investigation to a head which will be worth something yet." [15]

Intensifying Tourgée's continued interest in the Klan's activities was some notoriety recently gained for himself. Following the murder of John W. Stephens, the Judge had written an impassioned, essentially accurate letter to Joseph C. Abbott, United States Senator from North Carolina. Abbott had sent Holden a copy of the letter, which the Governor, to Tourgée's anger, presented to a northern reporter. When the letter appeared in the national press, not only did Tourgée's unkind depiction of conditions in the state arouse Conservative clamor, but the press had printed a garbled version of the letter, containing several inaccuracies. A state-wide furor followed,[16] and Tourgée was again subjected to a variety of threats and death notices. The usually staunch

[15] Tourgée to ———, August 14, 1870, Tourgée to Settle, August 30, 1870, Tourgée to Allan Rutherford, August 30, 1870, all in Tourgée Papers.

[16] Tourgée to Abbott, May 24, 1870, in N.Y. *Tribune*, August 3, 1870. Tourgée's figures on Klan outrages in his district had been increased, and he had mistakenly included two murders outside his district in the twelve that he reported. Actually this was not inaccurate, since he was unaware of two other murders that occurred, and three more victims soon died from the effects of Klan attacks. Hamilton (*Reconstruction*, 528, n. 1) errs in saying that Abbott proved he did not alter the letter, thus implying that Holden did. Abbott merely furnished another correct copy, and Tourgée believed that Abbott's copyist had erred initially. The *Sentinel* garbled the letter even further (Greensboro *Patriot*, September 29, 1870).

Judge was greatly perturbed, particularly because Emma was with child and had earlier lost an expected baby. He and Emma seriously considered leaving the state permanently, but instead they sought a temporary refuge, a foreign post, perhaps, where the Judge "wouldn't mind yellow-fever, cholera, fleas, earthquakes, vertigo, smallpox, cannibalism, icebergs, sharks, or any other name or shape of horror—provided always there are no K.K.K." Robert M. Douglas, a Greensboro Republican who was then serving as President Grant's private secretary, was prepared to offer Tourgée a consulate in Peru, provided that Douglas' brother-in-law, Thomas Settle, approved. Settle took the post instead, and the carpetbagger was left to continue his struggle.

Although the Judge was exceptionally worried and uncomfortable, he had by no means been cowed. He publicly repudiated threats from the Klan with "the utmost contempt," and he engaged in a testy exchange with the Guilford bar because they, who had never raised a voice against the Klan, had censured his letter to Senator Abbott.[17] Tourgée was also busily fighting a tendency within his own party to use carpetbaggers as scapegoats while catering to "any native or trimming Republicans." Also true to his character was the Judge's wily plan to protect Governor Holden against impeachment by a Conservative state Senate that had ejected a sufficient number of Republicans to guarantee a safe majority for conviction. Tourgée proposed that a select group of men engage in private conversation with the Conservative senators, confident that few would hesitate to declare their belief that Holden was guilty. Their right to sit in judgment with preconceived convictions could then be challenged at the trial. Tourgée was convinced the plan would work, but nothing ever came of it, and Governor Holden became the final victim of the militia affair when he was impeached and removed from office. He received little sympathy from Tourgée, who concluded that the trial illustrated that the Governor had been "at every stage, if possible, a more egregious ass than his bitterest enemy ever wished or thought him."[18]

[17] Greensboro *Patriot*, May 18, 1871; Tourgée to Guilford bar, August 16, 1870, Tourgée Papers.
[18] Tourgée to V. C. Barringer, February 7, 1871, Tourgée Papers. A Conservative rejoiced that Holden's policy had "more effectually broken up radical rule in N.C. than anything the wisdom of the Conservative party could have devised" (J. K. Ruffin to W. K. Ruffin, August 23, 1870, Hamilton [ed.], *Thomas Ruffin*, IV, 232–33).

Despite Tourgée's continued militancy, Conservatives fared unusually well in his courts during the remainder of the year. Considering a good part of the recent militia movement illegal and indictable, Judge Tourgée was prepared so to charge the grand juries, and a desire to avoid doing so had contributed to his earlier efforts to leave the state. Conservatives were soon pleasantly astonished to find the Judge approving indictments against Kirk and his militiamen and only blocking proceedings against Governor Holden because of certain technical errors. As Conservatives made these gains, the Republicans lost ground in several Ku Klux cases. The men held for Stephens' murder were released upon the recommendation of the Republican solicitor, and although this gentleman had a reputation for timidity, the lack of evidence left him little choice. Developments in Alamance were more disappointing. The guilt of at least one Klansman in that county had apparently been established, but these cases were dropped, a step attributed to the weakness of the solicitor and the failure of Governor Holden to provide needed encouragement and assistance. But Judge Tourgée may not have been as forceful as was often his wont, and some Republicans accused both Tourgée and the solicitor of having sold out to the Klan.[19] Tourgée would toil diligently in the future to prove that this was not true.

[19] —— [Many Persons?] to Tourgée, n.d., Tourgée Papers.

XIV

Portrait of a Carpetbagger

There was one house, standing far back from the street, its yard thickly shaded by elms and oaks, which was . . . a place of mystery, for here there lived that one-eyed scoundrel, that old carpetbagger, Judge Tourgée, . . . justly considered by all good people to be a veritable monster." So reminisced one North Carolinian about his youth in Greensboro,[1] and a playmate of O. Henry would recall:

> As to Judge Tourgée, we looked upon him as some sort of a pirate, mysterious and blackened by a thousand crimes, and we glanced at him covertly when he happened around. He was sort of an ogre, but even then we admired him for his courage and wondered at it, coming as he did from the North. Very dark stories were whispered of his doings out in far-off Warnersville, the negro settlement out by the Methodist graveyard. He held meetings out there that we were almost prepared to say were a species of voodooism.

As the Republicans waged a losing struggle to maintain their place in North Carolina after 1870, carpetbaggers were increasingly treated, by allies as well as foes, as a liability. Like Negroes, they were both a propaganda burden and a convenient scapegoat for the ills of Reconstruction. Doubly infuriating to Tourgée was the growing acceptance of the carpetbagger stereotype in the North, and by 1870 carpetbaggers

---

[1] Rufus W. Weaver, quoted in C. Alphonso Smith, *O. Henry Biography* (New York, 1916), 66. The following quotation is by Thomas H. Tate, in *ibid.*, 67.

had largely lost their influence and disappeared as officeholders in North Carolina. Little heed had been paid to the admonitions of one native white Republican that "we must keep together, scallawags, carpetbaggers & niggers. This is our safety—this is the hope of the South." [2]

Sometimes the belligerent Judge Tourgée found insult where none was meant, though more often there was abundant cause for his complaints. He waged a persistent campaign in defense of immigrants that ranged historically from Jesus of Nazareth to Jefferson Davis, and his home remained a center of Republican gatherings and discussions. The Judge also joined some Yankee friends in establishing a mock fraternal organization, the O.I.C.B. (Order of International Carpetbaggers?), which sought to explain and laugh away opprobrium with a newspaper printed on Independence Day, 1870. The order's symbol was an American eagle on the wing with a carpetbag in its beak, and the following poem, credited to A. Satchel, appeared:

> Let us have peace we cry to all,
> Union forever, freedom to all,
> Freedom of thought, freedom of speech
> Freedom for all men and for each—
> A Carpetbag

Trite humor provided needed relief, but even more helpful in easing Tourgée's existence were his continued achievements. The favorable impact of his code and judicial work has been noted, and although Chief Justice Pearson delighted in minor, stinging criticisms of the young Judge during his first year on the bench, Tourgée's judicial conduct continued to win respect. His ability and determination, combined with a predilection for secluded study, did keep Tourgée closer to wisdom than most, an indication of which were his three published volumes on North Carolina law (an "exceedingly valuable contribution to the legal literature of the state" [3]) and his articles on local legal history. On the bench the Judge displayed confidence, comprehension,

[2] Barringer to Tourgée, n.d., Tourgée Papers.
[3] Frank Nash, quoted in Ethel Stephens Arnett, *Greensboro, North Carolina, the County Seat of Guilford* (Chapel Hill, 1955), 269.

and tact. Though vexed by frequent racial injustice (he fined attorneys for addressing witnesses as "nigger"), he was quick to compliment the absence of prejudice, and he handled a variety of minor court incidents with attractive humor. In response to a violent fight in court between two attorneys, for example, the Judge levied huge fines while declaring that they would be suspended if the antagonists made up. A rapid reconciliation followed.

The Judge's persuasiveness was illustrated in 1873, when he exchanged courts with another judge and arrived in the new district with a reputation based almost solely upon the political slanders of past years. Received with stares, suspicion, and distrust, he tactfully surmounted several deliberate tests to win not only acknowledgment and praise but festive honors. Seldom had a stranger made a more favorable impression, confessed the opposition press, and to Emma the Judge boasted, "Everybody is praising me so that I am getting to blush by habit." In the words of one Conservative, Tourgée had presided "with becoming dignity, commendable firmness and acknowledged impartiality, and with marked courtesy to the Bar. If it is treason to say this of a political adversary it is treason to speak the truth." [4]

An indication of Tourgée's ability is afforded also by the record of cases appealed from his court to the state Supreme Court. Despite the complex legal impact of emancipation and radical legal, social, and political changes, there was little increase in the number of cases being appealed from the courts of Republican judges, and the young and inexperienced Judge Tourgée maintained a smaller than average number of such cases. It is true that a higher than average percentage of Tourgée's appealed cases were reversed (the total number remained comparatively small), but these cases reveal challenging controversy rather than inability. Judge Tourgée was prone to become involved in controversy both as a representative of the code commission and in consequence of his democratic sympathies, and he perpetuated certain disputes by making rulings that challenged or limited previous decisions from the higher bench. In complicated property, will, criminal, and constitutional matters, the higher court often chose a different but not

[4] Clipping, Goldsboro *Messenger*, n.d., Tourgée Papers. See also M. London to T. Settle, January 15, 1873, Settle Papers; Tourgée to his wife, January 12, 1873, Tourgée Papers.

necessarily wiser path than did Tourgée, who was at times supported
by a Supreme Court minority.[5]

There is no trace of objectionable influence on Tourgée's administration of justice, except insofar as Republicanism was reflected in his
insisting upon equal treatment for Negroes or securing heating systems
for the jails in his district (he had been thoroughly informed in 1867
of the discomforts of winter imprisonment by the imprisoned unionist
William S. Johnson). In only one decision favorable to Republicans was
Tourgée reversed by the higher court, but this case involved a debatable
constitutional question and had mixed political implications. Tourgée
also collided with Conservatives when he attempted to compel the
state to pay an admitted debt, but his earlier decisions upholding debts
contracted during the Confederacy indicate that the Judge was being
primarily guided by free-enterprise principles. The cases which might
arouse suspicion, however, were four decisions favorable to George W.
Swepson, all later overturned by the higher court. Although the notorious
Swepson was behind the loan to Tourgée of thirty-five hundred dollars
in 1869, there is no indication in the cases themselves of wrongdoing
or connivance, and the only evident contact between the two men
involved Swepson's request for a thirty-day delay of his trial as "a
matter of justice," which was granted, and an instance in which
Tourgée parried a request from Swepson for a secret meeting. Furthermore, Swepson was a Conservative who did not extend Tourgée a desired
business loan in 1871 and who displayed a subsequent hostility toward
him hardly suggestive of any past indebtedness. One might note, too,
that Judge Tourgée handed down a similarly favorable decision to an
intense opponent, William A. Graham, which was also reversed by the
higher court.[6]

The net result of Tourgée's behavior upon the bench was to secure
for him, especially in areas where he sat as judge, a reputation for
ability, impartiality, and the rapid dispatch of business. A number of

[5] See *North Carolina Reports,* LXIII (1868–69)–LXXX (1879). Cf. Kenneth E.
St. Clair, "The Administration of Justice in North Carolina" (unpublished Ph.D.
dissertation, Ohio State University, 1939), 210–14.

[6] See especially *University* v. *McIver,* 72 N.C. 76; *Shaffer* v. *Jenkins,* 72 N.C. 250;
Smitherman v. *Sanders,* 65 N.C. 447. See also Swepson to Tourgée, December 31,
1870, June 3, 1872, and Tourgée to Swepson, January 2, 1871, Tourgée Papers;
Swepson v. *Harvey,* 66 N.C. 436; *Swepson* v. *Harvey,* 69 N.C. 387; *Railroad* v.
Swepson, 71 N.C. 350; *Swepson & McAdoo* v. *Rouse,* 65 N.C. 34.

prominent lawyers who had been his political opponents concluded that
Tourgée "was the ablest judge that they had ever practiced under" and
one of the best the state ever had; generations later, a retired chief
justice of the Supreme Court of North Carolina applauded Judge Tourgée's legal wisdom and the rare breadth and depth of his decisions.[7]

Tourgée also engaged in a multitude of activities outside the realm
of law, and his accomplishments contributed to the political tolerance
that prevailed in Greensboro. He was an active trustee of the faltering
state university, and when he spoke at a meeting to promote education
in Guilford County, his efforts elicited praise from both political
parties and from "nearly all of the prominent citizens of the county."
Tourgée was an active member of the northern Methodist Episcopal
church, a church often disliked in the South, and he gratuitously
handled legal work for this church and helped it found a short-lived
seminary for whites at High Point and a Negro school (at which
Tourgée reputedly taught) that later became Bennett College for
Negro Women. Despite his disputes with local attorneys, the Judge
became a leader of the Greensboro bar association, and in 1873 he was
elected Master of the Greensboro Masonic Lodge. A year earlier, the
Judge had led in the organization of a needed hook-and-ladder fire-
fighting company for the city, and he was one of the founders, stockholders, and directors of the privately financed North Carolina Railroad,
which sought to build a railroad south from Greensboro.[8]

The varied accomplishments of the Judge encouraged respect and
pleasant relations, but this state of affairs was accomplished only by
mutual efforts and was comfortably established only after Republican
control in the state and county had been brought to an end. It was
similar to the experience of the Fool in Tourgée's noted novel: "There
arose a spirit of mutual forbearance; they forbore to take offense at his
views, and he forbore to express them; they excused his views because
of his Northern birth and education, and he excused their acts because
of their Southern nativity and training; they disregarded his political

[7] Hamilton, *Reconstruction*, 415; Milton *Chronicle*, April 16, 1873; William A.
Devin, "Footprints of a Carpetbagger," *The Torch*, XVII (April, 1944), 16–19, 21.

[8] Raleigh *Standard*, July 27, 1868; Greensboro *Patriot*, June 17, July 8, 31, October
14, 1869, January 18, 1872; property records of 1878, Court House, Greensboro;
Early Winfred Bridges, *Greensboro Lodge No. 76, A.F. and A.M.* (Staunton, Va.,
1951), 81–82, 261.

convictions because a method had been discovered to prevent their crystallizing into results, and he refrained from urging them because to do so was useless travail." [9] Reflecting the mellower mood were numerous friendly press items. One, in 1871, entitled "Ku Kluxed," described how a group of Conservative young men had serenaded the Tourgées' home, after which the youths were welcomed in for supper and entertainment. Nothing, concluded the writer hopefully, can sooner restore harmony "than musical instruments and a good supply of wine."

The Judge found more time for simpler pleasures as Republican political fortunes receded. The Tourgées' social activities increased, their circle of firm friends grew ever larger, and, returning to an earlier love, the Judge indulged more in the natural beauties of his home state— roaming the alternating hills and bottoms, woods and fields, rivers and streams of the piedmont; delighting in the colorful scented spring blossoms or vivid autumn foliage; and often seeking the excitement of the hunt or the pleasures of rod and reel. Sometimes his outings were a part of large community projects, such as the celebrated piedmont deer hunts, but more frequently they were family affairs. Despite increased pleasantries, the Tourgées remained outsiders, firmly knit together by years of danger, insult, and ostracism, which periodically reappeared. A new member had joined the family late in 1870, a daughter, christened Lodolska after her mother but soon called, more pleasantly, Aimée, and a closeness between the Judge and his daughter was increased by a longing for more children that was never to be fulfilled. Seldom was the Judge happier than when on an outing, on horseback or foot, with his wife and daughter, enjoying their companionship and the beauties and thrills of nature; but too often there were other things to be done.

Heavily bearded, stouter but still handsome, the Judge was the picture of health, although he remained seriously troubled by his injured spine. He sat at his desk or judicial post in frequent pain, was unable to exert himself physically, and suffered occasional attacks of prostration and paralysis. Fittingly, even his physical difficulty succeeded in arousing comment, when, in an effort to ease his back in court, the Judge introduced one of the newfangled spring and swivel chairs to the state. A lesser problem was his social shyness, and at one social event, the

[9] *A Fool's Errand*, 304.

Judge erred at the table, dropped a glass of water, sat on the back-gammon board, and finally, while endeavoring to recapture respect, unwittingly embarrassed the ladies with a word that had an offensive meaning in the local idiom.

Tourgée was also intriguingly involved in economic matters during these years, being enticed by thoughts both of profits and of the social benefits that would accompany southern economic development. Together with a group of Negroes and whites, he participated in the formation of the Guilford County Co-operative Business Company, which "without distinction of party" sought to assist mechanics and laborers "in procuring a home at a much more reasonable price than they now pay" and "incidentally, to foster the manufacturing establishments among us, and other material interests." [10] The results of this venture, to be capitalized at one hundred thousand dollars in ten-dollar shares, are unknown. Perhaps more significant were Tourgée's various articles encouraging the development of what he called "our wonderful manufacturing facilities." Pointing to advantages in climate, raw materials, and convenient waterways, the Judge advised that increased industrial activity would support a growing population, provide needed markets for agriculture, and improve the prosperity and intelligence of North Carolinians. Such manufacturing must be promoted, he warned, or the state would "grow poorer and poorer as the years elapse by supplying medium crops of raw materials to the busy hands and more enterprising brains of our sister states." [11] Tourgée suggested that bonuses, special privileges, and other inducements be offered to attract investment, an approach then being extensively utilized in northern states and which would become popular in the South a century later.

Anxious to play a more direct part in economic growth and impressed with the rate of profit that he encountered in a court case, Judge Tourgée himself launched a wood-turning industry early in 1871. Prepared to invest all his own funds in this project, he did not encounter similar enthusiasm elsewhere. An attempted loan from George W. Swepson was curtailed by Swepson's demand for twenty-four per cent interest; an appeal for local investment was adversely affected by "the political aspect of affairs"; and a requested loan from the Freedmen's

[10] Greensboro *Patriot*, September 30, 1869.
[11] Clipping, Tourgée Papers.

The North Carolina Code Commission (1868), which prepared the state's new code and much of its legislation: William B. Rodman, Victor C. Barringer, and Tourgée. Tourgée Papers, Westfield, New York.

"Carpet-Bag Lodge," located in Greensboro near the corner of Ashboro and Douglas Streets, in the 1870's. The balcony and most of the porch were added by Tourgée, and recently some of the oaks that he loved were still standing. Tourgée Papers, Westfield, New York.

A Split among the Truly Loyal Radicals!

Carpet-Bagger *vs.* Scalawag.

RUIN OR RULE! IN SPITE of the MULE.

To Congress.

JUDGE TOURGEE,
On the run, with his chief stock in trade—brass and negro.
" Hold on, little ' manhood,' we'll beat the mu-el man !"

WINDY BILLY
Takes the road indicated by the Radical finger-board,—
saying " I'll ride Darr's mule to Congress yet !"

The Greensboro *Patriot* of September 24, 1868, enjoys the intraparty congressional rivalry between William F. Henderson, indicted for mule stealing, and Tourgée. University of North Carolina Library.

Out of Doors
42 Brigade Red Men of Carolina

Dear Sir

This is to inform you to hold no more Courts in Carolina / you have had your day / if you ever hold another or attempt it you will share the fate of Jno W. Stephens / it is ordered you leave the state / we are bent on that / we give you fair warning / now go on and you will get it

by order of the 42 Brig Red Men of Carolina

Letter in the Tourgée Papers, Westfield, New York.

Bank encountered a "peculiar pressure against Southern investments." But the ever-enthusiastic Tourgée plunged ahead with twenty-four hundred dollars of his own money and the assistance of another carpet-bagger, W. H. Snow, who was already involved in the state's wood-turning industry. Soon Snow traveled north to purchase the necessary machinery, a dozen hands were employed constructing a plant, and the Judge, who had mortgaged all his property, was prepared to go on just "as if I had $20,000 in my hands." "I am just going to trust blindly in my usual luck, and go on until I come out or am stumped entirely." [12] Here was a venture that might help relieve the unfamiliar lull in the Judge's political life.

This shakily launched enterprise merged with a similar company in the fall of 1872 to become the North Carolina Handle Company. Tourgée was president of the company and contributed to the invention of a patented machine for producing wooden handles, and for some time his optimistic predictions were confirmed. The company prospered and expanded, specializing in the manufacture of ax, pick, and similar handles and referring to itself as "King of the handle makers," with the largest handle-turning capacity in the nation. By 1873, over sixty employees were working in the plant, and at one time seventy-four men were employed in cutting timber alone. Owned entirely by North Carolinians and with its market almost entirely in the North, the venture was drawing needed capital into the state, and a New York market of over twenty thousand dollars was hopefully anticipated. The details of the establishment, operation, and final demise of this enterprise were later fascinatingly described by Tourgée in the short story "Mamelon."

The initial success of the North Carolina Handle Company, together with the Judge's exuberance, encouraged dangerous expansion, and despite its early success, the company remained in a precarious financial state in the depression year of 1873. As a shortage of capital was felt because of the shrinking markets of that year, the firm began offering liberal discounts for advance payments, but with little success. The remaining customers were then antagonized when the desperate com-

[12] Tourgée to S. S. Ashley, February 22, 26, 1871, Tourgée Papers. See also two letter books of the North Carolina Handle Company, Tourgée Papers; Greensboro *Patriot*, March 16, 1871, November 20, 1872, January 15, 22, 1873.

pany drew advance drafts on expected orders without authorization, and when these drafts were not honored, the company's credit suffered. Several misfortunes intensified the squeeze. In March a broken steam-pipe closed the plant for two weeks, in May an expensive lathe was smashed, and shortly thereafter a fire destroyed over five hundred dollars' worth of property. The final blow was a rise in timber prices and railroad rates, although Tourgée's eloquent pleas for transportation rates that would enable the South to compete with northern rivals did induce the railroad to cut by one half its initial fifty per cent boost. Still, the company was in no condition to survive the major panic that hit in September, a panic that was the final blow to Tourgée's industrial dream, just as it was to the cherished railroad projects of the North Carolina Republican party. The Judge was caught "with rapidly maturing liabilities amounting to $30,000—and only bad debts and a big lot of unsaleable stock to meet it with." The company's operations sputtered like a dying hickory ember until early in 1874, when it was sold at auction, and Tourgée emerged "through it after a fashion, but *terribly shrunk.*" He had lost most of his property and savings but was sufficiently gratified at finding anything left to declare that he was glad he had not held "money and let it rust and canker but so used it that others received good from it though I have lost. I can sit by my window and see scores of snug homes that would never have been built but for the steady work and good wages which their owners derived from my enterprise." [13] And these jobs returned, for although Tourgée's connection with it was ended, wood-turning revived as an important local industry.

A new mellowness, tact, and compassion assisted Tourgée's adaptation to the partial defeat of Reconstruction. The Greensboro *Patriot* could say of Tourgée's Emancipation Day speech to the Negroes in 1872 that he gave "a very impressive talk and some excellent advice" and that it was "spoken of highly by everyone we have heard from on the subject." The Judge also captured Conservative compliments with several Decoration Day speeches during the 1870's, as well as by his lengthy sentimental poem on the Civil War, which was first read by the Conservative leader John Gilmer at the conclusion of his own memorial address in 1873. It was a somewhat different Tourgée who

[13] Tourgée to Martin B. Anderson, n.d., Tourgée Papers.

could ask that the scars of war be "so far as possible hidden and forgotten," that the bonds of union be strengthened by mutual sympathy and understanding, and that blows lately given be remembered with sorrow and those received, with pride. He spoke of reverence for Stonewall, admiration for Stuart, and pride in Lee, and he gracefully honored the men and motives (but never the principles) of the defeated Confederacy. The Yankee judge's views and eloquence could delight political opponents who had been steeped in the same flowery romanticism. "Never did language fall from human lips that excelled in grandeur and sublimity that which this eloquent orator entertained this assemblage of people with," said the Conservative Wilmington *Post* of Tourgée's speech there in 1874, before an estimated five thousand citizens, and his speech in Raleigh the following year was considered a "beautiful and touching discourse."

Everywhere in the 1870's, idealism among Republicans was declining or being curtailed, but the Judge remained too proud to play the sycophant and too sincere to surrender cherished beliefs, and he continued, as best he could, to promote his democratic idealism. He still publicly advocated full civil and political equality for Negroes, but he also showed restraint, as when he discouraged a mass Negro Republican victory celebration to avoid provoking a row, correctly surmising that the Negroes would suffer most from any disturbance. Tourgée also continued his religious and educational work among the recent slave population, and at the first commencement exercises of Bennett Seminary he advised the Negroes "to avail themselves of opportunities now offering to acquire learning, and after acquiring it, to put it to good use by assisting in the further advancement of their race." [14] His attitude toward segregation was flexible and unclear. In many areas, such as education, he accepted it without open objection, but elsewhere, whether from necessity or taste, he promoted integration. His private life was remarkably free of racial barriers, he succeeded in maintaining integrated juries without noticeable opposition, and the integrated baseball games at his handle works may have reflected his efforts. The Tourgée family also educated the two daughters of their light-skinned Negro cook, one of whose daughters later went north to pass as a white person but subsequently returned to Greensboro to become the founder of a

[14] Greensboro *New North State*, May 21, 28, 1875.

refined and prosperous Negro family. The Judge's involvement in this venture impressed him with how the slightest touch of Negro ancestry brought on all the stigma of color prejudice, a consideration that inspired several of his novels.

Judge Tourgée also stirred other currents of reform, such as helping secure the admission of the first female lawyer to the state bar. Tabitha A. Holton, the twenty-three-year-old sister of one of Tourgée's earliest unionist colleagues, had mastered the law while tutoring her brothers, and in 1878 she applied for her state license. A prominent attorney and persistent foe of Tourgée's code reform, William H. Battle, led a determined resistance, which objected to a southern lady's being "permitted to sully her sweetness by breathing the pestiferous air of the court room." The major technical argument against her admission was the use of the male gender in the pertinent legislation of 1854. Pleading the lady's case, Tourgée argued that a mere technicality of language could not halt social evolution, and he was able to utilize as a convincing precedent recent court decisions that had interpreted the term "free white" to include "free black" because of emancipation. A similar and no less remarkable emancipation of women was under way, insisted Tourgée, and he countered chivalrous objection by suggesting that freedom of choice and increased avenues of self-support would lessen feminine poverty, immorality, and vice. Whatever the influence of Judge Tourgée's efforts, even he concluded that it was primarily modesty, charm, and thorough mastery of the law that did win for Miss Holton her admission to the bar.[15]

In a reflection of his years of interest in free Negro workers, Tourgée also exerted reformist pressures in their behalf. Although Republican efforts in behalf of labor had always been minimal and much Republican legislation was sufficiently conservative to be retained for decades, legislation and law under Conservative auspices became ever more favorable to men of wealth or land. The particularly lowly cropper, who lacked independence, funds, or knowledge, faced the burden of initiating legal action in almost any matter of dispute, and the tenant was increasingly becoming subject to similar disadvantages. One very pertinent case was heard before Judge Tourgée, and, suggestive of the total implica-

[15] *Ibid.*, January 10, 24, March 7, 1878; clipping, *Current Thought*, February, 1878, Tourgée Papers.

tions, involved both a Negro and a white cropper. The suit was instituted by a landowner against a third party who had induced these two croppers to break their contract. The significant issue was the validity of an atrocious contract. If at any time the work of the two croppers did not suit the landowner, he had the right to discharge them and appropriate the entire crop to himself, and this could be done "not alone for unfaithfulness to their business, but for what he or any of his family may be pleased to consider disrespectful behavior to him, or to any of his family, in no way connected with their business, the mere flout of a child it may be." Judge Tourgée ruled that the two men could not in any way be bound by such an inequitable agreement, and dismissed the case. He was promptly overruled by a Supreme Court still controlled by justices elected on the Republican ticket of 1868. The fairness of a contract was not within its jurisdiction, declared the higher court, and the law could not permit anyone "to sow discontent between the head of a family and its various members, wife, children, and servants." The cropper was a servant and subject to all the inferiority that this implied. Justices Settle and Reade, however, upheld Tourgée in a vigorous dissent. The contract was an apparent fraud and imposition, stated the two dissenters, whereas the supposed right of recourse to the courts meant little to poor laborers who lacked the ability, money, or time to implement such a right. They feared that a "new *regime*" was being created "worse than slavery," wherein the laborer remained almost as thoroughly dominated and dependent as the slave, while the landowner retained none of the responsibilities and obligations of the past.[16]

It was another strange facet of Reconstruction that the court majority cited as precedent in this case a recent antiunion decision of the Massachusetts Supreme Court, a case also directed against a third party, a union organizer who had induced employees to leave their work. Judge Tourgée later provided an additional ironic touch. While so eager to champion agricultural labor, he proved less social-minded regarding the responsibilities of business. He had refused compensation to a passenger injured while alighting from a moving train, only to be again reversed by the higher court.[17]

[16] *Haskins* v. *Royster,* 70 N.C. 601. See also *Harrison* v. *Ricks,* 71 N.C. 7, and *Varner* v. *Spencer,* 72 N.C. 381.
[17] *Lambeth* v. *N.C.R.R. Co.,* 66 N.C. 495.

Obviously, Judge Tourgée had continued to make his presence felt. He had aroused both lasting enmity and admiration, and, several decades later, Tourgée's obituary notice in one of the state's leading newspapers reflected his confusing impact and continuing heritage remarkably well:

His was a striking personality, and none the less so because of the fact that he was for many years the most thoroughly hated man in North Carolina. The consensus of testimony from these sources shows that he was not a mean man. He was open, bold, determined, fearless and self-reliant. He neither asked nor gave quarter. He never betrayed his party nor sold a friend. He was neither a toady nor a humbug. He had convictions, and with them the courage and the resources with which to proclaim and maintain them. He was clean handed and clean of life. The bitterest foe in the darkest of those dark hours never [?] charged him with participation in the robbery of our people. His supreme effort to make Northerners out of Southerners was well meant, but it was more than a human task. With full knowledge of the dangers attending his mad course, in the face of the dire threats that were daily thrown in his face, consciously aware that there was dynamite under every foot of earth he trod, . . . he displayed the nerve of a martyr in his wild, mistaken attempt to make an Ohio of North Carolina. Calmly, tenaciously and boldly throughout the darkest of those years, he persisted in the advocacy of ideas wholly and offensively obnoxious to our people. Fearlessly and loyally he stood by his party in support of all these policies, which to the Southern mind were wicked and cruel.[18]

[18] Andrew Joyner, Raleigh *News and Observer*, May 28, 1905.

XV

A Tale of Redemption

The Conservative party had captured the North Carolina legislature in 1870, but it was not yet in firm control of the state. Not only did the Republicans retain executive and judicial dominance, but until 1876 they waged a spirited and telling struggle to recapture complete political control. Furthermore, the Republicans actually carried the state on certain issues in 1871, 1872, and 1875, all long after the supposed disastrous effects of their Reconstruction rule.

During these years, the Conservatives, who by 1876 accepted the Democratic party label, continued to denounce Republican extravagance, incapacity, and wickedness, to complain of the state debt, and to cultivate scalawag, carpetbagger, and Negro stereotypes. Undoubtedly more substantial, however, was this party's desire to minimize the political democracy that it feared and the social reform whose costs it resented. In response, the Republicans defended their idealism and reformism and identified their opponents with aristocracy and with the illegal terrorism of the Ku Klux Klan. Political rivalry remained emotional and intense, with Conservatives rigorously pressing the race issue as each election approached, and the Klan occasionally reappeared. Also of assistance to Conservatives was a gerrymandering of the state that enabled them to retain a large legislative majority in 1872 while winning only a minority of the state's popular vote. The Republicans did capture the governorship at that time for an additional four years. New electoral laws also handicapped the generally less literate Republican voters, and whatever the merits of such regulation, it was achieved with a surreptitiousness that reflected one of the most momentous accomplishments of the Reconstruction era—the triumph of the democratic idea. The opponents of Reconstruction now not only vigorously waved the banner of democracy for whites, but they even tacitly endorsed full political privileges for the Negro. White supremacy continued on a somewhat different plane, with Conservatives accepting "Negro equal political privileges" but vowing not to allow the Negro "and his peculiar leaders" to any "longer have *control*." [1] Whatever the reality of the situation, there was thereafter a lack of sophisticated argument against the principle of Negro suffrage. In another century this would tell.

Other developments were of greater immediate assistance to the Republicans, particularly the emergence of stronger Federal measures against the Klan. Congressional investigations verified the existence of Klan terror and violence and prompted Federal legislation and police action, and during the presidential election year of 1872 a great number of suspects were indicted and arrested by Federal authorities. Although these cases were dropped in a gesture of amnesty soon after President Grant's re-election, there was more substance to the matter than political maneuvering. A state of disorder had existed, and it had not been created by Republicans. Although Tourgée and other southern Republicans were not above selfish politics, in this instance they essentially sought to remove violence from the contest and appeared willing to accept their fortunes under a peaceful political process.

Judge Tourgée displayed an unusually persistent, even vengeful, interest in the new campaign against the Klan. Early in 1871 he had traveled to the national capital and urged Federal intervention, and in succeeding weeks he industriously accumulated the names of confessed Klansmen for the senatorial investigating committee. Later he himself was summoned to Washington, but, in accordance with his own advice that the national government should rely primarily upon native southern witnesses, he was never called upon to testify. Happily convinced that the government was finally *"awake"* to the problem, Tourgée returned to North Carolina and quietly launched his own investigation of past atrocities in the now peaceful Seventh Judicial District. The last month of that year brought success.

Shortly before Christmas of 1871, Tourgée wrote an excited letter to his wife from the town of Graham, the county seat of Alamance and

[1] Greensboro *Patriot*, April 6, 1871.

scene of the murder of Wyatt Outlaw two years earlier. "I think the time has come for *moving the waters*," exclaimed the Judge, while cautioning Emma to keep the matter "very quiet." A few days later George F. Bason, a prominent attorney, apprehensively wrote to the grand statesman of the Conservative party, William A. Graham, that "our worst fears are realized." Judge Tourgée had exploited a dispute between two Klansmen to secure certain revelations, soon followed by warrants and arrests. Among the local citizens called upon to assist in making these arrests was James Stockard, a former Klansman and "heretofore considered a staunch, determined man" by his allies. True to this estimate, Stockard had allowed two Klansmen left in his custody to escape, but Tourgée, who had the capacity to dominate, immediately arrested Stockard and "by some means got out of him the information that he was present at the murder of Outlaw, & many other important facts, upon which warrants were sent out all over the country; but by this time the news had spread, & nobody was found." Yet Tourgée could boast that he had "knocked a big hole in the bottom of the bucket." [2] A number of Klansmen had been arrested, two had confessed to participation in the murder of Wyatt Outlaw, and many had fled, including, as Tourgée feared, the major culprits.

The Judge held court at once on these cases. After levying a minor fine of court costs, he freed numerous individuals who confessed to mere Klan membership or minor crimes ("poor, ignorant, misguided men" enticed by "the ambition, lust and cowardice of their leaders," concluded Tourgée). Yet he strenuously sought indictments in a number of more serious cases. The Judge's conduct, complained the worried George Bason, "may have been all proper and right, & strictly within the province of his Honor," but it was certainly akin to intimidation. What was worse, the Judge's tactics were effective. A grand jury that Tourgée believed included "a large majority of members of Ku Klux organizations, including one Chief of a camp" actually "presented bills of indictment [against] sixty-three members of the Klan for felony and eighteen for the murder of Wyatt Outlaw." The jubilant Tourgée

2 Tourgée to his wife, December 13, 16, 18, 1871, Tourgée Papers; Bason to Graham, December 18, 19, 1871, Graham Papers. See also various confessions in the Tourgée Papers and Alamance Superior Court Minutes (1871–72), 94–121, Court House, Graham, N.C.

even wrote President Grant of his success, pointing out that in sixty-four previous cases against the Klan he had failed, but that now, thanks to recent Federal firmness, he had succeeded. Many of those indicted, the Judge noted, were members of the "most respectable families of the county." [3]

Conservatives were understandably upset. Many had joined or sympathized with the Klan, and fearing the legal and political effects of exposure, they reacted swiftly. Within several days they had introduced a bill into the state legislature repealing the law under which most of the Judge's indictments had been secured. In less than three weeks, this bill became law. The sixty-three felony indictments were thus negated, and in the succeeding session of Alamance court, Tourgée's efforts to renew the indictments were successfully resisted. [4]

The murder indictments still remained to worry the Conservatives. In addition, they accurately suspected that Judge Tourgée was uncovering facts concerning the murder of John W. Stephens, and there were rumors that one of the Alamance fugitives was threatening to surrender and confess unless substantial protection was forthcoming. To secure such protection Conservatives flocked to the banner of "amnesty and pardon" so recently raised by Horace Greeley and the Liberal Republicans of the North, and they were greatly aided by a new Federal policy of leniency that dismayed militant southern Republicans. Whether from unconcern, economy-mindedness, or beneficent expectations, Grant's administration had suspended its legal proceedings against the Klan in 1872, and during the following year all Klansmen who had been imprisoned by the Federal government were pardoned. Ostensibly in a similar spirit, North Carolina Conservatives introduced legislation granting a pardon for all crimes theretofore committed in behalf of any secret organization. Only after a lengthy debate, sufficient to ensure that Outlaw's suspected assassins would not come to trial in the spring of 1873, did Conservatives agree to exempt willful murder, arson, and burglary from such amnesty. But this was only a temporary tactical concession. The following year even these exemptions were removed, and an unrestricted pardon was extended to all past crimes by Klansmen.

[3] Tourgée to President Grant, December 28, 1871, Tourgée Papers.
[4] For documentation of this and the succeeding amnesty affair, see Olsen, "The Ku Klux Klan," *NCHR*, XXXIX (1962), 361–62.

Although several moderates defended the amnesty program as a magnanimous effort to restore peace and good will, Republicans were justly cynical. The extension of amnesty to Republican leaguers was considered a hypocritical blind, and Republican efforts to remove their own organizations from the act were repeatedly defeated by Conservatives, who had no desire to clarify the real intent of the act. Judge Tourgée, as usual, had become publicly involved in the controversy, and his bitterness was contrasted with the very spirit of the entire amnesty program. In particular, the Judge was erroneously accused of having recently threatened to give Orange County "hell." This, he responded, would be "carrying coals to Newcastle with a vengeance." The allegation against the Judge inspired a legislative call for an inquiry into his official conduct, with the indignant Judge challenging his foes to get on with it and either convict or clear him.[5] Neither was ever done.

The gesture of amnesty offered the Republicans was indeed hollow, there being no substantial protection, either retroactive or immediate, extended to Republicans. Several of the Negroes jailed for Klan-like crimes by Judge Tourgée lacked the required connection to any secret organization, and although Jayhawkers were covered by the amnesty act, this term applied only to six Negroes who were deprived of protection. They had been sentenced to long prison terms by Judge Tourgée for retaliatory arson against the Klan, and arson was not covered by the original amnesty act. When this crime was later included, it was provided that such pardon did not extend to those already convicted. The amnesty act also specifically exempted all matters connected with Republican railroad projects, and the idea of amnesty for the unjustly impeached Holden was openly mocked. Well might Tourgée admonish his sanctimonious opponents that the Bible said to forgive your enemies, but nowhere did it say to forgive your friends.

Objecting to the amnesty program as setting a pernicious precedent, North Carolina Republicans sought to settle for a lesser defeat by discouraging the further prosecution of the Alamance murder cases, and they applauded when a nolle prosequi with leave was entered before the disappointed Judge Tourgée early in 1874. This was the end of his pursuit of the Klan. Meanwhile he had turned the amnesty act to one

[5] Raleigh *Sentinel*, January 28, 1873; clipping, Tourgée to the Raleigh *Era*, February 28, 1873, Tourgée Papers.

Republican's advantage by dismissing an indictment against ex-Governor Holden, one that had arisen out of the Kirk-Holden war. "The one-eyed cyclopean," objected the *Sentinel* angrily, after "arguing the case himself ordered the indictment to be quashed, and hiding his head and face below the bench, laughed like a negro in old times when he had done a mean trick that pleased a mean master." [6]

Just two years earlier the Judge's reputation had been on the rise, but his campaign against the Klan, along with his continued political activity, had thoroughly revived the familiar mockery, ridicule, and denunciation. Helping to stimulate this increased involvement in politics, and also in private business ventures, was the insecurity of Tourgée's judicial post. According to a controversial clause in the constitution (the one inserted by the Judge himself), the terms of the first group of judges elected were to be extended for an extra two years. Tourgée's term was thus scheduled to expire in 1874, but because of Conservative hostility and the ease with which the similar provision respecting the legislature had been negated, Tourgée erroneously expected an earlier end to his judgeship. Therefore he was inclined to promote his political interests.

The most substantial party issue of these years was perhaps the continued Conservative criticism of the constitution of 1868, criticism that centered upon two constitutional items that Tourgée had been particularly responsible for and was anxious to retain—the new systems of law and of local self-government. The objections to the former have been discussed earlier, and Conservatives were anxious to restore legislative control over local government because of continued Republican success in certain counties, especially in those with large Negro populations. Conservatives desired the complete elimination of any possibility of subsequent Republican victory. Because of the popularity of the constitution of 1868, however, they proceeded with caution, and when Conservatives submitted an act calling for a constitutional convention, they attempted to mollify the state and nation by providing that delegates would be pledged not

to touch the homestead and personal property exemption clauses, to deprive colored persons of their rights, to compen-

[6] Clipping, n.d., Tourgée Papers.

sate former owners of slaves, to recognize the war debt, to restore corporal punishment, to abolish the public schools, to require an educational or property qualification for voting, to change the ratio between the poll and property taxes, to pass any ordinance of a legislative nature, except for a settlement of the public debt, to change in any way the mechanics' and laborers' lien, and the clauses declaring that there was no right of secession and that the paramount allegiance of every citizen is due the United States.[7]

This was both an answer to Republican demagoguery and an admission of the popularity of the reforms of 1868. Yet Republicans were justified in their continued suspicions, and the future fate of public schools and Negro equality would prove that Conservatives could willfully subvert what they hesitated directly to oppose. Magnifying suspicion was an extralegal step taken by the Conservative legislators in 1871. Unable to muster the required legislative majority to call a convention, they had submitted the entire question to a popular referendum.

Tourgée rushed to defend the Republican reforms. In an anonymous newspaper article he accused Conservatives of desiring to restore upper-class political control and predicted that their victory would serve to perpetuate in North Carolina the highest illiteracy and lowest wages in the nation, and thus also to discourage future industrial development. Privately the Judge feared that the outlook was bleak, especially because of weakness and division within his own party. Convinced that the referendum bill was unconstitutional, he was disgruntled by the state Supreme Court's refusal to intervene in the matter, and he feared that the Republican governor, Tod R. Caldwell, would "from fear of impeachment . . . perform the duties allotted to him in the bill." [8]

To his great delight, Tourgée found that he had underestimated Governor Caldwell, who flatly refused to implement the questionable referendum bill. But the issue was not to be settled so simply. Conservatives merely by-passed the governor by preparing a new bill (again

[7] Hamilton, *Reconstruction*, 564.
[8] Tourgée to J. C. Abbott, February 10, 1871, Tourgée Papers. See also speech manuscripts and Tourgée to Nichols & Gorman, February 8, 1871, Tourgée Papers.

without the constitutionally prescribed majority) that ordered the county sheriffs to conduct the election. The pessimistic Tourgée desired to boycott this election and fight the issue through the courts, and although he was convinced of the illegality of the legislative acts, his proposal was one that could well have resulted in the collapse of the Republican party and many of its reforms in 1871. Instead the Republicans fought at the polls, with Tourgée playing an active part but hoping to minimize his role because of the sensitivity of his judicial position. Republicans were aided by the popularity of the constitution, the questionable legislative procedures of the Conservatives, and fears of provoking Federal intervention, and the proposed convention was soundly defeated by a vote of 95,252 to 86,007. Of course, this was only a partial victory, for the Conservatives had obtained a majority of 10,000 votes and two delegates in the vote for convention members.

Encouraged by the election results of 1871, as well as by Federal activities against the Klan, Tourgée's own crusade was intensified. He wrote several anonymous newspaper sketches mocking Conservatives and the Klan, delivered several speeches within and without the state on the subject of the Civil War and Reconstruction, and was again considered as a congressional candidate. His speeches in the North during the summer of 1872 displayed a somewhat different spirit than his conciliatory addresses at home, and certain references to Confederate atrocities prompted a publicized exchange of insults with the recent war governor of North Carolina, Zebulon B. Vance. But Tourgée's main message to his northern audience concerned the significance of Republican defeat in the South. As Conservatives regained control, he predicted, they would by devious means soon deprive the poor, especially the Negroes, of the franchise: "The South will then be a unit. Every State District and County will be under the control of the same party and spirit that sustained slavery, brought on the war, supported the Rebellion, opposed Reconstruction and constituted the Ku Klux. The Democratic party of the North will be dominated and controlled by their voice and vote and the old slavocracy will rule again with a rod of iron. . . ." [9]

Meanwhile, following their defeat at the polls the Conservatives, with some Republican cooperation, resorted to the slower legislative

[9] Speech manuscript, July 18, 1872, Tourgée Papers.

method of constitutional amendment. A number of constitutional revisions were passed by the legislature of 1871–1872 but had yet to secure a second such passage in the succeeding legislature. In 1872 the Republicans carried a majority of the state's electorate, and despite gerrymandering, they sufficiently increased their representation to block these amendments. They proved willing, however, to accept some minor constitutional changes, and with bipartisan support eight amendments were approved and subsequently ratified by popular vote. None of these amendments significantly altered the political structure created by the Republicans, and consequently Conservatives were not about to abandon their attacks on the constitution.

In 1874 Judge Tourgée lost both his judgeship and his handle-making business and launched a serious quest for new office. Fortunately, he was in unusually good health at this time, a condition in part attributable to an operation the previous year that replaced his long-defective eye with a glass one. As the Judge undertook his pursuit with renewed vigor and need, the choicest political plum available was one he had long desired—a congressional seat. While denying, with calculated modesty, that he was an aspirant for this post, Tourgée made his readiness to serve quite clear. Nor was it mere disinterest that induced him to advise his party solemnly that it should select "the strongest candidate the party can put forward, without any regard to any personal preference or minor consideration whatever," since everyone admitted that he was "the only man who [had] a ghost of a chance to carry the Dist." But this hope was apparently rather thin. "I believe I can carry the Dist.," Tourgée noted, "but I *honestly think* I am the *only one* who does believe it." [10] Defeatism among his allies, together with Tourgée's northern origin and reputation for radicalism, were serious handicaps, but the highest hurdle was another candidate, William F. Henderson, Tourgée's opponent in the same contest six years earlier. To the discomfort of moderates, Henderson secured the nomination. Republicans were forced to swallow their own six-year-old depictions of Henderson's lack of education and ability and his antagonism toward the upper classes, and their hitherto successful appeals to moderates were seriously undermined.

[10] Printed circular, Tourgée to T. M. Owen, May 16, 1874, Tourgée to T. B. Keogh, May 25, 1874, and Tourgée to M. B. Anderson, May 11, 1874, Tourgée Papers.

Once again defeated in his congressional aspirations, Tourgée sought to renew his judgeship. He was considered the ablest and strongest Republican candidate for that position, although many doubted the chances of any carpetbagger. More important, the Conservatives had already nominated John Kerr, an extremist of questionable competence, and the Republicans maneuvered to find a compromise candidate among the moderate Conservatives who opposed Kerr. Reluctantly acquiescing to this strategy, Tourgée offered to withdraw if either Thomas Ruffin, Jr., a talented lawyer and son of an eminent statesman and jurist, or the Quaker Nereus Mendenhall would run. Accepting this bid, Ruffin sought the votes of members of both parties who were "desirous of having the law administered without the suspicion of partisanship." Republicans were overjoyed, considering Ruffin "the most prominent man in a large connexion" and his candidacy "a genuine *tremblement de la terre* in N.C." [11] In the approaching election, the contrast between Henderson and Ruffin would enable Republicans to test the comparative advantages of appealing to radicalism or moderation. As for the already twice-frustrated Tourgée, he made a bid for a Federal appointment, but as one of his cronies pointed out, he lacked the proper political character to secure an office through party machinery. Only one thing was left; the title Tourgée had earned on the bench stayed with him. He had always gloried in a title, and there was something mellifluous and fitting about the sound of "Judge Tourgée," even when pronounced with the hard g or long e, as was so popular among his foes.

Conservatives revived the effective race issue during the campaigning of 1874, while Republicans were further bewildered by the clash between principles and pragmatism. An idealistic Republican minority sought fuller Negro equality, while the party inclined to temporize on the touchy issue. Thus a Republican newspaper denounced recent legislative agitation for more equality, and when a Negro convention in the state advocated racial equality in public accommodations, Republicans feared to endorse it.[12] North Carolina Republicans also reacted against the Federal civil rights bill being considered in Congress. They had ex-

[11] Ruffin statement, Greensboro *North State*, July 15, 1874; S. F. Phillips to Tourgée, June 27, 1874, Tourgée Papers.
[12] New Berne *Republic-Courier*, November 29, 1873; Raleigh *Republican*, quoted in Greensboro *Patriot*, July 1, 1874.

perienced more than enough of the inability or unwillingness of the national government to implement its idealistic policies, and the views of the practical reformer Tourgée were indeed harsh:

> The bill—with all respect to its author, is just like a blister-plaster put on a dozing man whom it is desirable to sooth to sleep. The most important thing in the world is to let the South forget the Negro for a bit—let him acquire property, stability, & self-respect; let as many as possible be educated; in short let the race itself get used to freedom, self-dependence, and proper self assertion, and then let this bill come little by little if necessary. Of course, if it becomes law, it will be constantly avoided. No man can frame a statute which some other cannot avoid. For all its beneficent purposes it will be a dead letter. For its evil influences it will be vivid and active. It will be like the firebrands between the tails of Samson's foxes. It is just pure folly and results from what I have long claimed, that the people of the North and our Legislators, will not study the people of the South reasonably. . . . If we get this fool's notion imposed on us, good-bye schools in the South. It simply delays—puts back —the thorough and complete rehabilitation of the South ten or twenty years.[13]

When this bill passed the Senate, North Carolina Republicans responded with denunciations and a legislative resolution endorsing civil and political equality but opposing any social equality or "inter-mixing of the races, in the schools, churches or elsewhere." The southerner and Republican judge Robert P. Dick soon delivered a decision on this question that helped establish the long-lasting judicial doctrine of "separate but equal." [14]

Despite such Republican maneuvers, the race issue told heavily and "more than anything else, broke the last hold of the Republican party upon the State." [15] Moreover, Republicans suffered from a lack of leadership, funds, and newspapers, and their ostracism in the East

[13] Tourgée to M. B. Anderson, May 11, 1874, Tourgée Papers.
[14] Greensboro *Patriot*, April 7, 1875.
[15] Hamilton, *Reconstruction*, 599.

provoked one Republican to equate his party with the free-soilers in the ante-bellum South. Conservatives swept the state. Illustrative of the Republican dilemma, their only elected Congressman was a Negro, John A. Hyman. In Tourgée's area the Republicans retained some strength, electing legislators in four counties, but the congressional and judicial posts were lost. The adverse effect of Henderson's nomination may well have been decisive, for he was defeated by 1,260 votes, while Ruffin lost the judgeship by a mere 352 votes. Republicans may have committed one of their greatest blunders in not having chosen the able and respected Tourgée for the congressional race that year.

Conservatives announced their victory with an illustration of Miss Liberty, captioned "Sic Semper! White Supremacy," and the future was predicted in a prominently displayed letter from a "Democrat-Conservative." We assure the Negro equality before the law, it stated, but we also assure that we will strike down the Republican party forever "and proclaim to the world that the race of men, God saw fit to enslave for a time *never were*, and *never can be* our equals. . . ." [16]

[16] Greensboro *Patriot*, August 12, 1874.

XVI

Tourgée and
the Settlement of 1875

Although constitutional revision had not been made an issue in the elections of 1874 and many legislators had been instructed against a convention movement, the victorious Conservatives renewed their attack upon the constitution of 1868. Overcoming apprehensive recollections of the rebuke of 1871, they passed a new convention bill, this time with the required legislative majority. Republican suggestions that the entire question again be submitted to the electorate were soundly crushed, but delegates were pledged, once again, not to tamper with certain constitutional provisions.

Guilford County was entitled to two delegates in the new constitutional convention, and it was reflective of popular suspicions that Conservatives there nominated two moderates, John A. Gilmer and Nereus Mendenhall, the latter a Quaker-Unionist. With no remunerative office at stake, Republicans proved less reluctant to assume the burdens of a carpetbagger's candidacy and nominated Judge Tourgée, together with their state senator, A. S. Holton, a self-educated yeoman. Tourgée's popularity obviously concerned the *Patriot*, which warned against his talent, perception, and cunning. He was especially aided in this instance by his identification with the still-favored reforms of 1868, and he continued to command unusual enthusiasm among the Negroes, and understandably so. At the recent Raleigh Memorial Day celebration, while white Union and Confederate veterans had marched arm-in-arm, contingents of Negro firemen had not been invited for the first time

195

since 1868, but it was Tourgée who still spoke out, in the main oration, as a persisting champion of equal rights.[1]

During the convention campaign Conservatives were divided and worried enough to avoid specific proposals on the state level and to rely heavily upon general denunciations of the constitution as a product of militarism, ignorant Negroes, carpetbaggers, "sciolists and adventurers." William A. Graham conveniently suggested that "a constitution with such an origin and such features" required justification rather than criticism, and the state executive committee of the Democratic party apologized evasively that "limited space" did not permit it "to catalogue the numerous defects and imperfections of our present constitution or to enumerate the remedies to be offered." [2] Locally, Democrats were less restrained, but also inconsistent. Their several liberal suggestions in Guilford had actually been endorsed by, or had originated with, the Republicans and were not supported by the state Democratic party. More ominous were certain political desires of the Redeemers, especially their interest in legislative control of local government. Ignored in the west, this idea was popular in the east as a means of restoring Democratic control over ten counties still dominated by Negro Republican voters. So again the familiar theme of white supremacy was in the forefront, and it was additionally exploited by demands for constitutional segregation in schools, marriage, and other matters. "The issue is now well defined," stated the Raleigh *Sentinel*. "It is *Negro* vs White Man." [3]

There was reason enough for Tourgée to consider the gains of 1868 endangered, and, determined to preserve them, he labored mightily with voice and mind and pen to contribute to the campaign of 1875. Republicans were not above endorsing some constitutional reform but advised that desirable changes could be effected with less risk and expense through the legislative amending process. While a few Republicans actually had hopes of capturing the convention, most candidates joined Tourgée in a pledge to vote for immediate adjournment, a chal-

[1] Clipping, *Elevator*, n.d., Tourgée Papers.
[2] Democratic party address, Greensboro *Patriot*, June 9, 1875; Graham to Conservative senators, December 15, 1874, Graham Papers.
[3] Raleigh *Sentinel*, July 26, 1875, quoted in William Durham Harris, "The Movement for Constitutional Change in North Carolina, 1868–1876" (unpublished Master's dissertation, University of North Carolina, 1932), 51–52.

lenge intended to encourage a popular verdict on the convention itself.
A less effective contribution by the Judge was another round of dialect
poetry entitled "John Workman's Notions," a rather uninspiring version
of a yeoman's Republican rationale.[4] Tourgée again was subject to
scurrilous attack, as the various past incidents and accusations against
this "wandering political Arab" with "a chronic hankering for position"
were revived and a few new ones were added.

Republicans centered upon a defense of the work of 1868, when,
Tourgée stated, "for the first time [in North Carolina] the rights of the
masses were regarded above the interest of any aristocracy, and manhood regarded as of more value than money." Now the constitution
was being opposed "not because it was unjust to any, but because it
gave privilege, precedence and the power to oppress to none," and it
was indicative, he suggested, that a recent landlord and tenant act
sought "to reduce the poor man to a state of peonage—to make him
absolutely dependent on the landowners—to establish here a slavery
for the poor—whether white or black—worse than was ever known. . . ."
Republicans undoubtedly exaggerated (although Tourgée was correct
when he spoke of a desire to restore the whipping post), but their
accusations did serve to commit Democratic candidates more firmly to
that limiting pledge prescribed by the legislature.[5]

When, in the course of debate, earlier admissions by Tourgée that
Reconstruction was a failure were turned against him, he responded that
it was Federal weakness and inefficiency that he censured, and not
equalitarian principles. Mocking the reactionary blindness and many
past mistakes of the state's educated leadership, above all secession, he
remained a thorough democrat:

> If I were to write my political creed it would be Lincoln's famous
> aphorism. 'A government *of* the people, *by* the people, and *for* the
> people,' including in the term 'people' the entire population of
> the United States. . . . The whole, with the counter-checks of
> variant interests and conflicting views, is far more likely to do

4 Greensboro *North State*, July 16, 1875.
5 Manuscript, n.d., and clipping, n.d., Tourgée Papers; W. A. Graham to D. F.
Caldwell, June 10, 1875, Graham Papers. Said Graham: "We must do as Virginia
does, whip thieves, and turn them loose; and, if the crime is repeatedly committed,
hang them. . . ."

justice and promote the true interests of all, than any part or
class.

That theory, plan or idea, of government which brings the
government most nearly to the people—the whole people—
allows them most directly to control and direct it, does away with
political 'middlemen,' damns privileged classes, and trains the
people most rapidly and effectually in the management of public
affairs for their own good—that theory is the one to which I
give my unfaltering adhesion . . . the very assumption of ex-
clusiveness, or superior right to rule or govern in our land is
repellent to my instincts, my convictions, and my deliberate
belief as to sound policy.[6]

That race demagogy was not overpowering nor Republican persuasion
without effect was proven when Tourgée and his allies polled a slight
majority of the state vote. In Guilford the candidacy of a carpetbagger
had not been fatal; the Republicans there decisively won a state election for the first time since 1868. It appeared that the Republicans
had narrowly captured the convention, and the alarmed *Sentinel* scur-
ried to gather a list of those Republicans who had pledged an immediate
adjournment. But developments in Robeson County, a county of
heavy Negro population and Republican strength, revealed that the
Democrats were not easily to be denied.

On election day, the state chairman of the Democratic party dis-
patched a decisive telegram to four Democratic commissioners of Robeson County—"As you love the State, hold Robeson." [7] The five commissioners of that county, the fifth being a Republican, had appointed
all the registrars and judges of election, and all but one of the registrars
and a majority of the supervisors at each polling place were Democrats.
Even with such Democratic assurances, the total returns in Robeson
still gave the two Republican candidates a slight majority. As these
votes were returned from the local polling places, it was the duty of
the county commissioners to "proceed to add the number of votes
returned. . . ." Instead, without precedent or authority, they accused

[6] Greensboro *North State*, June 18, 1875.
[7] Hamilton, *History of North Carolina*, Vol. III: *North Carolina since 1860*
(Chicago, 1919), 185–86.

the judges of election in four townships of not having deposited the poll books with the register of deeds as required by law, and threw out those returns, to give the two Democratic delegates a majority.[8]

The Robeson action sufficed to shift the convention balance, and Tourgée quickly brought the matter before Supreme Court Justice Thomas Settle. Despite the obvious injustice and illegality of the Robeson commissioners' action, the Court had no more right to interfere with their behavior than they had had to interfere with the local returns, and Settle, a Republican, denied himself jurisdiction. Adding to the irony was Settle's belief that the clever legal complaint of Tourgée and his associates was based upon an unconstitutional law.

When the constitutional convention met a short time later, Justice Settle called it to order and swore in the delegates. Again he overruled Republican objections and accepted the certificates of election held by the Democratic delegates from Robeson as prima-facie evidence of their right to be seated. "No doubt," he noted, "this gives great power to dishonest election officers, but we know no remedy for this, but by the choice of honest men." Republicans could well boast of Settle's principled behavior, although privately, like Tourgée, they might bemoan it. Tourgée's only ultimate satisfaction in the matter occurred several years later, when he participated in another case wherein the state Supreme Court indicated clearly the illegality of the Robeson commissioners' actions. But this had a dismaying touch, since Tourgée had been defending similar illegal activities by Republican commissioners during the election of 1876.

Further court action on the Robeson matter in 1875 was impractical because time was of the essence. But there was still hope within the convention itself, especially when the death of a Democratic delegate, the able William A. Graham, further narrowed the margin. When the convention assembled there were fifty-eight Democrats, fifty-eight Republicans, and three Independents. Two of the last were considered Democrats, but Tourgée had been assured that one of the Independent Democrats would vote with the Republicans on organization. The final decision thus rested with the Independent Republican, Edward Ran-

[8] For the succeeding dispute, see especially *Report of the Select Committee on the Robeson County Contested Election Case* (Convention of 1875); Greensboro *North State*, August 20, September 3, 10, October 1, 1875.

som, who declined offers of the chairmanship from each party. The Democrats did nominate Ransom, however, and supported him with 59 votes, while the Republican candidate received 58 and the two candidates cast their votes elsewhere. Organization was thus blocked until the fourteenth ballot, when Ransom, whom Tourgée had described to Emma as "a fool, who in my opinion wants to be bought up," shattered the Republicans by casting his ballot for himself and becoming a chairman with Democratic proclivities. Tourgée, caucus president and apparent floor leader of his party, was furious, and angry denunciations by him and other Republicans further alienated the chairman. While the Judge considered him a purchased scoundrel, Emma chided her husband for the failure to buy Ransom first. "It seems to me," she concluded, that "the end would have justified the means." [9]

Democrats had finally secured *their* convention, and an election in Orange County to replace the deceased Graham widened their majority to two votes, leaving the discouraged Tourgée to lament that the recent "great Republican victory" had amounted to nothing. The struggle was quickly resumed, however. Tourgée's party could still speak effectively and with the authority of a popular majority, while the Democrats could hardly risk a split in their ranks. The situation minimized convention action, and Republicans continued to push for adjournment or control, centering their hopes upon the Robeson County matter, which was now buried in committee. Tourgée led a series of efforts seeking a hearing and decision on this issue, which the opposition sought to delay. The Democrats obviously intended to avoid endorsing the questionable actions taken in Robeson, while continuing to utilize the two disputed votes. Furthermore, the final decision might well go against them if the Robeson delegation was barred from voting upon its own eligibility.

Not until the sixteenth day of business was the matter returned from committee. The Democratic majority proposed a further investigation

[9] Tourgée to his wife, n.d., September 7, 8, 1875, and Mrs. Tourgée to Tourgée, September 8, 1875, Tourgée Papers. The convention proceedings may be followed in the Raleigh *Sentinel*, the Raleigh *Daily Constitution*, the Greensboro *North State*, and the *Journal of the Constitutional Convention of the State of North Carolina Held in 1875* (Raleigh, 1875), hereafter cited as *Journal*. For the final Robeson uproar, see especially *Journal*, 148–69; Raleigh *Sentinel*, September 28, 30, October 1, 1875; *Daily Constitution*, September 28, 30, 1875.

of the Robeson election, during which the disputed delegates would retain their seats. A Republican minority report, written by Tourgée, charged *"deliberate and intentional fraud"* and demanded an immediate decision. Newly manufactured charges of irregularity offered a further excuse for additional investigation, and after further delay, only eleven days prior to adjournment of the convention, the Democrats moved to return the matter to committee for a complete investigation. Republicans retaliated by insisting that the Robeson seats be declared vacant or that the convention be temporarily adjourned until the facts were decided. Tension mounted as, aided by decisions from the chair, Republican suggestions were by-passed without a vote and Tourgée's efforts to disqualify the Robeson delegates from the pending vote were blocked. When it became apparent that the vote on recommittal would be taken, Republicans fled the hall to prevent a quorum, but Chairman Ransom declared the motion passed. Two desperate, anticlimatic days of wrangling followed, culminating in several hours of angry disorder and confusion provoked by a dispute between Tourgée and the chair. All to no avail.

Some time earlier, hostilities had been briefly submerged in mutual tributes to the deceased William A. Graham, and in another illustration of a familiar Reconstruction dualism, it was "the genuine sensibility, the beautiful language, . . . and the impressive tone . . . of the eulogy of Judge Tourgée" that attracted special admiration.[10] Before long, of course, the Judge was inspiring less favorable judgments, and hopes of lasting harmony and good will were being dispelled by renewed partisan controversy. His prominence in debate has already been indicated, and he was also a member of the key committee on revision and editor of a short-lived newspaper founded to cover the convention, the Raleigh *Daily Constitution*. All together, he was conspicuous enough to win the distinction of being the most objectionable delegate present, and his vigor during the Robeson furor prompted demands for the bodily ouster of this "carpetbagger and negro-worshiper of the first order."

Who was the leader of Republican captious, causeless, obstructive, turbulent, and disorder tactics but Albion W. Tourgée, ex-Judge, ex-federal officer, a man trained in all the infamous arts

[10] Raleigh *Daily News*, September 7, 1875.

of the politics of his party, insensible to shame, bold in his purpose, unscrupulous in his means, insatiable in his rapacity, unmeasured in his ambition, unblushing in his audacity, he it is that has thrust upon the parliamentary usages of North Carolina practices which have found congenial soil in the hot beds of carpetbag legislation elsewhere, but except for a brief period, never took root here. He it is that has made violence take the place of order, has introduced dissension as the substitute for argument, and would substitute the operation of parliamentary law by the introduction of brute force.[11]

Tourgée's denunciations of Ransom prompted an amusing adventure, when the former was informed at dinner one evening that Ransom had threatened to shoot him on sight and was at that moment posted outside the dining room. His past experiences encouraged Tourgée's ready belief in the warning, and as he left the dining room, someone slipped him a revolver. Sauntering out to where Ransom stood, the Judge walked back and forth before the convention chairman and stopped to glare at him awhile. But no attack came, and Tourgée proudly left, convinced that he had cowed an antagonist.

Meanwhile, the convention proceeded with its business, the Republicans contributing to minor alterations of the constitution and to the securing of effective records of the convention's work. They also opposed several changes with some success, and at times they obviously enjoyed their new role as minority critics, especially in urging a rejected economy measure, a reduction in the number of state senators. A more significant controversy arose when the Democrats sought a constitutional provision for segregated schools. The Republicans endorsed school segregation but objected that making this a constitutional matter would multiply the injustices of white supremacy. A Negro delegate moved that "colored children shall have equal advantage with white children in their vicinage, and that all monies raised for school purposes shall be rationally divided between white and colored children of each race within school ages." [12] This was similar to Tourgée's proposal of 1868

[11] Clipping, n.d., Tourgée Papers. See also Salisbury *Watchman*, October 7, 1875, Greensboro *Patriot*, October 6, 1875.
[12] *Journal*, 130.

and was supported by the Republicans but defeated by the Democrats. Schools were meant to be not only separate, but unequal. After their school suggestions were defeated, however, the Republicans sought to prevent future political capital being made of their stand. Only three Republicans voted against a constitutional provision for segregated schools on its final vote. Even Tourgée joined the majority of 113.

A proposed constitutional prohibition of racial intermarriage encouraged Tourgée and a minority bloc of Republicans to exploit a certain suspicious flaw. Pointedly noting that the opposition opposed interracial sexual relations only on a level of equality, Tourgée moved that any illicit sexual intercourse between a white and a Negro should be a misdemeanor.[13] When this suggestion was defeated, on party lines, Tourgée wryly observed that while the constitution forbade interracial intimacy within the holy bonds of marriage, it condoned such contact outside this bond. When Republicans again bowed to political expediency on the final passage of the provision, Tourgée abstained.

Directly related to the race issue was the effort to restore "unlimited" legislative control over local government. Republicans argued in favor of local sovereignty and perceived that the proposed measure threatened poor whites as well as Negroes, but their efforts to preserve local popular elections were defeated. When the Democratic measure passed, Republicans mourned and Democrats praised the transfer of "the control of county governments from the hands of an irresponsible, corrupt, and ignorant mob of untutored barbarians to the Legislature of the State." [14] The Democratic party, with additional aid from stringent voting regulations, which disfranchised poorer whites and Negroes, would soon establish control over all county governments and further undermine the continuation of two-party politics in North Carolina.

Of similar but less significance were Democratic efforts to increase the judicial authority of the legislature. Republicans, understandably suspicious of the "justice" that would be dispensed by a Democratic legislature, defended an independent judiciary, and Tourgée was prominent in an unsuccessful effort to prevent a reduction in the number of judges and to continue their local popular election. Although endorsing some increased legislative control, Tourgée feared and resisted any

[13] *Journal*, 261–65.
[14] Goldsboro *Carolina Messenger*, October 18, 1875.

attempted restoration of the old county court system. His suggested prohibition of such a move was rejected, and the way was indeed left open for a variety of foolish efforts to return in part to the old, outmoded legal methods. Somewhat more technical was the convention's extension of legislative control over the actual jurisdiction of courts, a further infringement of judicial independence and a particular threat to magistrates. The somewhat general constitutional definition of jurisdiction that did remain was largely attributable to Republican efforts.

Throughout these matters the Democrats had maintained a rather solid front, but this unity broke, as it had in 1868, over economic questions. The internal division in 1875 involved the state debt, despite the fact that the Democratic rationale had rested so heavily upon denunciations of Republican fiscal behavior. Actually, Republicans sympathized with, or at least endorsed, the desire to reduce the state's burden of debt, but they were not willing to accept all the odium and shock themselves. A Republican initiated the fiscal furor in the convention by proposing that the payment of any debt be prohibited without the approval of both the legislature and electorate. Most Democrats were ready to utilize such a procedure against the Reconstruction debt but not against other portions of the state's indebtedness. Both parties split on the question of precisely what portion and what proportion of the debt was to be denied.

The finance committee proposed an equitable settlement providing for the payment of thirty-three per cent of most of the debt, five per cent of the disputed Reconstruction special tax railroad bonds, and no accumulated interest. Other Democrats, however, proposed and secured a substitute that prohibited payment, except by popular approval, of any state railroad bonds issued since 1868. They would repudiate the Republican debt while assuming most of the burden, but their desires were defeated by the combined strength of the Republicans and nine Democrats. All other suggestions were also defeated, and the debt question was not decided by the convention. Tourgée, who had been absent while these measures were being considered, had earlier proposed settlement of the question by an impartial outside tribunal. His plan was lost in committee.

As the convention drew to a close, it was clear that the Republicans

had fought with some success. Tourgée had made some additional contributions of his own by helping to preserve a state-supported system
of public education and by obtaining protective provisions for prisoners
leased as convict labor. He failed, however, in an effort to clarify the
presentation of the issues to the voters in the ensuing popular ratification of the convention's work, with the Democrats favoring a more
confusing ballot.[15] His final failure was in his effort to secure amnesty
for the impeached William W. Holden, a reflection of that continuing
Democratic curtailment of the scope of forgiveness. The Goldsboro
Record, in commenting on Tourgée's impressive speech in behalf of
Holden, declared that it "should be inclined to vote, after hearing him,
against any measure he might advocate, even when in favor of it
before." [16]

On its thirty-first day the convention of 1875 adjourned. The Democrats had been forced to minimize their intentions and had suffered
some defeats, and the greater number of constitutional changes were
minor ones supported by both parties and hardly necessitating a convention. More momentous were the various segregation, political, and
judicial measures ratified over Republican protest. Constitutional segregation exalted race prejudice and further degraded and hindered the
Negro. Legislative control of local government served to handicap
poorer whites and Negroes and to debilitate two-party politics, and
before long a Populist-Republican alliance would repeal this change.
The judicial alterations were also questionable. The rotation of judges
served little purpose other than to encourage confusion, cost, and
inefficiency, and eventually it was modified. The reduction in the
number of Supreme and Superior Court judges was unrealistic and
provoked complaints that led eventually to an increase in their number
far beyond that originally established in 1868. One major advantage
of the new judicial system was its flexibility, but negative-minded
legislators would long avoid any profitable utilization of this flexibility.
In the future, several efforts to restore portions of the ante-bellum
legal structure would end in failure, as would experimentation with
the county and circuit courts, and the ill-defined jurisdiction culminated

[15] *Journal*, 131, 140, 145–46, 259–60.
[16] Clipping, n.d., Tourgée Papers.

in somewhat of a hodgepodge.[17] The Redeemers could hardly claim the constitutional distinction achieved seven years earlier by the Republicans, and with some justification Tourgée returned to Greensboro in 1875 pleased only that the outcome had not been worse.

[17] Walter Clark, *Address on Reform in Law and Legal Procedures* . . . *June 30, 1914* (Wilmington, Del., n.d.); Albert Coates, "The Courts of Yesterday, Today and Tomorrow in North Carolina," *Popular Government*, XXIV (March, 1958); *Public Documents*, No. 1 (1881), 17–18, No. 1 (1883), 23–24, No. 21 (1885), No. 1 (1887), 29–30.

XVII

The Final Blows

During these years, Tourgée's problem of earning a livelihood had increased. After his business collapsed and his judgeship terminated, he formed a law partnership with a Greensboro lawyer, George H. Gregory, which did not prosper, a fact that he reluctantly attributed to political hostility. The partners did endeavor to overcome this handicap by establishing a reputation in criminal cases and succeeded in attracting attention by their defense of a Negro woman charged with killing her child. Tourgée's three-and-one-half-hour summation was followed by an acquittal on grounds of insanity, which induced the press to object that the skill of lawyers and the "over generous sympathies of twelve men" had secured a verdict that could "only have the effect of lessening the dread of punishment and encouraging indulgence in vice." [1]

Although few debts would ever be canceled with the remuneration obtained by the defense of impoverished criminals, such hostility was an obvious professional handicap. Tourgée's hopes for the financial success of his first novel, published in 1874, also proved vain, and the Judge was sufficiently reduced in circumstances to become overjoyed at earning a scant eighty-five dollars in legal fees. As for the future, he feared that only God could save his family "from complete wreck—as to estate and prospects." During the convention of 1875 he had sold copies of his novel, *Toinette*, to cover his expenses, while Emma lacked five dollars for necessities and warned her husband against bringing home guests to "spy out the barrenness of the land." In that same year Tourgée sought to exploit his speaking ability by giving lyceum lectures

[1] Greensboro *Patriot*, December 23, 1874.

on southern humor and on interpretations of modern civilization. His preferred talk, "The Ben Adhemite Era," attacked post-Civil War conservatism and identified the nineteenth century with the beginning of the march toward equality and brotherhood for all. Financially more significant was the Judge's attainment of a post as Federal pension agent in Raleigh, a position obtained despite many competitors and much objection to "such an infamous scoundrel" as he. In April, 1876, the Tourgées moved to their new residence and a few months later disposed of their Greensboro home at auction.

Within a short time after settling in Raleigh, Tourgée became involved in the election campaigns of 1876. The Hayes-Tilden presidential contest was itself unusually dramatic, and for North Carolinians a Republican governorship and the constitutional amendments of 1875 were also at stake. Pleading poverty and handicapped by his change of residence to Raleigh, Tourgée avoided a candidacy and pledged to work but not to pay for his party that year. In response to an assessment from the national Republican committee, he flatly refused to send "money to fight elsewhere while [North Carolina had] only about one speaker to fifty Democratic stumpers." "I will see you d - - d first," he vowed, and as for threats against his pension post, "if you think you can get a man to do more for the place I am in, let him have it." [2]

After announcing the purchase of several glass eyes in expectation of having a few shattered, the Judge undertook his usual vigorous stump campaign. It seems that he also wrote his party's state platform in 1876, one that extended beyond traditional commitments to censure Federal mistreatment of the Indian, to pledge completion of a railroad to the western border, and to denounce the recent landlord and tenant act as designed to "reduce the laborer to serfdom and restore to the landowner the autocratic power which Slavery conferred upon the Master."

Still militant, but fearing the permanent collapse of Republican power, Tourgée was prepared to sacrifice principles to expediency. He condemned efforts to revive the Union Leagues and counseled a Negro candidate for presidential elector, James E. O'Hara, to withdraw. O'Hara angrily refused, but Tourgée failed to see how O'Hara could justify a

[2] Tourgée to J. M. Edmunds, October 9, 1876, and Tourgée to R. C. McCormick, October 9, 1876, Tourgée Papers.

policy that might help weaken the Constitution of 1868 and sink Negro rights and Republicanism completely. Do not blame the Republicans, advised Tourgée. "It makes no difference how black or how white you may be you cannot subvert realities. . . . This is not a question of what *ought* to be but of what *is*. . . ." When O'Hara did finally withdraw, the Democrats were free to mock the absence of a Negro on the Republican state ticket.[3]

Not being a candidate, Tourgée attracted only limited insult in this campaign. He was mocked for having dined with a Negro and for a speech to his "sable brethren," and certain comments appearing in the Raleigh *News* prompted him to institute a suit for slander, which quickly induced the *News* to apologize and commend Tourgée as a lawyer, judge, and "fearless and uncompromising partisan."

Tourgée considered the state and national Republican tickets unusually strong and the constitutional issue a favorable one, and he was initially sanguine. The Democrats, however, played down state issues, other than Reconstruction stereotypes, while the Republicans bore the burden of Grant's discredited regime, unpopular Federal liquor taxes, and the continuing depression. In the Greensboro area the race issue had noticeably revived following the Tourgée-Holton victory of 1875, though generally this was a familiar rather than "a new era" in racist politics.[4] As the election approached, Tourgée's optimism declined, and privately he predicted that the "era of retribution [was] at hand." The center of campaign interest was the gubernatorial contest between Thomas Settle and the Confederate war governor, Zebulon B. Vance. Fifty-seven public debates between these two titans, at Settle's instigation but at locations chosen by Vance, made the campaign one of the most dramatic in the state's history, although "often the reasoning element" of Vance's friends "were disappointed in his speeches." [5] Apparently this consideration did not determine the election. The Conservatives swept the state, and the constitutional amendments were adopted.

"Righteousness by righteous methods had at last prevailed and

---

[3] Tourgée to O'Hara, August 4, 12, 1876, Tourgée Papers; Greensboro *Patriot*, July 19, 1876.
[4] Cf. Hamilton, *Reconstruction*, 636.
[5] *Ibid.*, 649–54.

Reconstruction in North Carolina was ended," or at least that was the conclusion of Professor J. G. de Roulhac Hamilton in his treatment of the period. Actually there had been a good deal of unrighteousness involved. Tourgée believed that the ballot boxes were freely stuffed, and his estimates, based upon the questionably low census figures of 1870, suggested that the total vote actually exceeded the voting population. Certainly the vote in counties controlled by Democratic registrars had increased far beyond that in counties controlled by Republicans, at times astonishingly so, and it is no secret that dishonest returns were thereafter a common means of keeping the Republicans down. Not only had southern Republicans been rather decisively crushed under a burden partially imposed by the North, but the disputed Hayes-Tilden election engendered a decisive betrayal.

With such a succession of defeats—constitutional revision, the loss of the governorship, and abandonment by President Hayes—it is little wonder that Republicans in North Carolina, among them Judge Tourgée, were discouraged and dismayed. The lengthy dispute that culminated in securing the presidency for Hayes added to tensions in the South. "I have never seen an hour when political bitterness has been so intense and hostility to Northern men so fierce as it is today," Tourgée complained in 1877. It was all he could do to "live among these people now," but he could not leave "without serious loss until times improve." [6] Meanwhile, he continued as pension agent and formed a new law partnership with William Horsfall, a Granville County attorney. The former position remained tenuous, since opponents sought his ouster by advising President Hayes that he was "about as unprincipled and obnoxious a carpet bagger as ever cursed this or any other state." Tourgée's supposed friend, Swepson, was also involved in efforts to displace him.[7] He soon lost the pension agency, but for somewhat different reasons. A bureau consolidation reduced the number of agents from fifty-eight to eighteen and despite lamentations to his superiors about his problems in the South and his Civil War injuries (to which,

[6] Tourgée to Dr. Sutherland, April 15, 1877, Tourgée Papers.
[7] C. H. Belvin to Secretary of Interior, March 23, 1877, and W. M. Robbins to Secretary of Interior, April 9, 1877, Department of Interior Records, National Archives; Swepson to Matt Ransom, November 11, 1876, Matt Ransom Papers, Southern Historical Collection.

questionably, he attributed the removal of his eye), Tourgée did not succeed in remaining as one of the eighteen.[8]

In several small ways he continued to receive attention. He was invited to deliver an obituary address upon the death of Chief Justice Richmond M. Pearson, and he was lauded for his two published legal works. But provocations also continued, as when Tourgée instituted a suit to block a partisan rearrangement of the government of Raleigh. The legislature had drastically gerrymandered the city, shifted the source of political power, and altered voting requirements and procedures. Although these steps seriously abridged the rights of Raleigh's Negro citizens, the legislature's position was strengthened by the adoption of the constitutional amendments of 1875, and Tourgée's case appears to have been dropped. He also became involved in a confusing case in which he defended some Republican county commissioners who had thrown out the returns from a township in the election of 1876, thus causing the election of three Democrats. The political complexion of this case was mixed, but Tourgée's defeat decisively established the illegality of the Robeson activities of 1875.[9]

Tourgée's pessimism increased after 1876, but he was not yet silenced, and his final contribution to North Carolina politics was the influential series of anonymous "C" letters, which exploited a rivalry among Democrats for the position of Chief Justice of the Supreme Court. William N. H. Smith was the candidate of a moderate and conciliatory faction, while the states' righters and extremists in the party preferred Daniel G. Fowle or David Schenck.

Tourgée's first anonymous letter, signed "C" (for carpetbagger?), appeared in March, 1878, and initiated a series of scathing and humorous delineations of the ambitions of Fowle, Schenck, and other Democrats.[10] The letters attained state-wide fame, intensifying the Democratic split and effectively discrediting the extremist wing. Fowle and Schenck were cleverly ridiculed as blusterers who sought judicial honor through reviv-

[8] Tourgée to Commissioner of Pensions, September 25, 1876, March 21, 1877, and Tourgée to Senate Committee on Pensions, January 18, 1877, Tourgée Papers; Tourgée to President R. B. Hayes, May 24, 1877, Department of Interior Records.

[9] *Moore* v. *Jones*, 76 N.C. 182.

[10] *The "C" Letters as Published in "The North State"* (Greensboro, 1878). Appearing initially in Greensboro *North State*, March through May, 1878, the letters were reprinted throughout the state.

ing memories of the war, although they had actually lurked safely in the rear during the war and only loomed "into prominence after peace was declared and treason was made safe and profitable." Democrats and Republicans alike paid tribute to the "master pen" of "C," but Democrats also cautioned against the divisions he inspired. "There has been no such writing in North Carolina in our day," the Wilmington *Star* thought. "No one can for a moment believe that Tourgée wrote them, after reading his literary abortion, Toinette, one of the most vicious of books without a spark of genius. . . . The author of the 'C' letters has genius, learning, and a rare combination of gifts. His style is infinitely superior to the productions of the carpet-bagger ex-judge that we have seen. 'C' has remarkable intellectual resources, and writes from a full mind." [11]

"C" levied his major attack against an old rival, Superior Court Judge Schenck, an impassioned defender of southern rights, who periodically aroused Tourgée's ire. Only a short time earlier, Schenck, who had anticipated a Supreme Court judgeship ("the goal of my ambition") since 1877, had been confidently thanking those who had helped him secure the post.[12] But "C" 's recollections about this "thirteenth hour Confederate" and his abasement before the congressional Ku Klux Klan investigators provoked some angry Democratic wrangling, particularly between the recent Klan leader, Randolph Abbott Shotwell, and Schenck's defender, Paul B. Means. Schenck's aspirations were thoroughly undermined. Overcome emotionally as well as politically, his grief was soon dispelled by a five-thousand-dollar post with some syndicate, a salary twice that of the judgeship. "I thanked God for His continued mercy," Schenck confided to his diary. "I now see that He had better things in store for me than a Supreme Court judgeship." A few years later he would actually turn down a nomination to that bench.[13]

Daniel G. Fowle was a less serious and less interested nominee for the justiceship, but Tourgée found him a more determined man. The angered Fowle suspected Tourgée's authorship and accosted him one day with a demand for denial or affirmation, and following Tourgée's

[11] Wilmington *Star*, quoted in Greensboro *North State*, July 25, 1878.
[12] Journal of David Schenck, VII, 441, Schenck Papers.
[13] *Ibid.*, VII, 456, 691, and X, 135.

refusal to comply, Fowle attacked him with a cane. In the brief flurry Fowle drew blood and Tourgée boasted of having left a fist mark visible for several days. The matter was then taken into court, Tourgée invoked the Fifth Amendment, and Fowle was fined a penny and costs. "C" was left free to jest at the unchivalrous attack, while Tourgée served notice that he had resumed carrying his pistol and welcomed all comers.

"C" also enjoyed a number of lesser criticisms of other Democrats, particularly those elevated to power because of their connection with the Klan at the expense of more capable men. Moreover, he offered several interesting reflections on Reconstruction, including a pronouncement that the Republican party in the South was dead beyond hope of resuscitation. But the Democrats, he added, while a party of intelligence and wealth, had yet to offer an effective answer to southern problems. Waving the Confederate gray might attract votes but did not solve the serious problems of the South.

"C" had achieved Tourgée's last victory in the South. Smith secured the chief justiceship, and not only had Tourgée contributed to this result and attained some measure of revenge for the besmirching of the past, but he had received encouraging literary acclaim as well. This, together with discouraging success elsewhere, helped maintain his interest in writing. A second series of "C" letters retained the wit and incisiveness, but not the political impact, of the originals. Lacking a convenient issue, "C" had become a mere critic of the Democrats.[14] Tourgée's efforts in the field of fiction were to be more significant.

In 1874, J. B. Ford and Co. of New York had published Tourgée's first novel, *Toinette*, under the pseudonym Henry Churton, the name of the original owner of the site of Hillsboro, North Carolina. An interest in southern race relations inspired the effort, but local ante-bellum tales, together with the Tourgée family's close friendship with their colored cook, shaped the plot of this story of a slave mother and daughter. Each of these beautiful, talented, and light-skinned slaves becomes her master's mistress. Each of the two intelligent and humane masters is deeply in love with his mistress but cannot overcome the barriers of race to fulfill his love properly. Southerners, comments Tourgée, could tolerate any white man's living with a slave and selling his own

[14] Clippings, second series of "C" letters, *North State*, June–July, 1878, Tourgée Papers.

children on the block, but "the spectacle of a white man defying the laws of God and man by living openly with a free-nigger, whose off-spring would also be free, and the mother not subject to execution for the debts of the father, was altogether preposterous!" [15]

Toinette's mother, cruelly victimized by the ways of slavery, tragically misconceives certain actions of her lover and murders him. The daughter's owner, Geoffrey Hunter, is a handsome gentleman of intelligence, culture, and courage, who begins a Pygmalion-like training of Toinette, his pet, only to become enamored of her. But despite his love for Toinette and his critical views of slavery, Geoffrey cannot conquer his prejudices. Certain circumstances then lead to Toinette's being freed and going north with her son just prior to the Civil War. As a Civil War nurse she again encounters Geoffrey, a wounded Confederate officer, at death's very door, and lovingly nurses him back to health. Upon his recovery, Geoffrey is astonished to discover Toinette passing as white and indignantly exposes her in a poignant scene.

> She deserved all he could make her feel for trying to pass for a white woman and a lady. This rushed through his brain in an instant, and then, with a voice hoarse with excitement, he cried out, imperiously: "I say, you girl, Toinette! Toinette!" Five years were brushed away in a second. Their months of toil and study were in vain. . . . The free, white, intelligent, interesting, beautiful Mrs. Hunter was lost for the moment. In her stead was the poor, abject, timid, pretty, "nigger gal." . . . She started like a guilty loiterer, and answered instantly, with that inimitable and indescribable intonation of the slave: "Sir?" [16]

Sobered by a realization of his own cruelty and his love for Toinette, Geoffrey later pleads with her to return to their ante-bellum illict relationship. But the free Toinette refuses to be sullied by that sin which slavery might excuse. In the author's mind slavery had more thoroughly

[15] *Toinette: A Tale of the South* (New York, 1874), 174–75. Revised and published as *A Royal Gentleman* (New York, 1880).
[16] *Toinette*, 377–78. A friend objected that no mulatto would ever be so virtuous as Toinette (W. H. Bailey to Tourgée, January 11, 1877, Tourgée Papers).

corrupted the master than the slave, and the subsequent scoffing by some ex-slaveowners at the very idea of a mulatto's being virtuous perhaps enhanced his point. In the original novel, love and need finally do conquer prejudice after Geoffrey suffers a stroke and becomes blind, and the tale concludes with a reconciliation and apparently an intended marriage. A revised version, *A Royal Gentleman*, ends more effectively with no solution at all.

In *Toinette* Tourgée intended to emphasize that the obvious physical evils of slavery had been exaggerated, while other subtle and neglected effects of that system were so deeply engraved, in differing fashion, upon the souls of master, freedman, and poor white that they could not be erased simply by law or proclamation. The necessary work of erasing this heritage had only just begun, and in his own efforts toward that end Tourgée's educated and accomplished heroine served to emphasize the illogic and injustice of white supremacy. Her experiences illustrated that racist fanaticism would make little concession to either great intellectual attainment or an extremely fair skin. This novel also attacked the popular northern myth that the nonslaveowning whites of the South were all poor white trash. The strikingly portrayed Betty Certain is a poor white woman of sufficient stature and sense to humble the aristocratic Geoffrey. She also displays a hostility toward slavery and the white aristocracy, and her race prejudice proves less enduring than that of the slaveowning class.

In method and content, *Toinette* resembled Tourgée's later fiction. While tendentious and partisan, the work revealed an astute and compassionate comprehension of many complex facets of society. The author's intense hatred of slavery did not prevent a portrayal of humane and sensitive slave masters, who were apologetic victims rather than champions of the system. He could censure the abolitionist movement and praise Lee while damning Davis, and although primarily critical of the South, he could mock the hypocrisy of race prejudice in the North, "which boasted of its freedom and equality." His praise of northern enterprise was also critically qualified and included the comment that "whatever of humbug and cheat and extortion and robbery under the name of trade and swindling and lying and defaming for lucre's sake, and forgery and burglary and sudden death and unpunished crime and honorable rascality—in short, whatever there is in infamy which can steal the livery of trade, finds its home and congenial retreat in New York." [17]

Nevertheless, *Toinette* was essentially a criticism of the South, and while its depiction of prejudice was in many ways effective and keen, it may have embedded the theme of slavery too firmly in its author's mind. Tourgée's first novel also revealed a very able prose and an unusual skill in dramatic narrative. Unfortunately, these abilities were accompanied by a reliance upon melodramatic plot and all the hackneyed techniques and values of traditional, sentimental romance. *Toinette* is filled with purity, honor, murder, ghosts, secret rooms, and fortunate but unlikely coincidences. The didactic author also allowed his verbosity to dilute his strength and frequently interrupted his entrancing tale with historical digression. Still, as Edmund Wilson has observed, "the verve of Tourgée as a storyteller does more or less carry it off." [18]

Toinette was endorsed by the press in dozens of cities, North and South, as "absolutely thrilling," a tale of "remarkable power," "an elegant romance," a "fervid and eloquent" depiction of slavery, and "superior to any novel which has appeared in a long time." Overcoming their scruples as to its sexual theme and its favorable comments on tobacco, the Protestant religious journals and newspapers were especially attracted to the tale and granted it thorough and appreciative treatment. There were unfavorable reviews, too, which found the tale boring or false or objected that it idealized the Negro or revived sectional and racial conflict.[19] A more vicious response appeared throughout North Carolina following the thoughtless revelation of the author's identity by a friend in the North. The volume was considered proof of the unlimited integrationist desires of Republicans. *"The real purpose of Tourgée was TO POPULARIZE INTER-MARRIAGE BETWEEN THE RACES IN NORTH CAROLINA."* [20]

Extensive reviewing only mildly encouraged sales, and the book brought little profit. But public and private praise, together with a second edition in 1875, encouraged the Judge, and in 1876 his short story

---

[17] *Toinette*, 487.

[18] Edmund Wilson, *Patriotic Gore: Studies in the Literature of the American Civil War* (New York, 1962), 534.

[19] Review clippings, Tourgée Papers.

[20] Charlotte *Observer*, September 24, 1874.

"Mamelon" appeared as a serial in Henry Ward Beecher's *Christian Union*. In intended contrast to *Toinette*, "Mamelon," like the already completed "John Eax," ignored the shadow of the Negro in its discussion of the South.[21]

Built about Tourgée's experiences in the handle business, "Mamelon" is, until its fantastic denouement, a realistic and believable story. The hero, Paul Dewar, an admirable southern aristocrat, so ingenuous that he cannot comprehend indirectness in others, is a Confederate general impoverished by the war. Through a long and arduous struggle, which seriously undermines his health and marriage, he rebuilds his plantation and then mortgages it to enter a partnership in the handle business with an enterprising Yankee immigrant. The prosperity of this business is just on the verge of solving all Paul's problems when the partners are ruined by the crash of 1873. The mortgage is due; a shot is heard from Paul's room; his wife, Sue, rushes in to find her husband, who had determined to secure her his life insurance money, lying on the floor. But Paul had suffered a stroke in the act of firing, the shot missed, and a visiting professor, who treats his stroke, is so entranced by Paul's archeological and geological collection that he offers enough for it to meet the mortgage payment. In addition, the spent bullet has lodged against a rock specimen, taken from Paul's plantation, which contains corundum, and so the professor, the carpetbagger, and the Dewars attain new wealth and contentment.

Its melodramatic ending aside, "Mamelon" is instructive and entertaining, and Tourgée succeeds unusually well in character portrayal and commentary on simple personal relationships. There is again some perceptive social commentary, and a deeper analysis of the caste structure of the white South is entwined in the more complex plot of "John Eax." Central to each of these tales is the death of the old South, while "the new South was springing into life about us—the spirit of the North and the manhood of the South its matchless elements."

Tourgée also produced additional articles and editorials, in which he continued to endorse the goals of Radical Reconstruction and to condemn the Federal government for allowing the landed aristocracy to suppress democracy and the Negro. There had been some gains, he felt, notably the surface endorsement by all of Negro legal and political

[21] *Christian Union*, April 19–June 14, 1876.

equality. Of course reality did not yet square with this endorsement, and Tourgée was opposed to the growing tendency to give the project up, though his remedies were mild. He encouraged Federal aid for education and for a transcontinental railroad through the South, and he accompanied this endorsement of Federal action with warnings against the reviving concept of states' rights. "It is as certain to be established as to-morrow is to shine," Tourgée predicted, "that the least right of the humblest citizen of the American nation is a nobler, worthier and diviner [sic] thing than any right or privilege which any state of this Union can possess." [22] Tourgée would not see that day, but such concerns continued to dominate his thought and writing, and early one Sunday morning in 1877 he arose from a restless night of pondering and announced to Emma that he was going to write a book and call it "A Fool's Errand." [23] He began the tale that morning, one that would promote his views on the postwar South with an effectiveness far greater than he dared dream.

Meanwhile, neither absorption in his writing nor political pessimism deterred the Judge from continued Republican activity. After losing the pension agency, the Tourgées returned to Greensboro, where the Judge renewed his pursuit of that long-elusive congressional candidacy. By 1878 competitors were few among the discouraged Republicans, although Tourgée's old nemesis, William F. Henderson, again stepped forth and added Greenbacker sympathies to his long-standing rivalry with the Judge. But after announcing his independent candidacy with the backing of the Greensboro Republican press, Tourgée secured the endorsement of the district Republican convention. He was finally able to make the race for Congress.

Somewhat hopefully, Tourgée launched his campaign on long-familiar principles and references to a supposed new era of "tolerance"

[22] "The New Theory of State Rights," manuscript, [1875], Tourgée Papers. See also "The Slave's Wages," [1873], and "God Out of Nazareth," 1876, manuscripts; also the clippings "Root Hog or Die," [1875], "One of Three Things," *The Advocate*, n.d., "Why Reconstruction Was A Failure," by Henry Churton, Northampton (Mass.) *Free Press and Journal*, [1875?]. See also Tourgée to Wilmington *Post*, May 22, 1875, and Tourgée to President R. B. Hayes, June 2, 1877, Tourgée Papers. One of Tourgée's articles was sent to a newspaper that he would become prominently connected with eight years later. See Tourgée to Editor, Chicago *Inter Ocean*, November 16, 1876, Tourgée Papers.

[23] Tourgée to James C. Young, August 24, 1903, Tourgée Papers.

and "mutual forbearance." The Democrats replied by ridiculing the possibility of a carpetbagger's promoting southern interests and by depicting Tourgée as a "political tramp" without a "throb of genuine sympathy for the people he is seeking to represent." The fact was, however, that Tourgée displayed an astute appreciation of North Carolina's problems. In a capable analysis of the much-criticized Federal liquor and tobacco taxes, he supported such luxury taxes while pointing out that the real inequity was an advantage accruing to larger distillers because of the advantage of consolidation. Tourgée proposed to relieve this inequity by a graduated tax on actual production. He did favor an outright repeal of the brandy tax, since it brought little revenue and neglected the need of southern fruit growers to preserve their crops from spoilage. With tobacco, too, the problem was consolidation; Tourgée accused the large Lorillard firm of securing a Democratic tax bill that would drive out the smaller competitors.[24]

Although a hard-money, high-tariff man, Tourgée was still clearly a reformer. He favored a graduated income tax and regulations upon "the rapacity of great [railroad] corporations," and he endeavored to make Federal aid to education a major issue. Holding the Federal government responsible, because of abolition, for the problem of illiteracy in the South, Tourgée proposed a national education tax to combat illiteracy. But currency was the only issue that succeeded in attracting much attention, and Tourgée's hard-money rationale had little appeal to a depressed agricultural area being swept up by the panacea of inflation. If Tourgée argued tellingly against the oversimplifications of this craze, he perhaps underestimated the benefits of inflation to farmers and the benefits of specie payment to wealthy bondholders. Unluckily, these views of a carpetbagger were easily identified with "the bondholders" and "the capitalists" of the North. To add to the Judge's woes, Emma, unwilling to endure the rigors of another campaign, fled north with Aimée for an extended stay.

And so the radical Tourgée approached his final test in the South, identified with a conservative currency stand. He and his allies, so recently reviled as "red Republicans," now spoke of the need "to sup-

[24] Broadside, *Judge Tourgée's Platform*, University of North Carolina Library; *Alamance Gleaner*, October 15, 1878; Greensboro *North State*, October 10, 24, 31, 1878. New "John Workman" poetry also appeared in *ibid.*, September 26, 1878.

press Communism." When the Democrats proved sufficiently inflationist to secure the withdrawal of a Greenbacker candidate, the contest was between Tourgée and Alfred M. Scales. In a series of stump debates between the two, the Judge displayed his old ability and fire, together with some welcome humor. When one debate was interrupted by a thundershower, which completely flooded Scales's open carriage, Tourgée effectively ventured that Scales's buggy held water much better than his arguments. In another instance, when Scales concluded his opening address with contemptuous references to carpetbaggers, Tourgée began by asking whether his opponent was proud of being a North Carolinian.

"Yes, of course," Scales responded.

"Well remember that I became one from inclination, you by accident."

Through the ensuing laughter, Scales countered, "But you came here a beggar, to make money."

"Yes, but had I come in only with rags upon my back, I brought more into the state than you did."

Clever retorts could not ward off Tourgée's defeat by the most decisive majority the Democrats had yet amassed in the district. With his family still absent, the depressed Judge momentarily envisioned his once-promising life ending in ruin and disgrace, revealing a tendency to despair which in the future would often have good cause to reappear. For several lonely months Tourgée continued to work on his legal and fictional volumes and to ruminate on the wisdom of leaving the state. While toying with prospects outside of North Carolina, he also resumed his legal practice, and during the spring of 1879 he produced a new series of anonymous letters, signed "Jeduthan Jeems," which castigated various Democratic policies and leaders, especially the Commissioner of Agriculture and subsequent champion of the Populists, Leonidas L. Polk. " 'J. J.' writes well; his wit and learning are superb and it is hoped he will continue," commented one Democrat, but warned against his promotion of quarrels inside the party. "We have the State now; let us not in a fit of envious folly or purblind selfishness return it to the hands of the thievish carpetbaggers and roguish scallawags." [25]

Fourteen years of attachments still bound this carpetbagger to his

[25] Clipping, Raleigh *Daily News*, June 26, 1879, Tourgée Papers. The Jeems letters appeared in *ibid.*, May–June, 1879.

adopted state. "I seem almost to have knit my heart into the land," he protested to Emma, and "I hate to leave." His words were more true than he knew. But conditions had changed for the worse over the past decade. The fight seemed over for good. Tourgée, the Negro, and the Republicans had lost. There were far too few young white Republicans appearing on the scene, and President Hayes had undermined the older radicals. There was little actual danger to life or limb, yet the hostility appeared more unanimous and pervasive than ever. The invisible but uncomfortable barrier remained—the stares and whispers, even from children—and the distressed Emma, who was still in Pennsylvania, urged her husband to leave for good. Primarily influenced by the conviction that he would always remain an alien Yankee, always be denied fair acceptance, Tourgée finally prepared to leave the South. Showing no interest in certain proposals that he edit a Raleigh newspaper, he began disposing of the family's Greensboro property and arranging for a move to Denver, Colorado. One final triumph was the appearance of his *Digest of Cited Cases* in the summer of 1879, which was quickly praised by Republican and Democrat alike as one of "the most valuable contributions" ever made to North Carolina legal literature.[26] Tourgée had also completed and made arrangements for the publication of two novels that year, *A Fool's Errand* and *Figs and Thistles*, and an anticipation of the southern reaction to these works may well have contributed to his decision to leave the state. On September 2, deeply touched by dozens of complimentary letters bemoaning his departure,[27] the forty-one-year-old carpetbagger bade a last fond farewell and left for Denver, for what he considered the challenging but more assimilative West.

Thus ended Tourgée's career as a carpetbagger, a career that stands not only as a particular repudiation, but raises some doubts as to the general validity, of a still popular stereotype. The clash between this Yankee and the redemption South had been a sharp one, clouded, it is true, by hate and imperfection, but in this clash Tourgée's personal

[26] John Manning to Tourgée, August 21, 1879, and many similar letters in Tourgée Papers.

[27] For example: "You have contributed more to the law and literature of this state than all the native Patrician class during generations" (Daniel L. Russell to Tourgée, October, 1879). "I venture to say—the State has never had a better servant than in you while you sat upon our Bench" (Edward Graham Haywood to Tourgée, August 25, 1879).

faults had been a decidedly secondary consideration. The basic dispute had been one of principles and ideas, and the carpetbagger's position must be judged as neither dishonorable nor unrealistic. His radicalism had been most ardent at a time when there was some chance for success, and although he later displayed a willingness to make concessions to reality, the new South's price was so high that it is not easy to dismiss as impractical Tourgée's refusal to pay. Finally, despite the bitterness and one-sided outcome, the clash had been mutually beneficial. Tourgée had succeeded in impressing not only the law but the spirit of his adopted state, while his experiences there provided the substance of a remarkable literary triumph and matured a social consciousness that thereafter dominated his life. The Fool's errand had not been all foolish, for Tourgée, the South, or the nation.

XVIII

A Fool's Errand
By One of the Fools

W hen the Tourgées headed west in the fall of 1879, the outlines of the future were indeed vague. Fourteen years, no matter how turbulent, had made North Carolina a home, while Colorado was a complete unknown. Following the welcome rest of a long train trip, the family established itself comfortably in Denver, where the Judge concluded arrangements for an editorial position on the Denver *Evening Times* and began investigating the local legal opportunities. Amidst the still-prevailing romance and excitement of the mining frontier, Emma was thoroughly smitten by the silver fever, and the Judge, together with several cronies, soon invested a small sum in real estate and mining. Entirely unrelated developments then brought an end to these fresh endeavors and directed the Judge's interest back toward those Reconstruction experiences which had so wrought his heart and mind.

A month after leaving the South, Tourgée's second novel, *Figs and Thistles,* had been released to a mildly favorable reception, and six weeks later A *Fool's Errand By One of the Fools* appeared anonymously. The former work was of little significance, but the latter, a thrilling and largely autobiographical account of Reconstruction, proved to be of high quality and published at a most propitious time. The Fool is Comfort Servosse, like Tourgée an educated Yankee of French origin, who travels South for similar reasons, behaves in similar fashion, and endures similar adventures, failures, and successes. Marking a high point in the Judge's power of thought and prose, possessed of "moments of pathos, suffering, and even stark tragedy," [1] the work appeared at a moment when the nation's population was still in a quandary regarding southern events over the past fifteen years. Not only did it offer the populace an astute and entertaining account of the Reconstruction puzzle, but it particularly pleased those Republicans who were reacting against the conciliatory tactics of President Hayes, and it provided the Republican party with a powerful campaign weapon for the approaching presidential election.

The nation's press, and soon its citizenry, were carried away by the exciting and convincing narrative of the Fool and intrigued by his anonymity. A book that had begged for a publisher in three cities and had been offered outright to Whitelaw Reid for one thousand dollars became a sensational success. The northern press was overwhelming in its recommendation, while even southerners found it "a powerfully written work" and fearfully wondered whether it would "do as much harm in the world as *Uncle Tom's Cabin*" or successfully demonstrate "the utter hopelessness of revolutionizing the politics and society of the South." More careful journals, such as the *Atlantic Monthly* and the Boston *Literary World*, were also impressed, the latter concluding that "the story throughout exhibits a naturalness, a composure, a reality, a self-restraint, which belongs to the best class of literary works. . . ." A more enthused New England reviewer wondered "in view of the power here displayed, whether the long-looked-for native American novelist who is to rival Dickens, and equal Thackeray, and yet imitate neither, has not been found. A romanticist, sage, publicist, politician, and philosopher in one, is a rare combination." [2] Such success encouraged public revelation of the author's identity, which further added to the novel's reputation and brought appreciative letters from fellow fools. In six months the Judge's profits reached twenty-four thousand dollars. Within a year sales reputedly approached one hundred and fifty thousand copies [3] and two foreign translations were under way. A *Fool's Errand* had become the best seller of its day, and Judge Tourgée found himself suddenly lifted to fortune and fame.

[1] John Hope Franklin (ed.), *A Fool's Errand By Albion W. Tourgée* (Cambridge, Mass., 1961), xix.

[2] Review clippings, Tourgée Papers.

[3] Mrs. Tourgée to Roberts Bros. Publishers, March 30, 1887, Tourgée Papers; John R. Howard, *Remembrance of Things Past* (New York, 1925), 316.

No doubt with recollections of the key that had been prepared for *Uncle Tom's Cabin,* early in 1880 Tourgée prepared a documentary supplement for some succeeding editions of *A Fool's Errand,* "The Invisible Empire," which remains a lively and superior interpretation of the dread activities of the Ku Klux Klan. Also at this time, one of the Judge's publishers ventured to Denver to persuade the somewhat reluctant author to undertake another Reconstruction novel, and soon Tourgée was working from earlier manuscripts on *Bricks Without Straw,* a venture that marked a decisive commitment to a literary and journalistic career. This decision, together with an urgent demand for the new work, induced the entire family to return east in July of 1880 and establish themselves in a rather stately mansion in downtown New York. Throughout the summer, the Judge toiled steadily in a sitting room overlooking an old, tangled garden just off Broadway, while each day Emma carried completed manuscripts to the publisher and returned with the previous day's proofs. About six, the family dined, after which Tourgée often was off to the city's Republican headquarters to partake in gratifying discussions about his book, the South, and the approaching election.

Judge Tourgées second Reconstruction novel, *Bricks Without Straw,* appeared that October. Again he presented a plot that was sometimes entrancing but too often contrived, in this instance primarily directed toward depicting the dilemma faced by the freed slaves. The central characters are an idealistic Yankee schoolmarm, Mollie Ainslee; an intelligent and noble southern aristocrat, Hesden Le Moyne; a crippled mulatto preacher, Eliab Hill; and a powerful, illiterate, black freedman, Nimbus Ware. Led by Mollie, Nimbus, and Eliab, the Negroes in *Bricks Without Straw* begin the postwar period by rather successfully exploiting the educational, economic, and political advantages of freedom. But while Mollie "enthusiastically prophesied the rapid rise and miraculous development of the colored race under the impetus of free schools and free thought," most southern whites "only saw in it a prospect of more 'sassy niggers,' like Nimbus, who was 'a good enough nigger, but mighty aggravating to the white folks.' " [4] As a result, race prejudice combines with aristocratic tradition and economic selfishness

[4] *Bricks Without Straw,* 147. For an illustration of the impact of this novel, see the review in *The Dial,* I (1880), 110–12.

to create a dogmatic resistance by the white South to Negro advancement. The nation had asked an impossible task of reform and Reconstruction, and the book ends with their collapse.

With the addition a short time later of "John Eax" and *Hot Plowshares*, Tourgée completed what was subsequently presented as a six-volume series on the origins and aftermath of the Civil War. In order of historical content, the set included *Hot Plowshares* (1883), *Figs and Thistles* (1879), *A Royal Gentleman and Zouri's Christmas* (1881), *A Fool's Errand* (1879), *Bricks Without Straw* (1880), and *John Eax and Mamelon, or the South Without the Shadow* (1882). Greatly varying in value, these volumes provided a provocative and significant contribution to American literature and thought, while also suggesting that the author was more successful as a reporter and historical analyst than as an artist.

The tragedies of the Civil War and Reconstruction, Tourgée suggested, had largely originated in mutually unrecognized differences between two essentially disparate civilizations, a North guided by the political and economic ideals of the modern world, especially those of democracy and freedom, and a South bound by an anachronistic slavery that had fostered racism and caste. "Why the Northern man felt as he did, believed what he did, and did what he did, and why the Southern man felt otherwise, believed otherwise, and did otherwise" were the perceptive questions Tourgée attempted to answer.[5] Although he placed undue emphasis upon the continuing impact of slavery and left his own preferences thoroughly undisguised, he still dealt critically and fairly with both sections, and his account was astute, compassionate, and just. Nevertheless, his thesis, and it remains a defensible one, was that southern society had been and was still in annoying constant conflict with freedom, equality and economic progress, all of which were identified with the North, with God, and with the inevitable course of human evolution. The South should and eventually would obtain more industry, more education, more freedom, and more equality, Tourgée wrote, but its traditions and its leaders were conspiring to hold it back, while sectional misunderstandings continued to confuse the picture.

Edmund Wilson has concluded that because of Tourgée's resemblance to southerners, his insolence and reckless independence, and his

[5] *Continent*, IV (December 5, 1883), 731.

romantic and chivalrous views, he succeeded in depicting the southern point of view "not merely from first-hand observation but with a sympathetic intuition such as, so far as I know, was exercised by no other Northern invader who has put himself on record. . . ." [6] But this ability also reflected a basic philosophy, one that combined environmentalism, compassion, a faith in mankind, and a national pride encompassing the South. Convinced of the essential goodness of people, Tourgée sought the origins and esteemed the sincerity of beliefs that he himself abhorred. He presented the clash between North and South as a clash between good and bad values, but not as one between good and evil men. Honorable men on each side were following the dictates of a conscience imposed by their respective societies, and Tourgée, while urging particular values, also sought to encourage mutual tolerance and understanding. "Which was right and which was wrong, abstractly, is of little moment to-day," he said of the Civil War, but "that all who were actors in that mighty drama should understand and appreciate the sentiments and motives of those who stood opposed to them is, at least, desirable. That our children should understand that the great cataclysm was sprung, not from passion, greed or ambition, but was based upon the deepest impulses of right and honor, is essential to that homogeneity of sentiment on which our future prosperity and happiness so much depend." [7] It was reflective of this attitude that despite vivid depictions of racist oppression and Klan terror, villainous personalities are lacking in Tourgée's fiction. Ironically, it was this same faith that produced in him not so much a jaundiced view of the South as an excessive trust in the idealism of the North.

Hot Plowshares, published last but historically the first of Tourgée's series, was necessarily a product of his imagination rather than his experience. The method and style is familiar. The tale revolves about the Hargrove and Kortright families, who represent, respectively, the substantial backbone of the slave South and of the free North, while an accompanying mystery of slavery and miscegenation again leads to a consideration of racial prejudice. In this instance, the moral of *Toinette* is carried to a logical but ludicrous end when the heroine undergoes the tortures of prejudice because of an erroneous assumption that she

[6] Wilson, *Patriotic Gore*, 537.
[7] *Hot Plowshares*, Preface. See also Tourgée, *An Appeal to Caesar*, 22.

is of Negro ancestry. Although Tourgée has been censured for escaping the racial dilemma by having the heroine prove to be white, here, as later in Mark Twain's *Pudd'nhead Wilson*, was a fitting means of ridiculing race prejudice itself.

The main intent of *Hot Plowshares*, however, was to expose the personal and regional impact of slavery as the source of anger, misunderstanding, and war. Thus the misfortunes of Hilda Hargrove and the burning of the town of Skendoah incite the North, just as the abduction of the slaves of Mallowbanks does the South. The thoughtful historical digressions accompanying this interpretation range from assertions of mutual sectional responsibility for slavery and war to a defense of the proslavery constitutional position and on to considerations of the role of radicals in history. For example, Jared Clarkson, the abolitionist, is depicted as one who "saw every wrong that scourged humanity, and hated it . . . sought out every good cause, and helped it," but "was like the comet among celestial bodies—bright, glowing, wonderful, upon which all gaze with admiration, but none set their watches by its movements." [8] Yet it is antislavery morality that is judged decisive in overcoming all other constitutional, judicial, religious, or economic considerations among the people of the free North. "What politician scheming for place and preferment could dream that a people's conscience would ever drive them so far?"

The next two novels carry us through the war years, in the South, with *Toinette*, and in the North, with *Figs and Thistles*. The hero of the latter, Markham Churr, relives Tourgée's boyhood and army experiences and is suggestive of many of his aspirations as well. A product of the democratic-religious tradition of the Western Reserve, Churr becomes the protégé of Boaz Woodley, a titan who typifies the honest accomplishment and skill, as well as the ruthless acquisitiveness, of the robber baron. After achieving wealth and a congressional seat under Woodley's tutelage, Churr finds himself morally opposed to certain of his mentor's tainted desires (which are obviously modeled after the Credit Mobilier scandal). Churr is torn between friendship, righteousness, and fear of his own egotism, but religious morality spurs him on to victory over Woodley, the political syndicate, and the controlled press. Although melodramatic and devoid of the perception and depth

[8] *Hot Plowshares*, 281–82. For the succeeding quotation, see *ibid.*, 226.

to be found in Tourgée's writings on the South, *Figs and Thistles* can be judged an early, significant critique of nineteenth-century American capitalism.[9]

But it is in depicting southern Reconstruction that Tourgée achieves a unique and vital place in American literature. The only carpetbagger and important participant to write pertinent fiction about this tragic drama, his work ably exploited his intense interest and firsthand knowledge without being crippled by an unconcealed commitment. Tourgée had much to say, and he said it powerfully and well. His balance and environmental emphasis are suggested by the following familiar section of *A Fool's Errand*, describing the contrasting thought of the North and South:

ANTE BELLUM.

Northern Idea of Slavery.

Slavery is wrong morally, politically, and economically. It is tolerated only for the sake of peace and quiet. The Negro is a man, and has equal inherent rights with the white race.

Southern Idea of Slavery.

The Negro is fit only for slavery. It is sanctioned by the Bible, and it must be right; or, if not exactly right, is unavoidable, now that the race is among us. We can not live with them in any other condition.

Northern Idea of the Southern Idea.

Those Southern fellows know that slavery is wrong, and incompatible with the theory of our government; but it is a good thing for them. They grow fat and rich, and have a good time, on account of it; and no one can blame them for not wanting to give it up.

Southern Idea of the Northern Idea.

Those Yankees are jealous because we make slavery profitable, raising cotton and tobacco, and want to deprive us of our slaves from envy. They don't believe a word of what they say about its being wrong, except a few fanatics. The rest are all hypocrites.

---

[9] For a doubtful view that *Figs and Thistles* is "better than Tourgée's Reconstruction novels," see William D. Dickens, "A Guide to the American Political Novel 1865–1910" (unpublished Ph.D. dissertation, University of Michigan, 1953), 77.

POST BELLUM.

The Northern Idea of the Situation.

The Negroes are free now, and must have a fair chance to make themselves something. What is claimed about their inferiority may be true. It is not likely to approve itself; but, true or false, they have a right to equality before the law. That is what the war meant, and this must be secured to them. The rest they must get as they can, or do without, as they choose.

The Southern Idea of the Situation.

We have lost our slaves, our bank stock, every thing, by the war. We have been beaten, and have honestly surrendered: slavery is gone, of course. The slave is now free, but he is not white. We have no ill will towards the colored man as such and in his place; but he is not our equal, and can not be made our equal, and we will not be ruled by him, or admit him as a co-ordinate with the white race in power. We have no objection to his voting, so long as he votes as his old master, or the man for whom he labors, advises him; but, when he chooses to vote differently, he must take the consequences.

The Northern Idea of the Southern Idea.

Now that the Negro is a voter, the Southern people will have to treat him well, because they will need his vote. The Negro will remain true to the government and party which gave him liberty, and in order to secure its preservation. Enough of the Southern whites will go with them, for the sake of office and power, to enable

The Southern Idea of the Northern Idea.

The Negro is made a voter simply to degrade and disgrace the white people of the South. The North cares nothing about the Negro as a man, but only enfranchises him in order to humiliate and enfeeble us. Of course, it makes no difference to the people of the North whether he is a voter or not. There are so few colored men them to retain permanent control of those States for an indefinite period. The Negroes will go to work, and things will gradually adjust themselves. The South has no right to complain. They would have the Negroes as slaves, kept the country in constant turmoil for the sake of them, brought on the war because we would not catch their runaways, killed a million of men; and now they can not complain if the very weapon by which they held power is turned against them, and is made the means of righting the wrongs which they have themselves created. It may be hard; but they will learn to do better hereafter.

there, that there is no fear of one of them being elected to office, going to the Legislature, or sitting on the bench. The whole purpose of the measure is to insult and degrade. But only wait until the States are restored and the "Blue Coats" are out of the way, and we will show them their mistake.

There was just enough of truth in each of these estimates of the other's characteristics to mislead. The South, as a mass, was honest in its belief of the righteousness of slavery, both morally and politically. The North, in like manner, was equally honest in its conviction with regard to the wickedness of slavery, and its inconsistency with republican institutions; yet neither credited the other with honesty. The South was right in believing that the North cared little or nothing for the Negro *as a man*, but wrong in the idea that the theory of political equality and manhood suffrage was invented or imposed from any thought of malice, revenge, or envy toward the South. The wish to degrade did not enter into the Northern mind in this connection. The idea that "of one blood are all the nations of the earth," and that "race, color, or previous condition of servitude," can not be allowed to affect the legal or political rights of any, *was* a living principle in the Northern mind, as little capable of suppression as the sentiment of race antagonism by which it was met, and whose intensity it persistently discredited.[10]

Still it was the "wise men" of the victorious North who were primarily responsible for the nation's postwar course, Tourgée insisted, and just as their initial understanding was clouded, so was their strategy absurd. Admirable goals were entrusted to the hands of the poor, the weak, and the idealistic, who were opposed by overwhelming power, wealth, and intelligence, and the South was inevitably "redeemed." "Like the ancient taskmaker, the Nation said: *'There shall no straw be given you, yet shall ye deliver the tale of bricks.'* " It was this tragic story that Tourgée narrated with the greatest insight, passion, and skill.

Undoubtedly, his two masterpieces were A *Fool's Errand* and *Bricks Without Straw*, which, together with the short stories "John Eax," "Mamelon," and "Zouri's Christmas," constitute the invaluable testament of a carpetbagger and provide a panoramic view and an astute analysis of the Reconstruction South. The entire story is there—the postwar suffering and confusion, the issues of unionism, race, and reform, the various contesting forces, the terrors of the Klan, and the final failure.

Tourgée's most significant accomplishment in literary realism may well have been his portrayal of such Reconstruction types as the aspiring white yeoman unionist and Republican; the illiterate but aware, and sometimes able, Negro; the enlightened southern gentleman, whose intellect overcame his prejudice; the respectable, capable Conservative influenced so decisively by caste and race beliefs; the race-conscious white commoner; and the idealistic but naïve Yankee teacher, Bureau agent, or carpetbagger. Sketching rather than developing these primarily political character types, Tourgée depicted southern Reconstruction as essentially a struggle of Republican political equality and reform against Conservative reaction, demagogy, racism, and power. Especially varied and valuable are his discussions of those still elusive Reconstruction figures the unionists, the Republicans, and the Negroes, and, indicative of his extensive reliance upon fact, almost every character and major

[10] A *Fool's Errand*, 121–23. For a related emphasis, see John H. and La Wanda Cox, *Politics, Principles, & Prejudice 1865–1866* (New York, 1963).

incident in *A Fool's Errand* can be at least partially identified with an individual or event in his Reconstruction experience. "He wanted to tell his bloodcurdling true story," Edmund Wilson has written, "to put on record his observations of the South and to explain the conclusions he drew from them, and he alternates his exciting episodes with chapters of political and social analysis; yet the latter does not deaden the narrative as happens so often with this kind of book." Tourgée's intense concern and immense knowledge of his subject had combined with sufficient literary skill to make him "one of the most readable . . . of writers who aim primarily at social history. His narrative has spirit and movement; his insights are brilliantly revealing, and they are expressed with emotional conviction." [11]

Discussions of prejudice and the Negro inspired some of Tourgée's finest writing—the confused but courageous adjustments to freedom of Nimbus Ware, the poignant exposure of Toinette, or the dialect, pathos, and humor of Berry Lawson. "Come up dar now an' wuk a farm on sheers," Berry jests with a friend, "an' let Marse Sykes 'llowance ye, an' yer'll come out like me an' git some good clothes, too! Greatest place ter start up a run-down nigger yer ever seed. Jes' look at me, now. When I went dar I didn't hev a rag ter my back—nary a rag, an' now jes see how I's covered wid 'em." [12] Subsequent encounters with stuffed ballot boxes and the unfair tenant laws of redemption exasperate Berry and drive him from the South. Of more heroic proportions than Berry is the once trusted slave Nimbus, whose visit to his impoverished and embittered former owner, Potestatem Desmit, helps establish the postwar setting of *Bricks Without Straw*:

> Nimbus stood before his master for the first time since he had been sent down the country to work on fortifications intended to prevent the realization of his race's long-delayed vision of freedom. He came with his hat in his hand, saying respectfully, "How d'ye, Marse Desmit?"

[11] Wilson, *Patriotic Gore*, 535.
[12] *Bricks Without Straw*, 190. For Tourgée's literary treatment of the Negro, see also two unpublished Ph.D. dissertations: Charles H. Nilon, "Some Aspects of the Treatment of Negro Character by Five Representative American Novelists: Cooper, Melville, Tourgée, Glasgow, Faulkner" (University of Wisconsin, 1952), and Helena M. Smith, "Negro Characterization in the American Novel; A Historical Survey of Work by White Authors" (Pennsylvania State University, 1959).

"Is that you, Nimbus? Get right out of here! I don't want any such grand rascal nigger in my house."

"But, Marse Desmit," began the colored man, greatly flurried by this rude greeting.

"I don't want any 'buts.' Damn you, I've had enough of all such cattle. What are you here for, anyhow? Why don't you go back to the Yankees that you ran away to? I suppose you want I should feed you, clothe you, support you, as I've been doing for your lazy wife and children ever since the surrender. I shan't do it a day longer—not a day! D'ye hear? Get off from my land before the sun goes down tomorrow or I'll have the overseer set his dogs on you."

"All right," said Nimbus cooly; "jes yer pay my wife what's due hcr and wc'll leave ez soon ez yer please."

"Due her? You damned black rascal, do you stand there and tell me I owe her anything?"

Strangely enough, the colored man did not quail. His army life had taught him to stand his ground, even against a white man, and he had not yet learned how necessary it was to unlearn the lesson of liberty and assume again the role of the slave. The white man was astounded. Here was a "sassy nigger" indeed! This was what freedom did for them!

"Her papers dat you gib her at de hirin', Marse Potem," said Nimbus, "says dat yer shall pay her fo' dollars a month an' rations. She's hed de rations all reg'lar, Marse Desmit; dat's all right, but not a dollar ob de money."

"You lie, you black rascal!" said Desmit excitedly; "she's drawn every cent of it!"

"Wal," said Nimbus, "ef dat's what yer say, we'll hev ter let de Bureau settle it."

"What, sir? You rascal, do you threaten me with the Bureau?" shouted Desmit, starting toward him in a rage, and aiming a blow at him with the heavy walking-stick he carried.

"Don't do dat, Marse Desmit," cried the colored man; "don't do dat!"

There was a dangerous gleam in his eye, but the white man did not heed the warning. His blow fell not on the colored man's head, but on his upraised arm, and the next moment the cane was wrested from his hands, and the recent slave stood over his former master as he lay upon the floor, where he had fallen or been thrown, and said: "Don't yer try dat, Marse Desmit; I won't bar it—dat I won't, from no man, black ner white. I'se been a sojer sence I was a slave, an' ther don't no man hit me a lick jes cos I'm black enny mo'. Yer's an' ole man, Marse Desmit, an' yer wuz a good 'nough marster ter me in the ole times, but yer mustn't try ter beat a free man. I don't want ter hurt yer, but yer mustn't do dat!"

"Then get out of here instantly," said Desmit, rising and pointing toward the door.

"All right, Marse," said Nimbus, stooping for his hat; "'tain't no use fer yer to be so mad, though. I jes come fer to make a trade wid ye."

"Get out of here, you damned, treacherous, ungrateful, black rascal. I wish every one of your whole race had the small-pox! Get out!"

As Nimbus turned to go, he continued: "And get your damned lazy tribe off my plantation before to-morrow night, if you don't want the dogs put on them, too!"

"I ain't afeard o' yer dogs," said Nimbus, as he went down the hall, and, mounting his mule, rode away.

With every step his wrath increased. It was well for Potestatem Desmit that he was not present to feel the anger of the black giant whom he had enraged. Once or twice he turned back, gesticulating fiercely and trembling with rage. Then he seemed to think better of it, and, turning his mule into a town a mile off his road, he lodged a complaint against his old master, with the officer of the "Bureau," and then rode quietly home, satisfied to "let de law take its course," as he said. He was glad that there was a law for him—a law that put him on the level with his old master—and meditated gratefully, as he rode home, on what the nation had wrought in his behalf since the time when "Marse Desmit" had sent him along that very road with an order to "Marse Ware" to give him "twenty lashes well laid on." The silly fellow thought that thenceforth he was going to have a "white man's chance in life." He did not know that in our free American Government, while the Federal power can lawfully and properly ordain and establish the theoretical rights of its citizens, it has no legal power to support and maintain those rights against the encroachment of any of the States, since in those matters the State is sovereign, and the part is greater than the whole.

The Negroes in Tourgée's fiction are idealized, it is true, but one must remember that this is true of all his characters, white or black, northern or southern, and this idealization did not preclude a critical reality. Admittedly "a slave may be freed in an hour; a free man cannot be made in many a day." [13] The ignorance and inability, the emotionalism and mistakes of the freed slaves are freely depicted, but the humanity and manhood of the Negro are properly recognized and maintained, and the rationalizations of prejudice are satirically crushed. In *Bricks Without Straw*, the frustrated valor of Nimbus Ware, the good-natured resignation of Berry Lawson, and the educational endeavors of Eliab Hill touch precisely those attitudes destined to dominate ideological conflict among Negroes for at least another century. It does not seem too much to say that Tourgée's accomplishments in Negro portraiture rank with those of George W. Cable and Mark Twain, while his interest in Negro dialect preluded the success of Joel Chandler Harris.

In his fiction Tourgée was also a pioneer in the destruction of various myths, as in his portrayals of a sturdy southern yeomanry, likeable slave overseers, and the fluidity of ante-bellum white society. While persistently repudiating his opponents' racial and political beliefs, Tourgée depicted the origins, nature, and sincerity of these beliefs with understanding and care. "There was never a kindlier, more hospitable, or more religious people on the footstool" than those of the South.[14] He recognized the honesty and ability of Conservatives and believed in their paternal interest in Negro welfare but considered this paternalism unacceptably limited by its insistence upon permanent Negro inferiority. Tracing the racist heritage primarily to slaveowners and their apologists, he also detected the intensity of newer racist demands from the poorer whites.

[13] *Hot Plowshares*, 175. See also *ibid.*, 148, note.
[14] *A Fool's Errand*, 104: "only they were kind according to *their notion*, as everybody else is, hospitable according to custom, like the rest of the world. . . ."

Tourgée's contempt for the cruel and cowardly atrocities of the Klan was accompanied by admiration for its daring and successful defiance of a recent conqueror. "It was a magnificent conception, and, in a sense, deserved success!" he could say,[15] while criticizing the North for its racial prejudice, its contributions to the existence of slavery, and its sole responsibility for the Reconstruction dilemma. The sincerity of his efforts even prompted praise from one of North Carolina's most determined Redeemers, Mrs. Cornelia Phillips Spencer, who concluded that *A Fool's Errand* was "the only book on South & North that presents a true picture. He has done it very well—& tells the truth as nearly as a c-bagger & a Tourgée could possibly be expected to do. I think he has *tried* to be fair." [16]

This recognition of Tourgée's contribution is not meant to deny the existence of weakness in content and technique. His reliance upon his own experience limits the validity of the picture he presented, since his judicial district was not typical of North Carolina and its resemblance to the South as a whole is unclear. A more serious failing is his relative neglect of pertinent topics or character types. Tourgée inclined to interpret Conservative behavior solely in terms of race, he provided only the briefest glimpse of the insincere Republican or of the momentous railroad fiasco, and personality faults were beyond the pale. In exaggerating slavery as the origin of southern peculiarities, he failed to detect the industrial strain in Bourbonism and minimized the extent of racism in the North and the progress of democracy in the ante-bellum South. He touched upon most of these factors, but so concentrated upon verifying his basic interpretation that he neglected qualifying material. His presentation of too pat an argument may have done more to undermine his work than did any general inadequacy of his thesis.

Attitudes toward Tourgée's artistic significance and skill have varied greatly, primarily in accordance with the degree of interest in the social content of his books, and recent attitudes toward Reconstruction and the Negro have brought him increasing praise. The most common criticism, and it does not lack substance, concerns Tourgée's adherence to the hackneyed methods of the traditional romantic novel—the idealization of character, the artificiality of plot, the morality and

[15] *Ibid.*, 289.
[16] Spencer to Charles Phillips, March 3, 1880, Spencer Papers.

sentimentalism, and the unconcealed tendentiousness. He has been accused, too, of poor dialect and an absence of humor, and his characters are usually lacking in "subtleties of character" or "nuances of human motivation." [17] Accustomed to, and still essentially involved in, debate, it was too easy for Tourgée to lapse into polemics, for his characters to become mechanical vehicles for his interpretations, and for his emotions to lose their poise—thus the frequent didactic excursions and the almost compulsive avoidance of ambiguity. Tourgée's greatest artistic tragedy was probably his failure to control this inclination by making his message a more integral part of his tale, a failing that was all the more deplorable because of the unusual power of his prose.

In recent reconsiderations of Tourgée's fiction, his faults are still recognized, but he is conceded an attractive and powerful content and style; George J. Becker judged him in 1947 as "perhaps the most neglected figure in American literature." [18] Tourgée's vigorous prose succeeds in retaining interest and in conveying his passion and intensity, his dramatic narrative achieves intense excitement and suspense, and he has a graceful descriptive ability. Alexander Cowie concluded that only a lack of emotional restraint kept Tourgée from becoming one of our greater writers, and he especially commends his "nice discrimination of phrase, his easy cadences, his distinguished talent for epigrammatic expression." [19] Tourgée's irony and satire, his humor and dialect, his "gracious vignettes of Nature," and, in the case of Toinette, his "shrewd comprehending analysis of character" have also been applauded.[20]

Tourgée's relationship to the emergence of fictional realism in the

[17] See especially Dibble, *Tourgée*; Theodore L. Gross, *Albion W. Tourgée* (New York, 1963).

[18] George J. Becker, "Albion W. Tourgée: Pioneer in Social Criticism," *American Literature*, XIX (March, 1947), 59–72. For earlier appreciations, see especially C. A. Smith, *O. Henry Biography*, 62–63, and Sterling Brown, *The Negro in American Fiction* (Washington, D.C., 1937), 71–75.

[19] Alexander Cowie, *The Rise of the American Novel* (New York, 1948), 521–35. The contrast between effective epigram and redundant didacticism in Tourgée's prose reflects, in part, a dichotomy in his thought between the old and the new, and between the agitator and the thinker. Consider his aphorisms: "A pound of justice would go further than a ton of charity" (on race relations); "The power of wealth is just as properly subject to restraint as the biceps and is even more liable to abuse"; "Solitude is the nurse not only of inspiration, but also of self-delusion."

[20] Owen N. Wilcox, "Albion Winegar Tourgée," *The Brief*, VII (1948), 7–54. For literary analysis, see Martin E. Hillger, "Albion W. Tourgée: Critic of Society" (unpublished Ph.D. dissertation, Indiana University, 1959).

United States has been less satisfactorily considered. This confusing literary development was itself a part of a broader intellectual adjustment between an older, idealistic teleology and the social problems and scientific views of the modern world. In his own resolution of this conflict, Tourgée displayed a dichotomy typical of the age, deriving both strength and weakness from his bonds with the past. Wedded to collegiately ingrained literary values and somewhat of an outsider among novelists, he was very little influenced by the attack upon romantic techniques by a Twain on one hand and a Howells or James on the other. The apparent lack of modernism and finesse in Tourgée's literature may be attributed largely to an isolation from the literary profession, together with the fact that he was more concerned with social interpretation and with serving and influencing his own generation than he was with perpetuating his name as an artist or contributing to the novel as an art form. In addition, he was, in his sectional novels at least, a representative, rather than a critic, of an older society. In resisting the abandonment of an earlier idealism and in assaulting the slavery heritage, there was something appropriate about a reliance upon the traditional values and literary forms of the free North. These considerations, plus a practical interest in reaching the public, contributed to the retention of artistic methods that were already being undermined by the early realists.

Tourgée also recoiled from the laborious character study and psychological emphasis with which Howells and James sought to depict and comprehend the modern world. On the other hand, he did contribute to the social stream of realism represented by Mark Twain and the local colorists. Drawing from personal experience and observation, he accurately portrayed and interpreted socially important characters and situations. His depictions of the South and the Western Reserve marked him as a uniquely diversified regionalist, but he also sought to combine different regional values into a truly national literature. Although his success was limited, the conception was rare.

To summarize, one might say that as an author Tourgée retained too much of romanticism, shunned psychological trends, and contributed to the sociological interest and insight of the newer American novel. His focus and his ties to past crusades had been a source of inspiration and power but had also encouraged outmoded techniques and a didacticism and sentimentalism that detracted from his powerful factual contributions. Thus, while in some respects old-fashioned, Tourgée was not an unsophisticated thinker. The idealism and nobility that he championed has often been too easily dismissed, and his attempt to utilize romance as a vehicle for fundamental truths anticipated the technique of Frank Norris. His social emphasis preceded that of Howells by a decade, and many of his conclusions were generations ahead of their time. A competent sociological awareness in his literature included an optimistic Darwinism, an environmental determinism (partially attributed by Tourgée to the influence of Oliver Wendell Holmes), and an acceptance of the primacy of collective over individual man. These particular views would become of increasing importance to his subsequent career.

While Tourgée does not stand among the great literary artists of the United States, his accuracy and significance easily equal that of many of the better regionalists and realists of his time. There is a perception, ability, and balance in his depiction of southern Reconstruction that differs markedly from the popular balderdash on that era subsequently presented by such writers as Thomas Nelson Page or Thomas Dixon, Jr. Within the confines of a skilled romantic technique, Tourgée captured much of the real tone of an age, and his conclusions regarding the Negro and the postwar South have increasingly gained credence. "A Fool's Errand," notes Edmund Wilson, "was received as a sensation in its day and it ought to be an historical classic in ours," a judgment that might well be extended to include Bricks Without Straw.[21] In their field these two works have never really been equaled; they stand among the few perceptive and satisfying accounts of that period to be found.

Neither the fortune nor the influence that accompanied this phase of Tourgée's literary career continued, primarily, perhaps, because the value of his early fiction was unique, although in good part his decline, like his success, was fortuitous. His was the voice of an old Republican idealism that was being swamped by a postwar wave of racism, materialism, and cynicism. Tourgée's never-ending support of the abandoned principles of Reconstruction, together with his newer critiques of the industrial North, launched him upon a crusade in the North as deter-

21 Wilson, *Patriotic Gore*, 536. Surprisingly, no paperback editions of these works are presently available.

mined as his previous one in the South. Again, his was an increasingly lonely cry. As the Negro became the forgotten man in the United States, his most vocal white defender was also forgotten. There was something tragic in the futile assault against prejudice that followed, and something heroic and prophetic as well. "It is . . . only in the element of simple, undoubting *faith,* that the kinship of genius and folly consists," Tourgée had written in *A Fool's Errand,* and for many years, as he had predicted: "Time smiled grimly as he traced anew the unsolved problem which had mocked the Fool's heart." [22]

[22] *A Fool's Errand,* 4, 359.

XIX

"Let There Be Light"

The appeal of *A Fool's Errand* to Radical Republicanism was based not only on its interpretation of the past, but on the fact that it kept the "irrepressible conflict" alive. Although slavery had been abolished, the Fool advised, the contrasting ideals of the "house divided against itself" would persist "in conflict until the one prevails, and the other falls." Furthermore, Reconstruction had not been a total failure but "a great step in advance," since "it recognized and formulated the universality of manhood in governmental power, and, in one phase or another of its development, compelled the formal assent of all sections and parties." [1] Tourgée perceived that the struggle to realize this commitment would extend far beyond the failure of Reconstruction in the South, and *A Fool's Errand* had a specific strategic recommendation to make regarding the new phase of conflict:

> The Nation nourished and protected slavery. The fruitage of slavery has been the ignorant freedman, the ignorant poor-white man, and the arrogant master. . . . Now let the Nation undo the evil it has permitted and encouraged. Let it educate those whom it made ignorant, and protect those whom it made weak. It is not a matter of favor to the black, but of safety to the Nation. Make the spelling-book the scepter of national power. Let the Nation educate the colored man and the poor-white man *because* the Nation held them in bondage, and is responsible for their education; educate the voter *because* the Nation can not afford that he should be ignorant. Do not try to shuffle off the responsibility, nor

[1] *A Fool's Errand*, 335–38.

cloak the danger. Honest ignorance in the masses is more to be dreaded than malevolent intelligence in the few. . . . Poor-Whites, Freedmen, Ku-Klux, and Bulldozers are all alike the harvest of ignorance. The Nation can not afford to grow such a crop.[2]

With the collapse of the Reconstruction political experiment, some more gradual and less controversial remedy, such as educational advancement, was a logical alternative, and it was not strange that a Radical Republican of Tourgée's experience would again look to the Federal government for aid. He had earlier been involved in postwar educational work and had been favorably impressed by the educational activities of a branch of the national government, the Freedmen's Bureau, as well as by private contributions from the North. The Judge urged a Federal educational program as early as 1870 in letters to Congress and to President Grant, and in the following year the introduction of George F. Hoar's educational bill into the United States Senate prompted Tourgée's appeal for a common school system "provided and controlled by the General Government, in the former slave states."[3] In his stress upon the human and political need for this step, the financial incapacity of the South, and the related responsibility of the entire nation, Tourgée achieved a rationale for Federal aid to education that was reiterated and elaborated upon for many years. During the remainder of the 1870's he petitioned the government and the Republican party toward this end, promoted it in his own congressional campaign, and, finally, popularized it through his fiction.

A Fool's Errand was widely read, but the precise influence of its educational advice cannot be gauged. Tourgée was wont to claim much credit for his own efforts in this direction, while disregarding other similar pressures. His was only one of several forces contributing to a Republican platform in 1880 that supported educational aid by Congress "to the extent of its constitutional ability." Tourgée asserted that this stand received the approval of all the state delegations to the Republican convention and the endorsement of several party giants, including the

2 *Ibid.*, 346–47.
3 Washington *Chronicle*, January 17, 1871, and clipping, "The President's Statesmanship," [1875?], Tourgée Papers; Tourgée, *An Appeal to Caesar*, 408–15.

presidential candidate, James A. Garfield. Tourgée attended this convention and conferred with Garfield, a previous acquaintance from the Western Reserve, and during the summer months that followed, he worked intently on *Bricks Without Straw*, which, upon its release in October, also helped to make the educational issue a part of the presidential campaign.[4]

In this novel, a southern aristocrat, Hesden Le Moyne, influenced by a Yankee schoolteacher and by the events of Reconstruction, eventually repudiates southern racism and caste to marry both the Yankee cause and schoolteacher. Clearly, Tourgée attached special significance to this type of intellectual southerner. While the poor white and Negro militant Republican leaders of his Reconstruction novels are ultimately killed or driven from the state, it is Hesden and his wife who remain, along with the Negro teacher Eliab Hill, to continue a lengthy and different kind of struggle against oppression and prejudice. Perceiving that the ignorance of many whites and blacks is contributing to the persistence of white supremacy and the disproportionate power of the landed gentry in the South and in the nation, Le Moyne becomes the advocate of Tourgée's long-range remedy: "Not *my* remedy, but the *only* remedy, is to educate the people until they shall be wise enough to know what they ought to do, and brave enough and strong enough to do it." The nation must help. Drawing from the example of the private Peabody fund, Le Moyne suggests that Federal funds be distributed directly, on a matching basis, to local schools in accordance with the amount of illiteracy in the region, thus attacking the basic problem, encouraging self-help, and by-passing the untrustworthy state governments. Tourgée's southern hero does not insist upon this particular plan but strives to "spur the national thought by every possible means to consider the evil, to demand its cure, and to devise a remedy."[5]

Following the completion of *Bricks Without Straw*, Tourgée plunged into the presidential campaign, where even the renowned James G. Blaine would find himself crowded from the platform by a popular demand for the Fool. Until the election, Tourgée steadily campaigned with an enthusiastic emphasis upon the critical and remedial suggestions

[4] *Continent*, V (March 26, 1884), 408; clipping, Emma K. Tourgée, "Memories of the Campaign of 1880," n.d., Tourgée Papers.
[5] *Bricks Without Straw*, 516–21.

of his novels. In the meantime, *Bricks Without Straw* became a success, and even *Figs and Thistles*, a less successful novel, created an unexpected and helpful stir when the mistaken notion developed that it was a fictional biography of James A. Garfield. According to Tourgée, both Charles A. Dana and the President-elect saw fit to credit a good part of the Republican electoral victory that November to his novels.[6]

In 1881 Judge Tourgée was at the pinnacle of his literary and political fame. He was a friend of the President-elect, and his novels had brought him a fortune of close to sixty thousand dollars and an honorary LL.D. from his alma mater (another would be granted by the University of Copenhagen in 1883). It was not too difficult to squelch a published challenge to his prestige entitled *A Reply to "A Fool's Errand By One of the Fools,"* written by William L. Royall, a Confederate veteran then practicing law in New York City. This was only the first of several books (one of which supported him) inspired by, or imitative of, the Judge's famous novel. Flaunting a paternalistic attitude toward the "savage" Negro, Royall's brief volume dismissed *A Fool's Errand* as "a wilful, deliberate, and malicious libel upon a noble and generous people" and drew particular attention to Tourgée's disputed loan from Swepson and Littlefield. A rebuttal by Tourgée and final response by Royall led the New York *Tribune* to conclude that the latter was "satisfied with pronouncing the statements of Judge Tourgée 'as false as hell'—a mode of reasoning which can hardly be called conclusive."[7] At about this same time, Tourgée's prestige was further enhanced by a gathering of political celebrities at a Union League banquet in his honor, and two months later Tourgée addressed this same organization regarding his new errand in behalf of Federal aid to education.

Shortly after the elections of 1880, President-elect Garfield sought Tourgée's advice respecting a proper southern policy, and the Judge, who had already volunteered some counsel, was eager to comply, especi-

---

[6] Manuscript biography, Tourgée Papers.

[7] March 15, 1881, quoted in Dibble, *Tourgée*, 81. Another attack was N. J. Floyd's *Thorns in the Flesh . . . A Voice of Vindication from the South in Answer to "A Fool's Errand" and Other Slanders* (Philadelphia, 1884). A confirmation was Harriet N. Goff's *Other Fools and Their Doings or Life among the Freedmen by One Who Has Seen It* (New York, 1880). See also *Not A Fool's Errand*, an 1880 re-edition of Joseph Holt Ingraham's *The Sunny South: Or, the Southerner at Home Embracing Five Years Experience of a Northern Governess in the Land of the Sugar and the Cotton* (Philadelphia, 1860).

ally by relating his educational recommendations to political as well as philosophical considerations. While warning Garfield against place-seekers in the South, Tourgée urged a reversal of Hayes's policies, believing that a southern Republican party could be built if Garfield announced his determination to appoint and heed only Republicans *"whenever"* qualified ones could be found, and pursued measures designed to attract moderate whites. "A large part of the very best men —I mean *truly* best and not *pseudo* best—will break away and go with us on the 'educational' idea," he promised.[8]

Later, this " 'educational' idea" was more intently considered by Garfield, Tourgée, and another Ohioan, Burke A. Hinsdale, a close friend of Garfield and president of Hiram College. Garfield had, of course, long been involved and interested in education and its relationship to the national government, and although he objected to the extent of Federal control in the original Hoar bill of 1871, he had supported a revised version the following year. Thereafter Garfield's interest apparently flagged, until 1880, when his acceptance of the presidential nomination included a strong endorsement of Federal aid to education. As between Tourgée and Hinsdale, it was clearly the former who persuasively continued to urge such a program upon the President-elect, while the more intimate Hinsdale served largely as a commentator upon Tourgée's proposals and appeared much more concerned with temperance, religion, and the Civil Service than with educational aid.[9] But Tourgée, too, had other interests, and, like Hinsdale and many others, sought a Federal appointment, despite his earlier denials of any such ambitions. But upon learning that some deserving officer might be removed because of this request, Tourgée protested strongly. "I would rather go into the wilderness and mount my Pegasus again," he wrote. "Fortunately I am not in need, am chock-full of day's works and rather enjoy being foot-loose so that I can shy a brick at any head I chance to

[8] Tourgée to Garfield, October 14, 1880, and December 14, 1880, James A. Garfield Papers, Manuscripts Division, Library of Congress. Professor Harry J. Brown, Michigan State University, kindly assisted my work with the Garfield Papers.

[9] Various correspondence, Garfield Papers, and Mary L. Hinsdale, *Garfield-Hinsdale Letters, Correspondence between James Abram Garfield and Burke Aaron Hinsdale* (Ann Arbor, Mich., 1949). Cf. Stanley P. Hirshson, *Farewell to the Bloody Shirt: Northern Republicans and the Southern Negro, 1877–93* (Bloomington, Ind., 1962), 88–94.

sight."[10] This was an attitude that a president besieged by office-seekers no doubt welcomed, and quite likely it increased his respect for the Judge.

In December of 1880, Tourgée sent a fourteen-page letter to Garfield with a proof copy of his educational article, "Aaron's Rod in Politics," which soon appeared in the *North American Review*.[11] During the following months, at a time when Garfield, struggling with his inaugural address, was in a most receptive mood, Tourgée pressed his views. Let me hear "your inaugural sing out clearly and unmistakably on the vital question—the keynote of an era at once sensible, practical and beneficent," Tourgée implored,[12] and he was to be more than satisfied. Almost a third of Garfield's address was devoted to the need for Federal aid to education, and it closely resembled, almost directly repeated, the general analysis that Tourgée had been championing. Subsequently, the Judge held two or more conferences with the President and showed the extent of his influence by securing the withdrawal of an appointment to the post of postmaster at Raleigh of William W. Holden, that long-suffering, but longer-suspect, Reconstruction ally.[13] But an assassin's bullet soon removed the promising Garfield, who, both Tourgée and Hinsdale were convinced, had been intent on making an educational program a keystone of his administration. His death appears to have been a mortal blow to the entire project, as well as to Tourgée's notable political influence.

Nevertheless, the educational issue remained, with Tourgée still in the midst of it. His second article on the topic, "The Education of the Negro," soon appeared, he initiated a related petition campaign, he wrote other articles and letters, and in the summer of 1883 he addressed the National Education Assembly, an organization formed in behalf of Federal aid.[14] Meanwhile, Tourgée also had begun publishing a magazine, *Our Continent*, which became a mouthpiece for these ideas. With his familiar exaggeration, he declared in its pages that "all other

[10] Tourgée to Garfield, March 22, 1881, Garfield Papers.
[11] Tourgée to Garfield, December 14, 1880, Garfield Papers; *North American Review*, CXXXII (February, 1881), 139–62.
[12] Tourgée to Garfield, February 14, 1881, Garfield Papers.
[13] Garfield Diary, April 7, 1881, Garfield Papers.
[14] "The Education of the Negro," *The Congregationalist and Boston Recorder*, XXXIII (November 30, 1881), 389; N.Y. *Tribune*, February 16, April 12, 1884; *Continent*, IV (October 3, 1883), 440.

questions affecting national life dwindle into insignificance" compared with the need for Federal aid to education.[15]

The Judge's views on the question became somewhat more controversial when he opposed the major, Republican-sponsored educational measure, the Blair bill, because it proposed to distribute funds through the state governments. This struck Tourgée as a repetition of the foolishness of 1867, for he feared that the southern states would so utilize Federal funds as to preserve the very inequality they were intended to destroy. Because of his intense recollections of Reconstruction, he was prepared to risk increased opposition to the entire idea of Federal aid by insisting upon the need to by-pass state governments. Although his own plan was designed to do this without interfering with the rights, privileges, or functions of state governments, he did weaken his position with the comment that it might be proper to see to it that Federal funds were not used to glorify the Lost Cause. Tourgée's fear of what might be taught continued to undermine his faith in education as an equalitarian remedy, but had as yet not seriously weakened it. Instead, his main concern was the continued failure of Republicans to carry through their educational pledge of 1880, although heavy losses from his magazine venture soon provided an additional personal worry. In 1884 Tourgée published a volume of nonfiction, *An Appeal to Caesar*, which he hoped would both save him from bankruptcy and arouse a popular clamor for educational action by Congress.

This volume, in which the term "Caesar" designated the citizenry, combined an espousal of Tourgée's particular educational program with a condensation of the sectional and racial interpretations found in his fiction. The book was a lively and provocative sociological tract, with flashes of brilliance. Tourgée, however, was haunted by declining success and influence, threatened with the immediate loss of his recently acquired fortune, and seriously ill, and unfortunately he pompously depicted himself in the book as a close associate of the murdered Garfield and the outstanding proponent of the educational remedy. "Mr. Tourgée," commented one newspaper, "has offended thousands of his readers by his overweening conceit and his stupendous egotism, so that much of the real merit of the work is overlooked." [16] Retribution

[15] *Ibid.*, V (March 12, 1884), 347. See *ibid.*, October 1883–May, 1884.
[16] Clipping, Albany *Argus*, December 14, 1884, Tourgée Papers.

occurred sixty-five years later, when a detailed history of the struggle for national aid to education did not even deign to mention Tourgée's name.[17]

An Appeal to Caesar was reminiscent of many years of radicalism; it declared that Negro equality was not only a moral necessity and a constitutional commitment but also an inevitable portion of the equalitarian trend of modern life. There was, in the long run, no choice of direction. The choice was whether or not intelligent guidance and a minimum of violence and suffering would characterize the change. Nothing, thought Judge Tourgée, could make a more desirable contribution than the elimination of illiteracy among the white and colored populations, and again he elaborated the many reasons why it was the duty of the Federal government to act. National responsibility for slavery and emancipation, justice to the freedman, the threat to social stability, and the impoverished condition of the South all warranted national action, while the resultant economic and political progress of the South would steadily win southern gratitude and diminish sectional hostility.

Tourgée's earlier assertion that "knowledge is not only the sole cure for barbarism, but the only remedy for *prejudice*" [18] perhaps demanded careful qualification, but essentially his position was sound. Admitting that prejudice and evil would not be automatically dissolved and might even be spread by education, he asked whether proper progress was not more probable in an educated than in an ignorant society, and whether education would not better equip Negroes to obtain their freedom and rights. As to theories of Negro inferiority, they were exposed as immaterial and unproven. "Whether the colored man is the equal, the inferior, or the superior of the white race in knowledge, capacity, or the power of self-direction has not been specifically revealed to me," he stated, but "some things are self-evident, and among these is the fact that every argument and demonstration by which the inherent inferiority of the African of the United States has been so frequently established has been shown by the irrefragable evidence of experience to be false." [19]

[17] Gordon Canfield Lee, *The Struggle for Federal Aid. First Phase. A History of the Attempts to Obtain Federal Aid for the Common Schools 1870–1890* (New York, 1949).
[18] *Continent*, V (January 30, 1884), 150.
[19] *An Appeal to Caesar*, 357.

In his anxiety to increase the impact of this volume, Tourgée resorted to one tactic, that of dire prophecy, which, like his pomposity, would occasionally reappear to lessen the accuracy and impact of his efforts. In this instance, underestimating the likelihood of heavy emigration, he erroneously predicted an imminent Negro majority and thus a much more explosive situation in the South, which conveniently intensified the necessity for some such solution as his own. In contrast to this error was Tourgée's rare awareness of the significance of increasing racial segregation, something not properly appreciated for at least another two generations. He recognized that the intimacy between Negro and white under slavery had, in some fashion, lessened racial antipathy, whereas the aspirations of free Negroes were creating new barriers of behavior and thought—thus the strange paradox of emancipation, that "the distance between the whites and blacks, though in fact very greatly diminished, seemed to have been as greatly increased." [20] This separation, he warned, was reducing contact and understanding and intensifying the need for education.

Whatever the strength or weakness of *An Appeal to Caesar*, it did arouse the public. It was reviewed widely and at length and prompted speeches and debates, and a comment by Bismarck was even attributed to the work. Although understandably not as successful as Tourgée's novels, still ten thousand copies were printed within six months, and the Toledo *Post* asserted that "no book of the past year has been more widely read, commented upon and criticised." [21] Reactions included endorsement, resistance, and unconcern. "We wish to do a piece of justice and frankly confess that we had a strong prejudice against Judge Tourgée as an embittered sufferer from dispelled illusions," stated the New York *Nation*, "but when we came to his plan of national education, we could not deny its reasonable and statesmanlike character." [22] While some readers found his general analysis reliable but his remedy absurd, others concluded the reverse. While many thought the work

[20] *Ibid.*, 103.
[21] Clipping, Toledo *Post*, n.d., Tourgée Papers.
[22] Quoted in Dibble, *Tourgée*, 96. Succeeding quotations are from various review clippings. See especially Atlanta *Constitution*, October 19, 1884; San Francisco *Chronicle*, October 19, 1884; Boston *Journal of Education*, November 16, 1884; Pittsburgh *Dispatch*, November 23, 1884; N.Y. *Tribune*, November 27, 1884; *Saturday Review*, December 20, 1884; and *Book Reviews*, February, 1885.

readable, factual, and powerful, others discovered "a mass of drivel" which was "grandiloquent and flippant by turns." While one admired the author's careful awareness of the limited possibilities of education, another scoffed at his "pupil-teacher's reliance on the infallible virtues of elementary education, an American child's implicit confidence in the self-evident truth of democratic principles." Behind these varying opinions, a basic acceptance or rejection of Tourgée's equalitarian predilections could usually be detected.

Despite the impact of *Caesar*, along with other forces, a Federal education program was not about to be secured. The Republicans, as Tourgée often complained, were increasingly guided by economics rather than ideals and were inclined to abandon the Negro. In addition, the proponents of an educational program were divided, the churches and many southerners were skeptical, and laissez-faire opponents of centralization were actively hostile. But Tourgée remained in a battle that was not yet over.

XX

The *Continent* Disaster

As the educational controversy proceeded, Tourgée continued, for a few years, to ride the tide of literary success. *Toinette* was republished in 1881 under a new title, *A Royal Gentleman*, and with a more appropriately tragic ending, and the following year *John Eax and Mamelon, or the South Without the Shadow* garnered a bit of praise and success. *Hot Plowshares* also appeared as a magazine serial that year, and a flow of articles, letters, and speeches expanded the Judge's commentary on the Negro and the South and extended it into such concerns as Christianity and civil service reform. For the first of many times, he addressed the Chautauqua Assembly in 1881, and a year later he effectively impressed a convention of newspaper editors with the neglected responsibilities of a free press.[1] Emma, who had endured such anguish in the South, delighted in her husband's new prestige and in the constant round of theater and opera, concerts and parties that it brought, with such highlights as an invitation to Harriet Beecher Stowe's seventieth birthday celebration, a visit from the Fisk Jubilee Singers, and a conversation with Oscar Wilde, whom Emma found "not anything overwhelming."

The Tourgées spent the winter of Garfield's election in Philadelphia, a good part of the time at the home of old friends from Ohio, and the Judge now added the lyceum circuit to his activities. His reputation ensured an initial success that his ability captured and retained.

---

[1] "Aaron's Rod in Politics," *North American Review*, CXXXII (1881), 139–62; "Reform versus Reformation," *ibid.*, 305–19; "The Christian Citizen," *Chautauquan*, II (1881), 86–91; "The Education of the Negro," *Congregationalist*, XXXIII (1881), 389; N.Y. *Tribune*, February 20, April 12, December 21, 1884; clipping, n.d., press club speech, Tourgée Papers.

On the platform his glistening eye and massive, bristling mustache seemed to convey the excitement of his Reconstruction experience, while his handsome appearance and casual dignity effectively dissipated the stereotype of the carpetbagger. He was credited with "a fascinating voice and manner, an easy, graceful style of speaking, and a humorous way of putting things." [2] Common sense and serious simplicity characterized his presentation, and reformism, his message.

One of Tourgée's many lecture tours led to the purchase of a family country house in western New York, in the little town of Mayville. While he was traveling by train to Chicago in the spring of 1881, the Judge's fancy was captured by an illustrated newspaper advertisement of a large, white house overlooking the northern end of Lake Chautauqua. On his return he stopped off to see it and was completely captivated. Reputedly built at a cost of over twenty thousand dollars as a wedding present for a daughter of one of the Tweed Ring, the twenty-three-room residence was surmounted by several attractive gables and towers and fronted by a large veranda, pleasantly reminiscent of the South. The area, not far northeast of the Western Reserve, resembled the surroundings and recalled the pleasures of both his and Emma's youth. Here was lovely countryside, Lake Chautauqua on one's doorstep, and Lake Erie only a few miles away. Here was a writer's welcome seclusion, together with a center of intellect and ideals only a few miles away at Chautauqua. Within a few weeks the Tourgées had purchased and entered their new home and christened it Thorheim, translated (with tongue in cheek) as "fool's home." Their arrival was a social event in Mayville, but it would be several years before the Tourgées actually settled down on Thorheim's fifty acres.

Meanwhile Tourgée had become involved in preparing a stage version of *A Fool's Errand* in collaboration with the actor-producer-playwright Steele MacKaye. Comparisons of Tourgée's work with *Uncle Tom's Cabin* helped encourage this project, as did the reported success of an unauthorized dramatization somewhere in the West, which was quickly broken up by Tourgée's legal threats. For the official dramatization, it was agreed that MacKaye's authority was to be supreme in matters of structure and Tourgée's in matters of fact, but the two proved difficult

[2] Clipping, Boston *Daily Advertiser*, December 13, 1811, and other clippings, Tourgée Papers.

to separate, and the author's didactics were inclined to clash with the playwright's dramatic sense. A more serious problem was provided by MacKaye's distressing immersion in certain fiscal and legal struggles, the result of which was that several days before the play's opening the last act had yet to be written, a leading actor quit, and several parts remained to be filled. Nevertheless, the play opened, a few days late, on October 26, 1881, at the Arch Street Theater in Philadelphia and met with a varied reception. Some critics were mildly encouraging and others strongly so, but objections to the play's length of four hours and to various dramatic faults were rather unanimous. MacKaye had added to the absurdity of plot and melodrama and was subject to special censure, but there was also opposition to the "bloody-shirt" theme, an attitude that boded much future ill for Tourgée. "It embodies the polemics of ten years ago," objected the Philadelphia *Times*, accusing the play of reviving an "excitement that has passed away and that nobody cares to recall." [3] MacKaye, who also played a leading role, was extremely satisfied, however, and concluded that he had so cut the "political verbiage of Judge Tourgée" as to produce an admirable play. "I have obtained laughter—applause—silence—tears, precisely where I calculated upon doing so," he boasted, but unfortunately the "money success" was "very moderate." [4] Two weeks later, despite a cut in length, the show collapsed from lack of funds.

Whatever Tourgée's business ability, he was invariably involved in ambitious undertakings, and the failure of his play was followed by an even costlier venture. It was simply impossible for the habitually active Tourgée to accept a life as placid as that of a writer. He liked influence and power and was anxious to invest his wealth in an attractive and profitable career, and what could be more fitting for one of his experience than a venture in publishing? So, in the fall of 1881, Tourgée participated in the formation of a hundred-and-fifty-thousand-dollar corporation, Our Continent Publishing Company, which was to publish an illustrated weekly magazine.

Tourgée was president of the corporation and editor of the weekly, *Our Continent*, although he later attributed its inspiration and initial

[3] Clippings, Philadelphia *Times*, October 27, 1881, Philadelphia *North American*, October 27, 1881, *American Register*, November 26, 1881, Tourgée Papers.
[4] Percy MacKaye, *Epoch: The Life of Steele MacKaye* (2 vols.; New York, 1927), I, 425.

policies to the treasurer, Robert S. Davis of Philadelphia. A third major investor and secretary of the firm was Daniel G. Brinton, an ethnologist of some repute, as well as owner and editor of the *Philadelphia Medical and Surgical Reporter*. Opportunity existed in the rapidly expanding magazine field, and the ambitious journal did anticipate an existing need in launching "the first serious attempt ever made to put into a weekly the attractions and excellences of our great monthlies." [5] Tourgée's fame provided excellent publicity, and among the minor investors were included the son of one of Tourgée's publishers and no less a personage than Ulysses S. Grant. But competition was keen, and the rate of failure among such enterprises was about fifty per cent.

The first issue of *Our Continent* appeared in February, 1882; it was a ten-cent illustrated quarto of sixteen pages that focused its interest upon quality, intellectual independence, and nationalism. The very title was designed to encourage "Americanism in literature and art," and a vow was made to present the "best" work of "our best writers" and "our best artists." [6] The venture started well, and like the best monthlies of that period, *Our Continent* was filled with prints and illustrations and carried short stories, serials, articles on an endless variety of topics, and such regular features as "Literary Notes," "The Household," "Science Jottings," "Our Society," "In Lighter Vein," and "Home Horticulture." Preparations had been lavish, and the journal has since been characterized by an eminent scholar as "a brilliant and ambitious attempt." "An unusual staff was assembled—Donald G. Mitchell in charge of art, Kate Field in a dressmaking department, Louise Chandler Moulton in a society section, Max Adeler for humor, and Helen Campbell editing household notes. All were stars; but with the exception of Adeler, they seem not to have been well cast in these rather humble parts." [7] More satisfactory were the illustrators, most of whom were competent, though academic, craftsmen associated with the Bozart Institute in Philadelphia, including Will H. Low, W. T. Smedley, Joseph Pennell, Howard Pyle, Kenyon Cox, Frank Bellew, and A. B. Frost. The staff and illustrators were "equaled by a remarkable galaxy of writers of articles, fiction, and verse," and in response to complaints

[5] *Continent*, II (October 18, 1882), 477.

[6] *Ibid.*, I (February 15, 1882), 8.

[7] Frank Luther Mott, *A History of American Magazines* (4 vols.; Cambridge, Mass., 1938–57), III, 42, 557–58.

that the weekly was of too high a quality for the average reader, Tourgée pledged to "stubbornly adhere" to the "theory that the best is none too good for 'the masses' of American readers." The first two issues contained poems or stories by Oscar Wilde, Sidney Lanier, Rebecca Harding Davis, Frank R. Stockton, and Hjalmar H. Boyesen, and "three days after the first issue was out, 58,000 copies of it had been sold." [8]

Fortune, however, did not remain so favorable, although extravagant expenditures continued (Tourgée was shocked at the fee of one thousand dollars paid Oscar Wilde for a single brief poem). When regular circulation failed to rise beyond about thirteen thousand copies, Davis and Brinton began to panic, but not the ever-determined and hopeful Judge. "At Albion's request," wrote Emma in her diary, "I write that his prediction is that one year from today he has $100,000 in the bank, outside of his property and Thorheim, and if this prediction is fulfilled, he goes to Europe and stays a year." [9] The following month Davis and Brinton sold out to Tourgée, who assumed full control.

Although altered in size to a smaller folio and changed in name to the *Continent*, the weekly retained its essential character under the Judge's editorship. He set policy and wrote for the journal but was frequently absent on lecture tours or stints of writing at Thorheim, which resulted in a visible increase in the activities of one member of the original staff, Helen Campbell, and in Emma's shouldering of much of the day-to-day management of the Philadelphia office. While Aimée and her father found need or excuse for frequent lengthy visits to the home at Mayville, the sometimes exasperated Emma seemed doomed to wearisome labor in Philadelphia, with her visits to the pleasant surroundings of Thorheim confined to summer weekends.

Tourgée's few literary contributions to the *Continent* included *Hot Plowshares*, a short story, and several poems. His poetry, like earlier efforts, consisted of story-sermons of little artistry, although the Negro theme could evoke such powerful touches as the following excerpt:

> Yet up from the Southland comes a moan
> Like Yesterday's ceaseless monotone.
> Hark! 'Tis the half-freed Slave's lament

[8] *Continent*, I (April 12, 1882), 130; Mott, *American Magazines*, III, 558–59.
[9] Mrs. Tourgée's Diary, May 17, 1882, Tourgée Papers.

For the bliss we promised and woe we sent!
The moan of the fettered, untaught soul
Charged with a freeman's power and dole! [10]

Reflective of the Judge's editorship and proclivity, however, were his more manifold and extensive thousands of words on literature, law, economics, education, and history. His initial editorials were replaced by a regular and opinionated column, "Migma," and he also wrote or contributed to "Literary Notes" and "The Bookshelf." Together with numerous articles, these columns soon placed his previous promise of "no axes to grind nor hobbies to ride" quite beyond his realization. Judge Tourgée was becoming a part of a much broader stream of the nation's critical life, although, as with his literature, he would never attain again the achievement or recognition that had marked his Reconstruction writings.

As was to be expected in a business venture, circulation was sought through the exploitation of accepted traditions and well-known names, but the literary and intellectual accomplishments of the *Continent* were not without merit. Its romance and sentimentality were provided by able and established stylists like Harriet Beecher Stowe, E. P. Roe, Julian Hawthorne, and Edward Everett Hale. But the magazine also presented the newer talent of Frank R. Stockton and utilized the more uncommon abilities of Charles G. Leland, the humorist; Anna K. Green, initiator of the popularity of the detective story; Joaquin Miller, then past his peak, who wrote on Indians and the West; and two delineators of urban life, Harriet P. Spofford and the satirical Edgar Fawcett. Although the *Continent* was inclined to rely upon popular competence and traditional style, it made a noticeable effort to encourage significant content in American literature. Among its romantic stories were plots ranging from the slave revolt, in a novel by Marion Harland, to economic problems, treated in Patience Thornton's "A Stock-Gambler's Daughter" and in the anonymous "On a Margin: The Story of a Hopeless Patriot." Important regionalists who appeared included Rebecca Harding Davis, Rose Terry Cooke, Sarah Orne Jewett, Constance Fenimore Woolson, and Joel Chandler Harris, and Tourgée applauded the realistic portrayal

[10] "Yesterday and To-Day," *Continent,* I (July 5, 1882), 328–29. See also "Their Monument," *Continent,* I (May 31, 1882), 249; V (May 28, 1884), 680–81.

found in Harris, Edward Eggleston, Charles Egbert Craddock, and George Cable, the last of whom turned down Tourgée's offer of seventy-five hundred dollars for a serial.[11]

Much less discerning was the *Continent's* attitude toward the emerging realism identified with William Dean Howells and Henry James. The magazine recognized this school, but denounced its literary attitudes, Tourgée's traditional biases having been ingrained by his collegiate training and dramatized by his life. The Judge's preference for an entertaining story was one consideration in the denunciation, but the real essence of the controversy was his prudery, his moral didacticism, and his exalted view of mankind. "The novel with a purpose is made a matter of artistic ridicule by over refined dilettanti," he complained, and endorsed the view that Howells and James were "novelists of first-rate abilities, writing with second-rate purposes, on second or third-rate materials." The reaction against romanticism had gone too far in Tourgée's view, and by shunning the reality of principles, ideals, and hope, "the modern novel—the artistic, analytic, realistic novel, as it is called in gushes of self-laudation by its prime votaries—becomes a false and distorted picture of life." Admittedly, there were "unpleasant, petty and debasing elements in human nature," but this, he insisted, "does not justify the novelist in dragging them always to the front. A picture is not truthful merely because it has dirt in it." [12] Tourgée demanded a fuller picture, not only the scabs and warts, but also the nobility, the courage, and the hope of mankind. "A ceaseless flood of epigram, eternal analysis of the most trivial and insignificant motives, the dalliance with vice as a common and familiar presence, and a belief that life has nothing good or noble in it worth the novelist's while to seek out and portray," [13] these were the tendencies he denounced in American fiction.

Tourgée failed, no doubt, to appreciate adequately the subtle perception and purpose of the realists, but there was much substance to his criticism. These writers could be boring, trivial, and, in their own fashion, trite, and the broader social interest of Howells had not yet developed. It is interesting to note that despite their literary antagonism, Howells and Tourgée were somewhat similar products of the ante-bellum

[11] Arlin Turner, *George W. Cable. A Biography* (Durham, 1956), 132.
[12] *Continent*, III (May 23, 1883), 669; IV (August 1, 1883), 159; IV (August 22, 1883), 252.
[13] *Ibid.*, IV (August 15, 1883), 219.

Western Reserve, sharing an equalitarian bias, a didactic commitment, and a puritanical morality. But while Howells was, in a sense, pursuing the tedious methods of science in creating character and scene, the impatient and involved Tourgée demanded synthesis and open commitment. A similarity was revealed, however, in their mutual appreciation of the entertaining and enlightening Balzac and Turgenev, although Tourgée's prudery hindered his full acceptance of such genius as that of Emile Zola, Leo Tolstoy, or Walt Whitman. This puritanical champion of freedom even favored the banning of "immoral" books from public libraries and refused, to his own detriment, to accept tobacco or liquor advertisements in the *Continent*. He did accept such ads as one for an electromagnetically charged corset calculated to cure everything from eczema to spinal ills.

In addition to literature, the intellectual interests of the *Continent* ranged from anthropology to zoology and attracted such contributors as the economist Richard T. Ely and three eminent university presidents, Charles W. Eliot, Daniel C. Gilman, and Noah Porter. The editor's most apparent bent was for sociology and history, and he served the latter profession well, drawing attention to the inception of the *American Historical Magazine* and praising the works of Moses Coit Tyler, Justin Winsor, John B. McMaster, Hubert H. Bancroft, and the lesser figures John Esten Cooke and George W. Williams.

The pages of Tourgée's magazine also flaunted his equalitarian idealism and began to define a newer reformism that he would champion throughout his life. Reconstruction was still a topic of vital concern to him, and although his specific emphasis remained upon Federal educational aid, this was but a step toward a larger goal announced in one of the first issues of the *Continent*. In Tourgée's eyes, the recent amendments to the Federal Constitution were based upon the "doctrine of equality of right," and, not content with the mere existence of such laws upon the statute books, he considered himself engaged in creating "a public sentiment that would not only permit but demand their enforcement, in letter and spirit, in every nook and hamlet in the land." [14] The focus of this interest was obviously the South. Tourgée believed that the final solution must be worked out within that section,

[14] *Ibid.*, I (May 17, 1882), 210. But see the stereotype Negro cartoon allowed to appear (*ibid.*, III [May 16, 1883], 640).

however, and looked especially to the influence of such enlightened southerners as Rev. Atticus G. Haygood, President of Emory University. At the same time, he believed that the North could and should exert an influence, and his hope in such a possibility was encouraged by his experiences with Garfield and other Republicans and by the continuing educational debate. But he had been aware of more discouraging trends for many years, and in the pages of the *Continent* he complained of the sacrifice of vital principles to reconciliation and gain, of the acceptance of millionaires as greater heroes than war-scarred veterans, and of the betrayal of the Reconstruction amendments by the nation's highest court. Adding to the Judge's exasperation at the changing tide was his conviction that, as earlier indicated by the Ku Klux Klan, it was the southerner who still displayed the most courage and pride in the defense of sectional ideals. The nation's history was being perverted, said the Judge, because the North was "too busy in coining golden moments into golden dollars to remember a past that is full of the glory of noble purposes. . . ." "The South surrendered at Appomattox, the North has been surrendering ever since." [15]

While thus continuing the Reconstruction dispute, Tourgée spoke, too, at this early date, of other evils—of a basic "wrong in the economic and social system," of mass poverty, of the dangerous power of corporate wealth, and of the world's dilemma in being "able to produce more than it is ready to use." [16] He applauded Henry George's *Progress and Poverty* and denounced the antilabor novel *The Breadwinners*, by John Hay. Bitterly critical of economic injustice and contemptuous of Herbert Spencer and the doctrines of *laissez faire*, he nevertheless opposed radical panaceas and favored corrective action by a democratic government, an approach that doubtlessly reflected his Civil War and Reconstruction orientation. Consistent with this reliance upon government was his support of various political reforms intended to enhance popular control. In its entirety, Tourgée's stand in the early 1880's displays a striking resemblance to the progressivism that would open the succeeding century, and suggests a neglected tie between this reformism and the old radical, anti-Liberal, and anti-Mugwump portion

[15] *Continent*, V (April 2, 1884), 444; VI (July 30, 1884), 156.
[16] *Continent*, V (January 23, 1884), 125–26; V (June 4, 1884), 730. See also *ibid.*, II, 503–7; III, 59; IV, 251; V, 59–60, 220, 728.

of the Republican party. Also related to progressivism was Tourgée's promotion of conservation and his partial and perplexed conclusion that imperialist expansion contributed to world progress despite its selfishness, brutality, and racism, all of which he denounced. Less immediately popular were his proposals for a government-owned communication system and, in a reaction against the expense and danger of armaments, for "an international court of arbitration *in perpetuo*." [17]

This expanded reformism did not destroy Tourgée's Republicanism. His Reconstruction experiences, the Negro issue, and the question of *laissez faire* remained rigid barriers against the Democrats, and, lacking any other promising alternative, he chose to do what he could to influence his once-idealistic party in the desired direction. During the early 1800's he urged reform and castigated his own party for promises betrayed, and, although he opposed the nomination of James G. Blaine and was disgruntled by an abysmally weak platform, he threw the support of the *Continent* behind the Republicans in the presidential election of 1884.[18] Nevertheless, he continued to bemoan the nomination of Blaine openly, and he found his speaking services resisted that year by the Republican National Committee because it had been decided to suppress the race question, which Tourgée most decidedly would not agree to eliminate from *his* speeches. The Judge's Republicanism was an older one, which, as it labored to return Republicans to earlier commitments and ideals, would increasingly fight as much within as without the party.

The *Continent*'s Republicanism in 1884 violated certain nonpartisan declarations of earlier years, but this was neither surprising nor the first time that such a thing had occurred, although it may have been inspired by hopes of patronage, for the *Continent* was foundering. Neither Tourgée's continued disbursements nor his proclamations of "assured success" had changed an outlook that had been doubtful from the first. But already heavily committed, he persuaded himself to continue his salvage efforts, and not only his recently acquired fortune but his income from lectures, a mortgage on Thorheim, the proceeds from the sale of

[17] *Continent*, III (February 14, 1883), 219.
[18] Tourgée's letter supporting Blaine (N.Y. *Tribune*, October 4, 1884) was reprinted as an expression of Republican views in Francis Curtis, *The Republican Party . . . 1854–1904* (2 vols.; New York, 1904), 153–55.

North Carolina real estate, and assignments on his copyrights were dropped into the abyss. Then, when appeals to the Republican editor and publisher James Gordon Bennett brought no succor, the Judge began to contract short-term loans at usurious interest rates and to surrender insurance policies and royalties as collateral. Late in 1883 he moved the magazine to New York in search of prestige and more local support and instituted various contests to stimulate interest. A slight increase in circulation and advertising may have made the magazine self-sustaining at its new location, but its position was precarious, and it remained heavily in debt.

The precise nature of several subsequent events is unclear. In the late spring of 1884, already exhausted in mind and body, Tourgée reinjured his spine while stepping from a curb and found himself bed-ridden. IIe had meanwhile become heavily indebted to, among others, one Charles H. Blair of New York. At this moment certain notes of Blair were due, and to secure a postponement, Tourgée went so far as to mortgage his future writings. He was then also desperately dictating *An Appeal to Caesar* from his sickbed, and Ulysses S. Grant, faced with misfortunes of his own, requested the return of the one thousand dollars that he had invested in the magazine. Upon learning of the predicament of the *Continent,* however, Grant apologized and begged the Judge not to give the matter another thought. Tourgée's efforts at fiscal and physical recovery were making encouraging headway, when a *Continent* stockholder suddenly instituted a "friendly" suit. This action frightened Blair, in turn, into demanding immediate payment, and the *Continent* collapsed.

It is not easy to evaluate this failure of what was, in some respects, an astute venture. Although the real breakthrough of the modern maga-zine occurred about two years later, Tourgée's weekly anticipated the popularity of the ten-cent, high-quality literary magazine that was timely and practical, partial to middle-class democracy, and not extremely genteel. The *Continent* displayed a nationalism and reformism of grow-ing significance, and its editor was imaginative, able, and widely in-formed. Even Tourgée's traditional idealism could have been of some assistance in achieving popularity, just as it was for another magazine editor, his onetime literary idol, Josiah G. Holland. But the *Continent* lacked the technical advantages of the inexpensive halftone illustrations developed a decade later, and the decision to make the *Continent* a weekly was of doubtful wisdom. Low-priced weeklies of this type that did succeed in the future could not afford the quality-consciousness of the *Continent*. Also, the trend toward briefness and crispness was not strong in Tourgée's magazine, and his puritanical code may have turned away subscribers as well as advertisements. Moreover, Tourgée denied the *Continent* his complete attention and supervision, and he had troublesome axes to grind, older ones that were losing public favor and newer ones that alienated business and political support.

The underlying difficulty of the *Continent* was, however, a business and fiscal one. As an entrepreneur Tourgée was perceptive but un-restrained, and his imagination, or his determination, or both, too easily outran his resources. The capital commonly required to succeed with a magazine such as he desired was far more than he could supply, while his independent and controversial position alienated other as-sistance. *Scribner's*, for example, expended half a million dollars to establish itself as a quality magazine at about this time, while Tourgée relied upon less than a fifth of this sum. As the well-known editor Edward W. Bok stated, "It was not so much a survival of the fittest as the survival of the largest capital." [19] A Philadelphia newspaper, com-menting on Tourgée's disaster, concluded that his magazine "was one of the best periodicals, taken all in all, that ever appeared in this country, which, if backed by sufficient capital and less persistently per-secuted by evil fortune, would have become in time a great financial success." [20] But one should balance this conclusion against the Judge's own conviction to the contrary, that his ex-partner, Davis, had misled him into an extravagant attempt, whereas had costs been drastically cut from the beginning, the magazine could have succeeded.

Instead, there had been another failure, and Tourgée collapsed with his magazine, a ruined and shattered man. "My poor husband!" wrote Emma many years later, revealing more of herself, perhaps, than of her husband. "How his life was embittered, ruined, by his trying to do what he had no capacity to do. His mind was too large to take in business details, and without that ability no one can succeed in such ventures as the *Continent*, which took all his fortune, his ambition, his

[19] Mott, *American Magazines*, IV, 15.
[20] Clipping, Philadelphia *Press*, n.d., Tourgée Papers.

hopes—everything but his wife." [21] The Judge spent that fall recuperating at a cousin's home in Canada, while the ever-faithful and helpful Emma endured a cruel fiscal examination that revealed a fortune lost and liabilities of over seventy thousand dollars. Near the end of the year, Judge Tourgée returned to Thorheim to begin again at the age of forty-six.

[21] Mrs. Tourgée to Mr. Moot, June 17, 1905, Tourgée Papers.

XXI

Recovering at Thorheim

Fame and fortune were now mostly behind the Judge, while before him was a huge debt and a vastly lessened earning power. Although he continued to lecture and write for a livelihood, his endeavors had only limited success, and the problem of the Negro and the South never ceased to confound him. By refusing to declare bankruptcy, the Tourgées retained certain possessions, including their heavily mortgaged home, but remained vexed by creditors and recurrent memories of lost wealth. The sale of Tourgée's books declined, half of his royalties were attached for debts, and creditors pursued whatever income arrived. Demands ranged from a humble plea for twenty dollars, which he owed for a Newfoundland dog, to a most annoying suit for twenty-five thousand dollars by Charles H. Blair, the man whose actions had toppled the *Continent* and who now unjustly sought to enforce his claim to all the Judge's new writings. Tourgée's intense worry and exasperation at such matters did not subside until eight years later, at which time a greatly reduced settlement was made with Blair, and not until 1896 was his last major debt fully extinguished.

Long before achieving such relief, Tourgée had abandoned his chivalrous visions of conquering the mountain of debt and turned his sole attention to keeping his family in reasonable comfort. Although some creditors were gradually paid, he was often reduced to blunt declarations of inability to pay, and he secured additional safety by copyrighting his works in Emma's name. Pennies were forever scraped and pinched, the Tourgée family peddled the Judge's books and produce from Thorheim's orchard, and it was not uncommon to find the mortgage overdue, the hired help behind in their wages, the coal bill mounting, or money being borrowed. The uncertain proceeds from writing and lecturing and the fluctuations in the Judge's health added to the family's discomfort. His back injury continued to bring recurrent attacks of prostration, as well as headaches and tremulous hands that made writing laborious and painful. He sought relief in medicaments that ranged from ice packs and strychnine to whiskey and rest.

The Judge's greatest difficulty, however, resulted from his persisting determination to unite his idealistic convictions with his mundane needs, a perpetual desire that was encouraged by fond memories of political and literary success. In succeeding years, while Tourgée was at times an avid seeker after political office, he was so not at the expense of, but rather for the sake of, his ideals. The wish to inform and better humanity, he wrote his daughter, "this and my ambition for the happiness of those I love is about all there is of me." [1] He feared neither would be realized, knew not where to turn, and confessed to Emma the bafflement of idle indecision. Yet his pursuit of satisfaction was intense and enticed him into so many commitments, for either principle or profit, that they threatened to work both him and Emma into the grave. The Judge carried "too many of the world's burdens on his shoulders & too many of its sorrows in his heart," a close friend observed,[2] and it was, above all, the difficulty of reconciling this dedication to justice with the needs of a family that contributed to the bickering and sorrow at Thorheim.

A directly related anxiety was provided by Tourgée's alternation of industrious and casual behavior. In the midst of accumulated obligations, his buggy rides or fishing trips for relief or inspiration left Emma fretfully confiding to her diary that he was wasting "away all the golden day, when honor, which means everything, is at stake." [3] Her husband also developed a consuming mania for invention, which was typical of that age and was stimulated by his romanticism and mild success with earlier patents on wood-turning machinery. He expended time and money on, among other things, steel implements, an improved propeller, portable housing, and especially on a wheel with a complex flexible

---

[1] Tourgée to his daughter, November 16, 1887, Tourgée Papers. Unless otherwise indicated, all manuscripts cited in this chapter are from the Tourgée Papers.

[2] A. O. Bunnell to Mrs. Tourgée, February 13, 1891.

[3] Mrs. Tourgée's Diary, October 8, 1886.

outer rim, a venture soon undermined by the pneumatic tire. All were a total loss.

The strain of this combination of frustrations can be seen in Emma's diary over a period of many years. On March 3, 1886, she wrote: "A letter from Albion at noon did not tend to raise my spirits, and one at night that nearly drove me to despair. I am so sorry for him because of the ill success of his enterprise, but I expected no other results." On June 2 of the following year this entry appeared: "A rainy, gloomy day with many sad accompaniments. Albion in despair over his work. Life does not seem worth the struggle anyhow." Four days before the Christmas of 1890, she complained of "a twelvemonth of more heart anguish than I have ever experienced before in my fifty years of life," and the following May 23 was "the end of another distressing, disappointing week. It does not seem as if this could go on much longer, but there is no telling."

Yet discomfort and somberness were clearly not the prevailing moods at Thorheim. The Tourgée family remained a vivacious and happy one, and the Judge obtained both satisfaction and profit from the platform and the printed page. His earnings did fluctuate wildly (he earned $725 one month and less than $100 another), but by March of 1886, Tourgée could delightedly report an advance of $2,500 for a new novel. "Thank God," he wrote Emma, "we are delivered from our extremity and you can now sleep *every night*. I shall expect the roses to bloom in your cheeks and the love lights to grow brighter in your eyes than ever." [4] There would be other such contracts, too, and eventually Tourgée's spinal injury brought a welcome veteran's pension.

The family never lost Thorheim, and a large and luxurious residence it was. There was often a cook in the house or workers on the grounds, and the Judge was obviously somewhat of a gentleman farmer; his orchard included a hundred and fifty varieties of plum trees, and he maintained a buggy, along with several dogs and spirited horses, his pride being a beautiful stallion, the namesake of Lollard in *A Fool's Errand*. During his working hours, Tourgée was comfortably ensconced in a spacious study filled with books, seated behind a handsome desk near a large bay window overlooking Lake Chautauqua. Emma's diary is filled with mention of "delightful days" with her husband, and his

[4] Tourgée to his wife, March 7, 1886.

return from a lecture tour was invariably an occasion for household gaiety. There were strolls over the beautiful acres of Thorheim and exciting buggy or sleigh rides through the pleasant, hilly countryside, and there were fishing trips, sometimes on the winter ice, and ice-skating or tobogganing, and pleasant evenings before the fireside. In prosperous years Aimée attended private school and the family vacationed at Lake Erie or in eastern New York. Emma even managed to spend a part of one winter with her daughter in Philadelphia, although the Judge lacked train fare for a visit and Emma's stay was cut short by a sudden dip in the family income.

Thorheim was usually a well-filled house, what with the Tourgées, one or both of Emma's sisters and their mother, and constant visitors from near and far. Old friends from Ohio and North Carolina, publishers and prominent Republicans, fellow reformers from as far off as England, and a growing circle of friends kept life entertaining and full. Tourgée's closest local companions were practical and successful but idealistic men—an eminent Buffalo attorney, a local banker, a prosperous horse-breeder, the proprietor of the Danville *Advertiser*, and the family doctor, who was the prototype for Dr. Colton in the novel *Black Ice*. Thorheim also functioned as a local social center and was the scene of numerous festive gatherings, at which the Judge enhanced his reputation as a lively conversationalist and welcome companion (he was still noted for a hearty and infectious laugh). Tourgée, clearly Mayville's leading citizen, joined in public activities ranging from the planting of locust trees along the village streets to fighting the district political machine.

Emma, of course, was manager of the household, as well as wife and constant comfort to the Judge. With the aid of her sister, Millie, she was also stenographer, copyist, proofreader, business manager, and nurse. Emma was somewhat of a welcome restraint on her impetuous and idealistic husband, but she remained primarily a factotum and go-between. Direction and policy were clearly set by the Judge. She strove endlessly and ably to serve him and to preserve, often by grieved silence, the beauty of their wedded life, but there were moments when she was a match for his faults with her own annoying complaints or mundane values, her social sensitivity or absorption in clothing or other petty matters. But these were rare interruptions in an unending idyllic romance that was the envy of many friends and was reflected in correspondence from the Judge such as this letter: "Well dear we have had twenty-six years of ups and downs, with a deal of happiness, some sorrow, bright hopes and many disappointments. On the whole, we have not done so bad. The world knows us; will not very soon forget us; we have done some good and will live again in our sweet daughter's life. We have the ripe autumn of life before us and please God may yet enjoy happy and prosperous days. God kccp you, my own true love, brave and bright as you have ever been and make you happier than ever before." [5]

The Tourgées' daughter, Aimée, was a delight. Bubbling with enthusiasm, artistic, intellectual, and emotional, she was clearly her father's child, a companion and correspondent, as well as something of a protégée. He fostered her interest in literature and art, and it was during their weekend buggy trips to and from Westfield, where Aimée attended the academy, that she became fascinated with an old house along the way and coaxed her father into undertaking the tale of *Button's Inn*. As Aimée became a mildly successful art student, the Judge served as her spur and critic, advising independence but also revealing and cultivating values of his own. "True, the individual may be sweeter than the mass," he counseled. "So too, he may be meaner, but the mass—humanity—how much of hope and fear and sweetness it represents. It does not seem to me very much to die for humanity. . . . An artist has a great debt always owing to humanity—he must make it better or worse. How shall he make it better? How shall he keep from making it worse?" [6] Technique must be developed, of course, but the Judge thought that significance should not be sacrificed to endless perfection, and he urged his daughter toward ambitious paintings of the sufferings of the poor, the cruel ostentation of the rich, or an heroic John Brown. He feared, however, that her talent was limited to competent illustration, and as the future revealed, her greatest success was as an illustrator for some of her father's writing. But Aimée's poor health was a far more serious concern, and brought on her early death not long after that of her father.

Tourgée's national prestige declined after his magazine's collapse, but

[5] Tourgée to his wife, May 14, 1889.
[6] Tourgée to his daughter, May 17, 1889.

there were continued small honors and endless but gratifying solicitations for his services from schools and colleges, aspiring writers, reformers, and various clubs and organizations. He held a professorship, without pay, in the newly formed Buffalo Law School, served as a Rochester alumni president, and was recruited for commencement exercises at the University of Buffalo. He exchanged letters on Reconstruction with historians,[7] while keeping alive his memories of that era by letters from both races and parties in North Carolina.

Of course the Judge delighted in such recognition and often gave graciously of himself. His most striking specific influence was upon two sharply contrasting individuals, one of whom was Charles W. Chesnutt, the Negro writer, whose literary efforts were in part inspired by Tourgée's work.[8] Following the Judge's early recognition of Chesnutt's accomplishment, a warm and lasting friendship developed between them. The other, and more famous, "protégé" was a North Carolina acquaintance who seriously accepted the famed carpetbagger's counsel during Tourgée's editorship of the *Continent*, and who several years later sent a letter of grateful acknowledgment to Thorheim telling of his progress and inviting Tourgée to his Boston home. This was none other than the popular Baptist preacher Thomas Dixon, Jr., soon to reap his greatest fame as the nation's leading literary racist, whose popular novels on Reconstruction represent the very antithesis of all that Tourgée stood for.[9]

During the years at Thorheim lecturing remained Tourgée's major source of income and chief didactic outlet, and between November and April of each year, the Judge was often to be found suffering all the inconveniences of the lyceum circuit somewhere between New Mexico and Massachusetts. His attire varied from casual to cutaway, touches of gray were beginning to crease his dark hair, he wore gold-rimmed glasses, and often leaned upon a cane. His mustache and eye and earnest ease still attracted notice, while his powerful voice con-

---

[7] Frederic Bancroft to Tourgée, October 27, 1887; Mrs. Tourgée's Diary, March 4, 1891 (concerning Moses Coit Tyler); Jacob E. Cooke, *Frederic Bancroft, Historian* (Norman, Okla., 1957), 19.

[8] Helen M. Chesnutt, *Charles Waddell Chesnutt: Pioneer of the Color Line* (Chapel Hill, 1952), 19–20; Tourgée to Chesnutt, December 8, 1888, Charles W. Chesnutt Papers, Fisk University Library.

[9] Dixon to Tourgée, February 25, 1888.

quered the largest auditoriums and could command attention for hours; the lyceum director Henry L. Slayton considered him one of the few really successful lecturers of the day. His inevitably humanistic speeches ranged through heroism, citizenship, economic justice, the Negro question, social evolution, urban evils, and the fast and foolish pace of modern life. If one correspondent is to be believed, his impact could be intense: "Why the whole town is in a blaze of intellectual excitement. We step high. We are breathing a rarified air. Your lecture has opened up our intellectual pores and we have laid aside our gossip, our horse talk, and our stale jokes and for the time we feel as if we are *men & women*." [10]

For the Judge, this was often a lonely and tiresome life of long, rough rides that aggravated his back, of late trains and missed trains, of barren waiting rooms, poor lodgings, and poorer meals. Schedules could be impossibly demanding; in one instance he had five lectures and fifteen hundred miles to be disposed of in five days. Even without such a rare rush, Tourgée, who was often preoccupied with his writings, had a perfect talent for losing his coat, his umbrella, his luggage, or even his manuscripts. The profits varied, and audiences were at times distressingly small, but the Judge often found enjoyment and success as well. He met old friends and gathered new ones, luxurious accommodations and gala receptions were provided now and then, and there was the repeated reward of attention and applause. The Judge could also roguishly grumble to Emma about prohibition towns or tease her about being welcomed by beautiful women at lonely hours or encountering lodgings of suspect propriety.

Tourgée also continued his writing, although his literary achievements now were being overshadowed by his journalistic contributions to a prominent Chicago newspaper, the *Inter Ocean*. One of the earliest signs of the Judge's recovery from the *Continent* debacle was, in fact, the appearance in this paper on December 13, 1884, of the first of a weekly series of anonymous "Siva" letters addressed to Grover Cleveland and entitled "A Man of Destiny: Letters to A President Elect."

In a disappointing attempt to match the earlier "C" letters, "Siva" 's efforts were an ungracious and ungallant attack upon Cleveland before

[10] E. G. Hubbard to Tourgée, December 24, 1887.

he even assumed office. The series marked a low point in Tourgée's writings. "I pity you as I do the snarling scavenger on the desert sands, because he is not fitted for better things," he wrote the President-elect. "I pity you standing before the world as the exemplar of the American people, as I would pity a Lilliputian leper put forward as representative and type of the unlettered giants of Brobdingnag." Soured by personal misfortune and the Republican nomination of Blaine, the Judge vented his anger on the first Democratic president since the war, castigating him for faults from his lack of military service to his obesity, and above all, for his allegiance to a do-nothing party led by Copperheads and "the ex-Confederate, kuklux, red shirt, bulldozing, fraud-protecting Bourbons of the South." There was, one reader acidly commented, "literary proficiency and rhetorical excellence" in Siva's work, but his words were no more than "spit balls" on a "deserted battlefield" with a few grains of truth buried in bushels of chaff.[11]

Nevertheless, in creating a stir, capturing the spirit of many Republicans, and winning the lasting gratitude of the *Inter Ocean*, the Siva letters were a publishing success. Hundreds of commentaries appeared on the series; Theodore Roosevelt was quoted as judging one letter the "equal to anything since the days of Junius." Guessing the authorship became a fad, and the guesses included Tourgée, as well as Benjamin F. Butler, Charles A. Dana, Frederick Douglass, James Redpath, and, of all people, Ulysses S. Grant. There was such enthusiasm that the entire set was published as a pamphlet, and the *Inter Ocean* later recalled that the "Siva letters did become popular, they did delight the readers of *The Inter Ocean*, they did achieve a universality of fame." [12] It was all a welcome boost to the pocketbook and confidence of Judge Tourgée and marked the beginning of years of writing for the *Inter Ocean*.

The Siva letters were succeeded in March, 1885, by another weekly column, "A Veteran and His Pipe," which was successively followed by "Letters to a Mugwump" and a second Siva series, "A Child of Luck." The first of these columns marked a return to quality and to the theme he handled best and was by far the finest. The Veteran's

[11] Quoted in Dibble, *Tourgée*, 97–98; *Inter Ocean*, January 3, March 7 (Rev. W. Rader to the Editor), 1885.
[12] *Inter Ocean*, January 4, 1885 (A. W. Edwards to the Editor), March 27, 1886.

Emma and Albion Tourgée in Philadelphia while editing the *Continent* magazine. According to occasional accounts in the press, Emma's hair had turned white overnight after a Ku Klux Klan raid on the Tourgées' North Carolina home. Tourgée Papers, Westfield, New York.

"Thorheim," Mayville, New York, some years before it was purchased by Tourgée. The far side of the house overlooks Lake Chautauqua. Courtesy of Mrs. Bess M. Hartmann and Mrs. L. C. Peterson, Mayville, New York.

Cover of the Continent. Library of Congress.

Tourgée at "Thorheim" in the late 1890's. Tourgée Papers, Westfield, New York.

soliloquies to his pipe are a carefully reasoned and eloquent lament of the dying idealism of the Civil War. The Confederates were "brave and earnest, but misguided men," who "must bear the stigma, not merely of defeat, but of a cause inherently wrong." Whatever the many faults of the North, its cause was just, but now, the Veteran moaned, its sacrifices were being betrayed. "The dead were to be mourned; the cause for which they died, forgotten." On the eve of Independence Day, the perplexed veteran asked: "Is it possible that right has its vanishing point? Do faith and doubt somewhere become indistinguishable? Is it true that assertion of abstract right sometimes becomes, in the concrete, an actual wrong? Is it true that while the colored man rejoices, the white man of the South must mourn? Is freedom right, and equality of power the true basis of government; or is the old-time Fourth of July only calculated for higher latitudes and for men with white skins?" A Confederate veteran forces upon him the sad truth that "we shall manage the Negro at the South as we choose, because the impulse of liberation and amelioration has spent its force, and for many years will lie dormant." [13] The source of future difficulty, this Confederate predicts, will not be the North but the Negroes themselves.

The two other weekly columns were partisan Republican documents, not without intelligence and skill but lacking the thoughtful charm of the Veteran's musings. "Letters to a Mugwump" exposed and denounced the aristocratic orientation of this faction, while the second Siva series consisted largely of new slurs on "the royal obesity" and the Democratic party. While both columns promoted Republicanism, some of Tourgée's doctrines left many party stalwarts shaking. Leadership should come from the wealthy and successful, he said, in mocking the Mugwumps, but unfortunately "the evils which threaten the peace and stability of the state come almost always from the rich rather than the poor. . . . The history of civilization is a struggle in which wealth has been the right hand of oppression." [14] Similarly, Siva was free in criticisms of "a tremendous conassociation of allied capital and organized fraud," which borrowed "the garb of patriotism in order to oppress the

[13] *The Veteran and His Pipe* (Chicago, 1886), 76, 78, 136, 158. Appearing in the *Inter Ocean*, April 25–September 19, 1885.
[14] "Letters to A Mugwump," *Inter Ocean*, October 3, 1885. This series appeared from September 26 through December 12, 1885.

people," which used "the ermine of the law to hide the most stupendous acts of plunder the world has ever known," and which was "drawing closer and closer the network of its power, gathering every year the many more helplessly and hopelessly within control of the few." [15]

It was a measure of Judge Tourgée's worth that he not only continued to develop such views but that, regardless of their threat to his own career, he continued to disperse them through one of the leading Republican newspapers of the West. His radicalism would prove a handicap to his political success in the North as well as in the South, and in seeking a state senatorial nomination in 1885, he suffered the first of several defeats from a northern Republican machine.

The conclusion of the second series of Siva letters in 1886 marked a change in Tourgée's writing activities, his next contribution to the *Inter Ocean* being the novel *Button's Inn*. Several magazine articles of distinction accompanied this literary revival, including what was probably Tourgée's most famous article, "The South as a Field for Fiction," [16] which in its power of ideas and expression, as well as its exaggeration, confidence, and florid style, was something of a prototype both of the Judge's weakness and his strength. The gist of this prophetic effort was that the South was "destined to be the Hesperides Garden of American literature." Pathos and agony, he asserted, are at the root of enduring fiction, and "in all history, no cause has so many of the elements of pathos as that which failed at Appomattox, and no people ever presented to the novelist such a marvelous array of curiously contrasted lives." He would not attempt to predict the form or guess the character of this literature, but he was confident that it would "certainly be great—greater than we have hitherto known, because its causative forces are mightier than those which have shaped the productive energy of the past."

Tourgée continued for years to expound his already familiar literary views—his moral and didactic preferences, his objections to formalism and lack of significant content, and his emphasis upon causative environment. Despite his endorsement of the banning of Tolstoy's *Kreutzer*

---

[15] "A Child of Luck," *Inter Ocean*, May 1, 1886. This series appeared from March 20 through December 4, 1886, with some omissions.

[16] *Forum*, VI (December, 1888), 404–13. See also "The Claim of Realism," *North American Review*, CXLVIII (March, 1889), 386–88; "The Literary Quality of 'Uncle Tom's Cabin,'" *Independent*, XLVIII (August 20, 1896), 3–4.

Sonata from the mails, his tolerance and appreciation of the realists had increased. "The simple fact is," he concluded, "that no novelist paints the real facts of any life"; each makes a selective choice, which may vary from the highest aspiration to the fit of one's trousers, and the only obligation is truthfulness. " 'Realist,' 'naturalist,' 'idealist,' 'romancist,' only that, and nothing more, can be demanded of them—that they paint life as they see it, feel it, believe it to be." [17]

This tolerance may have been encouraged by difficulties of his own; one newspaper rejected Tourgée's offer of some critical essays with the comment that realism was popular with "the people, and they don't want to be told anything to the contrary." He himself was tempted by "the fad of pschycic [*sic*] force and the other fad of *female lascivity*" to plan a story about a woman's spirit borrowing a man's body with which to seduce her rival.[18] He was sure he could make a hit with such a venture but doubted that he would consent to try.

There was insufficient enthusiasm for any such project, and the Judge's novels adhered to his earlier mode, though never again achieving the same descriptive or interpretive significance. He knew of the creative wealth still offered by the South, but absence interfered; he lacked the knack or will for new character study, and his old themes were exhausted. The inspiration to create enduring literature from lesser concerns was just not there. He needed another theme like Reconstruction. But when Tourgée did find a comparable topic, that of the problems of industrial society, he lacked the well of experience, for in the North he had remained something of an isolated celebrity, immersed in none of the real mechanics of society. Whatever his insight or comprehension, his knowledge was secondhand and could not provide the depth and brilliance that had shone from the pages of *A Fool's Errand* and *Bricks Without Straw*.

Nevertheless, the publishers of his previous successes, Fords, Howard & Hulbert, never surrendered their confidence, and while other publishers considered "his *great* popularity . . . a thing of the past," they were easily enticed by that recollection, as well as by sales that ranked

[17] "The Claim of Realism," 388. Tourgée believed in Tolstoy's right to publish but did not think the government should aid in the distribution of his work (*Inter Ocean*, August 9, 1890).

[18] Robert Bonner, N.Y. *Ledger*, to Tourgée, May 18, 1891; Tourgée to his wife, February 25, 1889.

Tourgée ninth among the most popular authors of that decade.[19] The Judge secured profitable serial publication for almost all of his new books, even contracting for them in advance, an important accomplishment in an age when the returns from writing were usually startlingly slim. Among those journals carrying his work were *Lippincott's Monthly*, the Chicago *Advance*, the New York *Ledger*, the Washington *National Tribune*, and *Cosmopolitan*; and in paying three thousand dollars for one novel, the *Inter Ocean* commented that it was paying him three times what it was paying Mark Twain for a comparable story.[20]

These arrangements had their disadvantages. It was understandably difficult to sell stories that were not yet written, while their hurried preparation was, to the annoyance of publishers and readers, most deleterious to their quality. While on speaking tours, the Judge was often hastily writing his latest work on anything from hotel stationery to telegraph blanks, in hotel lobby, parlor car, or waiting room. The helter-skelter preparation of his most serious new fictional effort, *Murvale Eastman: Christian Socialist*, was an indication of the problem. Although he pondered this serial for over a year, Tourgée did not put pen to paper until four days before the first chapter was sent off for publication. The plot was improvised as he proceeded, some chapters were rewritten as many as five times while others were rattled off in one day, and the entire effort was periodically interrupted by his weekly editorial column and proof corrections for another novel. In this fashion fifteen chapters were completed in eight weeks, at which time the work was interrupted by a lecture tour and trips to Washington, D.C., and Lake Mohonk in behalf of Negro rights. Finally, nine months after its beginning, the tale was completed.[21]

Relationships between Tourgée and his editors or publishers varied. They complained of delay and deficiencies in quality or content, and he could be stubborn and arrogant and occasionally picayune or nasty in defense of his income, principles, or pride. Responsibility for the cost of extensive proof corrections was a frequent source of dispute. His

[19] Roberts Bros. to Mrs. Tourgée, March 25, 1887; Arthur Hobson Quinn, *The Literature of the American People* (New York, 1951), 531. Quinn's sales rating for the years 1882–87, based upon very limited evidence, ranks Tourgée ninth at 54, with E. P. Roe first at 1,000, Cable and Howells at 14, and James at 1.

[20] W. P. Nixon to Tourgée, June 20, 1891.

[21] Mrs. Tourgée's Diary, September 17, 1889, to June 25, 1890.

publishers grumbled at disappointing sales and resisted Tourgée's reformism. When the Chicago *Advance* decided that its readers were repelled by Tourgée's bitter novel on the race question, it endeavored to break the contract for the work. "If it is an unpleasant truth," responded Tourgée, "I cannot help it," and the story continued. A year later the *Advance* enjoyed its revenge by censoring portions of another novel and interpreting Tourgée's anguished cry for free speech to mean that it was free to publish what it would and he was free to publish elsewhere. Censorship constituted a problem for the Judge's journalism and poetry as well. The press suppressed columns of his on the race question and politics, and the New York *Ledger* decided that one poem simply would not do because it depicted a southerner admitting that the Lost Cause was wrong.[22]

Of greater amicability and importance were Tourgée's normal dealings with the *Inter Ocean* and with his major publishers, Fords, Howard & Hulbert. A long and welcome employment with the former was attributable to the editor, William Penn Nixon, an ex-abolitionist and Quaker of Indian ancestry who partially sympathized with the Judge's racial and other crusades, and whose views were seconded by an editorial assistant, William H. Busbey, another idealistic Civil War veteran. In the publishing firm, John R. Howard, a fellow alumnus from Rochester, and George S. Hulbert served as close friends and understanding critics. With tolerance and humor, Howard bluntly exposed the Judge's weaknesses, but the impassioned Judge learned slowly, if at all. He will not "spare anything he has written," Howard complained. What he needed was a parish where he could "preach twice Sundays & once Wednesday night, that would relieve his internal moral commotion; then he could write *stories* without *sermons*, except as suggested by his graphic pen-pictures—& thus so much the more efficacious." [23]

Whatever his literary faults, in less than thirteen years after the move to Thorheim, Tourgée published an impressive total of fifteen books. Ten were works of fiction—four novels about the Lake Erie region, a critique of industrial society, an historical romance, a collection

---

[22] Tourgée to H. S. Harrison, March 26, 1889; Harrison to Tourgée, May 19, 1890; N.Y. *Ledger* to Tourgée, January 30, 1890; W. P. Nixon to Tourgée, July 7, 1892.

[23] J. R. Howard to Mrs. Tourgée, March 15, 1893.

of legal tales, a trio of short stories, and two novels reverting to the race and sectional themes. The other volumes consisted of an entrancing history of Tourgée's Ohio Civil War regiment, a series of lectures to young voters, a tract on the silver question, *A Veteran and His Pipe,* and a delightful tribute to his and Emma's marriage.

The local color novels—*Button's Inn* (1887), *Black Ice* (1888), *A Son of Old Harry* (1891), and *The Mortgage on the Hip-Roof House* (1896)—were of little social or artistic significance, although they did capture regional interest and elicit mixed responses from reviewers. For example, the melodramatic *Black Ice,* which drew freely from life at Thorheim, was ironically condemned by one newspaper as "almost as lacking in interest or incident as any one of Henry James' masterpieces of insipidity," while others found it "a lively story with plenty of go in it," one such reviewer "having read 400 pages at a sitting." [24] The Judge's horse story, *A Son of Old Harry,* was heartily recommended for its "rough strength and faithful realism" and impressed experts with the author's "keen instinct and accurate knowledge of the horse." [25] There was some such enthusiasm for each of these works, although the literary magazines were inclined to dismiss them as third- or fourth-rate fiction.

Throughout, these novels relied upon mystery, exciting incident, and a romance, and they were idealistic, melodramatic, sentimental, and weak in creation of character. They exuded an optimism and spirit of unlimited opportunity associated with an earlier free society of the North, while censuring materialistic and selfish trends. The more attractive prose consisted of picturesque sketches of small towns or countryside and of exciting narrative scenes such as the races in *A Son of Old Harry,* the near-drowning in *Black Ice,* or the mystery episodes of *Button's Inn.* Over all, Tourgée revealed himself to be less a novelist, perhaps, than a painter of pastoral scenes, a cracker barrel philosopher, and an historian. His analysis of the nation's religious heritage was astute, he recognized the nation's unique birthright as a people of plenty, and he clearly anticipated the frontier thesis, observing by 1886 that the "especial excellence [of the New World] consists not so much in its resemblance to the old-world life, as in the difference generated by

---

[24] N.Y. *Commercial Advertiser,* March 27, 1888, Nashville *Daily American,* March 18, 1888, Cleveland *Plaindealer,* n.d., and other review clippings.
[25] N.Y. *Sun,* n.d., *Turf Field & Farm,* n.d., and other review clippings.

new conditions." [26] He seldom succeeded, however, in integrating his environmental awareness effectively into the stories or characters he created.

Of similar limited significance, but more polished in structure, were the three trifling stories in *The Man Who Outlived Himself* (1898) and a more informative collection of legal stories, *With Gauge and Swallow, Attorneys* (1889), dedicated to the North Carolina gentleman Republican Samuel F. Phillips, then a prominent Federal officer in the national capital. In this volume, Tourgée carries the reader into some technical and personal intricacies of the changing legal profession, and two of the better tales return to the southern scene. One of these is a tale of miscegenation, in which an irreligious farmer is enticed by the pious into the community church only to take his vows so seriously as to attempt to end an unholy alliance with his Negro mistress by marrying her. This proves too much for the community and its minister. There were unusual plaudits for these stories, with even the Boston *Literary World* praising the volume, and several generations later Alexander Cowie concluded that they were "perhaps too 'technical' to be popular, but they contain some of his most delightful writing." [27]

At this point in Tourgée's career, it is convenient to step past three novels of serious social criticism to consider one uncommon product of his pen, an historical romance set in the Columbian era. Suggested for the centennial of 1892 by a friend and Federal official in the pension bureau, A. W. Fisher, this project revived a collegiate desire that thoroughly captured Tourgée's enthusiasm. Initially, ambitious arrangements were made for a joint project with the historian Hubert Howe Bancroft, who was to do a series of articles but withdrew. Tourgée proceeded with a topic splendidly equipped to give play to his historical, dramatic, and romantic predilections. The result, *Out of the Sunset Sea* (1893), with illustrations by Aimée Tourgée, was a finely written and entertaining adventure tale that captured the flavor and much of the pertinent fact of the era of expansion.[28] Environment and character

26 *Black Ice*, 10. See also *Button's Inn*, 235–42. Tourgée also anticipated future historians in his definition of the profitability of slavery, his conclusion that Lincoln overestimated the strength of unionism in the South, and his exposure of the dishonesty of the so-called Redeemers (see *Inter Ocean*, January 9, 1889, July 24, 1891, and December 21, 1894).
27 Cowie, *Rise of the American Novel*, 531.
28 Initially in *Inter Ocean*, December 18, 1892–March 26, 1893.

are integrated more successfully than usual, and the plot, with one outrageous exception, is believable and consistent, revolving about an Englishman who participates in the Spanish war against the Moors and accompanies Columbus on his voyage of discovery. Tourgée again conquered many reviewers, but the work antedated an approaching revival of interest in historical romance and may have been harmed by the depression that began in 1893. Except for a lucrative serial contract, the profits were slim. Nonetheless, it was reported to be considered superior to Charles Kingsley's *Westward Ho!* by no less an authority than John Fiske, and the *Inter Ocean* declared it one of the most popular stories it had ever carried and eagerly sought a projected companion piece.[29]

A year before the appearance of the Columbian story, Tourgée produced a similarly polished but otherwise different kind of romance, "An Outing with the Queen of Hearts," an idealized account of an isolated vacation trip by Emma and the Judge.[30] Wisely confined to a simple, though deeply felt, scene, this small work provides some delightful nature sketches and an impressive defense of the reality and beauty of romantic love and marriage: "All day long we wandered about, enjoying the solitude; prying into Nature's secrets; talking of old times; feeling the oneness which had grown with years, and is God's sweetest gift to man." There are some polemics, but they are well related and finely drawn, and there is an exciting adventure too, an unbelievable fishing incident that both Emma and the Judge privately insisted was true. Even the animosity of Tourgée's first biographer was softened by portions of this work, just as the Mobile, Alabama, *Register* concluded, on November 18, 1894, that although Tourgée was "a Black Republican of the deepest dye, a hater of the South and a misrepresenter of her people," this book revealed him as "a fanciful, entertaining and often graceful writer."

[29] W. H. Busbey to Tourgée, February 8, 1897.
[30] *Cosmopolitan*, XII (November, 1891), 70–84. Extended and revised in *An Outing with the Queen of Hearts* (New York, 1894).

XXII

The Bystander

The output from Thorheim appears impressive already, at least in bulk, but the major accomplishments of these unbelievably industrious years have hardly been touched upon. Not literature but social analysis and agitation, a constant and widely disseminated clamor for justice and intelligent reform in a distressing age, was to be Judge Tourgée's major new contribution to the nation. The outline of his position had been suggested previously, but now it was to be elaborated and extended, propagated and applied with all his familiar persistence and vigor. In the main it would all be another foolish errand, but time would reveal just how well the fires of war and Reconstruction had taught, tempered and hardened this "impassioned product of the Protestant-Revolutionary tradition."

Perhaps the most remarkable of these new activities began in April, 1888, with the launching of "A Bystander's Notes," a weekly editorial column prominently displayed in the various editions of the *Inter Ocean*, which some years later claimed the largest circulation of any morning newspaper in Chicago, as well as of any political newspaper published west of the Allegheny Mountains. With several interruptions, the two to three thousand weekly words of the Bystander reached as many as two hundred thousand subscribers,[1] in every state and territory as well as abroad, for over ten years. And what a column this was. Defying brief description, its commentary extended to strikes, tariffs, pensions, to lynchings, political parties, and depressions, to the silver question and the "bloody shirt." Lee and Grant were discussed, as were Beecher and

[1] *Inter Ocean*, February 24, 1894; Chicago Inter Ocean Press, A *History of the City of Chicago* (Chicago, 1900), 30, 319.

Blaine, Tolstoy and Scott, Froude and Von Holst, and others as well. Above all, though, the column was directed toward arousing the public against the social evils of the day, toward pleading for economic justice, popular rule, and equal rights throughout the nation and even throughout the world. Sometimes the Bystander column was superb; too often it was verbose; seldom was it trite. It was frequently eloquent in honest indignation, and it could be petty in its partisanship. The sarcasm and wit, the anger and determination, the frustration and conceit of the Judge were all to be found as his very soul seemed to flow into the crusade.

Tourgée was above all a propagandist, whose voluble disputation often outweighed objective study or the careful marshalling of fact. As with his literature, he did not cater fully to modern scientific demands, in this instance failing to exploit opportunities for careful investigation that were already being tapped by the early muckrakers or expressed in such articles as George W. Cable's "The Freedman's Case in Equity." In something of a postwar imitation of the abolitionists, Tourgée would agitate, agitate, agitate, and repeat, repeat, repeat. This lessened, of course, the variety, as well as the finesse, charm, and enduring value, of the bulk of his writing. Nevertheless, he wrote with courage, skill, and effectiveness, and he did so for a major newspaper at a time when the quality of editorial expression in the United States was seriously deteriorating. Not only can one cull from the Bystander one of the more perceptive social commentaries of that era, but such a column appears to have been a rarity in its day and may entitle Tourgée to some significant place in the evolution of the popular independent editorial column.

Nor was this the whole of Tourgée's agitational work. There were also hundreds of lyceum lectures and a number of major addresses in such places as Faneuil Hall, Lake Chautauqua, or the Summer School of Theology in Ocean Grove, New Jersey. There were novels of social protest, an ever-growing correspondence, and articles in the Forum, the Congregationalist, the New York Tribune, the Independent, Frank Leslie's Illustrated Weekly, the Golden Rule, the American Journal of Sociology, the North American Review, and elsewhere. By 1890 the Judge, now fifty-two, had achieved another new high in influence and activity, although there was no lessening of the distressing complaints in Emma's diary regarding impossible burdens of labor and debt.

Tourgée's efforts reflected attitudes that had changed little over many years. Religion still provided him with a source of ethics and optimistic faith, although the Judge claimed "no emotional religious suscep- tibility." "It seems to me," he wrote one minister, "that the chief func- tion of Christianity is to make the earthly conditions better, rather than to speculate upon or anticipate the heavenly ones." [2] The equality of all men under God and the Golden Rule were a major part of an equalitarian rationale, while Reconstruction had done more than all else to ingrain a conviction of the basic ability and goodness of the common man. He abhorred elitist views and was so extreme in his affirmation of the democratic dogma as to insist that "the great lesson of the world's history is, that oppression, evil and national debasement, spring always from the ambition, greed or lethargy of the rich, the wise, the strong, and never from the poor and weak." [3] But he was also con- fident that mankind was overcoming this exploiting minority and steadily progressing toward justice and right. The masses, responding to often unperceived environmental forces, were viewed as the root of this progress, and the real leaders of the world were those who helped point the way. "The man who finds at length the way to cure today's evils," wrote Tourgée, "will not be one whom the rich and cultivated will doat upon, but one whom they will *hate*. The *Christ* was not the tallow- faced mawkish sniveller our modern conception has made him; but a healthy mortal—so far as he was mortal at least—who scourged and cursed and waved over all men the rod of unrest and stirred in all minds the spirit of resistance to wrong. . . ." It is not easy to dismiss as presumptuous his own attempt to play a similar role, for there was an admirable sincerity in the effort. "Suppose there be or not be an eternal *right*—it is palpably evident that there is an eternal *better*," he wrote to Emma. "Man may be better, stronger, purer and man may help his fellow to become better and by so doing become better himself." He could not doubt "that human life has always been growing better, stronger, nobler. It has been going upwards ever since history or tradi-

<hr>

[2] Tourgée to Hull, n.d. [1889–90], Tourgée to Rev. Francis H. Rowley, September, 1893, Tourgée Papers. Unless otherwise indicated, all manuscripts cited in this chapter are from the Tourgée Papers.

[3] "The Rehabilitation of the Fourth of July," *Independent*, XLII (July 3, 1890), 8–9.

tion gave us any hint of its existence. And those who have lifted it most are not those who have passed their lives guessing at the end—puzzling over the infinite or speculating about whether there is a God or in making or overturning creeds—but he who has stopped to lift his fellow's burden, make his task easier, cure his woe or lessen his pain." [4]

Despite the vigor of his social criticism and the radicalism of certain of his views, Tourgée's position was essentially practical and moderate. Reconstruction had again been vital by helping instill a confidence in, and respect for, legality and for the possibilities of peaceful political progress. Under existing conditions he viewed illegality and violence with horror, whether it be by Klansman, Negro, or reformer. Solutions were not to be found in revolution, cynicism, or utopianism but in the fires of free debate and the democratic political process. Agitation was a necessary part of this process, but so too were the responsibilities of citizenship, which he especially urged in his series of essays to young voters, Letters to a King (1888). Although seldom a supporter of civil service reform, sometimes even doubting its wisdom, Tourgée did believe that a variety of political reforms would help, including female suffrage and not only a fair but a compulsory ballot, with time off from work with pay. The vital requirement, however, was the active participation of the people at a time when they appeared anxious to discover "not how the duty of the citizen may be best performed, but how it may be safely neglected." [5] Finally, ironic as it seems, his involvement in the largely futile struggle for Negro rights probably helped keep Tourgée away from more radical or visionary theories. His view of the Negro problem as essentially a southern one initially encouraged his continuing faith in the traditional values of the North, while later, as he became convinced of the decisively undermining impact of "race-prejudice on the part of the Northern people," [6] the evil and the need remained so apparent that no complex theory was needed to explain it. All that was required was the extension of accepted principles of justice and right; yet nothing

[4] Tourgée to ___?___, n.d. [1890]; Tourgée to his wife, January 27, 1889. Twenty-five years earlier he had written: "It is every person's duty in seeking to decide on any course of action, to ask himself, not what will bring himself most pleasure, most temporary enjoyment, but how he shall best perform his duty to God, himself and his fellows, how he shall best observe the purpose of his being" (to his wife, September 6, 1863).

[5] Letters to a King (New York, 1888), 58.

[6] Tourgée to W. A. Hazel, November 7, 1891.

was done. The obvious simplicity of this solution, no matter how exasperatingly out of reach, sharpened Tourgée's awareness of social paradoxes and encouraged his reliance upon a political and democratic structure that many other critics were, in one fashion or another, rejecting.

Second only to the question of Negro rights in Tourgée's agitational crusade was his castigation of the economic and political injustices of the late nineteenth-century United States. Here was a stalwart Republican who recognized and freely damned and fought the deleterious results of the callous search for profit and the increasing concentration of wealth. There was little that escaped his pen—the exploitation, the industrial accidents, the deadly conditions of urban life, the political power and Social Darwinian rationale of the wealthy, and even the mercenary Pinkertons, who were depicted as the equivalent of the Janizaries of the Air in Ignatius Donnelly's popular novel, *Caesar's Column*. Attracting national attention was Tourgée's caustic commentary, "Wanted a New Word," on the exemption of rich and respectable individuals from criminal responsibility for the thousands of deaths caused by the Johnstown flood. "The man who leads a riot is a murderer; the man who inaugurates a war, a patriot. He who kills by retail is a murderer; he who slays by wholesale, is, at the worst, only 'responsible.' " [7]

The social ills of that time, the Judge insisted, could be and should be corrected, and not through that crude and cruel "science of teaching the poor to be content with what they have, and the rich with what they can get." Justice and democracy demanded citizens who were "well fed, comfortably clothed, well housed, and well educated," and existing injustices should be primarily corrected by utilizing government—local, state, and national—to restrict the rich and assist the unfortunate.[8] "The power of wealth," the Bystander column stated, "is just as properly subject to restraint as that of the biceps and is even more liable to

[7] "Wanted a New Word," manuscript; Philadelphia *Press* to Tourgée, June 11, 1889.
[8] Bystander, *Inter Ocean*, January 25, 1890, May 7, July 2, November 5, 1892; Tourgée, "Political Economy, I," clipping. "The question which the world is now trying to solve is where the boundary is, or ought to be, between legitimate and illegitimate individual possession of the fruits of collective production" (Bystander, *Inter Ocean*, November 30, 1889).

abuse." [9] But Tourgée, unlike many others, did not seek the destruction of bigness, a return to the past, but a social intelligence that kept pace with economic progress. There was and could be "no inflexible line drawn between 'individual right' and 'collective right.' The best interests of society may draw the line in one place today and in another place to-morrow. . . . Where this line of demarcation shall be drawn depends entirely on the 'general welfare.' " [10] Furthermore, the Bystander believed that the world was "on the verge of great and radical changes in conditions and aspiration, and that in effecting these the power of government will be exercised in entirely new directions, and on a basis altogether unprecedented in political history; and this extension of the field of governmental function will be made in response to the universal demand of the best brains and truest hearts along the lines of universal equity and by peaceful and moral instrumentalities." [11]

The particulars of his stand were perceptive and practical. In supporting labor unions as a necessary equalizing device, the Bystander perceived that higher wages meant not only higher living standards but expanded markets and increased profits. Similarly, the tariff was viewed as a protection for jobs and wages even more than for industry, and although he was an advocate of sound money and aware of the usual lack of logic in the position of the silverites, the Bystander recognized the impact of deflation and favored an expansion of the currency supply. The Bystander noted the problem of technological unemployment; he advanced arguments in support of profit sharing, Federal insurance of bank deposits, regulated farm warehouses, and the compulsory arbitration of critical labor disputes; and he advised that the nation "tax a man in proportion as he grows rich" to thus "make him tired of growing rich." [12] He also advocated reform as a means of averting future turbulence and crisis. Often Tourgée's position was extremely independent, but its wisdom in substance or strategy defies easy judgment. For example, he supported Federal aid to education, farm warehouses, and currency expansion, and yet, with good reason, he opposed the powerful Blair bill, the subtreasury plan, and the silverite movement.

[9] Bystander, *Inter Ocean*, June 24, 1893.
[10] "John Workman's Notions," *Inter Ocean*, March 23, 1892.
[11] Bystander, *Inter Ocean*, January 25, 1890.
[12] Clipping, discussion by Thomas G. Shearman and Tourgée, Montclair, N.J., Outlook Club, March 20, 1891.

More censurable in these writings are a tedious pedantry and touches of annoying certainty, exaggeration, and alarmism. Just how far the Judge's passion could drive him was revealed elsewhere, in a personal incident arising out of the persisting clash with his stepmother. This antagonism reached its nasty climax in 1889, when Tourgée was not informed of his father's death until a neighbor wrote to question the Judge's absence at the funeral. His resultant fury actually provoked him into denouncing his father's widow in a public letter to the Kingsville, Ohio, press.

The Bystander column also expressed a callous demand for the exclusion of "all but the very best elements of foreign immigration," and, despite Tourgée's severe criticisms of anti-Semitism, he himself held a stereotyped view of the economic Jew.[13] Another great problem was one that had arisen earlier, that of the phenomenon of imperialism. Initially he treated the greed, cruelty, racism, and attempted sanctification of western expansionism scathingly, but gradually his patriotism, together with his sanguine hopes of principled behavior by the United States (another shade of Reconstruction), inclined Tourgée toward endorsing an expansionist role for his own country. This tendency was especially encouraged when the detested President Cleveland thwarted the annexation of Hawaii, an invitation to attack that Tourgée could hardly resist.[14]

When "A Bystander's Notes" first began in the spring of 1888, an unusual amount of serious critical writing by Judge Tourgée was under way. That same year *Letters to a King* was published, as was the first of three new novels of social criticism, all of which had appeared before the end of the following year.

The first of these, *Eighty Nine; or the Grand Master's Secret* (1888), was published under the pseudonym Edgar Henry, and arose from a unique but profitable contract between Tourgée and C. B. Matthews, president of the Buffalo Lubricating Oil Company, which was then angrily fighting John D. Rockefeller's Standard Oil Company.[15] The

---

[13] Bystander, *Inter Ocean*, April 18, 1891; *Button's Inn*, 69.

[14] For example, Bystander, *Inter Ocean*, May 23, August 29, 1891, November 26, 1892, November 10, 1894; "The Man of Destiny," *Inter Ocean*, January 20, February 10, 1894.

[15] Tourgée to Matthews, May 16, 1887, A. E. Moot to Tourgée, September 19, 1887, Tourgée to Moot, September 20, 1887.

novel's hero is Ryal Owen, son of a Georgia farmer and Confederate officer. By means of one of the many exciting horseback rides in Tourgée's fiction, Ryal meets and later marries Edith, daughter of Ambrose Fairbanks, a Union general and an older type of individualistic businessman. In the postwar period Fairbanks is crushed by the ruthlessly monopolistic Rock Oil Company in a series of events that also lead to Edith's death. Ryal then undertakes to carry out his father's last wish—the peaceful secession of the South as a solution to the continuing race problem. Secession is accomplished when northern monopolists, led by Mr. Stoningham of the Rock Oil Company, "a modern Midas with the virtues of a Puritan," join in the scheme as a means of enhancing their political control and crushing "socialistic" tendencies in the North.

The structure of *Eighty Nine* is trite, and digressions are more frequent and laborious than usual, one of them being a splenetic attack upon President Cleveland which virtually ruins the book and suggests that Tourgée sought to duplicate the influence and success of Siva and *A Fool's Errand* by playing a role in the presidential election of that year. At times the prose and melodrama carry the tale well, and there are several excellent observations on the society and history of the North and South, including the understandable but pertinent comment that the nation's raging economic conflict was "not, as so many short-sighted theorists have averred, between the capitalist and the mere laborer, but between the over-gorged capitalist and the great host of enterprising self-employers, whose hope is at the best to secure a modest competency." [16]

Despite such loyal service, the first person irritated with the novel was its sponsor, who had expected the advantage of Tourgée's name and who objected to his excursion into the southern theme. Actually, an alliance of northern and southern reaction was not an idle fear, and Tourgée intended to entice and provoke the citizenry in both sections, but secession as a *pièce de résistance* was another instance of injurious alarmism. The impact was sufficient to inspire many lengthy newspaper reviews, several of which denounced the work for abetting unrest and treason, although the New York *Tribune* found "a great deal of vigorous and even audacious thinking; much of it no doubt obsolete, warped,

[16] *Eighty Nine*, 413.

full of ingrained prejudice, but much also which is clear and incisive and goes straight to the mark." [17] But *Eighty Nine* never caught the public interest. It had sufficient weakness to merit its lack of success, and Tourgée may have erred in not exploiting his own name.

Tourgée's two succeeding novels divided the problems of *Eighty Nine* between them, while seeking their solution through shaming or persuading the nation into conformity with the professed principles of Christianity. "Pactolus Prime; or the White Christ" began as a Christmas short story in the Chicago *Advance* but expanded into a lengthy novel about the life and comments of its namesake, a Negro bootblack in Washington, D.C. There is again the factitious plot and annoying digression, especially into Christian Science, but the sardonic reflections of Pactolus do provide an intriguing discussion of Negro pride and shame, the crossing of the color line, the significance of Negro economic progress, the back-to-Africa movement, and Christian hypocrisy as revealed by slavery, imperialism, and color prejudice. The work was also another forum for advocating Federal aid to education while opposing the Blair bill. Undoubtedly it was a deleterious fact, as many reviewers noted, that the intent of this novel was "humanitarian, and not literary," but the book aroused a nationwide interest that was often favorable and sometimes enthusiastic. The southern response was particularly hostile. "What shall we say of such a writer?" exploded Joel Chandler Harris in the Atlanta *Constitution*. "Is he a monomaniac or simply a refugee from his race?" [18] *Pactolus Prime* certainly was an angry and bitter work, but it was also an essentially accurate exposé of a national shame so great that it may well have warranted the rancor displayed by its author.

It was, however, the last of these three critical novels, *Murvale Eastman: Christian Socialist* (1890), which was the Judge's greatest new achievement in fiction. Though hurried and haphazard in composition,

[17] Clipping, N.Y. *Tribune*, n.d. The Boston *Herald* commented (May 15, 1888): "He is no friend to the United States who sows the seeds of distrust among their people of all sorts and conditions."

[18] Quoted by Bystander, *Inter Ocean*, May 10, 1890. A denunciation of Tourgée's racial equalitarianism appeared in the Chicago *Times*, while favorable reviews appeared, among other places, in the Boston *Traveler*, the Philadelphia *Inquirer*, the N.Y. *Tribune*, and the Philadelphia *Press* (review clippings). The *Nation* said: "The hopeless agony in the lot of the black seeking to obtain among men the place of a man, this is what the book sets powerfully before us" (LI [1890], 195).

this was a heartfelt effort. "The agony—I can use no other word—of decision was intense," Emma confided to her diary as her husband began this tale. "He wishes to do so well—to put so forcibly the truths which have weighed upon him so long," and before long she cautioned the Judge against an application so strenuous that she feared it might kill or drive him into an asylum. But within a year the novel was finished, and the satisfied author was assuring his publishers that "it is not a graded track leading to Elysium but it does point out the pillar of fire that will lead over rocky and difficult desert paths to the only Promised Land which civilization can offer." [19]

The familiar combination of romance, mystery, tumult, and rosy resolution again carries the reader into serious social analysis, which in this instance obviously reflected and contributed to the Social Gospel movement. The hero, Murvale Eastman, is a young clergyman, inexpert only in courtship, who embarks upon a crusade against "a new feudalism" of wealth. Of course the rich were "not all bad" and like the lords of old had a proper claim to "a much higher level of intelligence, enterprise, and what is often termed public spirit." The root of the problem "was not in the men, but in the power they represented, the power to restrict opportunity and compel subservience. The evil lay in the power of the few and the helplessness of the many—the ability of the few to control and of the need of many to serve. It matters nothing whether this power is attested by the crest of a noble or the seal of a corporation, the effect is the same." [20]

In a sometimes entrancing quest for economic justice, Eastman battles the rich, becomes involved in a labor strike, uses the pulpit of the plutocracy as a forum for reform, and succeeds amazingly in all his endeavors. Despite its title and a truly trenchant description of economic evil and injustice, capitalism is endorsed, collectivism is strenuously denounced, and Christianity is championed as the source of a necessary ethic for practical action. The present-day demand upon Christianity, Eastman informs his shocked flock, is that it re-evaluate its faith in salvation and consider what it can "do for human betterment, to lessen

[19] Tourgée to J. R. Howard, November 4, 1890.
[20] *Murvale Eastman*, 251–52. This ran initially as a serial, "Nazirema, or the Church of the Golden Lilies," in the Chicago *Advance* from October 3, 1889, through July 3, 1890.

human woe, to increase the sum of human happiness, and advance the standard of human duty; to labor, in short, for human elevation on earth both as an end and as the surest method of effecting the eternal salvation of man." [21] Once this conviction is established (and this is primarily what the author urges), the methods will follow. Eastman does, however, go a step further in forming clubs of Christian Socialism, which accept anyone, atheist or believer, who will abide by the Golden Rule. These intended rivals of the Bellamite and Single Tax clubs were not intended to accomplish "impossible changes of human nature or the overthrow of all existing social conditions" but to act as publicity and action groups in behalf of sensible reforms. The novel's happy ending attests the author's faith, and it was precisely this ethical commitment to practical reform that would soon become and long remain the national pattern.

Murvale Eastman was clearly one of the Judge's superior works. There was artistry and originality in its many observations on the flaws and accomplishments of the rich and the poor, on the myopic views of management and labor, and on the delusions of human conscience and belief. Eastman's archrival, the millionaire Wilton Kishu, was especially well portrayed. He was a man whose conscience smote him for the smallest infraction of the law, but who, before his conversion, remained contentedly oblivious to the oppression and ruin caused by his business activities. One of the novel's most successful scenes was a satirical comparison of the care bestowed by the urban streetcar company upon its horses and upon its employees. The latter were piously consigned to the cruel but "divine law" of supply and demand, while the most fastidious care was lavished upon the horses by the company, one of whose directors was a leader in the S.P.C.A.[22]

Although artistic objections were again made and the New York *World* justifiably advised "a cold-blooded blue-penciled fiend to handle his manuscripts," *Murvale Eastman* was Tourgée's best-received novel, excepting his Reconstruction works. It was even praised by the *Yale Literary Magazine* and, since it did not emphasize the Negro question, by the southern press.[23] And, as always, there were strangely contrasting

[21] *Murvale Eastman*, 122–23.
[22] *Ibid.*, 142–46. For Kishu, see 384–86.
[23] Review clippings, N.Y. *World*, February 1, 1891, *Yale Literary Magazine*, February, 1891, Charleston, S.C., *News*, February 22, 1891.

evaluations of the Judge's thoughts, which in this instance were considered both practical and impractical, conventional and unique, conservative and dangerously radical. The famed Chautauquan bishop John H. Vincent hoped the work would be read "by every minister, mechanic, merchant, millionaire, and farmer in America," and the Los Angeles *Times*, while granting that Tourgée was not in the highest literary ranks, felt that there was "that in his style and method of treatment of whatever theme he handles, that compels attention. Keen, incisive, logical, and possessing the marvelous skill of a great word painter, he startles us into attention with facts that it is well for us to know." But the San Francisco *Examiner* best captured the author's intent with its comment that the novel had "in it all the motive power of something better than a social revolution: the direction of the thought and energy of Christian people into the right channels, the development of a practical Christianity, and the establishment of a kindly brotherhood between rich and poor, which shall be neither a burden to the former nor a curse to the latter." It was obvious that Tourgée was sowing seeds, a few of which sprouted as far off as in England, and some scholars of a later generation would conclude that *Murvale Eastman* was "the best known" work of Christian progressivism in the early 1890's and perhaps "the most carefully considered novel of Christian socialism" written.[24]

Other critical writings by Tourgée that merit attention include a discerning historical analysis, "The Anti-Trust Campaign," which appeared in 1893 in the *North American Review*, and a repudiation of Malthusianism printed several years later in the *American Journal of Sociology*.[25] The latter considered the problem of society to be "a steadily growing surplus of production, with its naturally depressing effect on prices and inevitable oversupply of labor," and urged as a remedy the general pursuit of social improvement rather than profit. Tourgée specifically suggested reduced working hours, public works, tariff protection and reciprocal trade, restricted production, the planned

[24] J. R. Howard to Tourgée, February 9, 1891; clippings, Los Angeles *Times*, January 28, 1891, and San Francisco *Examiner*, February 2, 1891. The book was discussed by a conference of about thirty ministers in England (Constance Shepard, England, to Tourgée, July 14, 1893). See also Walter F. Taylor, *The Economic Novel in America* (Chapel Hill, 1942), 100; Henry F. May, *Protestant Churches and Industrial America* (New York, 1949), 208.

[25] "The Reversal of Malthus," *American Journal of Sociology*, II (July, 1896), 13–24.

redirection of labor, and catering to the nonconsumer needs of the public. An anonymous column of economic ramblings in the *Inter Ocean*, "John Workman's Notions," also carried Tourgée's reformist thoughts for almost a year.

One indication of the impact of Tourgée's writings was his rapidly expanding circle of correspondents, which by the 1890's provided an extraordinary commentary on the nineteenth-century United States. There were letters from Negroes and whites, men and women, racists and equalitarians, college presidents and congressmen, clergymen and merchants, doctors and lawyers, and from farmers, laborers, and ordinary folk. Populists and socialists wrote to him, and Single Taxers and Greenbackers, suffragettes and temperance advocates, anarchists and Knights of Labor, Bellamites and idealistic Republicans. Negroes applauded his assistance, and southern Republicans described their travails. He was urged to campaign for a subtreasury plan and against the black-listing of employees and the sins of dancing. A Grinnell College debater sought his assistance, abolitionists welcomed his inspiration, and an Iowa farmer warned that half his neighbors were "ready now to take up arms against the existing conditions of things." [26] A businessman in Michigan was ready to follow wherever Tourgée would lead, the minister of the Park Street Congregational Church in Boston offered the use of his pulpit at any time, *Our Day* of Boston offered him an associate editorship, newspapers from Georgia to California to Illinois commented on the Bystander column, and, in the course of nature, there appeared a number of namesakes. Altogether, it was a revelation and an inspiration, and many of the readers affected were influential ones. There were clergymen of various denominations from many states, even including a missionary in Japan, as well as teachers, educators, librarians, and editors. Catherine Impey, the English Quaker, reformer, and publisher of *Anti-Caste*, was attracted by Tourgée's fight for Negro rights; a director at Hull House sought his advice; a governor of Minnesota appointed him to the Anti-Trust Association of the United States; Susan B. Anthony sent one of her books; and a congressman consulted with him about establishing a Federal economic commission. The associate editor of the *American Economist*, a high-tariff organ, was impressed by his economics, as

[26] A. J. Mansfield to Tourgée, 1894. See Tourgée's correspondence from 1889 to 1896.

were several minor economic reformers.[27] Julius A. Wayland, then publishing the *Coming Nation,* was a correspondent, as were newspaper editors or proprietors, Negro and white, from Boston, Omaha, Chicago, New York, Cleveland, New Orleans, and Detroit, and from small towns like Chautauqua and Danville, New York. A number of state legislators and congressmen, the most notable being Thomas B. Reed, were also directly influenced by Tourgée.

The precise impact of Tourgée's writings, however, cannot be easily assessed. Most of his program had little success, his supporters were usually lesser figures, and he was not a part of any really successful reform movement. In politics and publication he was a well-known but secondary figure, who fell just short of both power and technical perfection. Yet he remains an intriguing and important figure, operating on a decisive but unjustly neglected social level. His words were reaching thousands, despite some weaknesses they were persuasive and popular, and to some extent they were helping to establish the ground swell of the progressive future. For an impassioned reformer, the Judge also had a remarkable appeal for business and professional people, government administrators, and political leaders.[28] In part this may be attributed to his earlier fame, but it also reflected an effective manner combined with traditionalism, practicality, and a sympathy for the professional and business middle class.

Throughout these years of reformist agitation, Tourgée's major outlet for his writing had remained the *Inter Ocean,* a newspaper for the "solid respectable classes" whose motto was "Republican in everything, independent in nothing." [29] Little wonder that he had periodic spats with this paper over his wide wanderings from the party line and his denunciations of Republican spoilsmen, but his popularity and Editor

[27] Nicholas P. Gilman and George M. Ramsey (profit sharing), James M. Gale (banking), Albert Griffin and John A. Grier (currency).

[28] Congressmen William P. Frye (Maine), William E. Chandler (New Hampshire), Marriott Brosius and Thomas W. Phillips (Pennsylvania), Joseph D. Taylor (Ohio), John J. Ingalls and Harrison Kelley (Kansas), and David B. Henderson and Joseph H. Sweney (Iowa), and state legislators Charles T. Saxton and James T. Edwards (New York), Harry C. Smith (Ohio), and J. Gray Lucas (Arkansas) were friendly correspondents, as were such men as A. W. Fisher, Department of Interior; A. M. Robbins of Mark Hanna & Co.; John E. Burton, president of Hidalgo Smelting Co.; and Russell A. Alger, tycoon and politico.

[29] Mott, *American Journalism: A History* . . . *1690 to 1940* (New York, 1941), 463.

Nixon's sympathy maintained the tie, and the Judge actually was a firm, though maverick, Republican. He had little hope for, and several objections to, existing third-party efforts, and the Democrats remained openly racist and laissez-faire at a time when he increasingly looked to government, particularly the Federal government, as a positive agent for public welfare. Just as the Federal government, under Republican auspices, had preserved the Union, abolished slavery, and promoted prosperity, so, too, it should protect its citizenry from racist or economic oppression.

In a ceaseless campaign to redirect his party, Tourgée sought to convince party leaders that subservience to wealth and the abandonment of the Negro surrendered both principles and votes. He fought the Republican machine in his own local area and was active in several unsuccessful efforts to obtain the nomination of a reform presidential candidate. Although unusually active as a campaigner during presidential elections, the Judge sometimes found his activities curtailed by his refusal to shun the race question, and he persisted in reminding the party that it lost the presidency in precisely those years in which it most clearly abandoned an idealistic stand. To a great extent, Tourgée was, in fact, still continuing the Civil War and Reconstruction struggle. He believed that the desired victory could only come from the North, that it could be achieved by again endorsing humanitarian principles, and that while this victory would establish protection for all citizens from economic, political, and racial injustice, it would extend special Federal educational aid and protection into the South. As for the familiar cry of "bloody-shirt," Tourgée effectively rejected this as a counter-stereotype and a "petulant plea for exemption from the common lot of popular scrutiny and animadversion." [30]

Tourgée's hopes proved false. His concerns did not capture the interest of the Republican party, and reformers and eventually even Negroes increasingly turned away. The Judge was not naïve respecting the true state of affairs. He perceived Republican subservience to bosses and to wealth and was constantly urged by reformers to support third-party

[30] Bystander, *Inter Ocean*, April 22, 1893. For Tourgée's political rationale, see especially *ibid.*, April 28, November 17, 1888, July 2, 30, 1892, June 16, 30, 1894; Tourgée to Marriott Brosius, n.d. [1891]; Tourgée to President Harrison, April 12, 1890, September 25, 1891, Harrison Papers, Manuscripts Division, Library of Congress.

movements, but all things considered, there was hardly a better choice than the one he made. He had encouraging support within the Republican party, and he felt that honorable though futile combat was preferable to cynical resignation or surrender. He knew that many of his own allies considered him a disloyal and radical crank and a flayer of the dead horse of the Confederacy, but still he fought; he was prepared to sacrifice his literary interests to the cause and remained presumptuous enough to censure a Republican president and threaten him with the power of his pen.[31] To a congressman, Tourgée complained bitterly that the Republican bosses did not want individuality or responsible citizenship. All they desired was *"power."* And a Chicago journalist reported how a Republican banquet was left "in wild-eyed wonder" by one of his speeches, "which for brilliance of epigram, exquisite pathos, rich, broad humor has never been excelled at a political gathering in this state. . . . It seems to be the case with him not that he hates republicanism less, but democracy more. He made a rattling good speech and never condescended once to obtain applause by mere clap-trap. If Tourgée isn't a wonderfully earnest man he is a consummate actor, and at any rate he has the sardonic courage of a Lucifer with the inherent humanity of a St. Bernard." [32] Precisely these same qualities would continue to interfere with Tourgée's efforts to influence the northern Republican party or secure political position for himself, and it is a moot point whether he did more to enhance reformism within the party or to attract reformist support for a hopeless cause.

[31] *Ibid.*

[32] Clipping, Chicago *Herald*, March 4, 1891, and Tourgée to Marriott Brosius, n.d. "The question is not what is best, but which is better" (Bystander, *Inter Ocean*, June 30, 1888).

XXIII

Commitment Deferred

A variety of other activities also reflected Tourgée's crusading ardor. He received appreciative acknowledgments from penitentiary inmates in Minnesota for his prison reform work, and he was proud of promoting female participation in the New York State Prison Association. He supported relief and educational work among the Indians, and religious reformers sought his election, as a representative of women's rights and increased lay control, to the National Council of the Methodist Episcopal church. With uneasy memories of Baptist influence at Rochester University, he was also involved in efforts to reduce sectarian control of that school. Less disinterested, though in part patriotic, was his support of improved copyright laws and veteran's pensions. In 1890 the Judge became involved in an odd split in the temperance movement when he denounced the Woman's Christian Temperance Union and the Prohibition party for supporting the exclusion of illiterate Negroes from the ballot.[1] This incident reflected what had remained his central concern during all these years, the Negro question.

Not even the *Continent* debacle had seriously interrupted Tourgée's persistent demand that the nation fulfill its commitments to the Negro, and more than all else it was the evils of racism that infuriated and inspired and increasingly mocked this nineteenth-century Isaiah. No doubt the obstinate courage of a past commitment and fond remem-

---

[1] See, for example, Tourgée to Non Partisan Woman's Christian Temperance Union, January 22, 1890; N. T. Arnold to Tourgée, July 2, 23, October 19, 1891; T. J. Morgan, U.S. Office of Indian Affairs, to Tourgée, November 1, 1894; clipping, Minnesota *State Prison Mirror*, June 27, 1895, all in the Tourgée Papers. Unless otherwise indicated, all manuscript citations in this chapter are from the Tourgée Papers.

brances of past glory helped carry the Judge along, but they did not have the same force as did honest conviction.

This was an era when the Negro began his descent to a new low in American life: lynching and other forms of oppression were increasing and Jim Crow was becoming fashionable, the courts were emasculating constitutional protections and liberals were abandoning the cause, Republicans were renouncing their promises and the entire nation was accepting the rationale and the practices of racism. Tourgée was one of the few to pay the attention that this mockery of the national ethos deserved, and the fact that the final decision was still in the process of being made intensified his fiery concern. It may be no exaggeration to say that during the last two decades of the century Tourgée was the most vocal, militant, persistent, and widely heard advocate of Negro equality in the United States, black or white. He was the Garrison of a new struggle, but the times were wrong.

In his lectures and speeches, his articles and books, and above all in the Bystander column, with logic and passion, pathos and hope, Tourgée depicted in detail the origins of racism, smashed its rationalizations, and demanded its end. Again his writing was polemical and repetitious, but the extent and sophistication of his coverage, the fire and eloquence of his presentation, and the effectiveness with which he exposed and mangled the rationale of racism has been seldom, if ever, equaled. He demolished the innumerable varieties of anti-Negro thought and behavior and pointed out in forcible language the hypocrisy of the contrast between the professed principles of western civilization and its treatment of the world's colored population. He was aware of the depth, the sincerity, and the nature of such prejudice, but to him these considerations served neither as excuses for injustice nor deterrents to exposure and damnation. "I am a 'fanatic,'" he chided his opponents, "because I believe in the equal rights of all men, and in a God who is not partial to some of His children and cruel as an Aztec to others. . . . You think God is on the side of the white man; I think the white man would best be careful that he is on the Lord's side." [2] A portion of the Bystander

---

[2] Bystander, *Inter Ocean*, October 22, 1892. Permission has been kindly granted to reprint this and other items from Olsen, "Albion W. Tourgée and Negro Militants of the 1890's: A Documentary Selection," *Science & Society*, XXVIII (1964), 183–208.

column of March 4, 1893, captures the spirit of hundreds of thousands of similar words:

> The Bystander believes in the American Negro as a man and as an American. He believes in his capacity and the progress he has made. He would spare no exertion to right his wrongs, encourage his efforts, or show the world what he has done and what has been done for him. He regards the progress made since emancipation, in knowledge, in professional skill, in material acquirements, and in literary achievement as the most marvelous work of civilization.
>
> He counts the heroism, patience and faith of those who gave time, and strength, and opportunity, and money to set him afoot in the new career, as the crowning glory of American Christianity. Likewise he counts the spirit that bars him from equal right, equal privilege and equal opportunity, the most cowardly and infamous form of barbarism—the direct inheritance of that worst of all human institutions, Christian slavery. He believes in the same rights, the same remedies, the same law, the same opportunity, and the same privilege for one race as for another. "Good for white; good for black," is to his mind the sole test of methods, conditions, institutions, legislation and administration.

There was little regarding the race question that escaped Judge Tourgée, although, understandably, he focused his attack upon the South, the scene of the most intense and constant oppression. Portions of the southern press and leadership persistently provoked this emphasis with their demands for white supremacy and segregation, justifications of lynching, and racist declarations such as "as a general thing the educated negro is of all creatures the worst." [3] Tourgée responded by bitterly mocking the backwardness, selfishness, and foolishness displayed for so many years by a white supremacist South. At the same time he applauded departures from racist mores and anticipated eventual change.

---

[3] Clipping, Nashville *American*, March 17, 1889. Paternalism could be annoying too; for example: "The Negroes of the South today are the happiest and best contented class of laboring people on the globe" (clipping, Birmingham *Age-Herald*, April 20, 1890).

When the South did emerge, however, it would "no longer be 'the silent South' nor the subservient or palliating South, but the accusative and denunciatory South, which will realize that honor consists not in the concealment or denial of evils, but in their exposure and eradication." [4]

For his own time, however, the Judge had little faith in the white South. "Mr. Cable's 'Silent South,' " he wrote to a Negro leader, "is a silent humbug—and always will be silent." Such pessimism further encouraged his reliance upon Federal authority, and there was, perhaps, more than a little perception in the conclusion that "when the South is once convinced that the country is determined that the Negro shall have his rights as a citizen he will get them. Until that time he never will." This conviction was also eventually related to the efficacy of educational aid. Prejudice could not "be restrained by knowledge alone," Tourgée concluded in the 1890's, but if prejudice were effectively restricted by law, then it would "rapidly disappear with the spread of intelligence." [5] To justify Federal action he appealed not only to commitments, promises, and principles but to considerations of national dignity, southern progress, increased markets for the North, and potential violence. While in their immediate expectations his dire warnings of violence were exaggerated, racial injustice would yet bring much violence, and Tourgée's forebodings would be re-echoed by rather conservative spokesmen over seventy years later. [6]

During these years there was more than reason enough to despair of the fight, and many were the cries of anguish raised by the Judge against the failings of the Negroes and the callousness of the whites. But he continued to preach and apparently to believe that civilization was inexorably moving toward the desired goal, that the rise of the Negro was a part of a progression toward human equality and freedom for all that was already at full tide, and that the United States was the world center of this trend. The blessings of the Lord and the conscience of the multitude would inevitably bring about the triumph of justice, for "in the last analysis justice is the most powerful incentive of the Amer-

[4] Bystander, *Inter Ocean*, September 22, 1894.

[5] Tourgée to D. Augustus Straker, February 27, 1890; Bystander, *Inter Ocean*, January 12, 1889; manuscript essay on the Republican party, n.d. [1894?].

[6] Tourgée to John Mitchell, Jr., August 30, 1891. See Walter Lippman, Norfolk *Virginian-Pilot*, August 29, 1963.

ican people." [7] But he knew that it would take popular action by Negroes and whites to arouse this conscience and redirect the nation.

It is little wonder that the vociferous Judge became the special target of racist venom throughout the United States. He was considered a proper candidate for hanging and was freely and frequently described in such terms as "a vulture," "a fool yet unclassified," "a consummate liar and ass," and a "pestiferous mouther who for years has labored to incite an uprising of the Negroes in the South and whose fondest hope is that the white people of this section will be slaughtered by the thousands. . . ." [8] A somewhat different picture was revealed in the Negro press and in the Judge's mounting correspondence with the colored people's leaders.

Tourgée's involvement in the Negro issue approached a new intensity in 1888 with the beginning of the Bystander column, the appearance of *Eighty Nine* and *Pactolus Prime*, and a pertinent presidential campaign. Aided by his recollections of party failure four years earlier, Tourgée stood among a host of Republicans who were convinced either of the righteousness or of the potential popularity of a return to the struggle for Negro rights. But intraparty opposition was also powerful, consisting largely of high-tariff Republicans and Mugwumps. Although Tourgée participated in an attempt to nominate Robert Todd Lincoln for the presidency, he was not discouraged by the party's choice of Benjamin Harrison, a veteran who had displayed militancy regarding the race question and supported Federal aid to education. Soon after Harrison's nomination, the Judge, with appropriate flattery, presumed to make direct suggestions as to the proper campaign tactics. With warnings against relying solely upon the tariff issue and the support of the wealthy, Tourgée advised the Republican nominee to cultivate mass support by campaigning against concentrated wealth and for Negro rights. In addition he urged that a hundred leading conservative Republicans be sent to campaign in the southern states, a tactic no one had dared since Reconstruction. The Judge noted that this approach might not carry that section but would restore Republican prestige and

[7] Bystander, *Inter Ocean*, August 15, 1891.

[8] Clippings, Chicago *Herald*, March 31, 1892, Macon *Evening News*, June 12, 1892, New Orleans *Daily States*, June 14, 1892, New York *Mercury*, June 19, 1892, Mayersville *Spectator*, n.d.

help the conservative wing understand what the real situation was. In any event, he promised Harrison, "If you have nerve enough to order such an invasion of the South, you will find a 'Solid' North at your back." [9] To Tourgée this was not waving the bloody flag of the past but uncovering the present brutal truth.

The response was encouraging until the Republican National Committee succeeded in establishing a contrary policy, one that ignored the Negro and sought to cultivate southern white support by means of the tariff issue. There were few stronger tariff advocates than the Judge, but he was not about to consider "the American hog of more importance than the American citizen," and his scheduled campaigning was cancelled by the party.[10] He did retain a claim to notice by stumping on his own, although he did not enhance his influence by taking Harrison to task for slighting a request for an endorsement of *Letters to a King*, a book of political essays just published, which Tourgée hoped would influence the Republican campaign. "I have always taken my pay in more pulling," he informed the man who was soon to be president, "and have never been one of the crowd that is willing to kiss a presidential candidate's back side for the sake of hanging upon his coat tails." [11]

Harrison's victory strengthened the hand of those elements in the party who were disposed to abandon the Negro, but at the same time Tourgée considered any Democratic defeat a blow at white supremacy, and he had been encouraged by the public response to his campaign speeches. Also, there was reason for continued hope in Harrison, and, for the first time since the presidency of Grant, the Republicans controlled both houses of Congress. But it would be a year before the new Congress was seated, and things began to look worse before they looked better. Particularly annoying to Tourgée was a twisted application of his own strategy—the dispatching of prominent Republicans southward in quest of white voters only. As it developed, however, the poor results of

[9] Tourgée to Harrison, June 29, 1888, Harrison Papers. For the Republicans' tactical struggle, see Vincent P. de Santis, *Republicans Face the Southern Question* (Baltimore, 1959); Hirshson, *Farewell to the Bloody Shirt.*

[10] Bystander, *Inter Ocean*, November 17, 1888; Tourgée to Harrison, September 25, 1891, Harrison Papers. Cf. Harry J. Sievers, *Benjamin Harrison. Hoosier Statesman* (New York, 1959), 389.

[11] Tourgée to Harrison, September 15, 1888, Harrison Papers.

this effort in the southern elections of 1889 rekindled the tactical debate, while an obvious intensification of Negro oppression provided Tourgée with provocation, ammunition, and a widening circle of sympathizers. This new wave of racism, which was in good part a response to a spreading agrarian reform movement and an increasing Negro militancy, was characterized by an upsurge in lynchings and terrorization of Negro voters, followed by demands for "legal" disfranchisement and segregation laws. Noticeable signs of Tourgée's agitation at this time were his two superb articles, "Shall White Minorities Rule," in the *Forum*, and "Our Semi-Citizens," in *Frank Leslie's Illustrated Weekly*. The Judge was also gratified by increasing requests for lectures and an ever-mounting correspondence on this matter, and he was delighted by a request in 1889 for an article on the Negro from the New York *Tribune*, considering that newspaper hitherto "at the head of the mercenary branch of the Republican party," and its editor, Whitelaw Reid, "the real author of Blaine's policy in 1884, 'the nigger must go to the rear.' " [12]

Not only was Tourgée correct in hopefully anticipating a revival of the Negro question, but his own involvement was unexpectedly increased by an admirer from Kansas, Harrison Kelley, who had just been appointed to a vacancy in the House of Representatives and who seemed as anxious to represent Tourgée as the State of Kansas in the Fifty-first Congress. Welcoming this opportunity, the Judge warned the fledgling congressman against the pitfalls of selfishness and failure, while encouraging, as possible if improbable, the achievement of Federal aid to education and a Federal election law. Two such bills were actually written by Tourgée and introduced into the House by Kelley as a lesser part of a major congressional struggle soon under way over just these matters. In the course of this struggle, the determined Judge, although confined to a wheel chair at the time, traveled to the Capitol early in 1890 to testify before congressional committees on these topics. While in Washington he also lunched with the President, from whom he sought a judgeship, as well as support for Negro rights, and conferred for hours with the Speaker of the House, Thomas B. Reed. Whatever Tourgée's

[12] Tourgée to W. P. Nixon, August 29, 1889, and Tourgée to George C. Butterfield, January, 1890. Other articles included "Shall We Rebarbarize the Negro?" (*Congregationalist*, XLI [December 5, 1889]); "The Right to Vote" (*Forum*, IX [March, 1890]); "The Rehabilitation of the Fourth of July" (*Independent*, XLII [July 3, 1890]).

influence, both the President and the Speaker remained among the firmest supporters of an educational and an election bill. Tourgée also continued to promote these measures through the Bystander column, the novel *Pactolus Prime,* and extensive lobbying activities.

The first congressional dispute centered about the long-debated Blair bill for Federal aid to education. A decade of debate on this measure had actually strengthened the opposition. This opposition included foes of centralization, suspicious southerners, economy-minded northerners, and sectarians, and the sympathetic New York *Tribune* attributed an ominous shift in the attitude of some Republicans to the predominance of economic interest over principles. But another bit of opposition, which historians have neglected, came from Tourgée, who had influenced the debate for years and who objected to the Blair bill's reliance upon state governments and encouragement of certain inequities in the South. This bill allocated Federal funds in accordance with illiteracy rates but allowed the states to distribute the funds between the races on a per capita basis. Thus, as the Judge correctly pointed out, in a state with a colored population of one-third, if Negroes formed two-thirds of the illiterates, they would receive only one-third of the funds. This was certainly inconsistent with a system of a Federal distribution based upon illiteracy, as well as being a tacit encouragement of separate but unequal education. The Blair bill was finally killed by a very narrow Senate vote, Tourgée's views having been cited in debate and reflected in the views of at least five senators.[13] A shift of three votes would have passed the bill. The Judge may thus have contributed to the decisive defeat of a principle he had vigorously championed for many years, for his own bill was never considered and Federal aid to education was shelved for a generation. Tourgée, who was able to endorse segregated schools as better than no schools but not unjust Federal aid as better than no aid, watched approvingly from the Senate gallery as the bill was killed, and he continued to insist that "it was a lucky thing for the colored people of the South that the Blair bill did not pass." [14] The wisdom of his combination of principle and pragmatism was questionable, not only because of final defeat of the principle, but because

[13] Senators Spooner, Ingalls, Dolph, Hale, Plumb, and probably Frye, who was an admirer. See *Congressional Record,* 51st Cong., 1st Sess., 1874–75, 1998, 2192, 2436.
[14] Clipping, Tourgée interview. See also Washington *Daily Critic,* March 25, 1890.

VOLUME VII. NO. 26. DETROIT, MICH., NOVEM

AN IMPORTANT MATTER

OF NO PARTY, BUT AN APPEAL TO THE CONSCIENCE OF THE LAND.

The Great Weapon—Take Up the Cudgel—Power is the Only Guarantee For Right—Work, Tact, Silence and Self Abnegation.

Bystander in the Chicago Inter-Ocean.

One of the recent facts touching the question of the negro's relation to our National affairs is the proposed convention for the purpose of organizing a National league of colored men. The object of such an organization is, broadly stated to promote the interests of the colored race in the United States. The first thing to be done will, of course, be to determine what is practicable for the Negro to do to promote his own real enfranchisement, secure redress of the wrong which attach to his condition, and obtain for himself equal and unrestricted privilege and opportunity as a citizen and in business. From the point of view of an outsider who sympathizes with the work to be done, believes in the necessity of its being done by the race itself in a large measure, and realizes the difficulties in the way of its accomplishment, the proposed organization is a matter of very great importance.

* * *

Some Republican journals have seriously discouraged this project, insisting that the Republican party is devoted to securing equal rights and opportunities to the colored man, and that he needs no other organization to promote his interests. "What would be thought," asks one, "if a National convention of white men should be called to promote the interest of the white race?" Well, just such conventions are called and have long been in vogue. Until within thirty years such a thing as the interest of the colored man being considered in any political convention, except by the little squad of Abolitionists who persistently camped upon a neglected corner of the political field greatly to the annoyance of the other occupants, was never dreamed of. Even now the Democratic party boasts itself a "white man's party," and at the South never professed to be anything else.

In fact, our entire civilization has been either positively or tacitly white. In those regions where the Negro has not been actually distinguished against he has rarely been regarded as a fit subject for those influences which develop and exalt.

* * *

The claim that the Republican party is all the organization the Negro requires comes with very bad grace from the organs of a party which has shown itself thus far quite unable to deal with the questions touching his rights as a man and a citizen—a party with the record of inconsistency of 1876 upon its shoulders—an inconsistency so glaring that it seems impossible that any Northern Republican of average sensibility should ever ask a colored man to rely upon that party to remedy the evils which attach to his condition, at least until that crime against good faith and common sense has been retrieved.

* * *

The simple fact is that the Republican party is just like any other party. It seeks success and, within certain limits, it advocates and does whatever its leaders and manipulators believe will secure success and avoids what they believe will endanger that result. This is the very highest merit of the party system, which makes it the most perfect instrumentality of progress yet devised for a self-governing people. Strong; resolute, intense men, looking over the field of public sentiment, adjudge this idea or that to be uppermost in the popular mind, and so order an advance along this or that portion of the line of policy the party occupies and expect the rest without abandoning their position to remain comparatively quiet in any particular struggle. It is for this reason that the Republican party, after twenty-five years of aggressive movement along the line of individual right, turned again to the front the old Whig principle of protection and fought its battle almost solely on that issue. It was not because it had not abandoned the principle of equal right and privilege, but because the leaders believed that success was more probable if the attack was made on another part of the line. Many of its leaders, both during the campaign and since that time, have favored relegating the question of the rights of the colored man to the background. They have "had enough of the nigger," they say.

* * *

This is only natural, but it has an especial significence for the colored man. Whenever he shall make his rights and wrongs so prominent in the public mind that the leaders of the Republican party are morally certain of defeat unless they shall earnestly and effectually seek to secure the one and redress the other, then their coalition will receive its attention and remedial measures of a practical and effective character will be adopted or proposed as an issue on which it will join battle with its opponent. The purpose of such a league as is proposed, should not be either to antagonize or promote the interests of the Repubilcan party. That is a body quite as able to take care of itself. Its object should be to so present the interest and condition of the colored citizenship of the United States to the mind and conscience of the land, that no party will dare ignore the question—to compel the leaders of the Republican party to make the cause of the oppressed citizen their own, as they once did the cause of the slave. The hope of success is the mainspring of all party action. There may be wheels and balances and escapements, but the powe rwhich moves them all is the prospect of success. The politician may clean the works, oil the bearings, and adjust the movements, but public sentiment is the key which sets them all in motion and strains the spring which is the continuing motor.

* * *

But this is not the true test of the propriety and advisability of such a measure as the League proposed. Organization is the great weapon with which the battles of moderen civilization are fought. It is the common instrument by which the strong oppress the weak, and the weak resist the aggressions of the strong. It is the power which arms the hand of capital and makes the protest of labor effectual. The Negro race in America represents 8,000,000 souls having a common interest peculiar to themselves and laboring under specific disabilities. Their first duty to themselves and the world is to organize for the redress of grievances and use the power conferred upon them to compel the granting of equal privilege and opportunity to the Negro as a citizen. Let them hunt for redress just as the same number of white men having a common grievance would do—*with a club.*

* * *

It is high time the colored man took up the cudgels foa the assertion of his rights himself. There will never be any more Garrisons or Phillipses to fight his battles for him. It is not desirable that there should be. Liberty is a boon that can never be given to any race or a people. It must always be won by those who would enjoy it. All that others can do is to give a race a *chanee* to be free. The colored man in the United States has passed the period of tutelage. He must define and assert his strength—make himself felt—if he expects to win equal right and privilege as a man.

* * *

The first thing to be done in the assertion of his right is to show that he has power. Establish a colored League in the United States where a solid, earnest membership, large enough in half a dozen States of the North to turn the scale in an election, and the Republican party will no longer be apathetic in regard to his citizenship at the South. Even the Democracy may begin to have some respect for him. Let the Negro of the North use the collective force of his race, not to secure what is termed "recognition"—an office and a little pelf for individuals—but use it as his noble examplars the old time Abolitionists used their power—to bring fuller liberty to his race at the South. It amounts to nothing that A. B, or C. with the black skin is given an official position in some city or State in the North. It is civil and political liberty for the race at the South that is to be achieved. And this can only be obtained by compelling by united, harmonious action backed by demonstrable power, the active assertion of the rights of National citizenship to supplement and make effective its empty definition.

* * *

If the same number of native white citizens of the United States had a like common interest and common grievance there would have been such an organization long ago. Respect is always accorded to power and nothing but power. Weakness may awaken pity and pity may induce people to give alms; but power or the show of power is the only thing that gives equality or serves as a guarantee for right.

* * *

We have organizations of Irishmen, Germans and other nationalities for the benefit of their countrymen at home and abroad. Farmers assert their power as citizens in order to obtain their rights as producers. Workmen band together to defend themselves against associated employers. By all means let the colored men of the country form a National League to secure their rights as men and citizens.

* * *

Two objections are made thus far; the one that such an organization will be used by ambitious men to promote their individual aspirations. Very probably, that will be attempted; very likely it may be done to some extent. It certainly would if the members were white and there is no reason to believe that the colored man is exempt from such frailities. That is simply one of the things to be guarded against if possible, if not, the matter will end in failure, and the race must wait until it grows men big enough to see beyond the verge of their own shadow. It is better the Negro should fail in repeated efforts at self-assertion for a hundred years, however, than that he should let another year pass by without any effort in his own behalf.

* * *

It is also urged that such a movement will make trouble for Negroes at the South. No doubt it will. As soon as the "bull dozer" sees that the colored man is in earnest in his determination to enjoy the rights the Nation has granted him, another epoch of bloodshed is about as certain to be inaugurated as the sun is to shine. It is one of the inevitable consequences of having been once subjected by unlawful force, that such a crusade is certain to be begun against them without any fear of law and in utter contempt of National authority. It will probably require several hundred, perhaps several thousand lives, to organize such a league in the States of the South. It will be claimed that they are "organizing against the whites," and the world will be asked to listen to and believe once more, that fondly cherished lie, that men of Christain character have met together in the shade of the night to devise ways and means for "ravishing all the white women in the region," which has so long been declared the prime objection of "nigger risings," or to kill all the white men and burn all the white houses of a county or State. And thereupon a few "niggers" will have to be slaughtered here and there, to preserve "the peace of society," in defense of our white civilization" and the assertion of Christian purity!

* * *

These things may be expected. The question to be solved is whether the colored race in America has yet developed martyrs enough of that sort to make such a movement effective. It has produced thousands who have died in patient endurance of wrong, has it yet grown men brave enough to die—one—ten, a score, it may be—in every county of the South to secure their liberty? Such men will not die in vain. Those who come after them will dip their garments in their blood and press forward all the more steadily. There is nothing like the blood of martyrs to establish a good cause. They must furnish their own martyrs, however. The blood of the stranger has done all it can for the American Negro. There are some who believe the race is equal to the emergency. The Bystander is one of them—but it is not certain that any large number of the white people, even of the North, stand with him in this faith, or are even very earnest in the desire that the Negro should win and wear the crown of real enfranchisement.

* * *

Three things are all-essential to the success of this plan: 1. The Method: How shall it be most wisely and surely effected? The question is a very large one and will need serious consideration. A race which sent 30,000 refugees from bondage to freedom in twenty years with little to help them but the north star, can surely devise means for effecting such an organization. 2. What it shall do: Its first work should be to gather and disseminate facts. For this it must devise agencies. With Garrison and Phillips' warfare disappeared also their weapons. The people of the North—the conscience of the country—must now be reached in another manner. How? That is the question to be decided. 3. The man who shall direct such a movement. Such a man is born of any race hardly once in a century. Has the Negro race in the United States a man of nerve and power and self-forgetfulness enough, who is also gifted with the supreme quality of holding his tongue? Has it a man, harsh, relentless and self centered enough to ruthlessly put down the horde of self-seekers who always spring to the front in such a movement, and yet have tact enough to make them all work toward one end? It needs something of Cromwell and something of Parnell, but least of all does it require eloquence or display. Work, tact, silence, and an utter absence of self seeking—these are the prime qualities in the head of such a league. With such qualities in a leader commanding the confidence of the colored people and the respect of the country more may be done by such an organization toward the real enfranchisement of the Negro and the ultimate settlement of the race problem in two years than is likely to be done in a score of years without effective co-operation with existing instrumentalities by the colored men of the country themselves, acting distinctively and persistently as such, in furtherance of just and fair demands upon our Christian civilization.

ALBION W. TOURGEE.

Mayville, N.Y., Oct. 31.

ANOTHER CALL.

And an Appeal From Washington Afro-Americans.

The Central Bureau of Relief an organization of Washington Afro-Americans have issued an appeal to the earnest advocates of the equal exercise of political and civil rights for the colored American citizens. The appeal says in parts of this country—especially in the southern states—the colored citizens is prevented, by force and fraud, from exercising the rights of an American that are guaranted to them and other citizens by the Constitution and laws of our common country. This disgraceful and barbarous condition of affairs is assented to, if not encouraged, by the local governments of these states; and the general government has for nineteen years failed to apply any redress or remedy against these inhuman outrages upon its colored citizens. Believing, however, that a spirit of justice exists among the American people, this organization have issued this circular letter as an earnest appeal to all just and human citizens without regard to sex, race, creed, or political faith to assist their effort to remove this foul blot upon American civilization. The appeal is signed "in the behalf of seven millions of outraged colored American citizens" by the officers and executive committee of the bureau. A call has also been issued for a national convention to be held at Washington, D. C., on the first Monday in February, 1890.

One of the early militant calls of the Bystander, as reprinted on the front page of a Negro newspaper, the Detroit *Plaindealer,* November 15, 1889. Library of Congress.

CITIZENS' COMMITTEE.

❧❧❧ ORGANIZED SEPTEMBER I. 1891. ❧❧❧

To Test the Constitutionality of the Seprate Car Law.

ARTHUR ESTEVES, President.	FIRMIN CHRISTOPHE, Secretary.	G. G. JOHNSON, Ass't. Sec'y.	PAUL BONSEIGNEUR, Treasurer.
LAURENT AUGUSTE,	C. C. ANTOINE,	R. L. DESDUNES,	ALCEE LABAT
PIERRE CHEVALIER,	N. E MANSION,	A. B. KENNEDY,	EUGENE LUSCY,
M. J. PIRON,	R. B. BAQUIE,	A. J. GIURANOVICH,	E. A. WILLIAMS,
	L. A. MARTINET,	L. J. JOUBERT.	

New Orleans, La., ...Oct 5.............189 1

Hon A. W. Tourgée,
Mayville, N. Y.

Honored Sir + dear friend —

I should
have answered your generous letter at
once, but I was, as usual, busy, + there
was no need of being particularly in a hurry.

I thank you sincerely for the kind things
you say of me — thanks, thanks, but do not
call me a hero. I am a plain, ordinary
man. I prefer that. In that way
I'll not disappoint you.

Now to the question. The revival of
interest in the Jim Crow car matter
is owing to you more than to any one else,
+ I only hope that the people of other places
will do as well as our friends here. We
are not, however, without having some

[left margin, written vertically:] You can, in all amity, to advise with you in the case + let us know result. Still our counsel, you know &c.

The first page of a letter related to the origins of *Plessy* v. *Ferguson*, from Louis A. Martinet, militant Negro editor of the New Orleans *Crusader*, to Tourgée. Tourgée Papers, Westfield, New York.

his stand aroused some troublesome resentment among his usual allies.

Somewhat more involved was the fate of a proposed Federal election law primarily intended to protect Negro and white Republican voters in the South. Tourgée sought completely separate national elections under Federal control; he believed that this step would lessen southern resistance because it was not an immediate threat to state white supremacy. At the same time, the South supposedly would comply with the law in order to secure congressional representation, a precedent of Negro voting would be established, and Republicans would secure increased congressional strength as a basis for further reforms.

A favorable reception was initially accorded Tourgée's approach by the President, Speaker Reed, and some members of the House Committee on Elections. Reed continued to endorse similar views for a long time, and Kelley remained confident for weeks that a powerful bill was in the offing thanks to the Judge's impact.[15] "I doubt very much if he knows the great work he is doing," wrote Kelley to Mrs. Tourgée. "He is leading the leaders, and don't [sic] seem to know it." Actually, Tourgée was already fretting over signs of Republican vacillation, especially as revealed in a letter from his one strong ally on the House election committee, David B. Henderson, of Iowa. Nevertheless, a key bill presented by Henry Cabot Lodge did strike the Judge favorably, if only it could be strengthened. Instead, matters took an opposite turn in the form of suggestions to extend the supervisory election law of 1871. Tourgée tactfully appealed to the President, but to no avail, and apparently his stand was not even a serious part of the subsequent three days of caucus wrangling that culminated in an altered version of the Lodge bill based upon the earlier law.[16] Tourgée denounced this supervisory measure as impractical and a provocative form of espionage over state activities, and Kelley dolefully concluded that the only recourse left was agitation, with Tourgée to be "the Apostle of the agitation." [17] Rather pessimistically, Tourgée attempted to fill this role by continuing to push for

[15] D. B. Henderson to Tourgée, April 17, 1890, and Kelley to Tourgée, May 15, 1890; T. B. Reed, "The Federal Control of Elections," *North American Review*, CL (June, 1890), 671–80.

[16] Tourgée to Harrison, April 12, 16, May 2, 1890, Harrison Papers; Tourgée to J. C. Spooner, April 29, 1890, and Tourgée to Reed, n.d.; N.Y. *Tribune*, June 11, 1890; Washington *Post*, June 17, 1890.

[17] Kelley to Mrs. Tourgée, July 4, 1890.

alteration, two of his firmest allies being old southern cronies, Daniel L. Russell and A. W. Shaffer (the latter wrote a bitter polemic against the Lodge bill for the *North American Review*). But as the futility of this effort became apparent, and perhaps influenced by his experience with the Blair bill, Tourgée finally endorsed the Lodge bill as better than nothing. It then appeared destined for passage, when suddenly the Democrats arose in wrathful protest against this so-called "Force bill" to institute "one of the most dramatic political struggles the country had witnessed in years." [18] One of the senators most vociferous in conjuring up evil visions of Reconstruction and centralized tyranny was a North Carolina foe from Tourgée's past, Zebulon B. Vance.

When the election bill became so knotted in parliamentary maneuver and filibuster in the Senate as to block other legislation, a circle of economically oriented Republicans led in setting it aside in order to secure consideration and passage of a tariff bill. Although this move was ostensibly temporary, and sufficient votes had been pledged to ensure future passage of the election measure, the incident actually marked the decisive re-emergence of the primacy of pelf. With doubtful justice, the fall election losses also encouraged or excused abandonment of the bill, which was conveniently not even brought to a vote, thus enabling the Republicans to violate their earlier promises without incurring the embarrassment of going on record to do so. Judge Tourgée's disgust was intense. He not only recognized and denounced the motivation and treachery of certain Republicans but perceived that the event was another sad turning point for the Negro. "Who," the Bystander asked, "shall unlock the door of serfdom and subjection now closing on the Negro citizen of the South, and being locked with eager hands by the slavery-shaped dominants of American destiny amid the languid protests of Republican manipulators?" [19]

As these discouraging congressional events were taking place, Tourgée had been afforded an opportunity to goad white liberals by being invited to the Lake Mohonk Conference on the Negro in the summer of 1890. This all-white gathering of sincere and distinguished philanthropists would encourage an approach to the race problem that was soon to be

[18] Karl Schriftgiesser, *The Gentleman from Massachusetts: Henry Cabot Lodge* (Boston, 1944), 106.
[19] Bystander, *Inter Ocean*, December 27, 1890.

typified by the Negro leader Booker T. Washington, an approach offering moral advice and industrial training to the Negro while discouraging any agitation for equality. Judge Tourgée attended the conference to oppose this tack, and the very exclusion of Negroes from the conference typified a moderation and a catering to prejudice that he despised. To the delight of some observers, he disrupted the prevailing restraint on several occasions, and on the final day of the convention he delivered a major address described by one reporter as "a wonderful flaming" demand for a bold assault upon race prejudice in the United States. Advice and aid was fine, Tourgée insisted, but it was color prejudice that was the taproot of the Negro problem, and in this respect it was the whites who needed education.[20] As he warmed to his topic, a mighty thunderstorm moved over and darkened the valley of the Mohonk, and soon the Judge's forcible oration was being dramatically punctuated by lightening and bursts of thunder. Except for a fanciful touch of pride, it was a grand and eloquent plea and moved the conference to some platitudinous concessions, but basically these notables of influence and means were not to be diverted from their conservative path by Tourgée's or Nature's fury. The crusade sought by Judge Tourgée would not come from such a source.

As Tourgée's agitation among northern whites thus encountered repeated failure, he was more and more attracted toward a fuller involvement with the Negroes themselves. Late in 1889 he was heartened when several Negro leaders approached him regarding their civil rights efforts, and he welcomed their plans to launch an Afro American League as "the first step the race has attempted of its own motion toward self-assertive freedom—the only freedom that can ever be relied upon to give results." [21] The Judge's writings were used by the Negro press to stimulate enthusiasm for this venture, and early in 1890 not only the Afro American League but also the Citizens Equal Rights League was established, and several other national Negro conventions were held that year. But soon the Judge also detected intense controversies among the Negroes themselves regarding a proper response to the prevalent hostility or disinterest of white Americans.

[20] *First Mohonk Conference on the Negro Question . . . June 4, 5, 6, 1890* (Boston, 1890), 24–26, 54, 103–17.

[21] Tourgée to Robert Pelham, Jr., October 12, 1889, and Tourgée to William T. Green, November 7, 1889.

One reaction was a Negro "nationalism" that distrusted whites and encouraged a segregation of its own, and at the founding convention of the segregated Afro American League opposition was expressed even to acceptance of a letter of support and counsel from Tourgée because he was white. Mocked by white supremacists because of the rarity of Negro attendance at his lectures on the race question, Tourgée took the colored population to task for its limited appreciation of its white allies, and he deprecated the growth of caution and accommodationism among Negro leaders, many of whom supported the Blair bill or endorsed the Mohonk Conference. This was not the spirit sought by Tourgée. "I am so firm a believer in the Negro's capacity," he wrote one Negro leader, "that I cannot but be angry when I see their leading men striving for the reputation of being 'good niggers.' " [22] It would take courage and martyrs, and the Negroes must do it themselves, but Tourgée ventured that with a little fire and unity they could end "all oppression in half a decade without striking a [violent] blow."

Tourgée did not counsel a policy of violence, although he felt it might come to that, and endorsed self-defense, but he did urge a brand of Negro militancy that was not yet destined for success. Admitting the importance of economic and moral development, he also insisted that "neither wealth nor Christianity will bring justice unless joined with the steady, persistent, and resolute demand for right." [23] Negroes should organize, publicize, and agitate; they should sue for their rights, purchase homes in white neighborhoods, attend white churches, and defend their persons with force when necessary. Noting the impressive impact of Negro boxers, who were "doing the race good service," he wished "there were more of them." [24] Submission, timidity, and prayer would not do, and no Negro "should cast a ballot with any other object in view than his race's interest until every colored man is freely accorded every civil and political right a white man enjoys in every State of this Union." The colored people, Tourgée advised one of their leaders in 1891, must "convince the world that they are in earnest and are ready

[22] Tourgée to Anna J. Cooper, n.d. [1890].
[23] Bystander, *Inter Ocean*, October 27, 1894, a specific rebuttal of Booker T. Washington.
[24] Tourgée to John E. Bruce, July 31, 1891, John E. Bruce Papers, Schomburg Library, N.Y. Constance M. Green (*Washington: Capital City, 1879–1950* [Princeton, 1963], 213) finds Negro success in boxing contributing to race conflict.

to die if need be. Protest, remonstrance, denunciation—continuous, passionate, determined—these are, in my opinion, the only things that will save your people from submissive apathy and give them hope of final equality of privilege." He admitted the "difficulties attending such a course," but asked, "how shall a race reach a higher level of manhood if their leaders are silent when their rights are trampled upon?" [25] What he longed for and anticipated was a Promethean Negro leader prepared to sacrifice himself to these ends.

Perhaps Tourgée's insistence that Negroes both furnish their own leadership and adhere to his advice posed a paradox, but there were many from all ranks to inspire and agree with him. "Your notes are often read in Negro schools and churches in the South and the Negroes by the thousands send up their prayers to God in your behalf," wrote a Negro from Arkansas, while another Negro acquaintance in New York was doggedly asserting his rights and instituting legal suits against segregation by 1890. After a tour of the South, this New Yorker also reported that Negroes there were "determined to *Fight*. They say there are just three things for them to do, leave the south, fight, or be made slaves." [26] Portions of the Negro press were close followers of the Judge by 1890,[27] as were such prominent Negroes as Charles W. Chesnutt, Robert Pelham, Jr., and F. J. Loudin. Of lesser immediate impact was a small newspaper clipping, prized by Tourgée, which announced the award of a declamation prize to a Harvard University student in 1890, one William E. B. Du Bois. The most momentous encouragement came, however, from New Orleans.

With its Latin cultural heritage, Louisiana enjoyed a tradition of unusually relaxed racial contact, and many Negroes in New Orleans had been free for generations to accumulate dignity, influence, and wealth. This Negro community, which had once expected to serve in the Confederate Army, was aroused to indignation in 1890 by a proposed state law requiring railroads "to provide equal but separate accommodations for the white and colored races." Despite organized Negro resistance and aided by the naïve, if not treacherous, tactics of Negro

[25] Bystander, *Inter Ocean*, September 12, 1891; Tourgée to Joseph C. Price, April 3, 1890, and Tourgée to John Mitchell, Jr., n.d. [1890].

[26] A. M. Middlebrooks, Arkansas, to Tourgée, April 5, 1891, and Mack Caldwell, New York, to Tourgée, January 17, May 29, 1890.

[27] Detroit *Plaindealer* and Cleveland *Gazette* from September, 1889, on.

legislators, this Jim Crow bill became law in July, 1890. One of the most vigorous opponents of the measure, Louis A. Martinet, editor of the New Orleans *Crusader*, thereupon suggested that Negroes "begin to gather funds to test the constitutionality of this law," and steps taken in this direction included an appeal for support and advice sent to Judge Tourgée, who eagerly urged the project on.[28] Little more was heard of this matter until a year later, when eighteen substantial men of color in New Orleans announced a "Citizen's Committee to Test the Constitutionality of the Separate Car Law." Martinet credited Judge Tourgée, "more than any one else," for this "revival of interest in the Jim Crow car matter," and Tourgée was appointed the Committee's "leading counsel" with "control from beginning to end." Among those encouraging the venture was also a noted southerner, Supreme Court Justice John Marshall Harlan.[29] In this fashion another crusade began that culminated five years later in the nation's highest court.

The revival of the New Orleans Jim Crow fight late in 1891 also inspired other significant activities. Martinet was, like Tourgée, an ardent equalitarian, and, opposing the Afro American League because it was segregated, he had participated in the founding of the rival, biracial Citizens Equal Rights League in 1890. But a year later he and Tourgée agreed that the entire civil rights movement was plagued by doubt, inaction, and division, and was essentially defunct. Simultaneously, their exasperation was increased by signs of spreading oppression, and their hope, by signs of a Negro militancy that ranged from cries of protest in the Negro press to an attempted unionization of the lowly cotton pickers. In addition to Martinet, a number of other impressive Negro allies urged Tourgée on, especially the journalist John E. Bruce and Harry C. Smith, publisher and editor of a superior Negro newspaper, the Cleveland *Gazette*, and leader of one of the most effective state Negro organizations of the 1890's. Other supporters included W. A. Stowers and W. H. Anderson, who together controlled the Detroit *Plaindealer*, and John Mitchell, Jr., editor and later owner of the Richmond *Planet*. These were two unusually competent Negro news-

---

[28] New Orleans *Crusader*, July 19, 1890; Eli C. Freeman to Tourgée, August 4, 26, 1890. The relationship between Freeman and New Orleans events is unclear.
[29] Martinet to Tourgée, September 14, October 5, 11, 1891; Rodolph L. Desdunes, *Nos Hommes et Notre Histoire* (Montreal, 1911), 186.

papers, while Anderson was national secretary of the Afro American League and Mitchell headed the Afro American Press Association. This combination of circumstances and support,[30] together with a favorable response to certain suggestions ventured in the Bystander column, enticed Tourgée into an attempted reorganization of the equal rights movement. His prestige, his effective journalism, and his mounting influence among Negroes placed him in an unusually favorable position for just such an attempt.

[30] Tourgée also commended the policies of the Indianapolis *World* and the *Southwestern Christian Advocate*. Other friendly correspondents on the race question included Alex. G. Davis, Manager, Afro-American News Bureau; William T. Green, Secretary, Wisconsin Civil Rights League; W. A. Hazel, Secretary, Minnesota Civil Rights Committee; John L. Minor, Editor, New Orleans *New Era*; T. T. Harden, Associate Editor, Jacksonville *Southern Courier*; R. B. Cabbell, President, Chicago Colored Waiters Alliance; Robert McCoomer, President, Chicago fourth district Banneker League; S. Laing Williams and Ferdinand L. Barnett, Chicago attorneys; J. S. Wood, Editor, Decatur, Ill., *Afro American Budget*; T. B. Morton, President, San Francisco Afro American League; George M. Arnold, President, Bethel Literary and Historical Association, Washington, D.C., and Anna J. Cooper. Said one Negro leader: "As a race we owe more to Albion W. Tourgée than to any man living" (George E. Taylor, President, National Colored Men's Protective Association, to Tourgée, July 17, 1892).

❧ XXIV

The National
Citizens Rights Association

In October, 1891, Judge Tourgée's Bystander column urged all interested citizens to enroll in a new organization, under his provisional presidency, which was subsequently entitled the National Citizens Rights Association. The unique emphasis of this new mass movement would be the inclusion of southern Negroes and biracial action, and although Tourgée now held a more jaundiced view of northern whites, he anticipated sufficient response to create a powerful pressure group. If the Negro would but "manfully assert himself in this manner," the Bystander promised, he would "find the heart of the free North responding to his appeal and seconding effectually his efforts." To further assure white participation, the N.C.R.A. was to concern itself with the rights of all citizens and be led by men and women of both races (the Judge later decided that two-thirds of this leadership should be white). Appeals were directed toward both substantial and ordinary citizens, and to facilitate mass enrollment, especially in the South, membership was secret, the structure simple, and the cost a mere two cents to cover the expense of return mail. Tourgée aspired to create an organization numbering hundreds of thousands, which would collect and publicize the facts of oppression, utilize this publicity and the votes of its members to obtain remedial legislation, and attack segregation and other injustices through the courts. He began with a goal of one million members, and, convinced that Jim Crow laws were unconstitutional, he was sanguine of legal success. Of course the determination of his opponents, who spoke of segregation as "an unwritten law . . . direct from heaven

312

itself," was also recognized. It was like Reconstruction all over again, and the Fool marched into battle with hopes of adding "the Jim Crow Car, the Mississippi ballotorial law, and the assertion of the rights of citizenship in the different states" to his list of conquests.[1]

The initial response to Tourgée's announcement was impressive, as from throughout the nation thousands enrolled in the N.C.R.A.—whites and Negroes, southerners and northerners, individuals and organizations, the educated and the illiterate, the self-seeking and the selfless, the famous and the unknown. The letters of support were enough to make an entrancing book, and the Judge's influential allies responded with gratifying enthusiasm, none more so than the Cleveland *Gazette*, which would print almost every Bystander column for over a year. There were significant new endorsements, too, from a meeting of eight hundred Negroes in Topeka, Kansas, and from additional white and Negro publications in at least nine states, ranging from the Boston *Republican* and Denison, Iowa, *Review* to the daring *Gazette* of Huntsville, Alabama. Prominent supporters included Ida B. Wells, F. J. Loudin, F. L. Barnett, and Charlotte and Francis L. Grimke. Students at Oberlin announced a goal of five hundred members, branches were established at Grinnell College and the University of Iowa, and one application arrived from an American student studying overseas. A prominent Negro Republican, the president of the local Banneker League, was organizing a branch in Chicago, a Negro doctor headed one in Philadelphia, and steps were instituted to transform the entire Afro American League of Cambridge, Massachusetts, into Tourgée's N.C.R.A. Local Republican leaders, including postmasters in Minnesota and North and South Carolina, were active, and among the ministers involved were a Baptist in New Orleans, a Congregationalist in Topeka, a Presbyterian in Brooklyn, and Methodists in Indianapolis and in Lafayette, Alabama. From Chicago a Negro enthusiast wrote: "Don't let us alone for God knows I think ever black man in the worl loves you, at Quinn Chapel this afternoon call your name ever man and woman shoted and stamp thur feet and clap thar hand your name was jest as the day when thay

[1] Bystander, *Inter Ocean*, October through December, 1891; Cleveland *Gazette*, June 4, 1892; Tourgée to W. H. Anderson, n.d. [October, 1891], Tourgée to W. A. Hazel, November 7, 1891, Tourgée Papers. Unless otherwise indicated, all manuscript citations in this chapter are from the Tourgée Papers.

was set Free." [2] Clubs of 100 and 200 members were reported from Mississippi, of 220 from Chicago, of 60 from Urbana, Illinois.

From Texas a Union veteran expressed his desire to help achieve "the day when—we poor white trash—as well as the colored folks—will know and have the manhood to assert—our freedom," while another veteran in Illinois considered he had risked his life "for a Government of all the People" and wanted "the same treatment for my dusky Brother that I ask for myself. . . ." [3] There was a member in Mississippi, the brother of Confederate veterans, who was "fed up" with injustice and the Democratic party, and a white physician in Florida was organizing *"very* secretly for I value my life." [4] In Missouri a former lieutenant colonel in the Union Army found half the people he spoke to sympathetic, and from Joliet, Illinois, arrived a list of nine lawyers, one teacher, two physicians, and thirty-five business men. A group joining in Manhattan, Kansas, included a bookkeeper, a cashier, a professor, an old Tippecanoe Whig, the editor of a Populist newspaper, the local chairman of that party, a leader of the W.C.T.U., and a number of Negroes. At least two reformers in England joined.

The most moving and revealing response, however, came from the Negro South, a response of pathos and eloquence, of mingled anger, desperation, hope, and fear. Nothing did more to urge Tourgée on than the hundreds of letters that bared the horrors and sufferings of southern Negroes and revealed their sensitivity to a sad and terrible fate. Their letters told of invaded privacy, of deprivation of comfort and rights, and of intimidation, violence, and death. They told of hopeful desires in the face of hopeless conditions and of disillusionment with the Republican party, the Federal government, and Christianity. They sought aid, vowed support, and begged for secrecy, and they could be poignant even in their ignorance. "Dear Sir," wrote a Negro from Mississippi, "I write for advice The Light of Knowlledg is Dark in This part of the Land we are Locked up in Prision in a sence and in a Dark world of Ignence and is as Birds in Cages. . . ." [5] A Negro in Texas had no hope at all

[2] J. H. Jenkins to Tourgée, January 3, 1892.
[3] Horace Baker, Texas, to Tourgée, June 10, 1892; David T. Silver, Illinois, to Tourgée, September 7, 1892.
[4] C. W. Tompkins, Florida, to Tourgée, November 17, 1892.
[5] G. Wilson Stovall to Tourgée, November 27, 1892. For a collection of these letters, see O. H. Olsen, "Albion W. Tourgée and Negro Militants of the 1890's: A Documentary Selection," *Science & Society*, XXVIII (1964), 183–208.

that the government would ever "protect the Life of a poor unarmed inofencive niger from the Blood Thirsty Deamons of the South":

No no Sir the Federal government is not able for the Task nor never will be able we have found that out long ago   so we will go to Mexico as the only accesable Country where we will become Citizens and be protected as such and as we go we will sing
<blockquote>
My native land from thee
Oh land of misery from thee I fly
Land where we have often tried
Thy harsh laws to abide
</blockquote>
But we now will let you slid and go to Old Mexico where we will become Citizens and soldiers if she wants us.[6]

The "women of Wayne County," Mississippi, wrote because the men did not dare, and a college-educated teacher in Louisiana wrote of being outraged and banished for being an active Republican and local president of the Knights of Labor. A teacher in Georgia wrote of how the Bystander column moved him and his wife to tears, and in Dallas, Texas, a tree was planted in the Judge's honor by a Negro school. "We haven't much freedom in Texas and there is so much to discourage us," these pupils wrote, "but we mean to keep on trying." The many moving letters that honored the Judge defy adequate description, but some sense of their spirit and perplexity may be gathered from a letter dated July 4, 1892, from Duncan, Mississippi:

In your notes to the Interocean June 7th last, you give notice to all Lovers of Liberty, Justice and Freedom, and especially to those belonging to the National Citizens Equal Rights association to Form what is to be known as Local unions, accordingly We have met and considered the matter carefully, you are satisfied that there is no Law in this State to protect a Black man who makes any attempt to enlighten his Race on any political question; Surely you do not realize the situation as we do, who lives here, the man or Woman who attempts to strike a Blow here for Freedom must be killed out right—or he must

[6] Jas. W. Smith to Tourgée, February 21, 1892.

be Exiled from all he possesses at once as Miss Ida B. Wells of the Memphis Free Speech have been. In a word he must be made such an example of, untill no other Negro will attempt to do such a thing again, We are a little tired of having to show our Corpse to prove to the world that the Laws of this Country is not sufficient to protect the Black man as well as the white We read your notes Regular and Readily, our liberty have been taken from us so long untill we have almost got use to it, In a word we see no *possible* chance of ever being Free under The Flag of Liberty and christian civilization, Do you know my Dear Sir, that there are standing armies in every county in every Southern State called Malitia, and are at the command of the Governers of the different States, who are Negro haters and who are williug to sacrifice everything even Life in order to give the negro to know that he *must* obey the white man, These armies are always ready to go to any scene where a negro resist a White man no matter how small the case may be, or however wrong the white man may be, The *Negro must submit* It is no use to try the Law, Now what can people do who are Situated as we are, Just as complete into the hands of our Enemies in 1892 as we were in 1852 It is possible that something can be done, but how it is to be done, is as fare out of our sight as the God who created the heavens & the Earth, It took this government Four yrs with all of the modern artilry and the most skilful men of war, With as much money as they needed and more men than they did need, to drive these same men from the same power they have now, and how can we ever do such, with no men of war, no artilery, and no money. It is simply absurd, but we have deciden to do what you have requested even if we are exterminated we shall hope to hear from you as early as possible stating what you further will have us do

Very Respectfully
S. R. KENDRICK

During the first weeks following the launching of the N.C.R.A., as many as two or three hundred names arrived in a single day, but this burst of enthusiasm apparently spent itself within a few months. In any event, it was excessive for the Judge to speak of having two million names by the time of the Republican convention of June, 1892, a force with which he believed the race problem could right then "be practically settled." [7] A few months after the beginning of his efforts, Tourgée stated that an expenditure of $156 had brought twenty thousand recruits, and by March he ordered twenty-five thousand copies of an N.C.R.A. pamphlet he had written, *Is Liberty Worth Preserving?* By spring over one hundred thousand members were claimed, and later estimates would be over twice as high—impressive, if true, but still far short of two million. Meanwhile, a more formal structure had been announced for the N.C.R.A., an executive board, which included George W. Cable, a charter for one dollar, and dues of ten cents per month.[8] But there is no trace of any significant fulfillment of these arrangements.

Among the difficulties encountered by Tourgée's organizational venture was the presence of adherents some of whom were more anxious for position or pay than for the cause and others whose tactics were unwelcome. An indication of distressing divisions was the warning of white sympathizers in the South, who cautioned lest ignorant Negroes swamp reformism, and white-line Republicans in Dallas went so far as actually to endorse lynchings. More ominous were southern complaints that the Negroes were "getting to be rather too 'mouthy'" because of the Judge's efforts. He was accused of building a "Black Mafia" to murder whites and was threatened, by a letter in the press, with lynching.[9] One of the Judge's most industrious supporters, an almost illiterate but very courageous Negro in Mississippi, Dudley Stuard, was beaten and imprisoned for his work, but he was rescued by the intervention of the N.C.R.A. The situation in Mississippi grew worse as the election of 1892 approached, and Negroes armed themselves to resist intimidation by the whites. Some of the Judge's followers actually requested shipments of arms "marked hardware," and although he vigorously argued against such tactics, there was an outbreak that fall in which four Negroes were killed, seven reported missing, and

[7] Tourgée to Ida B. Wells, November 16, 1891; Mrs. Tourgée's Diary, November 30, 1891.
[8] Bystander, *Inter Ocean*, June 4, 18, September 3, 1892; Cable to Tourgée, December 19, 1891; Tourgée to Flavius J. Cook, August 23, 1893, Flavius J. Cook Papers, Duke University Library.
[9] Quoted in Bystander, *Inter Ocean*, July 30, 1892; clipping, Mayersville *Spectator*, n.d.; unsigned, to Tourgée, June 17, 1892; J. G. Sewell to Tourgée, October 17, 1892.

several wounded, all members of the N.C.R.A. Such brutal terrorism, protested the Bystander, was "necessary to secure the political ascendancy of the white man, and keep down the price of labor." [10]

Another element of tragedy involved a rumor or cruel ruse attributing to the N.C.R.A. promises of free provisions and transportation to homesteads in Oklahoma. Before this misconception could be corrected, a number of Negroes in Arkansas broke up their homes, sold their belongings and stock at depressed prices, and were left destitute and stranded.

The response of an emerging national Negro leadership concentrated in the North would be more vital to the success of Tourgée's entire venture. Impressive support from such circles has already been noted, but it was also clear that the N.C.R.A. was compounding existing jealousies and rivalries and encountering a profusion of apathy and opposition. The most sensible attitude toward this turbulence was undoubtedly that of W. H. Anderson of Detroit, whose *Plaindealer* complained that "as a race, we have produced more 'leaders' and fewer followers than any people under the sun." [11] Anderson sincerely continued his labors for the Afro American League while also encouraging and recognizing the potential of Tourgée's efforts. Quite different was the attitude of T. Thomas Fortune of the New York *Age*, an advocate of self-leadership, whose efforts to revitalize the Afro American League induced him to ignore Tourgée's N.C.R.A. Probably Fortune's most helpful victory was a successful suit against a restaurateur who had refused to serve him a glass of beer, an equalitarian triumph that earned the enmity of Negro prohibitionists.[12] Significant opposition to both Fortune and Tourgée centered in the aspiring editor of the Denver *Statesman*, Edwin H. Hackley, who was promoting an organization of his own. Asserting that "no white man" could "lead or direct" the colored population and specifically repudiating agitation, political action, and remedial legislation, Hackley helped to institute a widespread debate over "Tourgéeism." [13] All this tended to confirm the fact that accom-

[10] Walter H. Griffin to Tourgée, June 17, 1892, and Henry Williams to Tourgée, August 16, 1892; Tourgée letter, Cleveland *Gazette*, November 5, 1892.
[11] Detroit *Plaindealer*, May 6, June 3, 1892.
[12] N.Y. *Age*, October 31, 1892; Topeka *Call*, December 13, 1891.
[13] Detroit *Plaindealer*, April 15, May 13, June 3, 1892. See also Kansas City *American Citizen*, October 9, 1891.

modationism was increasing, that Tourgée's radical tactics were distrusted (the Blair bill was not forgotten), and that there was a reluctance on the part of Negroes to work with, much less to be dominated by, whites. The Judge's most bitter opponent was, perhaps, the conservative Indianapolis *Freeman*, which appeared as eager as any white supremacist to pounce upon "the ex-carpetbagger" and his "demagogury [*sic*] and rabid froth." The *Freeman* also sought a mess of pottage, saying of Tourgée's criticisms of the Grand Old Party that they required "no refutation at our hands, for the party's record of unparalleled service to the whole country, its great friendship, and greater legislation for the specific welfare of the Negro race in America, is spread upon the pages of history for all men to read, and the selfish ambitions of a thousand Tourgées cannot change a letter of the same or cast one doubt upon its authenticity." [14]

In the face of such difficulties, the Judge's pompous bearing and sometimes tactless words added to the aggravation, although, in the main, he and his allies persuasively continued to urge aggressive and interracial action and to protest the senseless and jealous opposition they encountered.

One clash of opinions not fully developing until 1893 involved the somewhat different equalitarianism of H. M. Turner of Georgia, a bishop of the African Methodist Episcopal church. Turner admired the Judge's hopes and efforts and wished them success, but he saw "no future in this country for the Negro" and desired congressional aid "to help the manly, and self-reliant black men to get out of this cruel nation. . . ." Tourgée deplored such a lack of faith in the United States (he would even take L. A. Martinet to task for wavering in this faith), recognized the obvious limitations of any such program, and helped to undermine it. Nor was his attitude softened by the popularity of this idea among white supremacists, one of whom published a book, *An Appeal to Pharaoh*, imitating one of the Judge's titles and utilizing his words copiously in behalf of deportation.[15]

The Judge and the N.C.R.A. (it was often difficult to distinguish the

[14] *Freeman*, October 31, 1891, June 25, 1892.
[15] Turner to Tourgée, November 2, 1892; J. C. Hartzell to Tourgée, November 29, 1892; Tourgée to Martinet, n.d. [1893]; Cleveland *Gazette*, December 9, 1893; Carlyle McKinley, *An Appeal to Pharaoh: The Negro Problem and Its Radical Solution* (New York, 1889).

two) did wield influence during these years. A visitor to Tourgée's hotel room in the national capital found the leading Negro politicians assembled there, and his contacts with Negro churches and colleges and such organizations as the National Colored Men's Protective Association increased. The Judge helped prepare petitions or resolutions for the Quakers, the Negro Catholic Congress, the Baptist Young People's Union of America, and state Republican conventions. He assisted a member of the Knights of Labor in preparing resolutions on race for the St. Louis industrial convention of 1892 (which chose, however, to sidetrack the issue), and he helped secure an effective civil rights clause for the constitution of New York state. The N.C.R.A. also helped spark a protest and boycott against the Chicago Exposition of 1893, and the Judge inspired the booklet by Ida B. Wells and Frederick Douglass, *The Reason Why the Colored American is Not in the World's Columbian Exposition.*[16] Tourgée did speak at the fair, however, on the appropriate subject of "Citizenship and Suffrage," sharing a week-long program with such speakers as John R. Commons, Clarence Darrow, Frederick Douglass, and Susan B. Anthony.

One enthusiastic ally in Kentucky busily promoted the N.C.R.A. program with mild success at Republican or Negro conventions in Lexington, Louisville, and Cincinnati during 1892, and Tourgée claimed political influence as far off as California. In politics the Judge and the N.C.R.A. continued the effort to divert the Republican party from "dollars and dimes" back to "human rights." At the presidential nominating convention of 1892 they claimed the balance of power in seven northern states and distributed N.C.R.A. circulars in support of the candidacy of Thomas B. Reed. That there was substance to their stand was indicated by the acceptance speech of the convention chairman and by the ringing declaration of Reed that prosperity had been achieved and that the future task of Republicanism was "to give every citizen of the United States liberty of thought and action (Cheers and applause). Wealth and prosperity are noble but human liberty is magni-

[16] See Ida Wells's notation on the copy of this pamphlet in the Tourgée Papers. For other items in this paragraph, see W. E. Turner, K. of L., to Tourgée, January 29, 1892; Society of Friends of N.Y. to Tourgée, June 17, 1892; J. T. Robinson to Tourgée, June 16, 24, July 4, 1892; Charles W. Anderson to Tourgée, May 1, 9, 1894; N.Y. *Age*, May 23, 1892.

ficent (Great applause)." [17] Reed's hopes were unjustified on both counts. The renomination of Harrison and a weak platform saw Tourgée again belaboring his party for driving voters out while striving himself to keep them in, but only two Republican newspapers would print an N.C.R.A. protest. Not only was the *Inter Ocean* not one of these two, but Nixon refused to print one of the Bystander columns and chastised the Judge for splitting the party. It is little wonder that Tourgée's endorsement of Harrison lacked vigor and that he advised support locally only for those Republicans who swore to support equal rights.[18]

Tourgée and the N.C.R.A. were undoubtedly establishing important precedents, but all their activity and influence had not brought much in the way of accomplishment. Perhaps their greatest triumph occurred in 1892, when the General Conference of the Methodist Episcopal church approved a strong resolution denouncing prejudice and segregation and calling for remedial action by churches, the press, and all levels of government. Although Tourgée was largely credited with this action, his precise role remains unclear, and many Negroes bitterly noted that the same convention failed to elect a Negro bishop or to reappoint the energetic equalitarian editor of the *Southwestern Christian Advocate*.[19] That same year, Tourgée exerted pressure upon the Presbyterian General Assembly, which also denounced outrages against the Negroes. Altogether, there was not much to compare with the mounting tide of racist oppression, and Cleveland's second victory was another discouraging blow. In reviewing the entire year, the Bystander could discover nothing more encouraging (outside the Negro community) than the fact that several additional journals were capitalizing the word Negro. The *Inter Ocean* was not yet one of them.

Harsh words meanwhile were still being exchanged with the *Inter Ocean* regarding Tourgée's radicalism, and objections to his column had increased. This conflict, along with some bitter words over a reduc-

---

[17] N.Y. *Tribune*, June 8, 1892; Bystander, *Inter Ocean*, May 28, 1892.

[18] Nixon to Tourgée, July 7, 1892, and Tourgée to Nixon, July 9, 1892; Bystander, *Inter Ocean*, July 30, 1892. There is "little hope of sensible progress . . . from either party," said the Bystander, although "with democratic control progress is clearly impossible; but with republican control serious retrogression is not presently probable." See Cleveland *Gazette*, September 24, 1892.

[19] Omaha *World Herald*, May 26, 27, 1892; Cleveland *Gazette*, May 28, June 4, 1892; C. H. Payne to Tourgée, June 1, 11, July 1, 1892; Ida B. Wells to Tourgée, July 2, 1892.

tion in salary and the impact of the crash of 1893, led to a temporary suspension of the Bystander column early that fall. Sparked by his indignation and his unemployment, the Judge turned to an idea that he had been considering for two years, the publication of an N.C.R.A. journal. His recent conquest of his major indebtedness gave him additional freedom for such a project. Despite the depression, the dissuasion of Emma and friends, and his own doubts, the Judge was sufficiently encouraged by his followers to plunge ahead with plans for a proposed monthly, the "National Citizen."

An engaging response to this venture came from T. Thomas Fortune of the New York *Age*. Fortune's Afro American League was now lifeless, and he and Tourgée had drawn closer in mutual anger at the outgoing President Harrison's appointment of a Tennessee Democrat, Howell E. Jackson, to the United States Supreme Court. Because of the New Orleans Jim Crow legal case, this was of special import to Tourgée, who wrote an angry editorial, "Ben. Harrison a Traitor Too!" for the *Age*. Actually, time proved Jackson to be a judge who won Negro respect. When Tourgée announced his proposed journal, Fortune, who had earlier been discouraged by the Judge from attempting a biracial journal of his own, sought to entice the proposed N.C.R.A. publication into locating in New York and absorbing the *Age*, which had a publishing plant, thirteen years' good standing, five thousand subscribers, and a "fair advertising constituency." If Tourgée agreed, Fortune promised to devote his "best efforts to placing the $5,000 of stock you have apportioned as the share of Afro-Americans." But Tourgée had distrusted Fortune for several years and also feared that the absorption of a well-known Negro newspaper would label the N.C.R.A. as a one-race organization, so he turned down the most substantial offer ever tendered him.[20] White participation was undoubtedly of central importance to the cause of civil rights, but the only practical possibility existing at that time may have been the more effective organization of the Negro. By his decision Tourgée surrendered a substantial basis for operation and a rare opportunity to secure support in the vital Northeast, where his influence was weak.

At that time, however, Tourgée anticipated the active participation of

[20] Fortune to Tourgée, November 16, 1893.

Charles W. Chesnutt as an associate editor. Chesnutt had displayed some initial enthusiasm, but was somehow frightened off, probably by Tourgée's excessive exuberance and his own pessimism regarding white support.[21] There was an additional discouragement when Thomas B. Reed and F. J. Loudin apologized that heavy depression losses prevented the investments they would have liked and were expected to make in the venture. The most significant investment discoverable was, in fact, fifty dollars from a New York horsebreeder, who may have been more sympathetic toward the Judge's love of horseflesh than toward justice. Meanwhile, Tourgée had restored his profitable relationship with the *Inter Ocean*, Nixon having bought out the interests opposed to the Judge, whose fans had been protesting. Then Tourgée increased his acceptability among the orthodox with a new series of Siva letters castigating Cleveland's second term. In April, 1894, much to Emma's relief, her husband deferred publication of the proposed N.C.R.A. journal. The following month the Bystander column was resumed in the *Inter Ocean*.

By this time the N.C.R.A. had almost disappeared, a fact that primarily reflected adverse national conditions but also certain internal features as well. The Judge was primarily an agitator with the Olympian leanings of a judge; he was as unenthusiastic as he was inefficient as an organizer. Some elaborate arrangements were announced, it is true, but they were never seriously implemented. Tourgée may have been involved in too many activities during these years to attend properly to an organization whose control he monopolized, and he lacked the wealth to exploit whatever opportunity did exist. Aside from several thousand dollars raised for the New Orleans segregated-car case, appeals for funds brought no significant response.[22] Opposition and dissension among the Negroes had been most discouraging; the Judge claimed that only ten per cent of the membership was Negro, of which most was from the South and almost none from the vital Northeast. In turn, his own manner was not accommodating, the lack of real progress against racism dissipated possible support, and his rejection of Fortune's offer destroyed one hope. There is also little doubt that Tourgée's

[21] Chesnutt to Tourgée, November 21, 27, 1893.
[22] There may have been one gift of one or two thousand dollars (Elsie D. Burnett to Tourgée, December 29, 1892).

continuing demand for economic reform alienated both Negroes and whites. Altogether, the simplicity of the N.C.R.A. and its domination by the Judge had been both a source of its rapid growth and strength and of its weakness. It had never been much more than a list of names, a personal possession of Tourgée's that added to, but was also dependent upon, his prestige and power. This was not enough, but there was not much else, and the organization continued to have a mild impact for several years.

In 1892 Tourgée, and therefore the N.C.R.A., participated in the election of a reform Republican, James T. Edwards, to the New York State Senate, an ironic contest in which the local Republican machine proved so strong that the reform Republicans had to nominate their candidate in the Democratic convention. Two years later, in his last bid for elective office, the Judge himself sought a congressional nomination under the auspices of the N.C.R.A. Championing his usual economic and racial program, he professed that his candidacy would recapture the votes of Populists and others who were leaving the party. This effort attracted unusual national attention but suffered from charges of party irregularity and the strength of a capable incumbent who had been promised another term and was the son-in-law of a wealthy banker. One sympathizer saw nothing but disaster in bucking this combination, while another lonely supporter, the Silver Creek *Gazette*, boasted that it was "the only Chautauqua county paper that stands for the people as against a rotten and corrupt political ring." [23] Understandably, Tourgée soon gave up the struggle. This famous judge, who had achieved such success as a young and unknown radical in the South, had been unable to overcome machine politics in the section he had glamorized as democratic and free. Little wonder that he sometimes expressed admiration for the independent nature of a southern politics that on other grounds he so despised.

More wrangling with the *Inter Ocean* also troubled Tourgée. The resumption of the Bystander in May of 1894 had occurred at a sensitive moment. Editor Nixon had at that time gone heavily into debt to purchase control of the newspaper, and he looked to party patronage for relief. Much to Nixon's embarrassment, the Bystander column

[23] Silver Creek *Gazette*, May 31, 1894. See also L. G. Raymond to Tourgée, May 5, 9, 1894.

severely censured the party during that spring and summer, and Tourgée was soon being reminded that he was paid "a higher rate per column than is received by any other political writer in the country" and warned to stop finding "fault with Republican leaders or with the Republican party as it now stands." [24] Additional difficulties were provided by the great Chicago Pullman strike that summer. This occurred during President Cleveland's administration, and while Tourgée again sought to gather Republican votes by focusing on the problems of the populace, the *Inter Ocean* blatantly catered to business interests and roundly denounced the strikers. As the strike raged, Tourgée carried on a cautious general discussion of the labor problem, a discussion that denounced excess profits, pointed to the justice and the helpful purchasing power of higher wages, championed compulsory bargaining, and found room for a strong endorsement of both unions and the strike weapon. One Bystander column was not printed because of its comments about the strike, and Tourgée suspected that his subsequent resuspension was due to his attitude respecting the labor question. Elsewhere, too, in 1894, the Judge bemoaned the stand of his party, accurately predicting the Populist-Democratic alliance that would come two years later and continuing to denounce the "tyranny of wealth": [25] "Already every branch of our government has lost touch and sympathy with the people. The idea is almost universal that money rules. We have a millionaire senate, a millionaire supreme court, the executive is wholly under the control of the rich men of the country, no matter which party is in power, and the general impression is that the enactment of law, its administration and enforcement, are also controlled by the power of money."

More fruitful was Tourgée's involvement in the struggle against what was probably the most dreadful manifestation of racism in that era, lynching. From the very first the N.C.R.A. had joined this crusade with proposals for a Federal law establishing local liability for such a crime. In 1894 the brutal killing of a Negro youth by an Ohio mob prompted Tourgée to write a letter to Governor William McKinley urging such a law. Also aroused by the incident was the rather strong Negro movement

[24] A. H. Busbey to Tourgée, August 13, 1894, Nixon to Tourgée, July 7, 1894, and Mrs. Tourgée's Diary, July 7, 1894.

[25] Bystander, *Inter Ocean*, April 28, 1894, May 19, 1894; for the following quotation, see Tourgée letter in clipping from Omaha *Bee*, May 8, 1894.

in that state, one of the leaders of which was Tourgée's ally, H. C. Smith, then a state legislator. Smith announced his intention to introduce the bill suggested by Tourgée, but a rival Negro legislator frustrated this effort by introducing a different plan. The legislature adjourned before agreement could be reached.[26]

At the next legislative session two years later, Tourgée's bill was introduced, and he traveled to Columbus to testify in its behalf before hundreds of interested spectators. The bill was then initially defeated, but, aided by the determination of its supporters and the endorsement of the outgoing Governor McKinley, it regained the floor and finally secured passage. Very shortly, however, it appeared that this, too, might be another fool's errand when a state court ruled the law in conflict with the state constitution. The Judge, whose wisdom was clearly impugned, promptly declared that "there was absolutely no doubt" that the state Supreme Court would uphold the law, and three years later his confidence was sustained. Meanwhile Tourgée's legal battle against Jim Crow had endured a much more significant test before the United States Supreme Court.

It will be recalled that Tourgée had been appointed in the fall of 1891 to direct a legal attack upon the Louisiana railroad segregation law. He momentarily questioned the wisdom of this attempt because of recent adverse court decisions. Since the Supreme Court had "always been the foe of liberty until forced to move on by public opinion," he wondered whether it would not be wisest to delay until the N.C.R.A. had generated favorable public pressure. "It is of the utmost consequence," he wrote, "that we should not have a decision *against* us," for the court "has *never reversed itself* on a *constitutional* question." This same fear turned some Negro leaders against the entire fight, while others were content to believe that the separate-car system would prove too expensive to maintain.[27]

Tourgée, of course, was accustomed to overcoming his fears, and there was good reason for legally resisting the spreading segregation laws. Although the Federal courts had already weakened the meaning of the

[26] For this entire issue, see Bystander, *Inter Ocean*, March 19, 1892; Cleveland *Gazette*, February 10, March 3, 10, May 5, 19, December 8, 22, 1894, and January 25 through May 30, 1896, June 19, 1897; T. Green to Tourgée, November 10, 1893, June 1, 12, 1894.

[27] Tourgée to L. A. Martinet, October 31, 1891; Kansas City *American Citizen*, December 8, 1891; Washington *Bee*, February 13, 1892.

Fourteenth Amendment, it was still held to bar discriminatory state action, and Jim Crow laws were a new form of state-imposed discrimination the constitutionality of which was extremely doubtful. After jealously but logically resisting efforts to arouse a clamor over the proposed case by involving other prominent individuals, Tourgée moved on. James C. Walker, a white criminal lawyer and one-time Republican in New Orleans, was paid a reasonable retainer to handle the routine procedures, while Tourgée served without a fee throughout. For the sake of certain legal arguments, the Judge advised that a "nearly white" Negro be used to establish a proposed test case, a matter that proved of some difficulty because such Negroes passed unchallenged and the darker population was complaining that those involved in the movement "were nearly white or wanted to pass for white." [28]

The railroads, though dreading public opinion, professed distaste for the costly segregation law and proved surprisingly co-operative. The Louisville & Nashville agreed to arrange a test case, although they would not bring the charges. In accordance with this plan, in February, 1892, a light-skinned young Negro, Daniel F. Desdunes, bought a ticket to Mobile, boarded a train, and took a seat in a white coach. Upon his refusal to move after the complaint of a white associate, he was arrested and committed to trial. This case was never heard, however, for in a separate decision the Louisiana Supreme Court voided the application of the law in question to interstate passengers as a violation of the commerce clause of the United States Constitution. This result was hailed with glee by Martinet's *Crusader*, which proclaimed that "the Jim Crow car is ditched and will remain in the ditch. Reactionists may foam at the mouth, and Bourbon organs may squirm, but Jim Crow is as dead as a door nail." [29] Martinet believed that Negroes could now force the Jim Crow car into disuse by enforcing their interstate rights, but although several such individual efforts were made successfully, they did not undermine the segregated-car system. Tourgée had judged the situation correctly when he advised keeping the interstate matter out of the Desdunes case, and he now proceeded with an intrastate case in an effort to destroy the principle of enforced segregation itself.

Within a few weeks of the dropping of the Desdunes case, a similar

[28] Martinet to Tourgée, December 7, 1891. For a brief account of the origins of this case, see also Desdunes, *Nos Hommes et Notre Histoire*, 183–94.
[29] Quoted in Detroit *Plaindealer*, July 22, 1892.

test was arranged with the aid of Homer Adolph Plessy, a gentleman of "one-eighth African blood," who bought a ticket in New Orleans for a trip wholly within the state and took a seat in the coach reserved for whites. Upon his refusal to move, Plessy was arrested and quietly accompanied the arresting officer. This action became the case of *Plessy* v. *Ferguson* after a lower court judge, John H. Ferguson, denied the arguments against the segregation law presented by Tourgée and Walker and they carried the case to the state's high court. Here they were again defeated in December, 1892. In the following month the case was carried, on a writ of error, to the United States Supreme Court, where final hearings were not initiated until late in 1895, with a decision handed down the following spring. Meanwhile, the very reverse of what Tourgée had hoped for had occurred. The climate had become ever more unfavorable, and was especially highlighted by Booker T. Washington's famous Atlanta Compromise speech of 1895, widely interpreted as a sign of Negro acceptance of an inferior status. In New Orleans, Martinet and his newspaper were on the verge of collapse at the end of that same year.

The legal attack against the Louisiana law by Tourgée and Walker relied primarily upon the Thirteenth and Fourteenth Amendments, and its essence had already been presented before the state courts.[30] Enforced segregation, they insisted, is a form of slave-like caste which violates the Constitution "because it denies equal protection of the law to all classes of citizens; perpetuates inequalities in the enjoyment of their rights; perpetuates race prejudice; and deprives citizens of liberty and immunity without due process of the law." Most of the elaboration of this stand before the Federal court was done by Tourgée, in bold and ringing phrases, while Walker concentrated upon establishing the impossibility of defining a Negro. A third brief, emphasizing certain unique technical points, was submitted by Tourgée's long-standing friend from North Carolina, Samuel F. Phillips, and his law partner, F. D. McKenney. It may have been reflective of pessimism that only Phillips presented his brief orally, although Walker pleaded illness and Tourgée was thoroughly involved in other difficulties at the time.

[30] See *U.S. Supreme Court Transcript of Records 1895*, XII (October term, 1895), Record Case 15, 248, and *File Copies of Briefs 1895*, VIII (October term, 1895), No. 210, U.S. Supreme Court Library, Washington, D.C.

Tourgée's personal absence did not, however, lessen the intensity of his commitment, and except for some bits of undue exaggeration, his brief was an eloquent composition of logic and law. Not until many decades later would Tourgée's interpretation of the related constitutional questions receive an appropriate affirmation,[31] and he outlined the heart of the entire matter with a clarity that a later generation could not have denied. "The trouble with this law," he insisted, was that it perpetuated "race prejudice among the citizens of the United States" and that it acted "to legalize caste and restore in part at least, the inequality of right which was an essential incident of slavery." It was "an act of race discrimination pure and simple" and was not passed, as claimed, "in the interest of public order, peace, and comfort" but was "manifestly directed against citizens of the colored race." Its object was "simply to debase and distinguish against the inferior race . . . to separate the Negroes from the whites in public conveyances for the gratification and recognition of the sentiment of white superiority and white supremacy of right and power." He challenged the justices to imagine their reaction if the tables were turned, and pointed to the exemption granted nurses as an indication "that the real evil lies not in the color of the skin but in the relation the colored person sustains to the white. If he is a dependent it may be endured: if he is not, his presence is insufferable."

One of Tourgée's arguments, that the light-skinned Plessy was being deprived of property (the obvious value of being considered white) without due process of law, suggests, it has since been noted, an unconscious paradox, for "this was not a defense of the colored man against discrimination by whites, but a defense of the 'nearly' white man against the penalties of color." [32] This was also, however, an eminently appropriate approach for that property-conscious age, and it was filled with ingenious portent. Tourgée was attempting to exploit the advantages of a lighter skin, for he knew that if Plessy's right could be established on this basis it would open a wide road. Not only would this impossibly complicate the enforcement of segregation, but, since

[31] Robert J. Harris, *The Quest for Equality. The Constitution, Congress and the Supreme Court* (Baton Rouge, La., 1960), *passim*.
[32] C. Vann Woodward, "The Birth of Jim Crow," *American Heritage*, XV (April, 1964), 101.

the holder of the smallest bit of property was entitled to the same rights as the largest, one drop of white blood would suffice.

None of the arguments in behalf of the Negro prevailed, and a Supreme Court that had already curtailed the range of the Fourteenth Amendment now further emasculated its content in endorsing discriminatory state action merely by denying that it was discriminatory. There was, of course, ample legal precedent for such a stand, and Justice Henry Billings Brown, a native of Massachusetts, in delivering the court's opinion relied heavily upon an oft-cited state decision upholding segregated schools in ante-bellum Massachusetts. The Jim Crow law of Louisiana, Justice Brown thought, was a "reasonable exercise of the police power of the state" which had "no tendency to destroy the legal equality of the two races, or re-establish a state of involuntary servitude." He found "the underlying fallacy of the plaintiff's argument to consist in the assumption that the enforced separation of the two races stamps the colored race with a badge of inferiority." There was only one dissenting justice, the one-time Whig and slaveholder from Kentucky, John Marshall Harlan, whose vigorous opinion echoed many of Tourgée's arguments and foreshadowed the reversal that came forty-eight years later. C. Vann Woodward has noted that it was thus the legal opinion of two sons of Massachusetts that bridged the gap in a national tradition of segregation that has been too often identified solely with the South, while it was an ex-carpetbagger and southern ex-slaveholder who championed equal justice.[33] The activities of the two scalawags Phillips and Walker should also be noted, although the greatest irony of all may have been the twisted logic of the court. It was certainly inconsistent, to say the least, for Justice Brown to include in his endorsement of Jim Crow the argument that social mores could not be established by law, for that was precisely what the court was allowing—the forceful imposition of segregated behavior by state law. The greatest weakness in the briefs in behalf of Plessy may have been the failure to exploit this fact more fully, and it might have been wise to have refuted the concept of separate but equal in greater detail. Of course, Tourgée did demolish this in essence, as did Justice Harlan, and

[33] *Ibid.*, 102. Almost twenty years earlier Justice Harlan spoke highly of Tourgée's brief in a homestead case (S. F. Phillips to Tourgée, April 4, 1878).

it is doubtful, after all, that more evidence of any kind would have then affected the court or the nation.

Confirming the predictions of Tourgée and Justice Harlan, the Plessy decision served as both an invitation and a rationale for a flood of oppressive segregation that followed, although the trend was already so apparent that the decision itself was anticlimactic. It attracted little national attention, except from the Negro press, which objected briefly, and it inspired no apparent reaction in the Tourgée family. Yet the Plessy decision did stand mockingly at the end of a long and bitter trail of folly, and Judge Tourgée had provided a strong and fitting rebuttal in his brief. Equality, he said, had become "the controlling genius of the American people," and the true meaning of the Fourteenth Amendment was "in strict accord with the Declaration of Independence, which is not a fable as some of our modern theorists would have us believe, but the all-embracing formula of personal rights on which our government is based and toward which it is tending with a power that neither legislation nor judicial construction can prevent." The battle might be lost, but he was ever confident of the war.

Last Errands—
The Basis and Bordeaux

T he Plessy decision was but one of many misfortunes besetting the
Tourgée family by the end of 1894. Even the winter seemed hostile,
as blizzards struck at Thorheim and the temperature dropped to 24
degrees below zero. The ill-fated Aimée was temporarily hospitalized
that fall, the Judge's royalties had dwindled to almost nothing, and
arguments with the *Inter Ocean* culminated first in a cut to half pay
and then in the indefinite suspension of the Bystander column, the
Tourgées' one steady source of income. Insult was added to injury a
few weeks later by that newspaper's strong endorsement of Booker T.
Washington's moderate tactics.

A more encouraging development was an apparent improvement in
the Judge's health, a factor that contributed to his decision to undertake the publishing venture dropped almost a year earlier. A publisher
in Buffalo, New York, together with several reformers and businessmen,
most of whom were also from that city, were attracted into the venture,
and in March, 1895, the first issue of a five-cent weekly, *The Basis: A
Journal of Citizenship*, appeared, dedicated to the encouragement of an
intelligent, responsible, and active citizenship. This effort was initiated
on a scant four thousand dollars, and disputes immediately erupted over
Tourgée's control. Even before the first issue was distributed, several
original backers withdrew, and the Judge was left in control with nothing
more substantial than permission to continue to publish without contracting any debt.

The *Basis* was published by McGerald & Sons of Buffalo, though its editorial and business office remained under Tourgée's firm control at Thorheim, where Emma, Aimée, and a clerk (probably one of Emma's sisters) wrestled with copy, subscriptions, advertisements, and other routine matters. An even larger task fell to the Judge, who wrote almost all the thirty-two pages of each weekly issue. Aimée also contributed several items, there was some additional fiction, and one of the investors, a Buffalo Unitarian minister, Thomas R. Slicer, gratuitously prepared a section on good government clubs. But the magazine's contents consisted overwhelmingly of Tourgée's skilled polemics, with some chapters of his regimental history, and the result was not unattractive. Among the more original observations were reflections on the still-raging currency controversy, praise for Harold Frederic's *The Copperhead*, and a unique interpretation of Booker T. Washington's Atlanta Compromise of 1895. Tourgée wrote that hitherto, in an effort to secure financial support, Washington stood "foremost among those who, if they did not encourage, were, at least, silent" regarding racial injustice, but at Atlanta he "rose above such sordid and fallacious considerations" to demand "for his people security and justice." That Tourgée's own tastes remained more belligerent, however, was made clear by his eulogy on Frederick Douglass delivered in Faneuil Hall two months after the Tuskegeean's famed address.[1]

One strength of the *Basis* was its low cost of operations, but while helping keep the magazine alive for thirteen months, such limited expenditures also made it impossible to reach effectively whatever market did exist and further limited that market by producing a journal representing little more than the voice of Albion W. Tourgée. He scarcely exaggerated in stating that the journal was essentially dependent upon his own "faith, courage, and ability to command support."[2]

The response to the *Basis* was typical of the response to Tourgée's recent endeavors—just favorable enough to keep it going, and occasionally more so. The Cleveland *Gazette* and one other magazine, the *Literary Digest*, were most attentive, and according to the Belfast *Northern Whig* Tourgée's work inspired "a national demonstration against American atrocities" in Great Britain.[3] There were also familiar disappointments.

[1] *Basis*, I (October 5, 1895); Boston *Globe*, December 21, 1895; *A Memorial of Frederick Douglass from the City of Boston* (Boston, 1896).
[2] Tourgée to C. W. Chesnutt, May 8, 1895, Chesnutt Papers.
[3] Clipping, November 7, 1895, Tourgée Papers.

The public remained uninterested in racial injustice, the Republicans were repudiating the Judge because of his reformism, and the reformers, because of his Republicanism. An attempted revival of the N.C.R.A. fell completely flat. The despondent Martinet reported only one subscription in all of New Orleans. Nor were attempted contests and appeals for funds any more fruitful.

Nevertheless, the *Basis* staggered on to a circulation of about twelve hundred, two staff writers were added, and late in 1895, at which time the magazine was converted into a monthly, the Judge entertained hopes of capitalizing on the coming presidential election. He hoped to become a voice for the candidacy of Thomas B. Reed. Pointing to the importance of the currency issue and to the powerful drive in behalf of McKinley, Tourgée implored the reluctant Reed to pursue the Republican nomination actively. All was in vain, and the April, 1896, issue of the *Basis* was its last.

This failure was accompanied by conflicting news. That same month some welcome information and acclaim arrived from Ohio, where the antilynching law had just passed, while a month later the Plessy decision was handed down. One day after this decision the Negro leader Ida Wells sent a cheering note, thanking Emma and the Judge for their constant inspiration, and on Memorial Day Tourgée continued the crusade with an oration in Boston. "Caste—the worst element of slavery —the legal subjection of one class to the domination and control of another, still exists," the Judge exhorted, "and, under the protection of a supreme court, which has always been the consistent enemy of personal liberty and equal right, may for a time triumph in the land. But this nation can no more endure a caste republic than it could endure a slave republic. The blood of yesterday flows too strong in the hearts of today to permit injustice long to prevail. Caste must die, as slavery died —accursed of God and despised of man." [4]

Despite this still flaming spirit, life for the Tourgée family had reached its nadir. The huge debt of ten years ago was gone, but the fifty-eight-year-old Judge felt the more frightening burden of exhaustion and despair. Not even a livelihood remained to him. His books were lying unsold. Two additional volumes, one already written, would bring almost no return, and because of his involvement with the *Basis*, his lecturing

[4] Boston *Globe*, May 31, 1896.

had become sporadic. Even more frightening was that sign of literary sterility, the rejection of new manuscripts by one journal after another. It is not surprising that the Judge longingly contemplated another book on Reconstruction and that one of his rejected manuscripts was entitled "A Failure." As the bills mounted, Emma's hopes, confided to her diary, were at their lowest ebb.

That spring the *Inter Ocean* provided one small ray of light by contracting for a series of Chautauqua articles by Aimée, and then the thrilling presidential contest of 1896 more thoroughly dispelled the gloom. Somewhat as Tourgée had predicted, the fire for this campaign was provided by a Democratic-Populist fusion in support of the free coinage of silver and the often vague, but always eloquent, reformism of William Jennings Bryan. The doctrines and popularity of Bryan frightened the Republicans into an unbelievably lavish publicity campaign, which, under the astute and free-spending direction of Marcus A. Hanna, sent hundreds of paid speakers and millions of pieces of literature into the campaign field. Tourgée partook gratefully of these expenditures.

Although he distrusted certain features of the Hanna-McKinley combine, Tourgée felt little reluctance in supporting the Republicans that year. He could not but recall hopefully McKinley's recent and decisive support of the Ohio antilynch law, whereas the Democrats as yet had offered no concessions on the race issue. In addition, Tourgée perceived that despite their humanitarian emphasis the Bryanites represented economic and political backwardness in an industrial age. He detected more than sufficient hokum in the theoretical position of the silverites to justify his hopes for a better approach from within the Republican ranks.

After preparing his own analysis of the currency dispute that summer, Tourgée borrowed twenty-five dollars to carry it to the national Republican headquarters in New York. Following some alterations suggested by the party, his manuscript, *War of the Standards* (1896), was printed by G. P. Putnam's Sons and endorsed and distributed as a Republican campaign document. The Judge was also employed as a campaign speaker, and the receipts from his new activities were soon being thankfully received at Thorheim.

War of the Standards approached the currency issue with intelligence at a moment when the silver cry had driven Republicans into a rigid orthodoxy of their own. Although it displayed obvious touches of the amateur, it possessed the graces of independence, ability, and sincere concern for the public. The London *Daily Chronicle* proclaimed it "the ablest work upon monetary science, from the point of view of the republicans, which the discussion of the currency problem in the United States has produced." [5] Properly rejecting the proposed free coinage of silver as based upon a false ratio of values and being a step backward toward bullionism, the volume also proclaimed the existing gold currency too scarce, too inflexible, too insecure, and too dependent upon private interests. The author was appalled by the recent reliance upon private bankers to rescue the nation from bankruptcy, and he advised a movement away from both business and bullionism toward greater government control and the more effective utilization of such credit mechanisms as Federal notes, Federal credit, and a Federal banking system. This accomplished conclusion was somewhat marred by the book's additional advocacy of an interest-bearing paper currency as a solution to the gold shortage.

Despite the competence of the Judge's brief volume and its Republican endorsement, it was too technical for widespread electoral use, and Tourgée's unorthodox agitation of this issue eventually exasperated Mark Hanna. Nonetheless, Tourgée's participation in the victorious electoral struggle contributed to his confidence as well as to his income, and his speeches in Pennsylvania were credited with defeating a popular silverite congressional candidate.[6] Soon after the Republican victory, the Bystander column was resumed in the *Inter Ocean*, and other writings of the Judge, including some currency articles, were being placed.[7] But the Tourgées were still far from comfort or security. The Judge displayed acute distress over a fruitless quest for an editorial position in New York,

---

[5] Quoted in Tourgée to William McKinley, March 5, 1897, Consular Recommendations, State Department Records, National Archives. The Glasgow *Herald* (December 31, 1896) said that "Tourgée is an economic writer endowed with quite an exceptional insight into the primary and ultimate forces of finance" (clipping, Tourgée Papers).

[6] Clipping, Washington *Evening Star*, May 12, 1897, Tourgée Papers.

[7] "The Best Currency," *North American Review*, CLXIII (October, 1896), 416–26; "Pending Problems," *ibid.*, CLXIV (January, 1897), 38–49; "Some Advice to Young Voters," *Golden Rule*, XI (October 1, 1896), 4–5. Several months earlier "The Reversal of Malthus" and "The Literary Quality of 'Uncle Tom's Cabin'" had appeared.

and Emma's continuing fears were confided to her diary on the last day of that year: "The close of the most distressful year of my life! Pray God the next may be different."

That it was to be different was due to a final twist in Judge Tourgée's troubled career, initiated by his application for a foreign consulate. This was a post traditionally bestowed upon authors, to which Tourgée strengthened his claim by invoking his past services to the nation and the Grand Old Party.

This was the only intent quest ever made for appointive office by the Judge, and it was aided by his recent labors and by heartwarming approval from many friends. It was as if a sudden flood of old Civil War idealism was bursting forth in honor of the famous fool. "No man in the country has done more than he for the good of the whole people," wrote a Chicago tycoon and reformer, H. H. Kohlsaat, formerly part-owner of the *Inter Ocean*, and variants of this opinion were echoed by Speaker Reed, Senator William E. Chandler, twenty additional congressmen, fifty members of the Pennsylvania legislature, forty prominent North Carolinians, several governors, a number of authors and college presidents, Negro leaders, and so on, down to a petition from fifty prominent citizens of Osborne, Kansas. Even Tourgée's powerful opponent in strategy, Booker T. Washington, joined the chorus of Negro support.[8]

For such a minor post, few could match the chorus of endorsements Tourgée enjoyed, but there was talk of administrative hostility toward all Reed Republicans, and Tourgée was embarrassed by his many years of conflict with the Republican party in his own state and district. Party protocol did allocate a consulate for his district that year, but this was to be dispensed by none other than the congressman whom Tourgée had tried to displace two years earlier and who had his own nominee in mind.

This circumstance would have negated the Judge's hopes but for the appointment of a sympathetic friend, the Michigan lumber king and politico Russell Alger, as Secretary of War. Alger beseeched the President to assist the impoverished Tourgée, whereupon McKinley, also subject to pressure from Negroes in Ohio, expressed a wish to the

[8] H. H. Kohlsaat to Mrs. Tourgée, February 27, 1897, and other letters, Consular Recommendations, State Department Records.

Secretary of State that "some suitable small consulship could be found for Judge Tourgée." [9]

The matter was not settled by this request, however, but was frustrated by one consideration or another for over a month. Tourgée, who meanwhile saw fit to urge upon McKinley a national campaign against lynching, had decided upon a trip to the capital to promote his interest, when an illness interfered. Emma then overcame her spouse's chivalrous objections and made the trip herself. If there was any need for tact, humility, or an admission of desperation, it was no doubt fortunate that the determined Emma appeared rather than her proud husband. For once, the Judge's illness may have been a blessing.

In Washington, Emma enjoyed visits with old friends and being squired about by the Secretary of War, Alger. More important, she received certain assurances directly from the President, although Speaker Reed, who supported the Judge's request, scornfully dismissed McKinley's pledge as a "Fairy tale!" [10] It was, in truth, dependent upon an endorsement of Tourgée by his hostile congressman. Reed brought pressure to bear upon this congressman, and two weeks later Emma again visited Washington and wrested an endorsement from the all-powerful New York senator, Thomas C. Platt. One day earlier, however, Alger had informed the Secretary of State that the President had determined upon the appointment, and Alger urged that he be relieved "from the constant importunities of the Judge and his wife, by sending the nomination over." [11] A few days later Emma left for home with McKinley's promise that her husband was being appointed United States Consul to Bordeaux, France. Not even a state assemblyman's disparaging remarks, which she overheard on the bus from the train station, could lessen the relief and joy Emma carried back to Thorheim.

The Judge's salvation by a party that he had labored, almost in vain, to redirect had about it the touch of both atonement and reward. The party sin was clear, and Tourgée had done Herculean service for a party

[9] Alger to McKinley, April 2, 1897, and McKinley to John Sherman, April 5, 1897. William McKinley Papers, Manuscripts Division, Library of Congress.

[10] Mrs. Tourgée, "How the Office Was Obtained," manuscript, n.d., Tourgée Papers.

[11] Alger to Sherman, April 30, 1897, and Platt to McKinley, May 1, 1897, Consular Recommendations, State Department Records. For Tourgée's embarrassing denunciations of Platt as "the most dangerous sort of a 'boss,'" see Bystander, Inter Ocean, October 10, 1891, and Basis, I (June 22, 1895).

whose glaring faults he deplored. Before long some of the buds he tended bore better fruits.

News of Tourgée's appointment brought a flood of congratulations into Thorheim, some lamenting the family's departure and others considering the reward tardy and meager. The irritation of the local Republican machine was unconcealed, while a friendly politician offered the wish "that the shekels" would now flow in the Judge's "coffer with the speed of the Empire State Express." From the South came regrets that Bordeaux was not farther off and that George W. Cable was not being sent away, too.

These signs of a lifetime of controversy were hardly noticed as the Tourgées prepared for their final errand. Amidst the busy preparations, the packing and the alterations of Thorheim for rental, there were many sad farewells, but joy was far more apparent than sorrow. Emma's sister left for a new home in Chicago, and Aimée for art school in Canada. In July, after borrowing funds for the voyage, Emma and the Judge embarked (much to the patriotic Judge's annoyance) upon an English ship. The crossing to Marseille was calm and restful, and a day of sightseeing there was followed by a long and uncomfortable train trip to Bordeaux. The new consul and his wife arrived near midnight, exhausted, and the next morning began a new career.

"Thank God—the light which has been so long hidden—shines," Emma wrote soon after their arrival, and for the Judge there was comfort in her joy and something soothing in the casual practices of the Old World and his physical separation from the problems that had plagued his past. Nevertheless, he was soon again busier than most men, vigorously involved in consular duties, in general affairs, and in writing the Bystander column for another year and a half, but he pursued his interests less incessantly than had ever before been true. The city's deity, Consul Tourgée soon learned, was Bacchus, and to speak evil of wine was blasphemy, but Bordeaux's Bacchus was neither ribald nor orgiastic. Like the grape fermenting in hundreds of cellars, the city's pace was gentle but steady, and encouraging this inactivity was the customary heavy noon meal with wine. "So you see the day is taken up with eating and sleeping," the Judge wrote his daughter. "Nobody hurries here; today is always tomorrow and tomorrow next week."

The consular building was conveniently situated near the water front, with the consul's living quarters provided in two upper stories. Furnishings were Spartan, and the location, at the center of the city's streetcar system, was sometimes noisy, but pleasant. Lovely trees shaded the lower windows of the four-story structure, while the upper windows looked across the avenue onto the greenery and parterres of a beautiful park, the Jardin des Plantes.

A consul's duties were far from burdensome, the income, while modest, was an improvement for the Judge, and Aimée arrived in time to gladden further the family's first Christmas abroad. Lack of acquaintances and language difficulties did impose a loneliness that only time could dispel, but meanwhile there was the enjoyment of foreign sights and sounds—"the quiet beauty" of Garonne, the complexities of marketing in France, and such intricacies of the wine industry as the entrancing *vendage* of Médoc, with its barefooted trampling of the grapes to the strains of wild music. Before long the Judge was an eager student of his new surroundings and was writing a history of what he concluded was the oldest continuous consulate in the world.

The daily routine at the consulate was complex for a novice. There were cargoes to clear, periodic reports to prepare, and a daily stream of callers to be met and placated. Protection and services had to be provided for American tourists, and there were letters to answer from businessmen and prospective travelers. Stranded seamen were aided, the births, marriages, and deaths of Americans were attended to, wills and estates were settled, and runaway daughters were rescued from amorous or ambitious gallants. Exporters were both fought and served, and while the Spanish-American War flared, a close check was applied to pro-Spanish activities. For several years the multiplicity of these tasks was complicated by impermanent vice-consuls and inadequate clerical help (attributable to the picayune funds allotted by the government), although this burden was more than shared by Emma and Aimée.[12]

A marked vigor and pride characterized the actions of Consul Tourgée. Uncowed by past misfortune, he was overly eager to influence and direct, as well as execute, policy. Unfortunately, his hopes exceeded his depleted reputation and the traditions of his post, and his efforts often were to

[12] For Tourgée's consular career, see Despatches from U.S. Consuls in Bordeaux, Register of Consular Communications Sent, and Instructions to Consuls, all in State Department Records, National Archives.

be annoyingly censured or ignored. It was neither the Judge's nature nor his tradition to be easily reconciled to expected standards of subservience and tact or to the haughty attitudes that so easily flowed from the State Department offices in Washington, while age and many failures had intensified his irascibility.

Tourgée was hardly settled in Bordeaux when the earliest of numerous collisions with his superiors was provoked by a Bystander column criticizing French legal procedures in the infamous Dreyfus case and making light of an official memorandum prohibiting the immigration of anarchists into the United States. To an immediate rebuke for a "breach of discipline" and a "violation of laws and regulations," the Consul responded by defending his humor and denouncing as "evidently unconstitutional" the exclusion of anyone from the United States "by executive order without law because of their political views." [13] The Judge also kept his superiors riled with communications bearing such titles as "Said Despatch Incomprehensible" or "Discussion of Mr. Elliot's Inquiry Why I Did What I Never Thought of Doing." It was usually little more than attempted sarcasm or wit that prompted several complaints of his "discourteous language" and warnings that "in the future all your communications to the department must be in terms becoming a subordinate in addressing a superior officer." Tourgée, in turn, could be pitifully sensitive and righteous in self-defense.[14]

His undiplomatic behavior proved a more serious matter when it extended beyond the confines of the State Department, and Tourgée was rebuked on several occasions. In one instance, although one of the Judge's reports was used, it had to be edited in Washington because he was "not authorized to criticize either the French Embassy at Washington or the Secretary of the Treasury." [15] Even innocent efforts could arouse a storm, such as Tourgée's conscientious encouragement of the French drink *piquette*, a mild concoction of apples and raisins. Endeavoring to encourage the export of American apples, he facetiously but accurately referred to the apples used as of the lowest grade, "sliced,

[13] Tourgée Despatch, March 21, 1898, Bordeaux Despatches.
[14] Tourgée Despatches, March 31, September 22, 1900, and Consular Memorandums, n.d. (attached to despatch of March 8, 1900), August 12, 1901, all in Bordeaux Despatches; Communications to Tourgée, September 7, 1900, and June 11, 1901, Register of Consular Communications Sent.
[15] Consular Memorandum, March 17, 1903, Bordeaux Despatches.

including skins, cores, and inhabitants," whereupon he found himself assailed for seeking to foist his nation's wormy apples on France. It appeared, however, that this *faux pas* aroused less anger than did his aspersions on certain wines and his intolerable assertion that French wine consumption was "steadily diminishing." [16]

Nor could Consul Tourgée aid the French with impunity. When he objected to American descriptions of *paté de foie gras* as "diseased" goose liver and to the labeling of certain varieties diluted for taste as "adulterated," he clashed with pure food enthusiasts and aroused mockery in the United States. The basic problem was that it was difficult to make an intelligent comment on economic affairs without arousing someone's ire, and while others might have preferred to avoid this difficulty, Tourgée quite obviously did not. In matters ranging from maraschino cherries and prunes to wines and walnuts, the Judge remained involved in controversy, and the unusual interest of foes and friends connected with the American press increased his impact. The Washington *Post*, for example, interpreted his reasonable description of European cultural resistance to mechanization with the headline, "French Labor is Stupid."

One ludicrous incident involving Consul Tourgée developed indirectly from his spinal injury. After five months of being bedridden during his third year in Bordeaux, the Judge's physician prescribed a move to the coastal resort of Archacon for hydropathic treatments. When the Tourgées subsequently moved into their rented "Villa Trocadero" in December, they were astonished to discover themselves locked out of the villa's bathroom, which they needed for the required treatments. A dispute with the landlord then culminated in the appearance of the police authorities at the villa with a writ authorizing entry and the seizure of the Tourgées' possessions for the withheld rent. Draping an American flag from the front balcony and claiming consular privileges, the Judge refused to honor the writ, whereupon the house was forcibly entered and searched. The Judge resisted throughout and later claimed that his remonstrances were dismissed with a curt gesture toward the flag and the comment, "Nous ne respectons pas ce drapeau-la," although the police attributed the latter accusation to the consul's poor hearing and poor French. In any event, his pride and patriotism had been thoroughly insulted, and the affair of Tourgée's bath soon occupied over

[16] Tourgée Despatches, March 19, 31, 1900, Bordeaux Despatches.

thirty pages of consular correspondence and became the subject of an international diplomatic dispute. Although Tourgée and the United States Department of State did not win their case for consular immunity, the "Tourgée case" succeeded in becoming a minor bit of diplomatic law.[17]

Such controversies over a period of eight years, illustrative of a lifelong pugnacity sharpened by age, cannot obscure other signs that Tourgée was a capable consul. With uncommon awareness of the commercial importance of his position, he wrote talented reports on conditions in France, fought against misconceived barriers to trade, encouraged American shipping, and aided American initiative with detailed descriptions of such French skills as the preparation of prunes and maraschino cherries. A great many of his efforts achieved recognition in consular publications and from business entrepreneurs. His most impressive report was, perhaps, a discussion of the reforestation of a vast sandy area of France with maritime pine, an account of successful conservation that aroused noticeable enthusiasm in the United States.[18]

Consul Tourgée was also aided by his legal skill. He was conscientious and anxious to serve. His patriotism and his ardent and obstinate nature did arouse resentment among the French, but, as in the South, his ability and understanding eventually won friendship and respect. More than once it was his propriety that drew him into controversy, as in the case of his refusal to extend questionable privileges to the president of the French Chamber of Commerce in New York. The Judge was rightfully proud of another controversy. Impressed with the dangers of transmitting livestock diseases, he insisted upon enforcing neglected disinfection laws regulating the export of hides and rags to the United States. His honest enforcement made a number of enemies in Bordeaux and diverted this trade to other, less scrupulously policed, routes. Tourgée's version of this affair received a decisive confirmation soon after his death, when his successor was approached with bribes and even with

17 John B. Moore, *Rights and Duties of Consuls: Chapter Sixteen of Moore's Digest of International Law* (Washington, D.C., 1910), 53–54; *Papers Relating to the Foreign Relations of the United States . . . 1900* (Washington, D.C., 1902), 429–56.

18 "Reforestation in France," *Consular Reports Commerce, Manufactures Etc.*, LXXIV (May–June, 1904), 647–52. See comments of Sioux City *Journal*, April 16, 1904, Jersey City *Journal*, May 6, 1904, and Charleston *News and Courier*, June 28, 1904 (clippings, Tourgée Papers.)

offers to construct a dummy disinfecting plant to provide the proper appearances.[19]

In the midst of Tourgée's absorption in consular affairs, he never quite abandoned his former activities and interests. The Bystander column continued until late in 1898, some final, mediocre fiction and several able articles appeared, and at least one more edition of A *Fool's Errand* was published. The Judge also contributed material to the presidential campaigns of 1900 and 1904, upon which his consulship was dependent, and, of course, he celebrated the results of each.

The fact that foreign affairs now became a topic of increased interest to the Judge was a reflection not only of his new post but of the pursuance of a more aggressive role in world affairs by the United States, the most dramatic sign of which was the outbreak of the Spanish-American War in the spring of 1898. In response to such trends, Tourgée's earlier perplexity regarding imperialism continued, and early in 1897 he feared lest sympathy for the Cuban rebels bring Cuba under the domination of the United States, believing that this would bring racism to the island and intensify it at home. But he also offered contrary rationalizations. Only a month after expressing these fears respecting Cuba, Tourgée declared that the time had passed when the United States could live wholly within its borders, for the national economy was expanding beyond that of any other country and must secure a part of the world's trade, and "that part must be just as large as we can make it. That way lies power and prestige and profit." [20] Since some nation would inevitably dominate these backward areas, far better that it be the morally superior United States.

So it was that Tourgée's voice was added to the rapidly swelling expansionist chorus, and his ardor was increased by the war against Spain. He wrote to impress upon the President the necessity of annexing the Philippines, and a later letter to McKinley applauding the decision to keep these islands revealed what a mockery the expansionist crusade could make of Tourgée's thirty years of equalitarian struggle. "I understand that the United States does not covet the task of bringing order out of chaos in the Philippines" and that "the natives are about as hard material as civilization ever had to deal with," he wrote. "I do not know

[19] D. I. Murphy Despatch, May 2, 1906, Bordeaux Despatches.
[20] Bystander, *Inter Ocean*, January 16, February 20, 1897.

what we can do with them, but even if we have to kill them off, it is better than to abandon the relics at Cavite." [21] The brutality of these comments was hardly extenuated by an obvious desire to cultivate the President's favor. Two days after this letter was written, a Bystander column appeared that spoke of "American enterprise, American intelligence, and the American sense of justice *toward all men*" creating "a new civilization in the gloom of Oriental darkness."

An extension of these considerations also led Tourgée into an analysis of world rivalry for power. Viewing "Prussian ambition and German industrial interest" as the main competitors of the United States, Tourgée predicted as early as 1897 that Germany would find her desired war of aggression in the Balkans. It was in response to this assumed threat that Tourgée, a one-time Anglophobe, became an earnest advocate of Anglo-American unity as the "only hope for free institutions" and the "peace of the world." [22] In an article in the *Contemporary Review*, a London magazine, he envisioned this English-speaking alliance as directed against autocratic governments, aggressive military designs, and oppressive colonial policies and in behalf of the interests of "the half-developed regions of the world." He also perceived that Anglo-American control of an excessive share of the world's food and raw materials increased the desperation of underdeveloped areas, but felt that it was England and the United States who could become "the efficient and unquestioned guarantors of the peace and prosperity of the world during the greater part of the twentieth century, with every prospect" of this also leading "to the establishment of international tribunals which may make warfare no longer the chief business of government." [23]

Theodore Roosevelt's assertive foreign policy appealed to this sense of mission, and in the last years of his life, Tourgée sought to compliment and advise Roosevelt, while apologizing for a boldness that stemmed from his being "so long accustomed to regard our country as God's instrument for good to the world." [24] He was again a soldier for liberty and the Union, and there was something reminiscent of the Civil

[21] Tourgée to McKinley, August 5, 1898, McKinley Papers.
[22] Bystander, *Inter Ocean*, February 20, April 24, 1897, June 5, 1898; "A Fool's Notions," I, II, III, manuscripts, Tourgée Papers.
[23] "The Twentieth Century Peacemakers," *Contemporary Review*, LXXV (June, 1899), 886–908.
[24] Tourgée to Roosevelt, November 9, 1904, Tourgée Papers.

War about it all. Whatever its merit, it was a point of view that retained no little respect over sixty years later.

Another of the Judge's concerns, which neither distance nor other activities could suppress, was the Negro question. The Bystander still found occasion to revive the familiar cry for justice, and the Judge wrote to Presidents McKinley and Roosevelt on the question. In an interesting letter to the former regarding the Boer War, Tourgée supported England's diplomatic demands by equating them with those of the United States during the Civil War, and he extended the parallel by noting that in each instance the challenger "regarded the right to enslave a colored race as an essential concomitant of freedom." [25]

Encouraging developments respecting the race question during these years were few. McKinley's first inaugural address contained a heartening attack upon lynching, and a colored midshipman was appointed to Annapolis, but there was not much else. Old memories were aroused when Negroes wrote from North Carolina to tell the Judge that the house once belonging to the martyred John Stephens was being converted into the Yanceyville Colored Academy. Bad omens were more frequent, and none was more infuriating than the great popularity of Thomas Dixon, Jr.'s racist fiction. These works had a particularly onerous impact because they were written by an acquaintance of Tourgée's and a renowned minister of that very Christianity to which he so often looked for justice. A review comparing Dixon's *The Leopard's Spots* with *A Fool's Errand* provoked a spirited thirty-two-page letter from the Judge denouncing Dixon and defending his own work. Later, after repeatedly receiving copies of one of Dixon's novels in the mail, Tourgée refused to touch the repulsive book but grasped it with tongs and dropped it into the fireplace.

Taking all this into consideration, it was not surprising that strains of despondency emerged from the Judge's isolation in Bordeaux. So much of his faith appeared to have been folly. "Every day I have grown less and less hopeful with regard to the outcome," he wrote McKinley in response to the Wilmington race riot of 1898. It appeared that Christianity had not condemned or prevented injustice but had excused and encouraged it. Rather than education's destroying prejudice, knowledge

[25] Tourgée to McKinley, December 11, 1900, McKinley Papers. Tourgée's progressive reformism had also continued in the Bystander column.

was resented in the colored man or used by the white to rationalize, refine, and strengthen exploitation. In defiance of justice and law, the subjugation of one race to the will and profit of another had not only been allowed but had been endorsed by the public and sanctified by the church, and there seemed to be "no present prospect for amelioration." Should "Christ make a second coming in the form of a Negro," Tourgée ventured, this would not provide enlightenment but "would disintegrate and destroy the christian [sic] churches of the United States. Then, indeed, might it be written, 'He came to His own and His own received Him not!' " [26]

The scope of the Judge's dismay was now extended. What he had once viewed as the nation's greatest problem became the "greatest of all world-problems," whose root was not slavery but race prejudice itself. "Slavery was merely an incident not the cause of a much deeper and more widely-prevailing evil—the fact that civilization and Christianity are irredeemably committed to the theory of white supremacy and the assertion in fact, if not in theory, of a world-wide difference between the inherent rights of a white man and a colored 'individual'; that the woeful 'burden' which the 'White Man' is compelled to bear, is to rule the colored races of the world and to compel the brown 'half-devil and half-child' to serve his interests, promote his comfort, and enhance his wealth." [27] In the face of this pervasive power, the Judge confessed to a curtailment of his own struggles out of both bewilderment and fear.

But one should not distort the Judge's passion, and the protest in his words is so clear that he who runs may read. He remained proud of the fight that his own words sometimes mocked, believing that it was in his expectations rather than in his tactics or goals that he had erred, and he was still confident in a just God who worked through man in mysterious, sometimes vengeful, ways. Were he to perceive the way ahead, he would speak, but as yet he could only say: "How it will be done, I do not know. That it will be done I do not doubt." Perhaps, he pondered, it would require not only generations of effort, but "some enlightening miracle or soul thrilling horror . . . to stir the hearts of Christendom and shame the pretensions of Civilization. . . ." It was

[26] Tourgée to McKinley, November 23, 1898, McKinley Papers; Tourgée to Roosevelt, October 21, 1901, Roosevelt Papers, Manuscripts Division, Library of Congress.
[27] "Black and White," manuscript, [1899], Tourgée Papers.

portentous that in these rambling thoughts he linked together the fate of the Negro, the colonial, and the Jew.[28]

One easily detects, too, a continuance of those efforts that Tourgée professed to have abandoned. While confessing his perplexity to President McKinley, he also humbly suggested that the President speak out in behalf of the Negro and that because of their admirable record in the recent war more Negro troops be recruited into the army. As for his pessimism regarding the automatic benefits of education, this was continuing resistance to the philosophy of accommodationism, and Tourgée continued to urge militant struggle upon Negro leaders. Victory would not come for the Negro "until for years the world and God have heard his agonizing cry for justice, liberty, equal rights and a freeman's opportunity. . . ." He predicted in 1900 that it would take a century to regain the rights destroyed since Reconstruction, and as the colored protest grew, he still expected the conscience and intellect of the whites to endorse its cry. It was fitting that the most promising sign of this hope, small as it was, would come in 1901 from a Republican president, by the simple act of inviting Booker T. Washington to dine. The furor that this invitation aroused recalled a similarly inspired attack upon Tourgée himself, a quarter of a century earlier. "You have lighted the fire and may be consumed therein," gratefully wrote the Judge, but "I am glad that I have lived to know that an American President is brave enough to ask a colored gentleman to his table. Whatever may hap, it is a brave man's act, a true christian's [sic] act which the world can never forget." [29]

While Tourgée thus retained his stand, idealistic concerns had become but a small part of his mild and comfortable life abroad. His circle of friends and acquaintances had slowly grown, and consular affairs had achieved a satisfying and decreasingly disruptive order. Pleasantness characterized his correspondence with old friends back home, while Emma and Aimée still provided "a heaven of earth." Tired in body and mind, content with his circumstances, the Judge was prepared to remain till the end in Bordeaux.

[28] *Ibid.*; Tourgée to F. L. Barnett, August 6, 1900, Tourgée to E. H. Johnson, May 15, 1902, Tourgée Papers.
[29] Tourgée to Barnett, August 6, 1900, Tourgée to E. P. Gould, November 23, 1903, Tourgée Papers; Tourgée to Roosevelt, October 21, 1901, Roosevelt Papers.

This expectation was rudely challenged in 1903, when, despite his earnest protests and the prediction of physicians that he could not survive the move, the sixty-five-year-old Tourgée was "promoted" to the post of consul general at Halifax, Nova Scotia. In fear and sorrow the move was begun, and Emma had actually embarked for New York before word arrived that in response to her final plea the transfer had been cancelled.

Tourgée's life then resumed its customary pace, and the entire crisis at least produced some gratifying support from the local business community. In the following year an operation on the Judge's hip, which removed a bit of shell embedded since the Battle of Perryville, did not prevent his renewed vigor and participation in the fall presidential election. But before the year ended, the Judge was seriously ill. Months of intense suffering followed, although "almost to the last day," the vice-consul reported, Judge Tourgée "gave directions in his usual intelligent manner, never losing interest in affairs, which for nearly eight years he had considered his highest duty to perform." On May 21, 1905, sixteen days after the completion of his last published consular report and one week after his and Emma's forty-second wedding anniversary, the Fool's errand ended. Among his last words were those recalled by Emma— "You have been the one perfect wife."

Epilogue

Following an honorary funeral service in Bordeaux, with the pall-bearers including the Mayor, the Prefect of the Department of Gironde, and the commanding general of the French Eighteenth Army Corps, Tourgée's body was cremated in Paris and his ashes were then taken to their final resting place at Thorheim. There, on November 14, 1905, the businesses of Mayville closed as the townspeople made their way through falling snow to the burial services at the village Methodist Episcopal church. The attendance of thirty or more Negroes from throughout the nation had been arranged chiefly by the Judge's staunch follower Harry C. Smith, who in his efforts had encountered continued difficulties regarding Tourgée. Booker T. Washington had not responded in kind to the dedication displayed by Smith, and the most prominent Negroes present were Tourgée's old militant allies—Smith, Ida Wells-Barnett, and Charles W. Chesnutt. But the moderates were represented, and Washington himself wired: "My race owes much to the courage, and helpful work of Judge Tourgée, which we shall not forget." This telegram did not suffice to prevent expressions of the community's bewilderment at the failure of the Negroes' presumed leader to appear.

The last rites for Judge Tourgée were simple ones, accompanied by several testimonials, including one by Chesnutt in behalf of the nation's colored population. Unfortunately, they were held without the presence of his ashes, which had been inopportunely delayed. Several hours later his remains were interred in another ceremony by the local post of the G.A.R. On the succeeding Memorial Day, the dearest of all commemorative days to Tourgée, a monument was dedicated at the grave, a twelve-foot-tall granite obelisk bearing a favored quotation that had long helped set the course of his life:

I pray thee then
Write me as one that loves his fellow-men

The Civil War had initiated the persistent errand that ended with this inscription, while the Reconstruction South had provided the vital touches of unforgettable evil and unquenchable hope. Political and literary success doubtless had helped to maintain the effort, but there is little to quarrel with in Emma Tourgée's conclusion that underlying all her husband's "matchless characteristics was his idea of Justice— justice to all men, no matter what their color or previous condition, because they were men." [1]

The best of intentions, however, could not hide the Judge's faults. His conceit, tactlessness, and pride were prejudicial to his efforts, and there were touches of selfishness. He was deficient as an organizer and leader, and at times his very passion warped his talent. But perfection is an idle dream, and, for all his faults, Tourgée was a Promethean figure, a partisan warrior true to conviction, who was loved and hated not for his defects, but for his ability and strength, for his powerful and original impact upon his time. Few could have fought this battle more effectively than he, and no one else made quite the same needed try.

It was Tourgée's misfortune and glory to assume a mantle that the nation was about to abandon. Preferring failure to hypocrisy, conscience to comfort, he elected to battle a monstrous evil that almost an entire civilization either endorsed or did not care or dare to defy. He fought in the South, then in the North, and by the side of the Negroes themselves, all to no avail. But there was no resolution of the dilemma that he faced, and who shall say that his achievement was not as great as his failure? "The life of the Fool proper," he wrote, "is full of the poetry of faith. He may run after a will-o'-the-wisp, while the Wise deride; but to him it is a veritable star of hope."

When Tourgée died, it was in many ways a dismal time for this poetry of faith, although the currents were still diverse. That very day, a race riot erupted in the city where the Bystander's appeals for justice had so long been published, and that year Dixon's racist play, *The Clansman*, made its triumphant national tour. Most of the post-mortem evaluations in the nation's press, while treating his memory with respect, repudiated

[1] Mrs. Tourgée to Charles L. Van Noppen, publishers, n.d., Tourgée Papers.

the disruptive impact of Tourgée's well-known crusade. Some, from New York to Georgia, adjudged his name "odious for all time to come," although there were others to extol his work and predictions.

So muffled was the Judge's cry that the very eulogy dedicating his monument expressly sustained the submissive tactics that he himself deplored. He would have been overjoyed, however, by a gathering of Negroes that took place not far from Thorheim less than two months after his death. This gathering at Niagara, Canada, instituted a vigorous demand for immediate and full racial equality under the leadership of William E. B. Du Bois, just such a Negro champion as the Judge had awaited. In its tactics and demands and its subsequent founding of the biracial National Association for the Advancement of Colored People, the Niagara Movement was clearly following a path that had been marked out by Judge Tourgée, and in November, 1905, the movement sponsored nationwide memorial services in behalf of three "Friends of Freedom," who were "William Lloyd Garrison, Albion Tourgée, and Frederick Douglass." [2] In response, the followers of Booker T. Washington pointedly ignored the memory of Tourgée and honored only the centennial of Garrison's birth.[3] Possibly Tourgée's failures and absence from the country for eight years hindered the restoration of his fame, but the Niagara Movement would grow, and there was satisfaction enough, perhaps, in the words of the noted Negro leader Archibald Grimké. Tourgée "will not have lived in vain," he wrote, "if the indomitable purpose which filled him shall live on still in the hearts of the race which he defended in its passage through the wilderness. . . ." [4]

Whatever the Fool's bequest, the passing years would often testify to his wisdom. Even before Tourgée's death, an era was under way that,

[2] *Voice of the Negro,* III (January, 1906), 19–20. "It is safe to estimate that 10,000 Negroes assembled on November 30th to keep green the memory of these great men" (*ibid.*). But the Niagara Movement did break with the Republican party. For a description of Tourgée's funeral, see Cleveland *Gazette,* November 18, 1905, and N.Y. *Age,* November 23, 1905.

[3] John A. Hagan to J. Francis Robinson, November 5, 1905, and Robinson to Booker T. Washington, November 6, 1905, Booker T. Washington Papers, Manuscripts Division, Library of Congress. The author is indebted to Professor Louis R. Harlan of the University of Cincinnati for these and other items in the Washington Papers.

[4] Grimké letter, N.Y. *Age,* August 3, 1905. But Tourgée would become so forgotten that future histories would write his name as Albert and Albinon and call his historical romance *Out of the Sargasso Sea.*

in its program and rationale, its internal reformism and its less appealing moral imperialism, closely resembled his familiar position. Five years later, another Republican, Theodore Roosevelt, expressed a similar repudiation of *laissez faire* and an endorsement of positive Federal action that did not receive its due until more than twenty years later. Nevertheless, the memory of Tourgée, who had so alienated others by his tenacious stand, was an unnoticed part of the dawning Progressive era. He could serve only as a reminder of a dark racist gap in its shiny humanitarian armor.

Although the longed-for assault against prejudice began soon after Tourgée's death, and the force of Negro wealth and achievement, together with ever-mounting numbers of white allies, was increasingly felt, there would be little apparent progress for decades. The world would, in fact, pass through traumatic purgings more dreadful than those the Judge had imagined before thorough opposition to racism would begin. And even more would be required to change the tide—the crumbling of colonialism and an ironic international competition in equalitarianism. Truly it was, as Tourgée had said, a world problem.

Not until half a century after Tourgée's death would the cry against racist oppression in the United States approach that crescendo and effectiveness of which he had dreamed, and his estimated date of fulfillment, the year 2000, begin to appear a reasonable goal. As this change occurred, the name of the forgotten carpetbagger sometimes reappeared, from a revival of scholarly interest in 1942 to headlines twenty-one years later in his southern home-town newspaper that told proudly of "A CHUNKY ONE-EYED GHOST" who was "haunting the halls of Congress" and cheering on "new champions of his program for federal aid to education." [5] Midway between these events, the United States Supreme Court was again considering the doctrines of Jim Crow, and Justice Robert H. Jackson wrote to friends living near Mayville, New York, of his having encountered the name of Albion W. Tourgée in connection with the school segregation decisions then pending before the court. The jurist wrote:

> The *Plessy* case arose in Louisiana, and how Tourgée got into it
> I have not learned. In any event, I have gone to his old brief

[5] Greensboro *Daily News*, December 15, 1963.

filed here, and there is no argument made today that he would not make to the Court. He says, "Justice is pictured blind and her daughter, the Law, ought at least to be color-blind." Whether this was original with him, it has been gotten off a number of times since as original wit. Tourgée's brief was filed April 6, 1896 and now, just fifty-four years after, the question is again being argued whether his position will be adopted and what was a defeat for him in '96 be a post-mortem victory.[6]

Four years later, the school desegregation decision of the nation's highest court did reverse the doctrine of *Plessy* v. *Ferguson*. Fifty-eight years after his defeat, the views of a Fool had won. Who can measure his own contribution to that end?

[6] Robert H. Jackson to Ernest Cawcroft and Walter H. Edson, April 4, 1950. The author is indebted to Professors C. Vann Woodward of Yale University and Paul A. Freund of the Harvard Law School for a copy of this letter.

I. Bibliography of Tourgée's Writings

The following partial listing does not include various clippings of additional articles, stories, and poems found in the Tourgée Papers the precise location or dates of which have not been ascertained, nor does it include the titles of the many unpublished speeches, lectures, poems, and articles also available in that collection. Additional information pertaining to re-editions and reprints, together with a detailed catalogue of Tourgée's writings in his own magazines, may be found in Dean Keller, "A Checklist of the Writings of Albion W. Tourgée (1838–1905)" (*Studies in Bibliography*, XVIII [1965], 269–79). An older bibliography may be found in Roy F. Dibble, *Albion W. Tourgée* (New York, 1921).

FICTION

"The Lagby Papers," Greensboro *Union Register*, precise dates unknown (January, 1867).

"God's Anynted Phue," letters, New Berne *Republican Courier*, February 3, 1872, and other unverified dates.

Toinette: A Tale of the South. New York: J. B. Ford, 1874. Published under the pseudonym Henry Churton.

"Mamelon," *The Christian Union*, XIII (April 19–June 14, 1876). Published under the pseudonym Henry Churton.

Figs and Thistles: A Western Story. New York: Fords, Howard & Hulbert, 1879.

A Fool's Errand By One of the Fools. New York: Fords, Howard & Hulbert, 1879. First published anonymously. The last discovered edition by Fords,

Howard & Hulbert was dated 1902, and in 1961 this work was reprinted under the editorship of John Hope Franklin by Harvard University Press, Cambridge. Two foreign translations have been located: *Eines Narren Narrenstreich* (3 vols.; Berlin: E. Pennet, 1882) and *Hullum Hritys* (2 vols.; Helsingessa, Finland: Waldamar Churberg, 1883).

Bricks Without Straw. A Novel. New York: Fords, Howard & Hulbert, 1880.

A Royal Gentleman and Zouri's Christmas. New York: Fords, Howard & Hulbert, 1881. *A Royal Gentleman* is a revised version of *Toinette*, published together with a short story, "Zouri's Christmas."

John Eax and Mamelon; or, the South without the Shadow. New York: Fords, Howard & Hulbert, 1882. Two short tales.

Hot Plowshares, a Novel. New York: Fords, Howard & Hulbert, 1883. First appeared as a serial in *Our Continent*, II–III (July 12, 1882–May 23, 1883).

Button's Inn. Boston: Roberts Brothers, 1887. First appearing weekly in the Chicago *Inter Ocean*, December 12, 1886–January 23, 1887, and in the Buffalo *Sunday Express*, December 19, 1886–January 30, 1887.

Black Ice. New York: Fords, Howard & Hulbert, 1888.

Eighty Nine; or, the Grand Master's Secret. New York: Cassell, 1888. Published under the pseudonym Edgar Henry.

With Gauge and Swallow, Attorneys. Philadelphia: J. B. Lippincott, 1889. Twelve short stories that first appeared in *Lippincott's Monthly Magazine*, XL–XLIV (December, 1887–August, 1889).

Pactolus Prime. New York: Cassell, 1890. Appearing as "Pactolus Prime; or the White Christ" in *The Advance*, XXII–XXIII (December 13, 1888–March 14, 1889).

Murvale Eastman, Christian Socialist. New York: Fords, Howard & Hulbert, 1890. First published as "Nazirema or the Church of the Golden Lilies" in *The Advance*, XXIII (October 3, 1889–July 3, 1890).

A Son of Old Harry. A Novel. New York: Robert Bonner's Sons, 1891. Initially appeared in the New York *Ledger*, XLVII (April 4, 1891–August 29, 1891).

" 'Corporal Billee,' " *Cosmopolitan*, XI (May, 1891), 96–108.

Out of the Sunset Sea. New York: Merrill & Baker, 1893. Published weekly in the Chicago *Inter Ocean*, December 18, 1892–March 26, 1893.

"An Astral Partner," *The Green Bag*, VIII (July–August, 1896).

The Mortgage on the Hip-Roof House. Cincinnati, O., Curts & Jennings; New York, Eaton and Mains, 1896.

The Man Who Outlived Himself. New York: Fords, Howard & Hulbert.

Three short stories: the title story, "Poor Joel Pike," and "The Grave of Tante Angelique." The title story ran weekly in the Washington, D.C., *National Tribune*, September 30, 1897–November 4, 1897.
"The Summerdale Brabble," Washington, D.C., *National Tribune*, March 7, 1901–May 2, 1901.

POETRY

Poll tax song, *National Anti-Slavery Standard*, November 9, 1867.
"Bring Flowers—Bright Flowers," Greensboro *Patriot*, May 14, 1873.
"John Workman's Notions," Greensboro *North State*, September 26, 1878.
"Monumentum in Aere," *Our Continent*, I (May 31, 1882), 249.
"Yesterday and To-Day," *Our Continent*, I (July 5, 1882), 328–29.
"Duplessis Mornay," *Our Continent*, II (November 29, 1882), 656–57.
"A Dirge," Chicago *Inter Ocean*, August 8, 1885.
"Childe Rob, of Lincoln," Chicago *Inter Ocean*, June 22, 1888.
"The Ballad of Gettysburg," Chicago *Inter Ocean*, July 4, 1888.
"Daniel Periton's Ride," *The Independent*, XLI (June 27, 1889), 1.
"The Christ," *The Basis*, II (December, 1895), 34.
"Tho He Slay!," *The Independent*, XLVIII (December 10, 1896), 37.

NONFICTION

The Union Register. Edited in Greensboro by Tourgée, December 1, 1866–June 14, 1867.
Election circular. Broadside. [Greensboro]: no publisher, October 21, 1867.
Wenckar and Winegar letters, *National Anti-Slavery Standard*, October 19, November 9, December 14, 1867, January 4, 1868.
"The Work of the Convention," Raleigh *Daily North Carolina Standard*, March 19, 1868.
Letters from Tourgée and from "C," Raleigh *Daily North Carolina Standard*, April 10, 1868.
A *Plan for the Organization of the Judiciary Department, Proposed by* A. W. *Tourgée of Guilford, as a Section of the Constitution*. Pamphlet. [Raleigh]: no publisher, [1868].
Tourgée to the Bar of the Seventh Judicial District, Raleigh *Daily North Carolina Standard*, December 29, 1868.

The Code of Civil Procedure of North Carolina, to Special Proceedings. With Victor C. Barringer and William B. Rodman. Raleigh: N. Paige, State Printer, 1868.

Tourgée letter defending his judicial conduct, Raleigh *Daily North Carolina Standard*, February 1, 1870.

Tourgée to Joseph C. Abbott, New York *Tribune*, August 3, 1870.

"National Education," Washington, D.C., *Chronicle*, January 17, 1871.

"Why Reconstruction Was a Failure," Northampton, Mass., *Free Press and Journal*. Published under the pseudonym Henry Churton; the date of the appearance of these articles has not been ascertained.

Memorial Day address, Greensboro *New North State*, June 24, 1874.

Tourgée to editor, Wilmington *Post*, Greensboro *New North State*, June 11, 1875.

Tourgée to S. C. Parker, Greensboro *New North State*, June 18, 1875.

"What the Pew Thinks. No. 2," Greensboro *New North State*, August 6, 1875.

The Daily Constitution. Edited in Raleigh by Tourgée, September–October, 1875.

"The Southern Question," Rochester, N.Y., *Democrat and Chronicle*, September 16, 1876.

Letter on the North Carolina elections under the pseudonym R. R. G., New York *Times*, February 10, 1877.

The "C" Letters as Published in the "North State." Greensboro: North State, 1878. Appeared initially in the Greensboro *North State*, March–May, 1878.

"The 'C' Letters. Second Series," Greensboro *North State*, June–July, 1878.

The Code of Civil Procedure of North Carolina, with Notes and Decisions. Raleigh: John Nichols, 1878.

Judge Tourgée's Platform. Broadside. [Greensboro]: no publisher, [1878].

Jeduthan Jeems letters, Raleigh *Daily News*, May–June, 1879.

A Digest of Cited Cases in the North Carolina Reports. Raleigh: Alfred Williams, 1879.

Statutory Adjudications in the North Carolina Reports. Raleigh: Alfred Williams, 1879.

A Fool's Errand and the Invisible Empire. New York: Fords, Howard & Hulbert, 1880. The second part of this work is a factual account of the Ku Klux Klan.

Tourgée's reply to William L. Royall, New York *Sun*, December 9, 1880.

"About Carpetbaggers," New York *Tribune*, January 31, 1881.

"Aaron's Rod in Politics," *The North American Review*, CXXXII (February, 1881), 139–62.

"Reform versus Reformation," *The North American Review*, CXXXII (April, 1881), 305–19.

"The Christian Citizen," *The Chautauquan*, II (November, 1881), 86–91.

"The Education of the Negro," *The Congregationalist*, XXXIII (November 30, 1881), 389.

"To the Readers of the Chautauquan," *The Chautauquan*, II (December, 1881), 182.

Our Continent. Edited by, and various writings by, Tourgée. Vols. I–VI (February 15, 1882–August 20, 1884). Title changed to *The Continent* on January 3, 1883.

"Give Us a Rest," Chautauqua, N.Y., *Assembly Herald*, August 6, 1883.

Tourgée letter on copyright laws, New York *Tribune*, February 20, 1884.

" 'Cash Down,' or a Percentage?," *The Critic and Good Literature*, I (March 1, 1884), 103.

"National Aid to Education," New York *Tribune*, April 12, 1884.

Tourgée letter endorsing James G. Blaine for the presidency, New York *Tribune*, September 24, 1884.

An Appeal to Caesar. New York: Fords, Howard & Hulbert, 1884.

"A Rare October," *The Independent*, XXXVI (October 23, 1884), 1,348.

A Man of Destiny. Chicago: Belford, Clarke & Co., 1885. Published under the pseudonym Siva. In part, originally appeared weekly in the Chicago *Inter Ocean*, December 13, 1884–March 4, 1885.

The Veteran and His Pipe. Chicago: Belford, Clark & Co., 1886. Published anonymously, although a 1902 edition carried the author's name. Initially appeared weekly in the Chicago *Inter Ocean*, April 25, 1885–September 19, 1885.

"Letters to a Mugwump," Chicago *Inter Ocean*, September 26, 1885–December 12, 1885. Appeared weekly, under the pseudonym Trueman Joyce.

"A Child of Luck," Chicago *Inter Ocean*, March 20, 1886–December 4, 1886. Published weekly, with some interruptions, under the pseudonym Siva.

"A Study in Civilization," *The North American Review*, CXLIII (September, 1886), 246–61.

"The Renaissance of Nationalism," *The North American Review*, CXLIV (January, 1887), 1–11.

"Logan the Loyal," Chicago *Inter Ocean*, February 10, 1887.

"Tourgée on Beecher," Chicago *Inter Ocean*, March 13, 1887.

"Old Abe's Son," Chicago *Inter Ocean*, August 20, 1887.

Letters to a King. Cincinnati, O., Cranson & Stowe; New York, Phillips and Hunt, 1888. These initially appeared in *Northwestern Christian Advocate*, XXXV (January 5, 1887–September 28, 1887). See also the Chicago *Inter Ocean*, June 11, August 6, 1887.

"A Bystander's Notes," Chicago *Inter Ocean*, April 21, 1888–August 12, 1893; May 5, 1894–January 5, 1895; November 21, 1896–October 2, 1898. Appeared weekly.

Tourgée letter on Reconstruction, Chicago *Inter Ocean*, May 15, 1888.

"Catching the Viper," Chicago *Inter Ocean*, September 28, 1888.

"The South as a Field for Fiction," *The Forum*, VI (December, 1888), 404–13.

"The Claim of Realism," *The North American Review*, CXLVIII (March, 1889), 386–88.

"Shall White Minorities Rule?," *The Forum*, VII (April, 1889), 143–55.

"To the People of Kingsville and Vicinity," Kingsville, N.Y., *Tribune*, May 3, 1889.

"A Tide Watcher's Thoughts," Philadelphia *Press*, June 2, 1889.

"A Queer 'Comedy of Errors,' " *The Congregationalist*, XLI (June 27, 1889), 214.

"Our Semi-citizens," *Frank Leslie's Illustrated Weekly*, LXIX (September 28, 1889), 122–23.

Tourgée letter on Negro rights, Cleveland *Plaindealer*, October 12, 1889.

"Shall We Re-barbarize the Negro?," *The Congregationalist*, XLI (December 5, 1889), 411.

"The American Negro: What Are His Rights and What Must Be Done to Secure Them," New York *Tribune*, February 16, 1890.

"The Right to Vote," *The Forum*, IX (March, 1890), 78–92.

"The Negro's View of the Race Problem," *First Mohonk Conference on the Negro Question . . . June 4, 5, 6, 1890*. Edited by Isabel C. Barrows. Pamphlet. Boston: G. H. Ellis, Printer, 1890, 104–17.

"The Rehabilitation of the Fourth of July," *The Independent*, XLII (July 3, 1890), 8–9.

"John Workman's Notions," Chicago *Inter Ocean*, July 1, 1891–April 20, 1892. Appeared weekly.

Tourgée letter on Tammany and the Negro voter, New York *Tribune*, October 29, 1891.

Tourgée letter on "Tourgéeism," Detroit *Plaindealer*, June 3, 1892.

"Christian Citizenship," *The Golden Rule*, VII (August, 1892).

Introduction to N. B. Ashby, "Wealth and Civilization," *Farmer, Field and Stockman*, XV (October 8, 1892), 829.

Tourgée letter on southern racial violence, Cleveland *Gazette*, November 5, 1892 [?].

Is Liberty Worth Preserving? Pamphlet. Chicago: Inter Ocean, 1892.

"The Anti-Trust Campaign," *The North American Review*, CLVII (July, 1893), 30–41.

Historical Souvenir of the 105th Regiment of Ohio Volunteers Prepared for the Nineteenth Annual Reunion. Buffalo, N.Y.: S. McGerald & Sons, 1894.

An Outing with the Queen of Hearts. New York: Merrill & Baker, 1894. A partial version appeared earlier in *The Cosmopolitan*, XII (November, 1891), 70–84.

"A Man of Destiny. Second Series," Chicago *Inter Ocean*, January 13, 1894–April 28, 1894. Appeared weekly.

Tourgée to Governor William McKinley and Tourgée to H. C. Smith, on lynching, Cleveland *Gazette*, March 3, 1894.

To the People of the 34th Congressional District. Pamphlet. Brocton, N.Y.: The Grape Belt Print, 1894.

Nominations and Principles. Broadside. N.p., no publisher, 1894.

"Vasco Da Gama," *Great Men and Famous Women*. Edited by Charles F. Horne. New York: Selmar Hess, 1894, III, 139–45.

"As a Public Man," *Martin B. Anderson, LL.D. A Biography*. Edited by Asahel C. Kendrick. Philadelphia: American Baptist Publication Society, 1895, 276–92.

The Basis. Edited and in the main written by Tourgée. Vols. I–II (March 20, 1895–November 9, 1895 [weekly] and December, 1895–April, 1896 [monthly]).

On the writing of *Button's Inn*, Dunkirk, N.Y., *Grape Belt*, June 29, 1895.

The Story of a Thousand. Being a History of the Service of the 105th Ohio Volunteer Infantry, in the War for the Union from August 21, 1862, to June 6, 1865. Buffalo, N.Y.: S. McGerald & Son, 1896. Portions appeared in *The Cosmopolitan*, XVIII (November, 1894–April, 1895), and in *The Basis*, May 25, 1895–November 2, 1895.

A Memorial of Frederick Douglass from the City of Boston. Pamphlet. Boston: By Order of the City Council, 1896.

"Yesterday's Duty and How It Was Done," speech, Boston *Globe*, May 31, 1896.

"The Reversal of Malthus," *The American Journal of Sociology*, II (July, 1896), 13–24.

"The Literary Quality of 'Uncle Tom's Cabin,' " *The Independent*, XLVIII (August 20, 1896), 3–4.

"The Literary Tendency," *The Author's Journal*, II (August, 1895 [?]).

The War of the Standards, Coin and Credit versus Coin without Credit. Vol. LXXXVIII of *Questions of the Day*. New York: G. P. Putnam's Sons, 1896.

"The Best Currency," *The North American Review*, CLXIII (October, 1896), 416–26.

"Some Advice to Young Voters," *The Golden Rule*, XI (October 1, 1896), 4–5.

"Pending Problems," *The North American Review*, CLXIV (January, 1897), 38–49.

Consular Reports. United States Department of State. Vols. LV–LXXIX (September, 1897–June, 1905) may be consulted for numerous reports by Tourgée, a complete listing of which will not be attempted here. See also *Special Consular Reports. United States Department of State.*

"The Twentieth Century Peacemakers," *The Contemporary Review* (London), LXXV (June, 1899), 886–908.

"A Quiet Corner in Europe," *The Independent*, LI (June 1, 1899), 1483–85.

"Our Consular System," *The Independent*, LIV (January 23, 1902), 208–10.

"The Unwritten Law and Why It Remains Unwritten," *The Green Bag*, XX (January, 1908), 8–17.

II. General Bibliography

The sources for this biography are primarily contained in several specific locations—the Chautauqua County Historical Museum in Westfield, New York, the Library of Congress and the National Archives in Washington, D.C., and the University of North Carolina Library in Chapel Hill. Also of major assistance in North Carolina were the State Library and the Department of Archives and History in Raleigh, the Duke University Library, and the Greensboro Public Library. The University of Rochester Library, the Moorland-Spingarn Collection at Howard University, the Schomburg Collection of the New York Public Library, and the Grosvenor Public Library in Buffalo were helpful for certain primary materials, and the general collection of The Johns Hopkins University Library was frequently of aid. The following listing of specific items encountered at these various locations will be confined to the more directly pertinent sources, although the author is also deeply indebted to various well-known secondary works and easily available bibliographical guides the inclusion of which was not deemed necessary. The nature and scope of Tourgée's activities as a carpetbagger, together with the unsatisfactory state of North Carolina Reconstruction historiography, contributed to the noticeable emphasis upon that aspect of his career.

MANUSCRIPTS

Most significant by far for this study were the Albion W. Tourgée Papers, located in the Chautauqua County Historical Museum, a collection abundant in personal, political, and professional material, including, among its more than eleven thousand items, letters received and sent, political and literary scrapbooks, pamphlets and newspapers, court records, and a variety of manuscripts. These papers vary in value; they are especially useful for Tourgée's carpetbagger days and his equalitarian activities of the 1890's, and an excellent guide is provided by Dean H. Keller's *An Index to the Albion W. Tourgée Papers in the Chautauqua County Historical Society, Westfield, New York* ("Kent State University Bulletin Research Series," Vol. VII; Kent, O., 1964). Additional material on Tourgée's military career was provided by the Army Muster Rolls, the Federal Pension Records, and the Judge Advocate General's Records, all in the National Archives, Washington, D.C., and by *The War of the Rebellion. A Compilation of the Official Records of the Union and Confederate Armies* (Washington, D.C., 1880). Reconstruction letters regarding Tourgée may be found in the Second Military District Records, and a file on his pension agency is in the Department of Interior Records, National Archives.

In utilizing Reconstruction manuscripts, an attempt was made to survey those North Carolina collections of particular import to the period or to the Greensboro area. The Nathan H. Hill, Benjamin S. Hedrick, William W. Holden, and William Lafayette Scott Papers in the Duke University Library contain material on Tourgée and early Republicanism, as do the George W. Swepson Papers, State Archives, Raleigh; the Douglas Family Papers, in the possession of Martin F. Douglas of Greensboro; and the Settle Family Papers, now in the Southern Historical Collection, University of North Carolina, but utilized by the author while they were in the possession of Mrs. Carl O. Jeffress of Greensboro. The Martin B. Anderson Papers, University of Rochester Library, contain interesting Reconstruction correspondence from Tourgée, and of some help were the property records in the Greensboro Court House and the Superior Court minutes in the courthouses of Graham and Raleigh.

In addition to those listed above, several sources were useful in a more general sense. The North Carolina Records of the Bureau of Freedmen and Abandoned Lands, National Archives, offer an excellent picture of postwar Federal policy and southern conditions, as do the Andrew Johnson Papers, Manuscripts Division, Library of Congress, Washington, D.C., the pertinent part of which may be found conveniently in Elizabeth Gregory McPherson (ed.), "Letters from North Carolina to Andrew Johnson" (*North Carolina Historical Review*, XXVII [1950]–XXIX [1952]). Another informative collection is James A. Padgett (ed.), "Reconstruction Letters from North Carolina" (*ibid.*, XVIII [1941]–XXI [1944]). Important for state political activities were the Governor's Papers of Jonathan Worth, William Woods Holden, and Tod R. Caldwell, State Archives, Raleigh. Additional appreciation of Republicanism is provided by the Daniel L. Russell, William J. Clarke, and Richmond M. Pearson Papers in the Southern Historical Collection; the Daniel L. Russell Scrapbook in the University of North Carolina Library; and the Tod R. Caldwell Papers, divided between the Duke University Library and the Southern Historical Collection. Family papers in the possession of Katherine Hoskins of Summerfield, North Carolina, were important in evaluating the career of John W. Stephens, and anti-Republican viewpoints are effectively presented in three manuscript collections edited by Joseph Gregoire de Roulhac Hamilton: *The Correspondence of Jonathan Worth* (2 vols.; Raleigh, 1909), *The Papers of Thomas Ruffin* (4 vols.; Raleigh, 1920), and *The Papers of Randolph Abbott Shotwell* (3 vols.; Raleigh, 1929–1936), all in *Publications of the North Carolina Historical Commission*. Of similar but lesser value were the following manuscript collections in the Southern Historical Collection: David F. Caldwell, the Cameron Family, the Patterson Family, Cornelia Phillips Spencer, Edwin G. Reade, David Schenck, William A. Graham, Matt W. Ransom, Bedford Brown, Samuel McDowell Tate, and the Pettigrew Family. Henry M. Wagstaff, *The James A. Graham Papers* ("The James Sprunt Studies in History and Political Science," XX; Chapel Hill, 1928, 91–324) was of some value, and Hugh Talmadge Lefler and Aubrey Lee Brooks, *The Papers of Walter Clark* (2 vols.; Chapel Hill, 1948–1950) contains a few items by and on Tourgée. Of some use for Tourgée's later political career were the papers of James A. Garfield, Benjamin Harrison, William McKinley, Theodore Roosevelt, Edward McPherson, and John C. Spooner, all in the Manuscripts Division of the Library of Congress, and of related significance was Mary L. Hinsdale (ed.), *Garfield-Hinsdale Letters. Correspondence between James Abram Garfield and Burke Aaron Hinsdale* (Ann Arbor, Mich., 1949). The Booker T. Washington Papers, also in the Library of Congress, were of use concerning Tourgée's Negro interests, as were the Charles W. Chesnutt Papers at the Fisk University Library and the John E. Bruce Papers and Booker T. Washington Papers at the Schomburg Collection of the New York Public Library. A few related items may also be found in the Flavius Joseph Cook Papers at the Duke University Library, the David J. Holl and E. S. Goodhuc Reid Papers at the University of Rochester Library, the Henry Vignaud and Russell A. Alger Papers at the University of Michigan Library, and the Frederick Douglass Papers and the Joshua Giddings-George Julian Correspondence, Manuscripts Division, Library of Congress.

MEMOIRS AND CONTEMPORARY MATERIAL

Among the numerous memoirs and contemporary pamphlets consulted, those few of direct pertinence to Tourgée's Reconstruction career included:

John W. Wheeler, *Reminiscences and Memories of North Carolina and Eminent North Carolinians* (Columbus, O., 1884); *The Southern Loyalists' Convention. Call for a Convention of Southern Unionists* ("The Tribune Tracts," No. 2; Philadelphia, 1866); "Proceedings of the Southern Loyalist Convention Held in Philadelphia, Pennsylvania, September 3, 4, 5, 6, and 7, 1866 . . . Washington City, 1866" (*The Reporter*, II, Nos. 33–40 [September 17–November 5, 1866]); *Ritual, Constitution and By-Laws of the National Council, U.L. of A. together with All Necessary Information for the Complete Workings of Subordinate Councils* (Washington, D.C., 1867); *Minutes of the North Carolina Conference of the Methodist Episcopal Church . . . 1871* (Philadelphia, 1872) and *ibid., 1878* (Greensboro, 1878); and the John G. Lea confession, released posthumously (State Archives, Raleigh, reprinted in the Greensboro *Daily News*, October 2, 1935). Relevant to Tourgée's later career were: William L. Royall, *A Reply to "A Fool's Errand By One of the Fools"* (New York, 1881); John Raymond Howard, *Remembrance of Things Past. A Familiar Chronicle of Kinsfolk and Friends Worthwhile* (New York, 1925); and Isabel C. Barrows (ed.), *First Mohonk Conference on the Negro Question . . . June 4, 5, 6, 1890* (pamphlet; Boston, 1890).

Among the memoirs of a more general significance were William James Battle (ed.), *Memories of an Old Time Tar Heel by Kemp Plummer Battle, President of the University of North Carolina, 1876–1891* (Chapel Hill, 1945); *The Life and Travels of Addison Coffin, Written by Himself* (Cleveland, O., 1897); *The Memoirs of W. W. Holden* ("The John Howard Lawson Monographs of the Trinity College Historical Society," II; Durham, 1911); Cornelia Phillips Spencer, *The Last Ninety Days of the War in North Carolina* (New York, 1866); and George F. Hoar, *Autobiography of Seventy Years* (New York, 1903). Reconstruction memoirs combining information or insight with unreliable gossip and tradition are John Alexander Brevard, *Reminiscences of the Past Sixty Years* (Charlotte, 1908); Joseph Blount Cheshire, *Nonulla: Memoirs, Stories, Traditions, More or Less Authentic* (Chapel Hill, 1930); Robert Watson Winston, *It's a Far Cry* (New York, 1937); and Mary Alves Long, *High Time to Tell It* (Durham, 1950). Brief anti-Republican interpretations may be found in W. H. Pegram, "A Ku Klux Raid and What Came of It" ("Trinity College Historical Society Papers," I; Durham, 1897); "Bartholomew F. Moore on Secession and Reconstruction" (*ibid.*, II [1898], 75–82); Thomas J. Jarvis, "The Conditions That Led to the Ku Klux Klan" (*North Carolina Booklet*, I [1902], 1–24); John T. Alderman, "Memories of 1865–1871" (*ibid.*, XIII [1914], 199–214); Haywood Parker, *Recollections and Observations of the Reconstruction Era* (pamphlet; Asheville, n.d.).

Political insight into various shades of political opinion was also afforded by the many Reconstruction pamphlets available in the University of North Carolina Library, the Duke University Library, and the North Carolina State Library at Raleigh. A complete listing of these titles was not thought advisable here.

NEWSPAPERS AND JOURNALS

Despite its intense partisanship, the North Carolina press affords a wealth of factual and interpretive material. The conservative weekly Greensboro *Patriot* (called the *Patriot and Times* from June, 1868, to February, 1869) was essential for the years 1865 to 1880, and the Raleigh *Daily Sentinel* (Conservative-Democratic) and Raleigh *Daily North Carolina Standard* and *Tri-Weekly Standard* (Union party-Republican) were read from 1866 to 1870, the most decisive Reconstruction years, and consulted for various subsequent incidents. The Republican Raleigh *Daily Constitution* was helpful for the convention of 1875, and of some pertinence were the Conservative Greensboro *Times* (February to June, 1868) and the following Republican newspapers: The Greensboro *Register* (July to September, 1868, and July to November, 1869), the Greensboro *Republican Gazette* (a few issues in 1869), the Greensboro *Republican* (a few issues in 1870), the Greensboro *New North State*, later called the *North State* (November, 1872, to December, 1878), and the New Berne *Republican & Courier* (a few issues in 1872). Also consulted were the Asheville *Weekly Pioneer*, *Daily Charlotte Observer*, Charlotte *Democrat*, Chatham *Record*, Henderson *Weekly Index*, Hillsborough *Recorder*, *Alamance Gleaner*, Raleigh *Farmer and Mechanic*, Raleigh *Daily News*, Salisbury *Watchman and Old North State*, Tarboro *North Carolinian*, Wilmington *Morning Star*, and Wilmington *Daily Journal*. Tourgée's Wenckar letters and several other items were obtained from the *National Anti-Slavery Standard*.

Of particular importance for Tourgée's post-Reconstruction career were his own writings in the Chicago *Daily Inter Ocean* and in his own two magazines, the *Continent* and the *Basis* (a complete file of which is available in the Grosvenor Public Library, Buffalo, New York). Of some value for Tourgée's Negro interests were the *Voice of the Negro* and the *Colored American Magazine*, while the Negro newspapers available in the microfilm collection prepared by the American Philosophical Society in co-operation with the Library of Congress, especially the files of the Cleveland *Gazette*, Detroit *Plaindealer*, New York *Age*, Richmond *Planet* and Indianapolis *Freeman*, were extremely useful. The New York *Daily Tribune Index* led to

various commentary on or by Tourgée in that newspaper, and various newspapers in Philadelphia, New York, Washington, Buffalo, Omaha, and St.
Louis were consulted for particular incidents. For the dispute over the
Lodge election bill, see Thomas B. Reed, "The Federal Control of Elections"
(*North American Review*, CL [1890], 671–80); "The Federal Election Bill
by the Hon. Henry Cabot Lodge, Representative in Congress from Massachusetts, and T. V. Powderly, General Master-Workman of the Knights
of Labor" (*ibid.*, CLI [1890], 257–80); Robert Smalls, "Election Methods
in the South" (*ibid.*, 593–600); A. W. Shaffer, "A Southern Republican
on the Lodge Bill" (*ibid.*, 601–9); and William E. Chandler, "National
Control of Elections" (*Forum*, IX [1890], 705–18), for a good review of the
entire subject.

PUBLIC DOCUMENTS

Among the invaluable state and Federal documents consulted were the
*Journal of the Constitutional Convention of the State of North Carolina
at Its Session, 1868* (Raleigh, 1868); *Journal of the Constitutional Conven-
tion of the State of North Carolina Held in 1875* (Raleigh, 1875); *Con-
stitution of the State of North Carolina together with the Ordinances and
Resolutions of the Constitutional Convention, Assembled in the City of
Raleigh, Jan. 14, 1868* (Raleigh, 1868); *Constitutional Convention of 1875;
Report of the Select Committee on the Robeson County Contested Election
Case* (Raleigh, 1875); and *Amendments to the Constitution of North
Carolina Proposed by the Constitutional Convention of 1875, and the Con-
stitution as It Will Read as Proposed to Be Amended* (Raleigh, 1875).
Useful for election statistics and other bits of political information is
Robert Diggs Wimberly Connor (comp.), *A Manual of North Carolina
Issued by the North Carolina Historical Commission for the Use of Mem-
bers of the General Assembly, Session 1913* (Raleigh, 1913).

Invaluable for material on Tourgée's legal career were the *North Carolina
Reports: Cases Argued and Determined in the Supreme Court of North
Carolina*, Vols. LXIII–LXXXII (1868–1880). A vast collection of informa-
tion, including code commission reports and the various governors' messages,
is obtainable in the *Executive and Legislative Documents Laid before the
General Assembly of North Carolina* (1865–1880), and bound separately
are the *Report of the Senate Railroad Investigation Committee, 1870*
(Raleigh, 1870) and *Report of the Commission to Investigate Charges
of Fraud and Corruption . . . 1871–72* (Raleigh, 1872). The North Carolina
University Library also contains a bound collection, *Documents of the Code*

Commission, 1868–1871 (n.p., n.d.). Also consulted were the *Public Laws of the State of North Carolina*, (1865–1880), the *Journal of the Senate of the General Assembly of the State of North Carolina* (1865–1878), the *Journal of the House of the General Assembly of the State of North Carolina* (1865–1878), and *House Bill No. 307, Session 1871–1872. A Bill to Be Entitled "An Act to Repeal the Code of Civil Procedure and to Enact a New Code in Place Thereof"* (n.p., n.d.). No attempt will be made to list the various North Carolina codes, revisals, and consolidated statutes that were consulted.

Federal documents were utilized for postwar conditions in the South, most notably Freedmen's Bureau and War Department reports and documents, convenient listings of which may be found in Paul S. Pierce, *The Freedmen's Bureau, a Chapter in the History of Reconstruction* (Iowa City, I., 1904) and George R. Bently, *A History of the Freedmen's Bureau* (Philadelphia, 1955). Both Federal and state documents are vital for the history of the Ku Klux Klan in North Carolina, particularly *Senate Report 1* (42d Cong., 1st Sess.); *Trial of William W. Holden Governor of North Carolina before the Senate of North Carolina on Impeachment by the House of Representatives for High Crimes and Misdemeanors* (Raleigh, 1871); and *Third Annual Message, W. W. Holden, Governor of North Carolina, Nov., 1870, Doc. No. 1., Session 1870–71* (Raleigh, 1870). Of lesser value were the *Testimony of the Witnesses in the Preliminary Examinations of the Lenoir County Prisoners. The Secrets of the Ku-Klux Klan, etc. etc.* (New Berne, N.C., 1869) and the extensive investigations of the Klan by the Joint Select Committee, *House Report 22* or *Senate Report 41* (42d Cong., 2d Sess., I and II). The *Congressional Record* (51st Cong., 1st Sess., 1890) was utilized in connection with the educational and election bills of 1890, and for the *Plessy* v. *Ferguson* case, the United States Supreme Court *File Copies of Briefs* and *Transcripts of Records* were utilized. For both this case and the Ohio antilynching law of 1896, the legislative journals and Supreme Court records of Ohio and Louisiana were of some use. Official consular reports by Tourgée may be found in *Consular Reports* (monthly), *Special Consular Reports*, and *Daily Consular and Trade Reports*, and in *Papers Relating to the Foreign Relations of the United States with the Annual Message of the President . . . December 3, 1900* (Washington, D.C., 1902).

SECONDARY WORKS ON TOURGÉE

The most complete biographical account of Tourgée is Roy F. Dibble, *Albion W. Tourgée* (New York, 1921), an unsympathetic and almost entirely literary treatment. The more important general sketches include a favorable one by Frank Nash in Samuel A'Court Ashe (ed.), *Biographical History of North Carolina from Colonial Times to the Present* (8 vols.; Greensboro, 1905–07), Vol. IV; one by J. G. de Roulhac Hamilton in *The Dictionary of American Biography*; and one in the *National Cyclopedia of American Biography*. Russell B. Nye's "Judge Tourgée and Reconstruction" (*The Ohio State Archaeological and Historical Quarterly*, L [1941], 101–14) is an early and significant reconsideration, as is Owen N. Wilcox, "Albion Winegar Tourgée," *The Brief*, VII (1948), 7–54. An appreciation of Tourgée's Reconstruction accomplishments was written by a chief justice of the North Carolina Supreme Court, William A. Devin ("Footprints of a Carpetbagger," *The Torch*, XVII [April, 1944], 16–19, 21). Margaret Toth ("Albion Winegar Tourgée, '62," *University of Rochester Library Bulletin*, VIII [1953], 57–82) includes a description of Tourgée's letters to Martin B. Anderson. For an appreciation of Tourgée's brief in the Plessy case, see Sidney Kaplan, "Albion W. Tourgée: Attorney for the Segregated" (*Journal of Negro History*, XLIX [1964], 128–33). See also the following by O. H. Olsen: "A Carpetbagger: Albion W. Tourgée and Reconstruction in North Carolina" (unpublished Ph.D. dissertation, The Johns Hopkins University, 1959); "Albion W. Tourgée: Carpetbagger" (*North Carolina Historical Review*, XL [1963], 434–54); and "Albion W. Tourgée and Negro Militants of the 1890's: A Documentary Selection" (*Science and Society*, XXVIII [1964], 183–208).

By far the most extensive consideration of Tourgée is in the field of his literature, and excerpts from, or minor comments upon, his writing occur in too many places to warrant a complete listing here, ranging, for example, from excerpts in Harry Thurston Peck, *Library of the World's Great Literature* (19 vols.; New York, 1898) or Willard Thorp et al., *American Issues* (Chicago, 1941), to friendly comments in James F. Rhodes, *History of the United States from the Compromise of 1850* (7 vols.; New York, 1893–1906) or William Coyle, *Ohio Authors and Their Books* (Cleveland, O., 1962), and to hostile comments in Paul H. Buck, *The Road to Reunion, 1865–1900* (Boston, 1937), or Arthur Hobson Quinn, *American Fiction. An Historical and Critical Survey* (New York, 1936). Following Tourgée's eclipse, early friendly judgments appeared in Theodore Stanton (ed.), *A Manual of American Literature* (Leipzig, Germany, 1909); C. Alphonso Smith, *O. Henry Biography* (New York, 1916); Vernon L. Parrington, *Main Currents in American Thought* (3 vols.; New York, 1927–30); Russell Blankenship, *American Literature as an Expression of the National Mind* (New York, 1931); and Sterling Brown, *The Negro in American Fiction* (Washington, D.C., 1937). See also Brown's "The American Race Problem as Reflected in American Literature" (*Journal of Negro Education*, VIII [1939],

275–90). The previously mentioned article by Russell B. Nye, written in 1941, marked a reviving interest in the controversial carpetbagger, and notable evaluations several years later included George J. Becker, "Albion W. Tourgée: Pioneer in Social Criticism" (*American Literature*, XIX [1947–1948], 59–72) and Hugh Gloster, *Negro Voices in American Fiction* (Chapel Hill, 1948), with increasing appreciation reaching its most significant level, perhaps, in Alexander Cowie, *The Rise of the American Novel* (New York, 1948) and Edmund Wilson, *Patriotic Gore: Studies in the Literature of the American Civil War* (New York, 1962). Tourgée has also been discussed at some length in at least six doctoral dissertations: Harry John Runyan, "The Backgrounds and Origins of Realism in the American Novel, 1850–1880" (University of Wisconsin, 1949), which accords Tourgée a place; Charles Hampton Nilon, "Some Aspects of the Treatment of Negro Characters by Five Representative American Novelists: Cooper, Melville, Tourgée, Glasgow, Faulkner" (University of Wisconsin, 1952), an apparent tribute; briefly, in William B. Dickens, "A Guide to the American Political Novel 1865–1910" (University of Michigan, 1953); Helena M. Smith, "Negro Characterization in the American Novel: A Historical Survey of Work by White Authors" (Pennsylvania State University, 1959); Martin E. Hillger, "Albion W. Tourgée: Critic of Society" (Indiana University, 1959), most persuasive and appreciative; and Theodore L. Gross, "Albion W. Tourgée: Reporter of the Reconstruction" (Columbia University, 1960). The last is the only one of these studies to utilize the Tourgée Papers, but while emphasizing the unique value of the writings of a carpetbagger, it does little more than reaffirm the earlier literary judgments of Roy F. Dibble. Reflecting the impact of Edmund Wilson's work, and somewhat friendlier to Tourgée, is a partial and revised version of Gross's dissertation, *Albion W. Tourgée* (New York, 1963).

Other recent articles on Tourgée's literature include Ted N. Weissbuch, "Albion W. Tourgée: Propagandist and Critic of Reconstruction" (*Ohio Historical Quarterly*, LXX [1961], 27–44); Theodore L. Gross, "The Negro in the Literature of Reconstruction" (*Phylon: The Atlanta Review of Race and Culture*, XXII [1961], 5–14), and "The Fool's Errand of Albion W. Tourgée" (*ibid.*, XXIV [1963], 240–54); and Monte M. Olenick, "Albion W. Tourgée: Radical Republican Spokesman of the Civil War Crusade" (*ibid.*, XXIII [1962], 332–45). Wallace Evan Davies ("Religious Issues in Late Nineteenth Century American Novels," *Bulletin of the John Rylands Library*, XLI [1959], 328–59) discusses *Murvale Eastman*, as does Charles H. Hopkins briefly in *The Rise of the Social Gospel in American Protestantism* (New Haven, Conn., 1940), and Henry F. May, in *Protestant Churches and Industrial America* (New York, 1949).

In addition to such standard works as those identified with Granville Hicks, Ludwig Lewisohn, Fred L. Pattee, and Robert E. Spiller, helpful literary interpretation or commentaries on Tourgée were found in George W. Cable. His Life and Letters by His Daughter Lucy Lefingwell Cable Bickle (New York, 1928); Phillip Butcher, George W. Cable: The Northampton Years (New York, 1959); Arlin Turner, George W. Turner: A Biography (Durham, 1956); Everett Carter, Howells and the Age of Realism (Philadelphia, 1954); Harry Hayden Clark (ed.), Transitions in American Literary History (Durham, 1953); Frank Luther Mott, Golden Multitudes (New York, 1927); Louis Wann (ed.), The Rise of Realism: American Literature from 1860 to 1900 (New York, 1961); and Herbert Edwards, "Howells and the Controversy over Realism in American Fiction" (American Literature, III [1931–1932], 237–48). Robert Lively (Fiction Fights the Civil War: An Unfinished Chapter in the Literary History of the American People [Chapel Hill, 1957]) presents a provocative, if unconvincing, challenge to Tourgée's assertion that Confederate ideals were dominating American fiction by the end of the century, which should be compared with Paul H. Buck or with Jay B. Hubbell, American Life in Literature (New York, 1949). Tourgée is also briefly considered in Lars Ahnebrink's The Beginnings of Naturalism in American Fiction . . . 1891-1903 (Cambridge, Mass., 1950), and, in noncommittal fashion, in Claude R. Flory, Economic Criticism in American Fiction, 1792 to 1900 (Philadelphia, 1936). Additional unappreciative views are encountered in William B. Cairnes, A History of American Literature (New York, 1912); John Nelson, The Negro Character in American Literature (Lawrence, Kan., 1926); Van Wyck Brooks, The Times of Melville and Whitman (New York, 1947); and Ernest Leisy, The American Historical Novel (Norman, Okla., 1950).

GENERAL SECONDARY WORKS

Information on Tourgée's ancestry was obtained from Charles W. Baird, History of the Huguenot Emigration to America (Vol. I; New York, 1885); Vital Records of Lee, Massachusetts to the Year 1850 (Boston, 1903); William A. McAusland, Mayflower Index (Vol. I; Clinton, Mass., 1952); James M. Arnold, Vital Records of Rhode Island, Vols. V and XIX (Providence, R.I., 1894–1910); and The Berkshire Hills, Compiled and Written by the Federal Writers Project of the Works Progress Administration for Massachusetts (New York, 1939). For Tourgée's youth, the following were helpful: W. P. Cooper, "The Old Kingsville Academy: A Biographical

Sketch" (in the possession of Dean Keller, Kent, Ohio); Rev. C. M. Hyde and Alexander Hyde (comps.), *Lee: The Centennial Celebration and Centennial History* . . . (Springfield, Mass., 1878); William W. Williams, *History of Ashtabula County Ohio with Illustrations and Biographical Sketches of Its Pioneers and Most Prominent Men* (Philadelphia, 1878); and Henry Andrew Wright, *The Story of Western Massachusetts* (New York, 1949). Exceptionally useful for background material were the following volumes from Carl F. Wittke (ed.), *The History of the State of Ohio* (Columbus, O., 1941–1944): Beverly W. Bond, *Foundations of Ohio;* William T. Utter, *The Frontier State, 1803–1825;* Francis P. Weisenburger, *The Passing of the Frontier, 1825–1850;* and Eugene H. Roseboom, *The Civil War Era, 1850–1873.* For Tourgée's college days, see Asahel C. Kendrick, *Martin B. Anderson LL.D.: A Biography* (Philadelphia, 1895) and Blake McKelvey, *Rochester the Flower City* (Cambridge, Mass., 1949). Pertinent to Tourgée's military career were Charles Bryant Fairchild, *History of the 27th Regiment N.Y. Vols., Being a Record of* . . . (Binghamton, N.Y., 1883); Charles Elihu Slocum, *The Life and Services of Major General Henry Warner Slocum* (Toledo, O., 1913); and Whitelaw Reid, *Ohio in the War, Her Statesmen, Her Generals and Soldiers* (2 vols.; Cincinnati, O., 1868).

The general accounts of North Carolina history found most useful were Samuel A'Court Ashe, *History of North Carolina* (2 vols.; Greensboro, 1908 and 1925); Robert Diggs Wimberly Connor, *North Carolina: Rebuilding an Ancient Commonwealth, 1584–1925* (4 vols.; Chicago, 1929). Reliable but brief is Hugh Talmadge Lefler and Albert Ray Newsome, *North Carolina; the History of a Southern State* (Chapel Hill, 1954). An excellent prewar account is Guion Griffis Johnson, *Ante-Bellum North Carolina: A Social History* (Chapel Hill, 1937), while Henry McGilbert Wagstaff, *State Rights and Political Parties in North Carolina, 1776–1861* ("The Johns Hopkins Studies in Historical and Political Science," XXIV, Nos. 7–8; Baltimore, 1906) depicts the Unionist and democratic sentiments later apparent in the Republican party. Joseph Carlyle Sitterson, *The Secession Movement in North Carolina* ("James Sprunt Studies in History and Political Science, XXIII; Chapel Hill, 1939) is a competent account. Revealing but nonanalytical is Mary Shannon Smith, "Union Sentiment in North Carolina during the Civil War" (*Meredith College Quarterly Bulletin,* IX [1915], 3–21), while the best account of this subject is found in Georgia Lee Tatum, *Disloyalty in the Confederacy* (Chapel Hill, 1934). See also John C. Barrett's competent *Sherman's March thru the Carolinas* (Chapel Hill, 1956) and *The Civil War in North Carolina* (Chapel Hill, 1963); A. Sellew

Roberts, "The Peace Movement in North Carolina" (*Mississippi Valley Historical Review*, IX [1924], 190–99); Horace W. Raper, "William W. Holden and the Peace Movement in North Carolina" (*North Carolina Historical Review*, XXXI [1954], 493–516); Ina W. Van Noppen, "The Significance of Stoneman's Last Raid" (*ibid.*, XXXVIII [1961], 19–44, 149–72, 341–61, 500–526); and Richard Bardolph, "Inconstant Rebels: Desertion of North Carolina Troops in the Civil War" (*ibid.*, XLI [1964], 163–89).

The standard work on Reconstruction in the state is J. G. de Roulhac Hamilton, *Reconstruction in North Carolina* ("Columbia University Studies in History, Economics, and Public Law," LVIII; New York, 1914), a reliable and mainly political history which is marred by a hostility toward Republicanism and a readiness to accept political slander as fact. Another work by Hamilton casts further light on the later 1870's—*History of North Carolina*, Vol. III: *North Carolina since 1860* (Chicago, 1919). The most important revisions of Hamilton are unpublished doctoral dissertations, such as Kenneth Edson St. Clair, "The Administration of Justice in North Carolina" (Ohio State University, 1939), which stresses the moderation of Federal military policy and the significance of race prejudice and raises doubts of a Republican crime wave. Another competent dissertation, weak in detailed treatment because of its scope, is Jack Benton Scroggs, "Carpetbagger Influence in the Political Reconstruction of the South Atlantic States, 1865–1876" (University of North Carolina, 1952), which emphasizes the positive contributions of carpetbaggers and concentrates largely upon Tourgée and North Carolina. A competent and analytical treatment placing responsibility for the railroad fiasco on members of each party is Charles Lewis Price, "Railroads and Reconstruction in North Carolina, 1865–1871" (University of North Carolina, 1959). Emphasizing the positive as well as negative features of the Union League but lacking in depth and conclusions is Austin Marcus Drumm, "The Union League in the Carolinas" (unpublished Ph.D. dissertation, University of North Carolina, 1955); and a work hostile to the League is Susie Lee Owens, "The Union League of America: Political Activities in Tennessee, the Carolinas, and Virginia, 1865–1870" (unpublished Ph.D. dissertation, New York University, 1943). William Donaldson Cotton, "Appalachian North Carolina: A Political Study, 1860–1889" (unpublished Ph.D. dissertation, University of North Carolina, 1956) offers a valuable, though somewhat undigested, accumulation of Reconstruction material. Also useful were Henry Lee Swint, *The Northern Teacher in the South: 1862–1870* (Nashville, Tenn., 1941); Frank W. Klingberg, *The Southern Claims Commission* ("University of California Publications in History," L; Berkeley, Calif., 1955), which contains material on Unionists during and after the war; and Ralph E. Morrow, *Northern Methodism and Reconstruction* (East Lansing, Mich., 1956), an account stressing the crusading arrogance of the church in which Tourgée was active.

The following unpublished Master's theses, all from the University of North Carolina, were also of use: John Blount McLeod, "The Development of North Carolina Election Laws, 1865 to 1894" (1947), a good account of political immorality the origins of which are attributed largely to postwar military rule; Elaine Joane Nowaczyk, "The North Carolina Negro in Politics, 1865–1876" (1957), partial and undigested; Douglass Charles Dailey, "The Elections of 1872 in North Carolina" (1953); William Durham Harris, "The Movement for Constitutional Change in North Carolina, 1863–1876" (1932), which is careless but includes such useful material as Judge Robert W. Winston's estimation of various Republicans; Henry C. McFayden, "The Administration of Governor Jonathan Worth" (1942); Richard Lee Hoffman, "The Republican Party in North Carolina, 1867–1871" (1960); and Willie Grier, "North Carolina Baptists and the Negro 1727–1877" (1944), which finds the humanitarian efforts of the Baptists undermined by radical Reconstruction.

There are a number of articles by J. G. de Roulhac Hamilton, most of which contribute little beyond what he subsequently published in his volume on Reconstruction, with the exception of "The North Carolina Convention of 1865–1866" (*Proceedings and Addresses of the Fourteenth Annual Session of the State Literary and Historical Association of North Carolina* ["Publications of the North Carolina Historical Commission," Raleigh, 1913], 56–68). Kenneth Edson St. Clair, "Judicial Machinery in North Carolina in 1865" (*North Carolina Historical Review*, XXX [1953], 415–39), well portrays the period of combined civil and military rule; and "Debtor Relief in North Carolina during Reconstruction" (*ibid.*, XVIII [1941], 215–35), by the same author, is an analysis of a major economic problem. Another friendly account of the role of the Federal military is Max L. Heyman, Jr., " 'The Great Reconstructor' General E. R. S. Canby and the Second Military District" (*ibid.*, XXXII [1955], 52–80). Also useful were James B. Browning, "North Carolina Black Code" (*Journal of Negro History*, XV [1930], 461–73), a critical view of the code; William A. Russ, Jr., "Radical Disfranchisement in North Carolina, 1867–1868" (*North Carolina Historical Review*, XI [1934], 271–83); Jonathan Truman Dorris, "Pardoning North Carolinians" (*ibid.*, XXIII [1946]), which stresses political considerations; and Leonard Bernstein, "The Participation of Negro Delegates in the Constitutional Convention of 1868 in North Carolina" (*Journal of Negro History*, XXXIV [1949], 391–409), which is valuable but slightly careless. A comparative analysis of the impeachment trials of Holden and Andrew Johnson is contained in Cortez Arthur Milton Ewing's "Two Reconstruction Impeachments" (*North Carolina Historical Review*, XV [1938], 197–230), and the controversial fiscal situation is treated in Albert Ray Newsome, "Report of an Investigation of the Passage of the Reconstruction Bond Ordinances and Acts of North Carolina in 1868–1869" (unpublished manuscript in Mrs. A. R. Newsome's possession) and in Benjamin Ulysses Ratchford, "North Carolina Public Debt, 1870–1883" (*North Carolina Historical Review*, X [1933], 1–20, 157–67). General interpretation is available in William Alexander Mabry, *The Negro in North Carolina Politics since Reconstruction* ("Trinity College Historical Society Papers," XXIII; Durham, 1940); and Robert Diggs Wimberly Connor ("The Rehabilitation of a Rural Commonwealth," *American Historical Review*, XXXVI [1930], 44–62) perceptively argues that the political turbulence of Reconstruction seriously retarded the economic recovery of the South. Also of some use were Daniel J. Whitener, "Public Education in North Carolina during Reconstruction, 1865–1876" (*Essays in Southern History Presented to Joseph Gregoire de Roulhac Hamilton . . . by His Former Students*, ed. Fletcher M. Green [Chapel Hill, 1949]) and "The Republican Party and Public Education in North Carolina, 1867–1900" (*North Carolina Historical Review*, XXXVII [1960], 382–96), both accounts favorable to Republican educational policies. More thorough treatments of education, unduly hostile toward Reconstruction and a supposed threat of integration, are Edgar Wallace Knight, *Public School Education in North Carolina* (Boston, 1916) and Marcus C. S. Noble, *A History of the Public Schools of North Carolina* (Chapel Hill, 1930).

Reconstruction articles of less value to this study included Joseph Carlyle Sitterson, "Business Leaders in Post-Civil War North Carolina, 1865–1900" (*Studies in Southern History in Memory of Albert Ray Newsome, 1894–1951, by His Former Students*, ed. J. C. Sitterson ["James Sprunt Studies in History and Political Science," XXXIX; Chapel Hill, 1957]); Johnny W. Barnes, "The Political Activities of the Union League of America in North Carolina" (*The Quarterly Review of Higher Education among Negroes*, XVIII [1952], 141–50); Harley E. Jolley, "The Labor Movement in North Carolina" (*North Carolina Historical Review*, XXX [1954], 354–75), which contains some material on the class origins of early political divisions; Benjamin Franklin Lemart, "Geographic Influences in the History of North Carolina" (*ibid.*, XII [1935], 297–319), an excellent treatment; John Bell, "The Presbyterian Church and the Negro in North Carolina" (*ibid.*, XL [1963], 15–36); Douglass C. Dailey, "The Elections of 1872 in North Carolina" (*ibid.*, XL [1963], 338–60); Sanders Dent, *The Origins and Development of the Ku Klux Klan* ("Trinity College Historical Society Papers," I; Durham, 1897); Jedith R. Davis, *Reconstruction in Cleveland County* (*ibid.*, X; 1914); Bryant Whitlock Ruark, *Some Phases of Reconstruction in Wilmington and the County of New Hanover* (*ibid.*, XI; 1915), a moderate Conservative view; and R. D. W. Connor, "The Ku-Klux Klan and Its Operations in North Carolina" (*North Carolina University Magazine*, New Series, XVII [1900], 224–34).

The main works consulted for local history and government were: James W. Albright, *Greensboro, 1808–1904* (Greensboro, 1904); Ethel Stephens Arnett, *Greensboro, North Carolina, the County Seat of Guilford* (Chapel Hill, 1955); Sallie W. Stockard, *The History of Guilford County, North Carolina* (Knoxville, Tenn., 1902); Early Winfred Bridges, *Greensboro Lodge No. 76, A.F. & A.M. A Historical Survey of One of North Carolina's Outstanding Lodges* (Staunton, Va., 1951); Charles Christopher Crittendon and Dan Lacy (eds.), *The Historical Records of North Carolina*, Vol. I: *The County Records Prepared by the Historical Records Survey of the Works Progress Administration* (Raleigh, 1938), which contains a useful survey of local political history; Hugh Talmadge Lefler and Paul Wager, *Orange County: 1752–1952* (Chapel Hill, 1953); and Paul Wager, *County Government and Administration in North Carolina* (Chapel Hill, 1928).

Legal history constitutes a field in itself. Works consulted for the history of codification include: David Dudley Field, *The Argument in Favor of a Code Contained in the Introduction to the Civil Code of New York* (London, 1867); Henry M. Field, *The Life of David Dudley Field* (New York, 1908); William Seagle, *The Quest for Law* (New York, 1941); Charles E. Clark, *Handbook of the Law of Code Pleading* (2d ed.; St. Paul, Minn., 1947); Allison Reppy, *David Dudley Field Centenary Essays Celebrating One Hundred Years of Law Reform* (New York, 1949); James Willard Hurst, *The Growth of American Law: The Law Makers* (Boston, 1950); W. J. Wagner, "Codification of Law in Europe and the Codification Movement in the Middle of the Nineteenth Century in the United States" (*St. Louis University Law Journal*, II [1953], 335–59); and "The Future of Codification: Essays in Honor of the Centennial of the Tulane Law School" (*Tulane Law Review*, XXIX [1955], 177–327).

Useful for North Carolina legal history is the *Scrap Book of Addresses by Walter Clark* available in the University of North Carolina Library, including *Address by Chief Justice Walter Clark . . . 8 May, 1913. The Legal Status of Women in North Carolina: Past, Present, and Prospective* (n.p., n.d.); *Lecture—American Correspondence School of Law—Pleading and*

Practice (Chicago, 1908); and *Address on Reform in Law and Legal Procedure by Hon. Walter Clark Chief Justice of the Supreme Court of N.C. . . . June 30, 1914* (Wilmington, Del., n.d.). See also Justice Clark's *The Code of Civil Procedure of North Carolina with Notes and Decisions to July 1900 . . .* (Goldsboro, N.C., 1900). Useful articles included Robert Watson Winston, "A Century of Law in North Carolina" (*North Carolina Reports,* CLXXVI, 763–91); William J. Adams, "Evolution of Law in North Carolina" (*North Carolina Law Review,* II [1923–1924], 133–45); and William B. Aycock, "Homestead Exemption in North Carolina" (*ibid.,* XXIX [1950–1951], 143–67). Very useful is Henry G. Connor and Joseph B. Cheshire, *The Constitution of North Carolina Annotated* (Raleigh, 1911); and Dillard S. Gardner, "The Continuous Revision of Our State Constitution" (*North Carolina Law Review,* XXXVI [1957–1958], 297–313) is a useful brief review. Marjorie Mendenhall Applewhite, "Sharecropper and Tenant in the Courts of North Carolina" (*North Carolina Historical Review,* XXXI [1954], 134–49) is a helpful historical treatment, and some historical information is available in Charles S. Mangum, *The Legal Status of the Tenant Farmer in the Southeast* (Chapel Hill, 1952).

Although too frequently uncritical, various Reconstruction biographical material proved invaluable. The sketches in Ashe's *Biographical History of North Carolina* are eulogistic but competent, and the unpublished manuscript of a proposed ninth volume in this series is available in the Van Noppen Papers, Duke University Library. Also reliable are Jerome Dowd, *Sketches of Prominent Living North Carolinians* (Raleigh, 1888); Charles Hunter Hamlin, *Ninety Bits of North Carolina Biography* (n.p., 1946); and John Wheeler, *Reminiscences,* mentioned earlier. The files of the Greensboro Public Library and Bettie D. Caldwell, *Founders and Builders of Greensboro, 1808–1908* (Greensboro, 1925) contain relevant information on local figures.

Pertinent full-scale Reconstruction biographies are rare. Most important were two informative works by Horace Wilson Raper, "The Political Career of William Woods Holden with Special Reference to His Provisional Governorship" (unpublished Master's dissertation, University of North Carolina, 1948) and "William Woods Holden: A Political Biography" (unpublished Ph.D. dissertation, University of North Carolina, 1951), the latter sympathetic toward Republicanism. For a competent appreciation of Conservatism, see Richard L. Zuber, "Jonathan Worth—A Biography of a Southern Unionist" (unpublished Ph.D. dissertation, Duke University, 1961). William Kenneth Boyd, *William W. Holden* ("Trinity College Historical Society Papers, III; Durham, 1899) is a competent work concerned largely with Reconstruction, and interesting background material is provided by Hope S. Chamberlain, *Old Days in Chapel Hill, Being the Life and Letters of Cornelia Phillips Spencer* (Chapel Hill, 1926) and Phillips Russell, *The Woman Who Rang the Bell: The Story of Cornelia Phillips Spencer* (Chapel Hill, 1949). Of limited use were Clement Dowd, *Life of Zebulon B. Vance* (Charlotte, 1897) and Richard Edwin Yates, *The Confederacy and Zeb Vance* ("Confederate Centennial Studies," No. 8; Tuscaloosa, Ala., 1958). The latter contains interesting Civil War material, some of which is elaborated in two earlier articles by Yates, "Zebulon B. Vance as War Governor of North Carolina, 1862–1865" (*Journal of Southern History*, III [1937], 43–75) and "Governor Vance and the Peace Movement" (*North Carolina Historical Review*, XVII [1940], 1–25, 89–113). A recent entertaining account of the notorious carpetbagger Milton S. Littlefield, which emphasizes the involvement of natives as well as carpetbaggers in Reconstruction fraud but remains a superficial account throwing little new light on the era, is Jonathan Daniels, *Prince of Carpetbaggers* (New York, 1958). Stuart Noblin, *Leonidas Lafayette Polk* (Chapel Hill, 1949) was pertinent to Tourgée's letters from "Jeduthan Jeems." A variety of useful but generally uncritical sketches may also be found in the files of the *University Magazine*, *North Carolina Reports*, *Quaker Biographies*, "James Sprunt Studies in History and Political Science," and *The State*, as well as in various state legislative manuals. See also John Spencer Bassett, *Anti-Slavery Leaders in North Carolina* (Baltimore, 1898) and Katherine Hoskins, "Lawyer Reid, Victim of the Ku Klux" (unpublished manuscript in the possession of Miss Hoskins).

John W. Stephens has been the subject of a number of sketches of limited value: A. J. Stedman, *Murder and Mystery: History of the Life and Death of J. W. Stephens of Caswell County* (Greensboro, 1870); Luther M. Carleton, *The Assassination of John Walter Stephens* ("Trinity College Historical Society Papers," II; Durham, 1898); Frank Nash, "John Walter Stephens" (*Biographical History of North Carolina*, ed. Samuel A'Court Ashe, IV, 411–21); Thomas J. Henderson, "Murder of 'Chicken' Stephens" (*The State*, March 25, 1939) and *Ann of the Ku Klux Klan: A Partly Fiction Story of the Old South* . . . (pamphlet; Yanceyville, N.C., 1942); Manly Wade Wellman, *Dead and Gone, Classic Crimes of North Carolina* (Chapel Hill, 1954).

The major source for Tourgée's post-Reconstruction career is his own writing, although in addition to standard accounts of the period and the previously discussed literary works, a number of other items were of particular value. *Epoch: The Life of Steele MacKaye Genius of the Theatre in*

Relation to His Times & Contemporaries. A Memoir by His Son Percy MacKaye (New York, 1927) and Arthur Hobson Quinn, *A History of the American Drama from the Civil War to the Present Day* (New York, 1936) were useful on the dramatization of *A Fool's Errand*, while Frank Luther Mott, *A History of American Magazines* (4 vols.; Cambridge, Mass., 1938–1957), was pertinent to Tourgée's editorial career. Helpful in evaluating Tourgée's journalistic significance were Frank Luther Mott, *American Journalism: A History of Newspapers in the United States through 250 Years, 1690–1950* (New York, 1950), and Alfred McClung Lee, *The Daily Newspaper in America: The Evolution of a Social Instrument* (New York, 1937).

Of particular assistance in understanding Tourgée's place in the continuing stream of Republican idealism were Vincent P. De Santis, *Republicans Face the Southern Question: The New Departure Years, 1877–1897* (Baltimore, 1959); Stanley P. Hirshson, *Farewell to the Bloody Shirt: Northern Republicans and the Southern Negro, 1877–1893* (Bloomington, Ind., 1962); and Mary R. Dearing, *Veterans in Politics: The Story of the G.A.R.* (Baton Rouge, La., 1952). Also helpful were Eric F. Goldman, *Rendezvous with Destiny: A History of Modern American Reform* (New York, 1952); Richard Hofstadter, *The Age of Reform: From Bryan to F. D. R.* (New York, 1955); Sidney Fine, *Laissez Faire and the General Welfare State. A Study of Conflict in American Thought, 1865–1900* (Ann Arbor, Mich., 1956); Horace S. Merrill, *Bourbon Democracy of the Middle West, 1865–1896* (Baton Rouge, La., 1953); and Russell B. Nye, *Midwestern Progressive Politics: A Historical Study of Its Origins and Development* (East Lansing, Mich., 1951). In tracing Tourgée's efforts in behalf of Federal aid to education, the above-mentioned volume by Stanley Hirshson was pertinent, as were Gordon Canfield Lee, *The Struggle for Federal Aid. First Phase. A History of the Attempts To Obtain Federal Aid for the Common Schools, 1870–1890* (New York, 1949); Burke A. Hinsdale, *President Garfield and Education. Hiram College Memorial* (Boston, 1882); Theodore Clark Smith, *The Life and Letters of James A. Garfield* (2 vols.; New Haven, Conn., 1925); Elvena S. Bage, "President Garfield's Forgotten Pronouncement" (*Negro History Bulletin*, XIV [1951], 195–97), and Allan J. Going, "The South and the Blair Education Bill" (*Mississippi Valley Historical Review*, XLIV [1952], 269–90). Daniel Walker Hollis, "The Force Bill of 1890" (unpublished Master's dissertation, Columbia University, 1947), was of some assistance, while for an understanding of political and congressional events the following, in addition to the standard accounts, were particularly helpful: Francis Curtis, *The Republican Party . . . 1854–*

1904 (2 vols.; New York, 1904); George F. Hoar, *Autobiography of Seventy Years* (New York, 1903); Leon Burr Richardson, *William E. Chandler: Republican* (New York, 1940); John A. Garraty, *Henry Cabot Lodge: A Biography* (New York, 1953); Karl Schriftgiesser, *The Gentleman from Massachusetts: Henry Cabot Lodge* (Boston, 1944); Samuel W. McCall, *The Life of Thomas Bracket Reed* (Boston, 1914); William A. Robinson, *Thomas B. Reed: Parliamentarian* (New York, 1930); and Herbert Croly, *Marcus Alonzo Hanna* (New York, 1912). See also Dean H. Keller, "Albion Tourgée and a National Education Program" (*Peabody Journal of Education*, XLI [1963], 131–35).

In dealing with Tourgée's relationship to the Negro, two doctoral dissertations provided unusual insight: Jack Abramowitz, "Accommodationism and Militancy in Negro Life, 1876–1916" (Columbia University, 1950), and August Meier, "Negro Racial Thought in the Age of Booker T. Washington; Circa 1880–1915" (Columbia University, 1957). A revised version of the latter has since been published as *Negro Thought in America, 1880–1915: Racial Ideologies in the Age of Booker T. Washington* (Ann Arbor, Mich., 1963), and see Abramowitz, "Crossroads of Negro Thought" (*Social Education*, XVIII [1954], 117–20). Also helpful were Herbert Aptheker, *A Documentary History of the Negro in the United States* (New York, 1951); Helen M. Chesnutt, *Charles Waddell Chesnutt: Pioneer of the Color Line* (Chapel Hill, 1952); Rayford W. Logan, *The Negro in American Life and Thought: The Nadir: 1877–1901* (New York, 1954); Richard Bardolph, *The Negro Vanguard* (New York, 1961); Francis L. Broderick, *W. E. B. Du Bois. Negro Leader in a Time of Crisis* (Stanford, Calif., 1959); and Elliott M. Rudwick, *W. E. B. Du Bois: A Study in Minority Group Leadership* (Philadelphia, 1960). See also Rudwick's "The Niagara Movement" (*Journal of Negro History* XLII [1957], 177–200). Among various articles and books consulted on *Plessy* v. *Ferguson*, special assistance was provided by Rodolph L. Desdunes, *Nos Hommes et Notre Histoire* (Montreal, 1911); Robert J. Harris, *The Quest for Equality. The Constitution, Congress and the Supreme Court* (Baton Rouge, La., 1960); Joseph S. Ransmeier, "The Fourteenth Amendment and the Separate but Equal Doctrine" (*Michigan Law Review*, L [1951], 203–60); Barton J. Bernstein, "Case Law in Plessy v. Ferguson" (*Journal of Negro History*, XLVII [1962], 192–98), and "Plessy v. Ferguson: Conservative Sociological Jurisprudence" (*ibid.*, XLVIII [1963], 196–205); and C. Vann Woodward, "The Birth of Jim Crow" (*American Heritage* XV [April, 1964], 52–55, 100–103).

In addition to the familiar *Dictionary of American Biography* and *Biographical Directory of the American Congress*, the following provided information on minor incidents or various individuals associated with Tourgée: Philip D. Jordan, *Ohio Comes of Age 1873–1900* (Columbus, O., 1943); John Phillips Downs (ed.), *History of Chautauqua County New York and Its People* (3 vols.; Boston, 1921); William J. Doty (ed.), *The Historical Annals of Southwestern New York* (3 vols.; New York, 1940); Jesse Leonard Rosenberger, *Rochester: The Making of a University* (Rochester, N.Y., 1927); *The University of Rochester the First Hundred Years Centennial Issue* . . . (Rochester, N.Y., 1950); Paul Gilbert and Charles Lee Bryson, *Chicago and Its Makers* . . . (Chicago, 1929); Bessie Louise Pierce, *A History of Chicago,* Vol. III: *The Rise of a Modern City, 1871–1893* (New York, 1957); Henry Justin Smith, *A Gallery of Chicago Editors* (pamphlet; Chicago, 1930); Chicago Inter Ocean Press, *A History of the City of Chicago Its Men and Institutions* . . . (Chicago, 1900); and Ida H. Harper, *The Life and Work of Susan B. Anthony* (2 vols.; Indianapolis, Ind., 1898).

Index

A

Abbott, Joseph C., 167: and state debt, 105, 110
Abolitionists, 53: in Tourgée's fiction, 228. *See also* Antislavery movement
African Methodist Episcopal Church, 319
Afro American League, 308, 310, 311, 313, 318, 322: origins of, 307
Afro American Press Association, 311
Agrarian Society: legal problems of, 134–36
Agricultural labor. *See* conflict; Landlord and tenant acts; Lien laws; Negro question
Alamance County, N.C., 184: Republicans gain in, 125; Ku Klux Klan in, 149, 150, 159, 161, 162, 165, 169, 186, 187
Albright, William R., 161
Alger, Russell, 337, 338
American Economist, 293
Amnesty and crime, 151: and Ku Klux Klan, 186–88
Anderson, W. H.: and Negro rights, 310–11, 318
Anglo-American unity: Tourgée on, 345
Anthony, George L., 73
Anthony, Susan B., 293, 320
Anti-Semitism: Tourgée and, 287, 348
Antislavery movement: influence on Tourgée, 5, 12, 24–25. *See also* Abolitionists
"Anti-Trust Campaign, The," 292
Appeal to Pharaoh, An, 319
Arkansas: Negroes in, 318

B

Atlanta *Constitution*, 289
Atlantic Monthly: on *A Fool's Errand*, 224

Bailey, William H., 139
Bain, Rev. Hope: unionist, 51
Balzac, Honoré de, 259
Bancroft, Hubert Howe, 259
Banneker League: in Chicago, 313
Baptist Young People's Union, 320
Barnett, Ferdinand L.: and Negro rights, 313
Barringer, Rufus: supports U. S. Grant, 123
Barringer, Victor C.: code commissioner, 130, 139
Basis, The, 332–34
Bason, George F.: and Ku Klux Klan, 185
Battle, William H.: and female lawyers, 180
Becker, George J.: on Tourgée, 238
Beecher, Henry Ward, 217
Belfast (Ireland) *Northern Whig*, 333
Bennett College: and Tourgée, 76, 174
Biracial unity: in South, 69–70, 71, 80–81, 91–92, 125; Tourgée seeks, 312
Black Codes of North Carolina, 31, 34
Blaine, James G., 244: Tourgée opposes, 261, 303
Blair, Charles H., 265
Blair bill: Tourgée opposes, 248, 286, 288, 304–5, 319
Bok, Edward W.: quoted, 263
Bordeaux, France, 339–40, 342, 348, 350

383

D

E

CARPETBAGGER'S CRUSADE
The Life of Albion Winegar Tourgée
OTTO H. OLSEN

designer:	Athena Blackorby
compositor:	Vail-Ballou Press, Inc.
typefaces:	Electra text, Deepdene display
printer:	Vail-Ballou Press, Inc.
paper:	Perkins and Squier, GM
binder:	Vail-Ballou Press, Inc.
cover material:	Columbia Riverside Linen